LACAN AND THE MATTER OF ORIGINS

SHULI BARZILAI

Lacan and the Matter of Origins

STANFORD UNIVERSITY PRESS

STANFORD, CALIFORNIA 1999

Stanford University Press
Stanford, California
© 1999 by the Board of Trustees of the
Leland Stanford Junior University
Printed in the United States of America
CIP data appear at the end of the book

For Eli

Acknowledgments

Parts of this book have previously appeared in several journals. I would like to thank the editors for granting permission to reprint, with alterations, the following materials: Chapter 3 appeared as "'History Is Not the Past': Lacan's Critique of Ferenczi" in *The Psychoanalytic Review* 84 (1997): 553–72; an abbreviated version of Chapter 4 appeared as "Models of Reflexive Recognition: Wallon's *Origines du caractère* and Lacan's 'The Mirror Stage,'" in *The Psychoanalytic Study of the Child* 50 (1995): 368–82; a slightly different version of Chapter 7 appeared as "Augustine in Contexts: Lacan's Repetition of a Scene from the *Confessions*" in *Literature and Theology: An International Journal of Theory, Criticism and Culture* 11 (1997): 200–21; and the Epilogue appeared as "Borders of Language: Kristeva's Critique of Lacan" in *PMLA: Publications of the Modern Language Association of America* 106 (1991): 294–305. I would also like to thank W. W. Norton and Company for permission to quote from the English translations of the works of Lacan.

I am grateful to a number of institutions for assistance extended to me during the period in which this work was in progress: the Israel Science Foundation, administered by the Israel Academy of Sciences and Humanities, for a grant that enabled me to benefit from the skills of Hannah Ovnat, in whom I found not only an excellent research assistant but also a fine person; Harvard University for appointments as a visiting scholar and the granting of library privileges; and the Hebrew University of Jerusalem for a sabbatical leave and several grants.

While working on *Lacan and the Matter of Origins*, I benefited from the suggestions, corrections, and encouragement of many good people. I acknowledge these debts to my family, friends, university colleagues, and students with a keen sense of accounts to be savored rather than settled. H. M. Daleski of the Hebrew University and Zephyra Porat of Tel Aviv University, who have been my lynx-eyed guides for many years, read and reread the chapters in various draft forms with rare patience, insight, and intellectual generosity. I have been blessed by their inestimably valuable and sustaining presence, as well as by their astute criticisms over the years. In addition, from the Epilogue, which was completed first, to Chapter 1, which was completed last, this work is indebted to the influence of a very great teacher and critic, Harold Bloom. It is a sign of the spaciousness of what could as easily be called his soul as his genius that my study of Lacan, written at times fiercely against the grain of Bloomian poetics, may also be offered with deep respect and affection as a tribute to his teaching. Other individual debts that I have accrued to students and colleagues are acknowledged in the endnotes to this volume. As the book took shape, my conversations with numerous colleagues were beneficial in ways whose traces are evident to me throughout its pages. It is with pleasure that I express my gratitude to Mara Beller, Virginia Blum, Antal Bókay, Daniel Boyarin, Gerald L. Bruns, Gerda Elata, Richard Feldstein, Shoshana Felman, Elizabeth Freund, Christine Froula, Jane Gallop, Ruth Ginsburg, Judith Feher Gurewich, Geoffrey Hartman, Norman Holland, Susana Huller, Alice Jardine, Robert Kramer, Judy Levy, E. James Lieberman, Deborah Anna Luepnitz, Nancy K. Miller, Alicia Ostriker, Ellie Ragland, William J. Richardson, Shlomith Rimmon-Kenan, Peter Rudnytsky, Henry Sussman, Tamise Van Pelt, Graham Ward, and Jon Whitman.

And not least, this book is dedicated to someone who didn't type the manuscript, didn't prepare cups of coffee, and countered every boast of achievement with the claim that I could do better. I don't know if I finally did but it made me mad enough to try.

S.B.

Contents

Abbreviations

When a source text is available in English translation, the translation is quoted and its page reference is given, set off by a slash mark, following the page reference to the source. When a text is not available in English, I have provided my own translation.

CF   Jacques Lacan, *Les complexes familiaux dans la formation de l'individu* (1938; Paris: Navarin, 1984). Translated by Carolyn Asp in abridged form under the title "The Family Complexes," *Critical Texts* 5 (1988): 12–29.

GW   Sigmund Freud, *Gesammelte Werke*, ed. Anna Freud et al. (17 vols. in 16; London: Imago Pub. Co., 1940–52)

OED   *Oxford English Dictionary*

SE   *The Standard Edition of the Complete Psychological Works of Sigmund Freud*, ed. and trans. James Strachey (24 vols.; London: Hogarth Press, 1953–74)

Seminar   *Le séminaire de Jacques Lacan*, ed. Jacques-Alain Miller (Paris: Éditions du Seuil, 1975–91) / *The Seminar of Jacques Lacan*, trans. John Forrester et al. (New York: Norton, 1988–98). In process of publication: 26 vols. are scheduled to appear in French, and 5 vols. have thus far appeared in English. Full references to these texts will be found in the Bibliography.

LACAN AND THE MATTER OF ORIGINS

Introduction

From "Maternal Presence" to "Maternal Object"

As Jacques Lacan elaborates his theory of the processes that constitute the human subject, his conception of the mother's role also changes. That is, the trajectory of the mother—or what Lacan sometimes designates the "maternal object"—closely correlates with his views on the origin and formation of the individual psyche. Lacan's thinking on these issues may be broadly divided into three main periods:

In *Les complexes familiaux dans la formation de l'individu* (1938), written for volume 8 of the *Encyclopédie française*, Lacan argues that separation from the mother at birth and weaning (*sevrage*) are crucial to subsequent psychic development. An awareness of the maternal presence orients the life of every subject. Above all, Lacan posits a dialectical mental organization that originates in the infant's experience of primordial ambivalence (acceptance/rejection) toward the archaic imago of the maternal breast.

Approximately ten years later, in "Le stade du miroir comme formateur de la fonction du *Je*" ("The Mirror Stage as Formative of the Function of the

I") and related essays written in the late 1940s and early 1950s, the powerful maternal imago undergoes erasure. Consigned to the biological-material realm, the mother is peripheral to Lacan's revised conception of the "coming-into-being" or advent of the subject. From among the three complexes described with equal attention in *Les complexes familiaux*, Lacan now foregrounds the second complex, called the "mirror stage": the encounter with a specular counterpart that precipitates the bipolarity of identification/alienation in the subject. This theoretical development entails not only the revision of psychoanalytic tenets concerning the Oedipus complex but also the readjustment of his previous formulations.

During the mid 1950s, Lacan found another place for the mother in his philosophy. The idea of the "paternal metaphor," which he introduced in his seminar on *La relation d'objet* (1956–57) and developed in other works, enables the reconceptualization of the mother's role. She appears as the one who instills in the child a desire to be the phallus that she desires and thereby completely to fill her lack. However, insofar as the mother indicates her dependency on and subordination to the Name-of-the-Father (see, for example, *Écrits*, 557 / 200),[1] she fulfills her mediatory role in the symbolic order. Her mediation, which assumes a prior acknowledgment of the paternal metaphor (also called the phallic signifier and paternal function), is deemed necessary for the child's libidinal normalization. Although Lacan's formulations about feminine sexuality underwent further modification, especially in the early 1970s with the publication of *Seminar XX: Encore*, his views on the mother remained largely unaltered.

Such is the basic itinerary of the mother in Lacan's works. The mother is first conceived of as fully present, then as almost absent, and finally—after a period of occlusion—she returns under the aegis of the phallus. Nevertheless, the formidable imago of the first period continues to haunt his later texts. Her resurgence may be discerned, for instance, in certain vitriolic references to Melanie Klein. Thus, after implicating Klein in the erroneous redirection of psychoanalysis toward the "frustrations coming from the mother, not that such a distortion has shed any light," Lacan addresses the urgent need "to deflate the monstrous conceptualization whose credit in analytic circles [he] challenged" (*Écrits*, 725, 732 / "Guiding Remarks," 87, 94). Contrary to Marcelle Marini's assertion that the "maternal theme in Lacan's works is as sparse as the paternal theme is abundant" (78), my analysis will try to demonstrate that the "maternal theme" is amply, albeit varyingly, present throughout his writings.

In tracing the shifts in Lacan's ideas about the constitution of human subjectivity, I examine his dialogic relations with his foremost precursor—the famous "return to Freud"—as well as with Sandór Ferenczi, Melanie Klein, Alexandre Kojève, Otto Rank, Henri Wallon, and others. In addition to exploring this immediate theoretical environment, I propose to show that certain pre- or nonpsychoanalytic texts, such as Prudentius's *Psychomachia* and Saint Augustine's *Confessions*, may also contribute to an assessment of his complex articulations of the mother's role in individual formation. In what follows I offer an overview of this study.

Chapter 1 tells of how Lacan came to acquire Gustave Courbet's mid-nineteenth-century painting *The Origin of the World* and what he did with the work after it entered into his possession. In detailing this history, I also recount in what ways the previous (as well as the present-day) owners have chosen to display Courbet's partial image of a female nude and discuss some possible implications of these modes of exhibition.

Taking the 1938 *Les complexes familiaux* as a starting point in Chapter 2, I examine the various means by which Lacan adopts, modifies, or thoroughly revises the works of Freud and of his dissenting followers in the early psychoanalytic movement. The controversial thesis of Otto Rank's *The Trauma of Birth* (1924), as will be seen, is particularly significant for Lacan's own formation (and formulations) of this period; and, at the same time, his revisionary recourse to the writings of Ferenczi and of Klein is also already evident. Similarly, Lacan's initial and subsequent readings of the concept of the death drive, as introduced in Freud's *Beyond the Pleasure Principle* (1920), and its relevance to a nostalgia for the maternal body instantiate his avowed fidelity to—and occasional radical swerves away from—the Freudian discovery.

In Chapter 3, I attempt to track a major alteration in Lacan's conception of psychical causality and temporality: from a basically genetic or developmental view to a structural or deferred-action view. In addition to discussing Lacan's extensions of the Freudian notion of deferred action (*Nachträglichkeit*), the question of his vituperative critique of Ferenczi also arises in this chapter. Why, indeed, does Lacan single out Ferenczi's 1913 article on "Stages in the Development of the Sense of Reality" for such strongly negative notice? This question leads me to the theoretical-tactical positions (mainly, the rhetorical strategies of defense and persuasion) that link the careers of Ferenczi and Lacan—with Freud always presiding in the background and providing the reference point for their departures *qua* returns.

Chapters 4 through 8 deal with different aspects of Lacan's theory of the mirror stage and take up several questions concerning the specular image. Whom does the child see? What exactly is in Lacan's mirror apparatus as compared with, for example, that of D. W. Winnicott? With whom does the primary identification that structures all subsequent interhuman relations take place? How does the fraternal rather than the paternal rival come in? Why and how is the maternal excluded?

Chapter 4 opens with an account of the convoluted publication history of Lacan's "The Mirror Stage." The chapter primarily focuses, however, on mirroring theories and theories on mirroring. The empirical research of the French psychologist Henri Wallon in the 1930s, although rarely acknowledged by Lacan himself, serves as a major resource for his articulation of the onset of subjectivity through reflexive recognition. Wallon's and Lacan's writings raise specific questions concerning both the phenomenological status of the mirror (real or metaphorical reflector?) and the identity of the specular image (who's in the mirror?). These issues in turn point to several conjunctions/disjunctions between Lacan's fully developed concept and Winnicott's thesis in "Mirror-Role of Mother and Family in Child Development" (1967). In concluding this chapter, I suggest that the considerable influence of the Lacanian theory of the mirror stage on twentieth-century thought derives from its elaboration of a new secular myth of genesis: "The mirror is the mother of the ego. But the mother is not in the mirror."

Chapter 5 deals with the *machia* in the mirror stage. Conflict is a constant feature of Lacan's teachings about interhuman relations throughout his long career. In the late 1940s, Lacan reformulated both his earlier insistence on the dialectical operations triggered by weaning from the imago of the maternal breast and the agent-provocateur role assigned to the Oedipal father in Freudian theory. He presents the idea of the mirror stage as the originary arena of confrontation through which the ego is constituted. The specular image is, in Lacan's revised view, the child's primary ambivalent object. This chapter also attempts to map what I identify as a "genre shift" in Lacan's writings: from psychological realism in Les *complexes familiaux* to an account of the subject's emergence out of the chaos of natal prematurity and fragmentation (the "body-in-pieces") that is structurally analogous to Christian allegory. Whereas the Hegelian-Kojèvian notion of the deadly struggle for "pure prestige" or recognition provides a paradigm for one type of conflict described by Lacan, in several respects his presentation of intrapsychic conflict bears a strong resemblance to Prudentius's epic poem about the fight for the soul. The final section of this chapter explores the implications of yet another departure from psychoanalytic doctrine: Lacan's revision of the classical stories of Narcissus and Oedipus through an isomorphic graphing or grafting of the one onto the other.

Chapter 6 traces the divergent trajectories of the idea of primary identification in Freud's and Lacan's writings. In contrast to Freud's emphasis on modes of imitation and incorporation of the *father*, Lacan's early work links identificatory fusion to the child's emotional tie with the *mother*. According to *Les complexes familiaux*, primary identification involves a wish to merge with the maternal imago through oral ingestion. However, in the 1940s and early 1950s, Lacan developed his theory of capture-captivation (*captation*) by a specular image; in this view, the subject's erotic and aggressive investments throughout life both derive from and depend on an imaginary relation. His remarkable response to Françoise Dolto's presentation of her successful treatment of two psychotic girls by means of the "flower-dolls" fashioned by their mothers serves to dramatize the preeminent status that Lacan accords visuality and the semblable during this period. Lacan's marginalization of the mother also appears in his detachment of such terms as "pregnancy" and "matrix" from the maternal realm. In his revised lexicon, these terms become realigned with the imaginary (fraternal) and the symbolic (paternal) registers of human experience.

In Chapters 7 and 8, I turn to the many references in Lacan's texts over a thirty-year period to a seemingly mundane anecdote from book 1 of Saint Augustine's *Confessions*. In attempting to motivate the privileged status of this brief anecdote about sibling rivalry, I examine various interrelated factors: its specific content and wider contexts in the *Confessions*, the different theoretical grounds for the citation of the same passage in Lacan's own writings, and the extratheoretical territories on which it possibly encroaches. If the Augustinian scenario may be read as a trace of Lacan's unwritten autobiography—that is, as the "confession" of a generally reticent and private author—

then significant parallelisms, especially concerning the relation to the mother, connect between the individual histories of Augustine and of Lacan.

Among the scenes of repetition discussed in Chapter 8, the reappearance of the anecdote at the close of Lacan's four-chapter section "Of the Gaze as *Objet Petit a*" in *Four Fundamental Concepts of Psycho-Analysis* (1964) receives particularly close attention. In this later citation, the jealous gaze of the child who watches a nursing sibling entails once again the occlusion of the maternal presence. As developed by Lacan, the gaze becomes coextensive with a series of related concepts: the *objet a*, desire, lack (*manque*), castration, and the phallus. Moreover, in connection with Augustine's scene of lactic rivalry, Lacan mentions the widespread folk belief in the evil eye and its reputed power of drying up milk. This linkage points to a crucial but less frequently remarked evolution in his work: the transformation of the human eye into a kind of mouth. In analyzing this theoretical development by means of diverse anthropological evidence, I arrive at a provisional explanation for why it is highly recommended in locales ranging from Greece to Rumania to Sweden that you learn to spit if you propose to stare.

Chapter 9 presents Lacan's conception of the mother-child relationship and its restructuration via the paternal metaphor in the late 1950s. His redefinition of the Oedipus and castration complexes results in a cautionary formula: "The mother is a big crocodile, and you find yourself in her mouth," as well as in a view of the paternal signifier as the child's chief defender against maternal rapacity: "It is a [phallic] roller which protects you, should the jaws suddenly close" (*Seminar XVII*, 129; trans. Fink, 56–57). Lacan's recasting of the Oedipal situation recalls another highly dangerous aggressor, namely, the big bad wolf who gobbles up a little girl and her grandmother. In conjunction with the varied configurations of the mother *qua* crocodile–tiger–petrifying Gorgon in Lacan's texts, I present several folkloric and fairy-tale variants of Little Red Riding Hood's story. My discussion chiefly draws on two psychoanalytic sources: Rivka Eifermann's self-analysis in three essays on the Grimms' "Rotkäppchen" and Ferenczi's hypothesis in his "Confusion of Tongues Between Adults and the Child" about the defensive mechanisms that sexual abuse and violence sometimes activate in young children. But numerous mythic and literary allusions in Lacan's texts considerably complicate any attempted critique of his theorization of the maternal role. His insistence on the negative elementary character of the mother is neither consistently nor one-sidedly upheld. Victor Hugo's images of the sickle and the sheaf in his poem "Booz endormi," for instance, apparently elicit Lacan's references to ancient myths about terrible divine fathers and their murderous sons.

In the Epilogue to this study, I have included an essay that engages Julia Kristeva's ongoing challenge to the superordinate position of the symbolic order in Lacanian theory and practice. Her most concentrated critique appears in an essay entitled "Within the Microcosm of the 'Talking Cure.'" This essay constitutes an important part of Kristeva's attempt to shift the psychoanalytic focus away from its preoccupation with the signifying chain and speech toward operations that are "pre-meaning and pre-sign," in brief, to move from the symbolic toward the semiotic. Her corollary investigation of the bond with / separation from the mother redresses the preeminence granted the phallic signifier and linguistic interpretation of the unconscious. Nevertheless, even while calling into question Lacan's position on these issues, Kristeva fully acknowledges his contribution to a psychoanalytic understanding of the speaking subject who is subjected to the grid—and grief—of language.

In concluding this prologue, I would like to make the claim that my argument is the product of a sustained and cultivated ambivalence.[2] But to my own ears the word "cultivated," with its implications of control and deliberation, is suspect. And to further underscore the happenstance, the oftentimes accidental and compelled (as opposed to cultivated) dimension of this study, I learned about the history of Lacan's possession of *The Origin of the World*[3]—a history that seems expressly designed to serve as a synopsis and allegory of the readings to follow—only after my manuscript was, or seemed to be, complete.

CHAPTER I

A Brief History of *The Origin of the World*

Courbet and Lacan

A visitor to La Prévôté, the country home of Jacques Lacan, purchased after World War II and situated in Guitrancourt, near Mantes-la-Jolie, might be shown to a large room called the *atelier* ("studio"). Lacan had set it up as a library and filled it with art objects, like Freud's office-study in Vienna and later in London. Among the objects that might have engaged the privileged visitor's gaze was a "strange diptych" in a loggia overlooking the room. However, rather than side-by-side or juxtaposed panels, this "double" painting consisted of a wooden screen that concealed the oil painting behind it. A secret mechanism enabled the screen to slide back. The screen, which was commissioned from the artist André Masson (brother-in-law of Sylvia Bataille, whom Lacan married in 1953), reproduced in abstract form the elements of the recessed work: "a Courbet canvas representing a female sexual organ" ("une toile de Courbet, représentant le sexe écarté d'une femme") (Roudinesco, *Jacques Lacan & Co.*, 294 / *Bataille de cent ans*, 305).

In thus briefly identifying the painting-behind-the-painting, Elisabeth

Roudinesco might be said to describe the essential. In *La bataille de cent ans*, her history of the French psychoanalytic movement, she also discloses the identity of the painting's owners and its exact location, a carefully guarded secret after Sylvia and Jacques Lacan bought it in 1955. But it is no less accurate to note that Roudinesco leaves out, or forgets (just as her translator omits the word *écarté* "opened, outspread"), the essential, neglecting to mention the title: *L'origine du monde*. The title contributes to the scandal as well as to the representational status of Gustave Courbet's painting. For while the canvas seems intended to image an object of male desire—"le sexe écarté d'une femme," the title makes ambiguous or opens up the question of this object: what might man want? Nevertheless, the partial disclosure just quoted may be deemed highly, if unintentionally, appropriate. *The Origin* not only has accrued "a series of repeated descriptions," a literary series in which Roudinesco's passage participates, but is also known for the history of concealments that have accompanied its exhibition by various owners (Nochlin, "Origin Without an Original," 77).

In the late nineteenth century, for instance, Maxime du Camp—"*littérateur*, photographer, member of the Académie Française, friend of Flaubert, man about town" (Herz, "Medusa's Head," 168)—published a description of *The Origin* as part of an attack on Courbet's politics, aesthetic theories, and decadent practice of realism in art. Du Camp apparently viewed the painting while it was still in the possession of Khalil Bey (Khalil Sherif Pacha), a Turkish diplomat and art collector living in Paris, who had commissioned it in 1866. In a highly indignant and not quite accurate account, du Camp describes what he sees in Courbet's "difficult" canvas:

> To please a Moslem who paid for his whims in gold, and who, for a time, enjoyed a certain notoriety in Paris because of his prodigalities, Courbet, this same man whose avowed intention was to renew French painting, painted a portrait of a woman which is difficult to describe. In the dressing-room of this foreign personage, one sees a small picture hidden under a green veil. When one draws aside the veil one remains stupefied to perceive a woman, life-size, seen from the front, moved and convulsed, remarkably executed, reproduced *con amore*, as the Italians say, providing the last word in realism. But, by some inconceivable forgetfulness, the artist who copied his model from nature, had neglected to represent the feet, the legs, the

thighs, the stomach, the hips, the chest, the hands, the arms, the shoulders, the neck and the head. (quoted in Herz, "Medusa's Head," 171–72)

The painting reveals both more and less than what du Camp attributes to it. Among its "remarkably executed" details are the very thighs, stomach, hips, chest—in fact, the torso in its entirety and part of one breast—said to be forgotten. Feet, arms, shoulders, neck, and the woman's head are indeed not represented.[1] But to call her body "convulsed" (rather than, say, "relaxed") is perhaps to project onto the figure an orgiastic pleasure that is the mirror-complement of the moral outrage and displeasure du Camp claims the portrait aroused in him.

Courbet's painting does, however, seem to be "difficult to describe." In a catalogue account published on the occasion of the first-ever public exhibition of *The Origin* (at the Brooklyn Museum in 1988), approximately 100 years after Maxime du Camp's diatribe, Linda Nochlin sees something else in the same canvas:

> The painting, a small but richly detailed one, representing a woman's torso, her thighs, and a single breast in extreme foreshortening, certainly falls under the rubric of pornography, as that term is generally understood, and was intended as such. . . . The analogy between this "strange diptych" and Marcel Duchamp's final work, *Étant donnés* ("Given that . . . ") of 1946–66. . . is striking. *Étant donnés* consists of a large wooden door with holes bored in it through which the viewer is forced to peep like a voyeur at the realistically constructed simulacrum of a nude woman's lower body and sex organs. (Nochlin, "Origin of the World," 177–79)

It is once again a question of sexual politics. But the cause for censure and moral dismay here fundamentally differs from du Camp's. That the painting "certainly falls under the rubric of pornography," with its attendant connotations of sexually exploited or fallen women, could not only be supported by way of analogy with Duchamp's *Étant donnés*. It was in two books about sex, not art, that photographs of *The Origin* first appeared during the late 1960s.[2] Furthermore, it is in mid-nineteenth-century erotic or pornographic photography, as Laurence des Cars notes in the Musée d'Orsay's 1990–96 catalogue, that Courbet's "radical composition, which does not conceal its intention behind any historical or literary artifice, finds without doubt one of its sources" (31).[3] The 1862 photograph *Feminine Anatomy* accompanying this claim is indeed remarkably similar to *The Origin* when seen in grainy, black-and-white reproductions.[4]

For des Cars, however, the elaborate care and technical virtuosity that Courbet lavished on the image problematizes its proximity to contemporaneous quasi-anatomical views of female genitalia and, apparently, removes it from classification as pornography ("as that term is generally understood"— in Nochlin's phrase) to the realm of high art. In fact, after almost 130 years of clandestine and sporadic viewing, *The Origin* now hangs in permanent exhibition on the walls of a famous national museum where, according to des Cars's implied defense, it rightly rests: "In sum, it's a question of a great piece of painting" ("En somme, il s'agit là d'un grand morceau de peinture" [31]). Yet to speak of "a great piece" is not a colorless, unmarked usage in this context. With the addition of a word—"piece"—instead of simply "a great painting," the expert revokes or, at least, undermines his own assertion by evoking once again the fragmented body-image of *Feminine Anatomy*. This pornographic instance, which is subcaptioned "element of a stereoscopic view," may provide an illustrative origin not only for *The Origin* but also for the expression *un joli* [or *un beau*] *morceau*—that is, for somewhat informal reference to a sexually available or attractive woman as a nice bit of stuff.

The rhetoric of the *femme-morceau*, however, is not all that might disturb the viewer of Courbet's image. Nochlin, a distinguished feminist art historian and critic, presents another dimension of her critique in an earlier essay written while she was preparing for the exhibition of Courbet's work at the Brooklyn Museum: "[R]epressed or displaced in the classical scene of castration anxiety, it has also been constructed as the very source of artistic creation itself" ("Origin Without an Original," 77). The painting is, in short, not only a "pussy shot" that would deliver the female body to the male gaze for delectation. The subject of the Courbet canvas is not only completely fetishized and profanized. *The Origin of the World* also reenacts the story of Genesis by representing the creation of woman out of male materials. In other words, the origin of the world is not to be found in the represented image, in the partial figure of the female nude, but rather in the male artist-creator-originator who gives shape and meaning to that body as to the blank matter of a canvas surface.

Even more expressly in Courbet's self-reflexive *The Painter's Studio: A Real*

Allegory (1854),[5] a nude model stands slightly behind the seated artist while, according to Nochlin, the "patriarch-painter is absorbed in his act of pro-generation, the supremely originating thrust of brush to canvas." The woman serves here as an empty and passive surface awaiting the fulfillment of phallic inscription. Completing this familial configuration, a little boy ("the son," Nochlin writes) stands before the artist and looks up at him. Thus the painter penetrates and leaves his mark in yet another way. In effect, "Courbet has locked into place patriarchal authority and pictorial original-ity. . . . [A]t the crucial heart of a crucial painting, Courbet-as-patriarch is represented as inscribing sheer matter—the actual pigment on the palette—as the origin of his creation" ("Origin Without an Original," 82). The ear-lier *Painter's Studio* is, then, entirely compatible with the thematics of *The Origin of the World*. Courbet's images of the female body (be they offered piecemeal, as it were, or whole) arguably demonstrate what Lynda Nead calls the "feminization of the canvas/surface" in which sexual and colonial ideologies combine to uphold "the male artist as productive, active, control-ling, a man whose sexuality is channelled through his brush." An exemplary instance of this dominant stereotype may be found in Wassily Kandinsky's 1913 evocation of his relationship to the canvas: "'I learned to battle with the canvas, to come to know it as a being resisting my wish (dream), and to bend it forcibly to this wish. At first it stands there like a pure chaste virgin. . . . And then comes the willful brush which first here, then there, gradually con-quers it with all the energy peculiar to it, like a European colonist'" (quoted in Nead, 56).

In Courbet's *Studio*, the painterly practice of colonization may be found in the portrayal of a landscape, rather than the model-mother-muse, on the canvas at the structural center of his composition. "Courbet goes so far as to cross out woman," Nochlin contends, "by substituting 'nature' for her as the signifier of his creation on the canvas-within-the-canvas. . . . This easy re-placement of the woman's body by landscape . . . bears a precise relation to the almost infinite mutability of the feminine itself under patriarchy" ("Courbet's Real Allegory," 31–32). The interchangeability of woman with landscape or nature suggests a series of metaphorical-political equiva-lences—a lump of clay, a blank page, a piece or bit of stuff—and this series could continue to gather figural surrogates.[6] But perhaps most important, the trope of Mother Nature as a terrifying and uncontrollable force is tamed, contained, subordinated to art; that is, the domain of culture is left to man. From this perspective, what *The Studio* (like *The Origin*) images and clarifies may be called, in Jean-Joseph Goux's terms, "the *masculine* profile of metaphysical hegemony": "Matter, along with nature, has always had a maternal semantic archaeology (reactivated by Plato and Aristotle themselves). . . . If (paternal) form is invariant, (maternal) matter is the changing and relative receptacle that possesses no determination or consistency apart from the imprint of this ideal form" (5).

The methods and mechanical devices invented for viewing *The Origin* seem to heighten an already offensive content. At the home of the Turkish ambassador Khalil Bey, the woman was kept, appropriately enough, behind a veil. She was sometimes shown to selected dinner guests. Here is one brief and often-cited reminiscence: "'A nude woman, without feet and without a head. After dinner, there we were, looking . . . admiring. . . . We finally ran out of enthusiastic comments. . . . This lasted for ten minutes. Courbet never had enough of it'" (quoted in Nochlin, "Origin Without an Original," 80; also in des Cars, 26, and Teyssèdre, 98–99). Had their host possessed a literary bent of mind, he might have quipped as he drew aside the curtain for them, "That's my last dessert. . . . " The painting was also a good resort when the extravagances of this collector and bon vivant required the reorganization of his finances.[7] Baron Francis Hatvany of Budapest purchased the canvas in about 1910 from the Bernheim-Jeune Gallery, where it was held in a double-locked frame. A panel showing a "castle in the snow," apparently *The Château of Blonay* by Courbet or his assistant, concealed *The Origin of the World* from immediate view (Teyssèdre, 86–87). The visitor had to get beyond the locks and castle in order to behold his object of desire. Presumably, the captive beauty was sleeping or simply waiting. Yet although the subject of this panel does invite speculation, it is unknown whether the castle view was especially commissioned from Courbet's studio or considerations of availability and appropriate size determined this choice of concealment. *The Origin* disappeared from Budapest during World War II and eventually returned to Paris, where Lacan acquired it after the war.

Lacan did not merely continue the tradition of his predecessors and conceal the work behind a screen. From the time of his acquisition, he consigned *The Origin of the World* to a regime of silence. He avoided letting it be known that he possessed the canvas. He also apparently rarely displayed it to his guests. He did not lend it for the 1966 exhibition *Courbet in Private French Collections*, an event that would have marked the centennial of its creation. For years nobody seemed to know what had become of the picture (Teyssèdre, 233). So here is something whose details are "excessively *odd*," as a certain prefect of police would have said (Poe, "Purloined Letter," 7). At considerable expense, one purchases the work of a grand master, constructs an elaborate mise-en-scène for its display, but then veils it in silence. *The Origin* became Lacan's well-kept secret, a secret maintained up to his death in September 1981 and for several years thereafter, until Roudinesco disclosed its place in his collection.

Thus in the gallery within the studio of a psychoanalyst, as in the dressing room of a collector of erotic exotica, the Courbet canvas is doubly recessed. It is contained by both its actual frame and its situation in a private space, a secret precinct to which visitors have access only via rare and special invitation. These arrangements may be variously interpreted, but one function is that of control, of mastery; they are designed to assure continued containment as well as erotic titillation. For the pleasure derived from this *objet* is due not only to the artist's mastery, the minutely detailed representation of the female sex, but also to the pleasurable sense of mastery over that which the painting, however ambiguously, names: the maternal body. On the one hand, Lacan treats himself (and his particularly valued visitors)[8] to a peepshow of an unknown naked woman, a profane and illicit, if not pornographic, spectacle. On the other, he constructs a cabinet in which an all-too-familiar site of fascination is lodged in relative safety just like a sacred text or relic of divinity that may be taken out and viewed only under special, ritual circumstances. The image is protected from the beholder-possessor, or the beholder-possessor from the image, by means of a system of controlled disclosure. Silence is also a kind of solution to personal dissonance.

Moreover, just as Lacan did not tell, so he did not sell *The Origin of the World* during his lifetime, even though it was, to put it baldly, worth the earth. When the painting ceremoniously entered into the collection of the Musée d'Orsay on June 26, 1995, it was the heirs of Sylvia and Jacques Lacan who "donated" it in payment of estate taxes. For weeks the press was busy with the body ("offered . . . to the minister of finances," for instance, is how the editors of *Elle* signaled the occasion) and the "fiscal secret" behind the transaction (see Teyssèdre, 388–89). Installed behind a pane of antireflective glass and assigned a bodyguard, Courbet's canvas is secured from vandals but not from the scandal of image and title. It is finally out, full in the view of every visitor. A transparent screen nevertheless mediates between the viewer and the viewed. Bernard Teyssèdre, historiographer and romancer of *The Origin of the World*, elegiacally sums up: "For one hundred and thirty years the painting was hidden, almost nobody saw it. Now that the whole world may see it, nobody, absolutely nobody, will see it any longer" (415).

To punctuate this history of *The Origin of the World* with a different description, Christine Froula's response to the meaning of the title, as well as to what its veiled scenes of exhibition signify, might provide a further explanation of why Lacan became a lifelong closet owner of the painting:

> The invisible "reality" that *L'Origine* foregrounds signals not female lack, the sight of which Freud insists, arouses male castration anxiety, but female "have," the recognition of which . . . can arouse male fear of his own (*étant donné* or always-already) lack—an anxiety that the very notion of castration defensively dissimulates by projecting the specter of lack back upon the maternal body that arouses it. *L'Origine*, in other words, punctures the similarly structured illusionist scenarios of Genesis and Freudian castration anxiety, both of which exchange weakness for power across lines of sexual difference. . . .
>
> If *L'Origine* lures the male viewer into the position of the erotic voyeur, then, it also confronts him with an image that may evoke not only sexual desire but buried emotions of desire, fear, grief, and loss that pertain not to the threat of "castration"—that is, to his actual body parts . . . but to a lost illusion, to phantom female body parts he once felt himself to possess in his early identification with his mother. (Froula, 7–8)

Among the legion of mysteries still surrounding *The Origin of the World*, it remains a riddle when or with whom the title originated. But when Lacan purchased the painting in 1955, it already bore this title.[9] The designation of the work cannot be severed from a central equivocation of the represented image. It is an image of great vulnerability, exposure, subjection to male desire and exploitation. The woman is, after all, literally effaced. In this context of viewing, and whether the artist himself bestowed the title on the work or not, it may be more suitably entitled: *A Master's Piece*. "Il s'agit là d'un grand morceau de peinture." At the very same time, however, the painting as named and known arouses anxiety through the recollection of total dependency, of the gift of life endowed by the mother, of a debt that may be displaced or repressed but never repaid in full, of a sacred mystery that mitigates any illusion of mastery and self-origin. In such a context, the title constitutes an act or profession of veneration, an entitlement that recognizes both the vulnerability of the viewer and the agency of the maternal body. The juxtaposition of two divergent feminist readings underscores this ambiguity. For Nochlin, the painting's title is part of an authoritative masculine assertion of originality, while for Froula, the title implies a subversive acknowledgment of and a tribute to the maternal.

Whatever might be the ultimate aim, meaning, or message of Courbet's representational politics, *The Origin* is evidently more complex and disconcerting than a traditionally eroticized image of the female body. It is also an image of the source of life whose visual analogue in Courbet's oeuvre is, as scholars have often remarked, the representation of the cave that is the origin of the river Loue.[10] *The Source of the Loue* (ca. 1864), painted in four versions within a year or so of *The Origin of the World*, has a comparable morphological as well as thematic figuration. With its precisely executed details of the cave entrance that is the origin of the river's life, Courbet's work may be compared to a "close-up shot" of an unseen but material reality—the womb—that is the origin of the world. In one version of *The Source*, the artist "allows the cave itself entirely to fill the painted surface, making the viewer feel that he could be sucked into its inky depths." Another rendering of the same scene contains a human figure: "a solitary fisherman who stands on a pier projecting out into the water, his tiny figure dwarfed by the awesome magnitude of the cave. Though he seems to be spearing fish, the man's gesture also suggests a boatman ferrying his way across the water into the fathomless depths of the cave" (Dumas, 154–56). Courbet's suggestive and powerful images of the river source repeatedly reveal that which the successive owners of *The Origin of the World* have taken pains to conceal or repress.

Masson's *panneau-masque* for the painting, while following the contours of the original, is thus ingeniously styled to evoke a landscape, thereby condensing *The Source of the Loue* and *The Origin of the World* into one abstract design with traces of an ulterior (or anterior) reality. Ambiguity once again enters into the frame of reference. On the one hand, the painted panel could be read as yet another representation that conspires to turn a questionable ratio into a declaration of foundational principle: female is to male as nature is to culture.[11] On the other, Lacan's positioning of *The Origin* behind the abstract painting commissioned from Masson, a brother-in-*law*, may well serve as a symbolization of his own lifework: the creation of a theory, often highly abstract and impenetrable, that grants preeminence to the phallic signifier and paternal-social pact (the Name-of-the-Father), behind which there is another scene where the mother plays her part.

All kinds of prophylactic measures—the wooden panel, the concealed mechanism, the loggia in the private study at a country residence—are adopted to insulate and distance that scene. This is not simply a commanding distance. The Master, or he who might be called (after Lacan) *le sujet supposé avoir*, requires protection from what he presumes to possess. The very devices that herald his possession of the "key" to *The Origin of the World* also function to disclose the precariousness of this claim. In Froula's strongly argued reading, "[a]s Lacan's *objet* figures a concealed, fetishized maternal body (the realist Courbet) as the repressed 'origin' of masculine symbolic culture (Masson's abstracted image), so his theory veils the sexual dialectics . . . behind the Law of the Father, the material womb behind the symbolic 'phallus,' repressed womb envy behind defensive castration anxiety, women as human subjects behind masculine projections of 'woman'" (9–10). Speaking more generally of Courbet's work in conjunction with Gustave Flaubert's, Neil Herz describes a significance to be sought in the "traces of a period in infancy when elementary acts of representation, of self-representation, and of sexual identification begin to distinguish themselves," even while becoming entangled in the infant mind. "It is not fortuitous," Herz acutely continues, "that the thematics of the Mother often surface in the work of these realists; nor is it surprising that these men . . . in the course of their work, should display both a profound identification with the women they portray and a defensive misogyny when such identifications come to seem threatening" ("In Reply," 214).

And yet, the sheer theatricality of Lacan's exposition or "setup" for this painting, whose appeal is undoubtedly to the male gaze, also implies a moment of mimicry. It could be intended not only flagrantly to declare a dialectics of male domination / female subordination but also to represent a self-conscious and self-reflexive parodic gesture that enacts—and, literally, imposes on the visitor to his gallery—the morally suspect and always somewhat ridiculous posture of a peeping Tom. *Étant donnés*: the display of *The Origin* simultaneously participates in a pattern of misogyny in which art cannot easily be differentiated from fetishism, pornography, or the profanation of the female body, and stands outside or beyond that pattern.[12] In this latter reading, the phallic "have," the position of symbolic privilege, deliberately recalls its interlinkage with other installations of the masculine imaginary.

As a woman and reader of Lacan, I do not have and possibly, in keeping with one phase of his psychoanalytic theory, cannot "have" a fixed or final position on this issue, which clearly impinges on so many others. This uncertainty could denote the fickleness and frailty—in a word, the "feminine" structure—of a readerly character conditioned by the symbolic paternal register. It may be further compelled by the convolutions of the Lacanian position itself that both sustains the phallus and, so to speak, gives it the axe.[13] However, what has tempered—or tampered with—my reading of Lacan is also, I would hope, the desire to avoid, even if such avoidance is only illusory, transfixion in the atelier of a master.

CHAPTER 2

Early Hetero-Orthodoxies

Lacan's Family Complexes

In 1938 Lacan contributed a book-length essay to volume 8 of the *Ency-clopédie française*. The essay, widely known as "*La famille*," was reprinted in 1984 under the title he chose when it initially appeared: *Les complexes famil-iaux dans la formation de l'individu* (Family Complexes in the Formation of the Individual). Lacan's full title presages the main argument of his text. It is familial-cultural factors and not instinctual forces that determine individual development. Moreover, the "subversion of all instinctive rigidity" is the distinctive mark of the human experience, as well as the source from which "fundamental forms of culture arise" (*CF*, 23 / 13).[1]

Compare the full title of Lacan's best known essay in the English-speaking world: "Le stade du miroir comme formateur de la fonction du *Je* telle qu'elle nous est révélée dans l'expérience psychanalytique" (The Mirror Stage as Formative of the Function of the *I* as Revealed in Psychanalytic Experience). The words that link the two titles—*formation* and *formateur*—

signal a special area of interest. In "The Mirror Stage," as in *Les complexes familiaux*, Lacan continues to pursue the phenomenological questions raised but left unanswered at the end of his 1936 essay, "Au-delà du 'Principe de réalité'" (Beyond the 'Reality Principle'). How is reality constituted for human consciousness? How is the *I* in which subjects recognize themselves constructed?[2] But, although in 1938 Lacan highlights the formative value of the family complexes, broadening the psychoanalytic focus to include culturally conditioned phases prior to the Oedipus complex, by 1949 his emphasis has shifted from the affective and familial domain to the visual determination of the subject. In brief, the specular image (in)forms the "I."

Despite this basic alteration in Lacan's thinking about subjectivity, and his apparent objection to the retrospective reading of his work,[3] several lines of continuity may be traced between *Les complexes familiaux* and his later writings:

First, the "intrusion complex" of 1938 is a harbinger of his fully developed concept of the mirror stage. Second, his future insistence on the decisive role of language and law, as opposed to instincts, is also evident in the encyclopedia article ("the complex is dominated by cultural factors" [22 / 13]). Third, in the section devoted to family pathologies ("Les complexes familiaux en pathologie"), Lacan's claim that the father is essential to the social integration and stability of the child, as well as his critique of the "decline of the paternal imago" in contemporary society (72/23), anticipates his conception of the Name-of-the-Father and the psychically devastating effects (psychosis) that attend its foreclosure.

A fourth, and possibly most profound, continuity does not involve any specific content or idea but rather a mode (which could also be called a strategy) of interpretation. *Les complexes familiaux* already exhibits the complexities of Lacan's "return" to Freud and dialogic stance toward other precursors. He engages throughout his essay in an exposition that, at times, radically revises the psychoanalytic doctrines he undertakes to explicate. Although Lacan occasionally notes his divergence from Freudian theory, fundamental differences are often left unsaid or half-said. The essay on the family therefore constitutes a breach of the generic expectation that an encyclopedia be a storehouse of past knowledge. A straightforward recapitulation of basic psychoanalytic tenets is not to be found in it. Lacan stakes out his own position in relation to earlier theories. He builds on psychoanalysis only to begin its reinvention. With varying degrees of explicitness, he interpolates his own distinctive views into the commissioned presentation of a prevailing doctrine.

Yet Lacan not only reads—and rereads—Freud throughout his fifty-year career. He also rereads himself. The importance of *Les complexes familiaux* for an understanding of Lacanian theory derives from its establishment of a point of departure that leads in different directions. As will presently be seen, a close examination of *Les complexes familiaux* does not uphold the back-cover claim of the 1984 Navarin edition that this text presents "no obstacle" to Lacan's later teachings. In introducing the reprinted work, Jacques-Alain Miller explains that his editorial decision not to include it in *Écrits* was due to considerations of its length ("en raison de sa longueur"). By implication, the work of 1938 could have been seamlessly inserted into the essays collected in 1966. The old text bears witness to the new. Significant differences do exist, however, and point to a pattern of modulation and revision. What sometimes complicates or obscures these differences is Lacan's practice of verbal recycling: that is, a tendency to conserve old terminology despite altered meanings. Certain terms or near equivalents ("castration" and "bodily fragmentation" are two examples discussed below) reappear in his texts even though emptied or half-emptied of their former content.

Les complexes familiaux thus calls for attention to a twofold revisionary movement. In what follows, I try to present the various ways in which Lacan's earlier views converge with and also diverge from his later work; and—in a second critical effort not always easily separable from the first—I examine several crucial junctures at which he adopts, modifies, or completely overturns the ideas of Freud and other theorists.

I

In the opening section of *Les complexes familiaux*, "The Complex: Concrete Factor in Family Psychology," Lacan announces a comprehensive genetic or developmental study: "Complexes, imagos, feelings and beliefs will be studied in their relation to the family and in terms of the psychical development that they organize" (25). The following sections provide a detailed mapping of the child's formative experiences within the family group. Lacan identifies three distinct stages of early childhood:

Stage 1, the *weaning complex* (*sevrage*), primarily designates the nursling's loss of the breast but also other crises caused by separation, particularly the expulsion from the mother's body at birth;

Stage 2, the *intrusion complex*, involves the child's interactions with the same-age counterpart, be it sibling or playmate; and,

Stage 3, the *Oedipus complex*, situates the child in the social-cultural context through the mediation of the father and other paternal representatives.

The predominance of a different imago or mental representation (maternal-fraternal-paternal) characterizes the child's progress from one stage to the next.[4] At the conclusion of the third section, Lacan insists on the linkage between processes of socialization and the paternal imago. Any decline of this imago—"his absence, his abjectness, his ambivalence, or his hypocrisy"—during the Oedipal stage is said to have wide-ranging consequences. The "deficiency of the father's personality" all too often seriously impairs the individual's capacity to avoid narcissistic disorders and to achieve culturally valuable sublimations. "Like evil godmothers at the very cradle of the neurotic," Lacan warns, "powerlessness and visionary impracticality surround his ambition so that he stifles the achievements the world expects from him" (*CF*, 73 / 23). Yet the emphasis on the father's crucial role in this section, unequivocal though it may be, does not characterize the essay as a whole and, in fact, is undercut at several points by divergent claims.

Foremost among these claims is Lacan's repeated assertion that the weaning process constitutes the determining factor in individual and cultural development and, consequently, in clinical treatment. In other words, "the mother is father to the man" is a recurrent motif of his 1938 essay. Lacan thus recasts Freud (and Wordsworth). Here are a few examples:

> It [*sevrage*] establishes the most archaic and stable feelings that link the individual to the family. We touch here on the most primitive complex in psychical development, on that which forms a part of all subsequent complexes. (26)

> Thus constituted, the imago of the maternal breast dominates all of man's life. (32 / 15 [trans. modified])

> The [maternal] imago, however, must be sublimated so that the child can make new connections within the social group. . . . Even sublimated, the

imago of the maternal breast continues to play an important psychic role. (33–34 / 15–16)

These statements raise a question about the consciousness that presumably registers the existence of the mother or other primary nurturers. How can an "awareness of the presence which fulfills the maternal function" exist, as Lacan argues (*CF*, 29 / 14), in view of what he also recognizes as the absence of an ego during the rudimentary stages of human life? Ontologically, how can an as-yet-to-be have any sense or understanding of an (m)other's being? To explain the constitutive functions of the mother even before the infant's self-differentiation and recognition of independent object-forms take place, Lacan calls upon both organic (instincts) and sociocultural (complexes) factors. While carefully differentiating complexes from instincts throughout *Les complexes familiaux*, he nevertheless acknowledges the material, biological basis of the first complex. "Whether traumatizing or not," he writes, alluding for the first time in his essay to Otto Rank's theory of the birth trauma, "weaning leaves a permanent trace in the human psyche of the biological relationship it interrupted" (27 / 14). Although the infant's tie to the mother may vary greatly from culture to culture, its vital organic foundation accounts for a universal phenomenon: "the fact that the maternal imago possesses the very depths of the psyche and that its sublimation will be particularly difficult" (32–33 / 15).

Lacan posits here a primal affective relationship ("archaic and stable feelings"), as well as an infantile groping after comfort and care. He even goes so far as to evoke "the child's attachment to its mother's 'apron strings'" (33 / 15). This dyadic arrangement is not, however, idyllic. *Sevrage*, in the narrow sense of weaning from the breast, repeats a more obscure and painful *sevrage*: "a primordial weaning which separates the infant at birth from its matrix" (31 / 15). In view of Lacan's subsequent usages, it is noteworthy that the term "matrix" expressly denotes the mother in this passage. The prematurity of human infants at birth—or, as Lacan elaborately puts it, "an insufficient adaptation to the rupture of the environmental and feeding conditions which maintain the parasitic equilibrium of intra-uterine life" (30 / 15)—generates a profound malaise and anxiety for which no amount of nurturing can compensate. Distress not only dominates the first months of life but also shapes the emotional-ideational organization of the psyche.

This argument in itself constitutes a major deviation from Freudian doctrine. In "From the History of an Infantile Neurosis" (1918), for instance, Freud describes the father as the child's "first and most primitive object-choice" (*SE*, 17: 27), whereas in *Les complexes familiaux*, Lacan speaks of how weaning from the breast gives "the first and most adequate psychic expression" to the separation from the maternal body at birth (31 / 15). But Lacan goes a step further. He also contends that the effects of primordial weaning or separation take precedence over any experiences of sexual repression. Although unmarked by flamboyant declarations of insurgence, his reordering of these events (first, separation from the mother; then, sexual repression) unmistakably departs from established tenets. In a key statement, Lacan argues: "If the psychic traits which escape from ego control first appear as the effect of sexual repression in infancy, their formation reveals itself . . . always closer in time and in structure to the situation of separation that the analysis of anxiety holds to be primordial, that is, to birth" (93 / 25; trans. modified). Like his earlier argument that weaning—be it "traumatizing or not"—leaves an enduring psychical trace of an interrupted physical bond, this formulation once again recalls the controversial thesis of Rank's *The Trauma of Birth* (1924). "[W]e have come up against the final origin of the psychical unconscious in the psycho-physical," Rank announces in his preface, "which we can now make biologically comprehensible as well. In attempting to reconstruct . . . the to all appearances purely physical birth trauma with its prodigious psychical consequences for the whole development of mankind, we are led to recognize in the birth trauma the ultimate biological basis of the psychical" (xiii).

By putting the birth trauma and, secondarily, actual weaning *before* the prohibition against incest, Rank proceeds to supplement (or, as his rival colleagues Karl Abraham and Ernest Jones viewed it, to supplant) the Freudian theory of psychosexual development, particularly the roles of the Oedipus and castration complexes. "The threat of castration," according to Rank,

> hits not only the vaguely remembered primal trauma and the undisposed-of anxiety representing it, but also a second trauma, consciously experienced and painful in character, though later obliterated by repression, namely weaning, the intensity and persistence of which falls far short of that of the first trauma, but owes a great part of its "traumatic" effect to it. Only in the

third place, then, does there appear the genital trauma of castration *regularly phantasied* in the history of the individual. (21)

In this passage and many others, Rank becomes a forerunner of future trends in psychotherapy such as the British school of object relations. The emphasis repeatedly falls on the pivotal influence of the mother rather than the father in human development. Rank's theoretical position in 1924 may be summed up, and parodied, in a single phrase that is attributed to him: *"Im Gegenteil, die Mutter! On ze contrary, ze mozer!"* (Lieberman, 235; also quoted in Gay, *Freud: A Life*, 477).

A double connection, then, may be drawn between Lacan's early views and Rank's. Conceptually, Lacan repeats the Rankian "heresy" by according a predominance to infantile experiences of separation from the mother; institutionally, both theorists profess unswerving loyalty to Freud (Rank made a gift of his book to Freud on 6 May 1923, Freud's birthday),[5] while following an independent path. In the case of Rank, however, the founding father was alive and complexly responsive to his disciple's maverick writings.

In the balance hung Freud's own work on the Oedipus complex and its implications for the treatment of neuroses, as opposed to his extremely close and mutually productive, almost twenty-year long relationship with a gifted, hitherto devoted follower. Prior to the publication of *The Trauma of Birth*, Rank had done much to promote the ideas (and business) of psychoanalysis. As Freud recorded in 1914, "I gained in Otto Rank a most loyal helper and co-worker" (*SE*, 14: 25). He also found and freely acknowledged an ideal son and successor: "the youngest and freshest among us while one knows that [being] so near seventy is quite a serious matter" (Freud to Rank, letter dated 4 August 1922; quoted in Taft, 77). An often reproduced photograph taken in 1922 shows the seven-member "Committee," or inner circle, of the Vienna Psychoanalytic Society. Freud sits regally in a massive leather chair that is placed at a slant and slightly apart from five members (Karl Abraham, Max Eitingon, Ernest Jones, Sándor Ferenczi, and Hans Sachs), who gaze at the camera. Only Rank stands directly behind Freud himself, with his forearm resting in an appropriating manner on the chairback. The heir is apparent. "Rank had entered Freud's circle with only his native abilities," Paul Roazen observes in *Freud and His Followers*, "and Freud was able, metaphorically, to give him birth" (395). Nevertheless, approximately two years after Rank's "birthday gift" appeared in print, and after a period of painful vacillation, Freud definitively rejected it in his *Inhibitions, Symptoms and Anxiety* (1926).

The notoriety surrounding Rank's book on birth trauma is unlikely to have escaped Lacan's notice while he was preparing his encyclopedia article for publication.[6] As what Jessie Taft calls the "blight of Freud's rejection" took its toll within the psychoanalytic profession, Rank became "nonexistent" even to his own students and former adherents (128, xv). The controversy and the ostracism to which it gave rise may partly explain why Rank is never named in *Les complexes familiaux*. Self-preservation is an excellent motive for silence. But the attendant emotional consequences were also harrowing to contemplate. In effect, Freud had drawn himself up in Lear-like rage and dignity and said to Rank, his former favorite son, "Here I disclaim all my paternal care . . . and as a stranger to my heart and me hold thee from this forever."[7] A persistent tension or difficulty characterizes the presentation of the parental imagos in Lacan's texts. His dual attitude toward the work of Rank, as will be seen, also signals that familial-professional disturbance.

II

To assess further the stakes involved in Lacan's concept of the weaning complex, I want now to reevoke in greater detail the ideological basis for Freud's reluctant quarrel with Rank. I propose to track this quarrel (whose personal and political convolutions have already been amply documented)[8] through a series of footnotes and endnotes that Freud appended to his works during the 1920s. Not only the actual content but also the changing positionality of these addenda signpost the shifts in Freud's attitude to Rank and his innovative thesis.

In "The Infantile Genital Organization" (1923), an essay contemporaneous with the completion of *The Trauma of Birth*,[9] Freud emphasizes the indissoluble link between the male genitals and the castration complex: "*the significance of the castration complex can only be rightly appreciated if its origin in the phase of phallic primacy is also taken into account.*" A footnote directs the reader to the reiteration of an already underscored argument:

> It has been quite correctly pointed out that a child gets the idea of narcissistic injury through . . . the experience of losing his mother's breast after suck-

ing, from the daily surrender of his faeces and, indeed, even from his separation from the womb at birth. Nevertheless, one ought not to speak of a castration complex until this idea of a loss has become connected with male
genitals. (*SE*, 19: 144)

Freud initially seems to concur with some unidentified person or persons
("It has been quite correctly pointed out . . . "), and yet does so only to qualify, in fact—to negate, his concession in the very next sentence. The silent
referent of Freud's canceled concession ("quite correctly. . . . Nevertheless,
one ought not to speak") is the recent work of Otto Rank. Freud does not
seem fully to acknowledge to himself, as well as to others, the adversarial position of his disciple. It is therefore hardly surprising that the published expressions of his disagreement tend to turn up, at first, in subtextual addenda.
As Peter Gay comments, "The last adherent Freud expected to give him
trouble was his valued and, he thought, wholly dependable psychoanalytic
son" (*Freud: A Life*, 470).

In a lengthy footnote added in 1923 to the case history of "Little Hans"
(1909), Freud repeats his opposition to the conflation of the castration complex with the child's prior experiences of loss and separation. Although he
mentions several contributors to this contested viewpoint, including Lou
Andreas-Salomé, A. Stärcke, and F. Alexander, the activities of Rank may
only be inferred from "and others." Indirection is still his preferred mode of
disputation:

> It has been urged that every time his mother's breast is withdrawn from a
> baby he is bound to feel it as castration . . . ; that, further, he cannot fail to
> be similarly affected by the regular loss of his faeces, and, finally, that the act
> of birth itself . . . is the prototype of all castration. . . . I have nevertheless
> put forward the view that the term "castration complex" ought to be con-
> fined to those excitations and consequences which are bound up with the
> loss of the *penis*.

Freud's concern in this footnote would seem to be the necessity for terminological consistency and clarity among his colleagues. In the interests of
the science of psychoanalysis, he would avoid a loosely metaphoric recourse
to the term "castration complex"; nevertheless, he claims a willingness to
recognize the "roots of the complex" in diverse infantile experiences of separation (*SE*, 10: 8).

A similarly covert strategy recurs in "The Dissolution of the Oedipus Complex" (1924). Freud initially acknowledges the existence of attempts to expand the castration complex in order to include two earlier types of separation: "Psycho-analysis has recently attached importance to two experiences which all children go through and which, it is suggested, prepare them for the loss of highly valued parts of the body. These experiences are the withdrawal of the mother's breast . . . and the daily demand on them to give up the contents of the bowel." A third type of separation—namely, birth—goes unmentioned at this point, as does the agent-provocateur behind such catchall phrases as "[p]sycho-analysis has recently attached importance" and "it is suggested." Yet the reason given for his reservations differs. Freud no longer characterizes these attempts merely as terminologically dubious but, rather, as empirically unfounded: "[T]here is no evidence to show that, when the threat of castration takes place, those experiences have any effect. It is not until a *fresh* experience [i.e., the sight of female genitals] comes his way that the child begins to reckon with the possibility of being castrated" (*SE*, 19: 175).

Freud's reassertion of the restricted conception of the castration complex is unequivocal. Concurrently, the issue of the redefinition of castration as primary separation from the mother has moved upwards, quite literally, from the margins to the main text of his essay on the Oedipus complex. It is not until the concluding paragraph, however, that he explicitly mentions the work of Rank and expresses his growing unease. The last paragraph may thus be read as, still defensively, occupying the place of an endnote. "Since the publication of Otto Rank's interesting study, *The Trauma of Birth*," Freud writes in 1924, "even the conclusion arrived at by this modest investigation, to the effect that the boy's Oedipus complex is destroyed by the fear of castration, cannot be accepted without further discussion. Nevertheless, it seems to me . . . perhaps inadvisable to begin a criticism or an appreciation of Rank's view at this juncture" (*SE*, 19: 179). The promised "appreciation" appeared two years later in the monograph entitled *Inhibitions, Symptoms and Anxiety*.

By 1926, and under the impact of mounting pressure from other members of the Vienna Psychoanalytic Society, Freud's criticisms of the birth-trauma theory had become numerous and trenchant. Certain inhibitions seem to linger, however. Rank himself is named only a few times, even though Freud carries on "a silent debate" with him throughout the book (Gay, *Freud: A Life*, 485). As in "The Dissolution of the Oedipus Complex," Freud specifically addresses the idea of the birth trauma only in his closing paragraphs, that is, in an endnote fashion. But the tone and the substance of his criticisms have greatly changed: "[T]he main objection to it [Rank's theory] is that it floats in the air instead of being based upon ascertained observations. No body of evidence has been collected to show that difficult and protracted birth does in fact coincide with the development of a neurosis" (*SE*, 20: 152). Freud's final words of outright repudiation and rebuke occur in an addendum whose title, "Anxiety from Transformation of Libido," seems no less significant than its placement in his text: "Rank's contention— which was originally my own—, that the affect of anxiety is a consequence of the event of birth . . . obliged me to review the problem of anxiety once more. But I could make no headway with his idea that birth is a trauma, states of anxiety a reaction of discharge to it and all subsequent affects of anxiety an attempt to 'abreact' it more and more completely" (*SE*, 20: 161). This statement marks the end of a road—"I could make no headway"—long traveled together. If previously Freud's footnotes suggested a hesitation, a dilemma, or a willingness to grant the benefit of some doubts, the location of this addendum corresponds to the finality of its content.

III

The reception of *The Trauma of Birth* may well have generated certain impasses in the usually rigorous and coherent argumentation of *Les complexes familiaux*. Rank himself represented an ambiguous model and precedent. Lacan wanted all his life, I think, simultaneously to occupy two positions: both that of beloved son and intellectual companion, held by Rank before his break with Freud, *and* that of independent, ambitious, even renegade, creator, held by Rank thereafter. However, in the usual course of events, "before" and "after" are (not unlike, say, loyalty and liberty) temporally irreconcilable. What Lacan tries continually to do is to negotiate a position between them.

And so he maintains that although sexual repression exerts a formative influence on childhood development, another event or crisis takes precedence over it. On the one hand, he does not hesitate to define this crisis as "the situation of separation that the analysis of anxiety has caused to be recognized as primordial, namely, that of birth" (*CF*, 93 / 25; trans. modified). On the other, because such formulations might seem uncomfortably close to Rank's heretical thesis, he also disparagingly refers to "the supposed trauma of this situation." In other words, Lacan repeals his appeal to the anxiety associated with natal separation and affirms his affiliation with Freud. However, the key terms of Rank's concept of the birth trauma and Lacan's category of *sevrage* continue to slide over similar, if not quite identical, experiential territory. Hence negation is repeatedly needed. In yet another oblique reference to Rank, Lacan categorically denies any connection between the weaning complex and the birth-trauma theory: "[I]t is nonetheless impossible to make of birth, as certain psychoanalysts do, a psychical trauma" ("il est pourtant impossible de faire de la naissance, avec certains psychanalystes, un traumatisme psychique"). The word "nonetheless" is doubly freighted here. First, Lacan repeatedly evokes "the anxiety [*l'angoisse*] born with life" and other phrases that resonate with Rankian formulations (*CF*, 31, 32). As Rank recapitulates in a letter to Freud dated 9 August 1924, "the anxiety basic to all symptoms was originally tied to the maternal genital" (quoted in Taft, 100). Second, Lacan's "nonetheless" is suspect also, and possibly more so, because of the explicit connection between the weaning complex and the concept of castration in his 1938 essay.

It may be helpful to recall at this point that, according to *The Trauma of Birth*, the ubiquity of the "so-called *castration anxiety*" in both sexes may be explained by the universal experience of birth. "[I]t seems to me quite intelligible," Rank argues, "that the childish primal anxiety, in the course of its development, should cling more especially to the genitals just on account of their vaguely imagined (or remembered) actual biological relation to birth (and procreation)." When Rank situates the castration complex "*[o]nly in the third place*," that is, after birth and actual weaning, he also contrasts the traumas accompanying these two lived or real events with the fantasized component of the castration threat, which, precisely "on account of its unreality, seems predisposed to take upon itself the greatest part of the natal anxiety-affect as guilt feeling" (20–21; emphasis added). Historically speaking, Rank's classification of the castration complex in third place was far more than a mere rearrangement of the psychosexual phases. It represented a red-flag statement for Freud and his adherents by calling into question a foundational principle of psychoanalysis.

Analogously, Lacan parts company with Freud when he elaborates the weaning complex and its effects on the mechanisms of psychical functioning. His valuation of the birth trauma, or what he prefers to call "the very obscure imago of a primordial weaning which separates the infant at birth from its matrix," cannot but subvert the hegemony of the Oedipus and castration complexes (*CF*, 31 / 15). The question implicitly posed in his discussion of castration anxiety is: what can account for the prevalence of this anxiety as manifested in dreams and other symptomatic formations of the individual?

For Lacan (as for Rank), the conundrum may be resolved if the constitutive role of *sevrage* as severance from the maternal body is acknowledged. In Lacan's redelineation of the concept of castration, the dread of irreparable loss, of separation from a highly valued object—a dread not merely fantasized but actualized during the weaning process—first emerges in relation to the mother. Castration anxiety is born with the moment of birth, with the primal passage from the womb into the world. For Freud, a different problem concerning the anxiety-affect of castration arises. He does not question its ubiquity in all human beings but, rather, the causes for its specific presence in the female psyche: what can account for woman's fear of the loss of something she never possessed?

In little boys, the castration complex is, after all, easily understood: it begins when they learn upon seeing the female genitals that the "organ which they value so highly need not necessarily accompany the body" (*SE*, 22: 124–25). But since little girls soon discover that their mothers failed to bestow on them "the boy's far superior equipment" (22: 126), the reason for their castration complex is a puzzle. Self-observation should eliminate any possibility of castration anxiety in girls. The concept of penis envy (*Penisneid*) attempts to address this issue, as well as to reassert the asymmetry between the sexes, by identifying two different manifestations of the castration complex. As Freud summarily puts it, "in boys, anxiety about the penis—in girls, envy for the penis" (14: 92). The girl's castration complex is not at all commensurate with the boy's. Rather, "in accordance with an ancient symbolic equivalence"—namely, a substitutive relation between phallic object and child—"the wish for a penis is replaced by one for a baby" (22: 128). This formulation expands the girl's expression of her complex ("envy for the penis") to encompass the compensatory activity of motherhood. *Neid* (envy) and *Wunsch* (wish) become inextricably linked in this view. Just as smoke is read as an index of fire, so Freud deciphers a woman's wish for a child as the sign or symptom that establishes the prior existence of penis envy.

Lacan generally explicates Freud's texts disingenuously, claiming merely to extract a meaning overlooked or misunderstood by previous commentators. His rereading or "return to Freud" is articulate. Only its implied swerve is silent. At this juncture, however, his critique of Freud's indexical alliances becomes overt: "[O]bserving the existence of the same fantasy in girls [as in boys], he was constrained to explain these facts by precocious revelations of male domination, revelations that led the little girl to nostalgia for virility." The "surcharge of mechanisms" that Freud required in order to motivate the castration complex of girls is, in a word, "erroneous" (*erronée*) (*CF*, 59). Lacan proposes another explanation for the prevalence of castration fantasies in both sexes:

> [T]he material of analytic experience suggests a different interpretation; the fantasy of [penile] castration is preceded, in effect, by an entire series of fantasies of bodily fragmentation that go back in a regressive sequence from dislocation and dismemberment through actual castration [*éviration*], disemboweling, even to [fantasies of] being devoured and entombed. (59–60 / 20; trans. modified)

It is noteworthy that this interpretation appears in the "The Oedipus Complex" section of Lacan's encyclopedia essay; however, the serial movement back to reentombment as revealed in the analytic situation disrupts the model of the Oedipus complex, with its emphasis on the father-child relationship. Once again the ultimate reference point for the castration complex predates the onset of Oedipal conflict. Prior to any real or fantasized threat of penile loss, the child undergoes an actual crisis precipitated by the rupture of archaic ties to the mother. For altogether unlike a newly born animal, which rapidly progresses to motoric coordination and physical self-sufficiency, the human infant is always born too soon. Castration anxiety appears with life, with the first painful intake of air.

IV

Is anatomy, therefore, destiny or not according to Lacan? As is by now evident, there is no simple "yes" or "no" to the question. Lacan gives new meaning to Freud's famous paraphrase of "Napoleon's" epigram "Character is Destiny."[10] On the one hand, he finds the anatomical distinction between the sexes to be irrelevant to castration anxiety; on the other, he does not completely discount biological or organic causes. Together with the distress of bodily dismemberment (*l'angoisse du déchirement vital*), the physiological-psychical experiences of weaning accompany the individual throughout life. The clinical analysis of fragmentation (castration) fantasies, as presented in *Les complexes familiaux*, reveals their association with "a destructive and probing form of penetration, which seeks the secret of the maternal breast" (60 / 20)—as if such a return to the mother could undo or repair the anguish of primary separation.

In thus describing the destructive infantile wish to penetrate the maternal body, Lacan relies on, and revises, the work of Melanie Klein. For example, in her essay on "Early Stages of the Oedipus Conflict" (1928), Klein portrays the mother from the perspective of a raging and vengeful child: "She has frustrated his oral desires, and now she also interferes with his anal pleasures." In retaliation, children of both sexes desire "to get possession of the mother's faeces, by penetrating into her body, cutting it to pieces, devouring and destroying it" (73). Directly after Lacan speaks of the infant's corollary wish to destroy the maternal breast, he mentions Klein, albeit parenthetically, for the first and last time in his 1938 essay. By coincidence (or perhaps divination?), the sentence in which her name appears is omitted in the English version: "But the researchers who have best understood the maternal origin of these fantasies (Melanie Klein) are interested only in the symmetry and extension that they bring to bear on the formation of the Oedipus complex, for example in revealing the boy's yearning for maternity [*la nostalgie de la maternité*]" (60).

In Lacan's view, Klein got it only half right. Whereas she recognizes that the mother is the originary cause of castration fantasies, she negates her own important insight, or defends against it, by predating the Oedipal phase and finding evidence of its effects in the earliest human experiences. Klein does not posit that the drives and anxieties common to both sexes are an outcome of separation at birth and weaning. Rather, backshifting the Oedipus complex to prior stages, she advocates a notion of womb envy ("yearning for maternity") in boys that symmetrically corresponds to penis envy in girls.

What Klein proposed, in her own view, was a theoretical direction that correlated with the Freudian doctrine. Unlike Rank, Klein did not diminish the Oedipus complex but, on the contrary, enhanced it by extending its sway over the infant psyche. It is exactly this extension, however, that aroused a furor within the British psychoanalytic movement during the 1930s and early 1940s. At a meeting of the British Society held on 7 April 1943, Anna Freud dissected the differences between "psychoanalytic theory as I understand it" and Klein's writings with a clarity and precision that her father, in particular, would have applauded. Most pertinent to the present discussion is this distinction: "One of the outstanding differences between Freudian and Kleinian theory is that Mrs Klein sees in the first months of life evidence of a wide range of differentiated object relations, partly libidinal and partly aggressive. Freudian theory . . . allows at this period only for the crudest rudiments of object relationships and sees life governed by the desire for instinct gratification" (quoted in King and Steiner, 421, 420).

The crux of this debate, then, is a question of dates and points of origin. Behind all the details of disagreement, as Anna Freud's analysis clarifies, there remains a "serious divergence of views about the sequence of development and the dating of certain all important events and functions: the beginning of object relationship; the onset and climax of the Oedipus complex; the formation of the superego" (424). Put another way—on a sliding scale, if Klein pushes the Oedipus complex back from ages 3–5 to 0, Freud and his followers would hold it at around 3–5. In objecting to Klein's backshifting of the Oedipus complex, Lacan might appear to join forces with her critics and detractors. In fact, his rejection of the Kleinian viewpoint does not return him to the accepted or orthodox position but, rather, removes him even further from it. He takes up a theoretical stance that is both counter to Klein's and, at the same time, to the more conservative factions opposing her. Again on a sliding scale, he would advance the weaning complex from 0 to 3–5 years and beyond.

For Lacan sees the long shadow of the mother, as well as "the play of forces arising from weaning," cast forward from the very first phase of life to all other phases of human development (*CF*, 56 / 20). Expelled and exiled in a state of unaccommodation that persists well beyond the first months of life, every subject is constrained to follow in the stumbling, postlapsarian footsteps of the primal parents. As Lacan proposes in 1938, "the metaphysical mirage of universal harmony, the mystic abyss of affective fusion, the social utopia of totalitarian guardianship"—each of these forms of individual and collective nostalgia derives from a longing for the "paradise lost before birth" (35 / 16). While comparisons of the intrauterine state to paradise are common enough, Lacan's imagery echoes one of the dominant tropes in Rank's *Trauma of Birth*. A short list of examples would include: "in the *anxiety dream* the *birth trauma*, the expulsion from Paradise, is often reproduced with all its really experienced physical sensations and details"; "[i]n the legends of Paradise and the Golden Age we have before us a description of this primal [pre-parturition] condition"; and "we must bear in mind that the pleasurable primal state is interrupted through the act of birth . . . and that the rest of life consists in replacing this lost paradise" (75, 116, 187). For Rank, the expulsion from paradise in the Book of Genesis constitutes an allegorical incarnation of the birth trauma. Moreover, he places the biblical story of Eve's creation from Adam's rib among the numerous deliverance myths "where, as a direct reversal of the real occurrence, the woman is cut out of the man. . . . The ensuing expulsion from Paradise, which has become . . . the symbol of the unattainable blessed primal condition, represents once again a repetition of painful parturition, the separation from the mother" (113). At the core of Rank's interpretive activity (and, to a comparable extent, Lacan's) is the trace of the maternal effect on all that may be called human.

V

To turn to a metacritical perspective, issues of origin, in both the senses of causality and priority, are overdetermined throughout *Les complexes familiaux*. The aim is not only to define first causes but to be first to discover them. "In order to define the genesis of repression according to a psychological schema," Lacan contends, "we must recognize in the castration fantasy . . . the mother as the object which causes it" (61 / 21). However, other "Explorers of the Unconscious"—to borrow Rank's dedicatory phrase to Freud in presenting him with the birth-trauma book—were there before Lacan.

Ten years prior to the publication of *Les complexes familiaux*, Klein had observed in her essay on Oedipal conflict: "[T]he mother who takes away the child's faeces signifies also a mother who dismembers and castrates him." In addition to withholding the breast and removing the faeces, the mother imposes other types of separation on the infant. "Not only by means of the anal frustrations which she inflicts," according to Klein, does the mother "pave the way for the castration complex: in terms of psychic reality she *is* already the *castrator*" ("Early Stages," 74). Moreover, as already noted, Rank's idea of castration anxiety arising from separation from the womb and the breast precedes both Klein's and Lacan's formulations: "[T]he importance of the castration fear is based," Rank writes in 1924, "on the primal castration at birth, that is, on the separation of the child from the mother" (20). In a remarkable footnote to this statement, he adds that "at the end of the analytic cure [he] found the phallus often used as 'symbol' of the umbilical cord" in the dreams of patients (20 n. 2).[11] By implication, when a degree of psychic (re)integration sufficient to end the treatment takes place, one indicator is that the phallic organ reveals its function as a displacement of or, in Lacan's later terms, a metonymy for maternal attachment. The umbilical cord between analyst and analysand, as Rank might have said, is ready to be cut.

But while the idea of the mother as the origin of castration anxiety does not originate with Lacan, his discussion of *sevrage* as castration differs from the Rankian and Kleinian views in two distinct ways. Lacan situates what Rank calls the "primal trauma" (birth) and "second trauma" (weaning) under the single category of the weaning complex; and, most notably, he introduces the intrusion complex (mirror stage) between the crisis of weaning and the Oedipus complex.

For all three theorists, however, the anxiety associated with loss of the penis is an ancillary and belated formation. As the contents of the infant's primal separation experiences evolve in patriarchal societies, the penis becomes their differentiated form. What analytic practice repeatedly demonstrates, according to Lacan, is that the fear of castration (in the narrow sense) represents a "radical form" of the subject's "primordial loss," a loss correlated with the maternal object. He further explains: "The subject responds to the anguish this object evokes by reproducing a masochistic rejection [of the object] . . . but he acts outs this rejection according to the structure that he has acquired, i.e., in imaginary localization" (*CF,* 61 / 21). That acquired "localization" or structure is the fantasy of penile castration whose manifest expression on the collective-societal level can take various ritualized forms of defense, as in "rites of circumcision that, in order to sanction sexual maturity, demonstrate that the subject accedes to it only at the price of corporeal mutilation" (61). Put another way, circumcision symbolically repeats the cut of the umbilical connection that sometimes is reconfigured as the "apron strings" between mother and child.

One of the difficulties in reading Lacan, as I indicated at the outset of this chapter, is his practice of retaining identical or similar terms even though their meanings and frameworks of reference have changed. Such a key term is "castration." In *Les complexes familiaux*, the term clearly has a less-than-literal signification. Lacan redefines the role of the male organ in the psychical constellation known (since Freud) as castration. To the extent that the concept of castration designates an irrecuperable loss, it may be grouped together with the terms "phallus," "lack" (*manque*), and the untranslatable "*objet a*" in his later writings. However, castration eventually comes to represent a *noncorporeal* cut, absence, or void that marks all human experience. In 1964, when elaborating on the "imaged embodiment of the *minus-phi* [(-φ)] of castration," Lacan points to symbolic representations (specifically, to the memento mori floating across the floor in Hans Holbein's *The Ambassadors*) of a pervasive lack that governs human drives and desires (*Seminar XI*, 83 / 89). The term "castration" thus no longer has phenomenological moorings in the separation inflicted at birth or in the withdrawal of the breast. By contrast, in 1938, the loss for which varied symbolizations of castration perform a substitutive function does have a concrete, albeit irrecoverable, referent. Lacan counts *éviration*, or deprivation of the penis, as only one in the series of dismemberment fantasies that may be traced back to weaning from the maternal body (*CF,* 60 / 20).

Yet another term that recurs with a significant difference more directly concerns the subject's—rather than the mother's—body: namely, the notion of "bodily fragmentation" (*morcellement du corps*) in *Les complexes familiaux* and of the "fragmented body-image" (*image morcelée du corps*) in "The Mirror Stage." These terms seem at first indistinguishable from each other. Lacan indeed links both of them to natal prematuration and motoric incapacity. At the deepest levels of the psyche, a dismembered imago of one's body prevails that harks back to "the fact of a real *specific prematurity of birth*" (*Écrits*, 97 / 4). The word "image," however, is appended in the interval (1938 to 1949) that separates the two essays. The "fragmented body-image" posits a visual-spatial recognition of the body as the necessary prelude to a cognition of being. The most critical event for the constitution of subjectivity is, in a phrase, "the mirror stage *as an identification*" (94 / 2). Lacan's emphasis on visuality and identification with the fraternal counterpart (I shall return to this emphasis in later chapters) coincides with the marginalization or repudiation of the mother's agency.

According to Lacan's account in *Les complexes familiaux*, the accent falls quite differently. Throughout life, the individual reproduces patterns of renunciation and restitution with the imago of the maternal breast at their core. (Lacan cites the *Fort/Da* game recounted in Freud's *Beyond the Pleasure Principle* as a prime example of this seesaw movement.)[12] The expulsion from the womb, or what he calls "the prenatal habitat" (34 / 16), does not only inculcate feelings of fragmentation and castration anxiety in the subject. Lacan also attributes the inception of ambivalence to processes of actual weaning; the withdrawal of the breast activates an affective polarity, an oscillation between acceptance/refusal. The weaning complex is, he emphatically, even dogmatically, states, "without a doubt the first crisis whose resolution will have a dialectical structure." Whatever attitude finally prevails—be it one of acceptance or refusal of weaning—the binary tension initially experienced in relation to the primary nurturer persists and structures the individual's mental life. "It seems that for the first time," Lacan argues, "a basic tension resolves itself through an intellectual intention" (27 / 14).

In the light of Lacan's later work, this contention is striking on three counts: first, in its implication of a dialectical *démarche*, a form of Hegelianism that will feature prominently in his writings about the narcissistic (imaginary) register; second, in its assumption of the maternal imago as the source of this dialectical structure. Whereas the first represents a strong point of continuity with his future views of the ego, the second will turn out to be thoroughly disjunctive. The phrase "for the first time" contains a third and possibly less evident presupposition. Whereas from Lacan's structural perspective of the 1950s and on, the subject's history is not to be understood by analogy with any notions of growth or of linearity, his survey of the family complexes is still basically genetic.

Hence another terminological shift needs to be noted. The term "complex" is a developmental concept in 1938. Moreover, it is also inherently "dynamic" in the psychoanalytic sense of a conflict between contrary mental forces.[13] Lacan's definition of psychical integration as "a dialectical process that makes every new form of conflict emerge from preceding conflicts with reality" encapsulates the organic and dynamic trends in his early thought (*CF*, 23 / 13; trans. modified). His exposition of the three complexes is consonant with this principle of growth through conflict. The intrusion and Oedipus complexes are inconceivable without the weaning complex; the second and third stages repeat with variations the stage that precedes them.

Lacan thus speaks of the "reenactment" (*reproduction* in the French) and "renewal of the pathos of weaning" during the intrusion complex. Stressing repetition-in-development, he notes the continued predominance of the mother in this later stage: "The sight of the unweaned sibling provokes a special aggression only because it repeats for the subject the imago of the maternal situation." The mirror stage is the self-inflicted replication of the weaning crisis. In Lacan's own words, "[C]'est le pathétique du sevrage que le sujet s'inflige à nouveau" (40–41 / 17; trans. modified). He also characterizes the second complex as marked by a dynamism that carries over from the first. Two attitudes simultaneously compete for ascendancy in the field of psychical forces: an intense feeling of fusion in which the child identifies with the sibling or playmate as opposed to a surge of love that recognizes an existent apart from the self. "Identification" and "love," seemingly nondichotomous terms, denote an affective bipolarity whose "opposition will be profound in later stages of development" (39 / 17). In sum, identification leads to fusion or desire for fusion; love, to alienation.

Lacan's analysis of these tendencies constitutes another of his silent swerves from Freudian theory. In "On Narcissism" (1914), Freud classifies the various types of identification that may develop into love (*SE*, 14: 90). In *Les complexes familiaux*, instead of narcissistic identification resulting in love, as Freud claims it does, love (defined as a recognition of the object as other than one's self) undoes identification and triggers aggression. The very term "intrusion" indicates that aggressive impulses already feature in this early version of the mirror stage. It is not that love is not enough. Love is basically impossible. By rearticulating the notion of love in dynamic opposition to identification, Lacan disarticulates it, destroys it; or, at least, he implies a profound suspicion of its sustained experiential reality between subjects.

Just as the intrusion complex resonates with the weaning complex and its "basic tension" (27 / 14), so the affective residues of the first two stages resurge during the third. Ambivalent feelings toward the father reenact the dialectical patterns of acceptance/rejection (stage one) and identification/love (stage two). The young child's new object of ambivalence—the paternal imago—"usually stands in the place of the double with which the ego first identifies" (64 / 21). In Lacan's view, this tension acquires "a profound genetic importance since it remains inscribed in the psyche in two ineradicable ways": on the one hand, identification with the father brings about the formation "called the ego ideal" and produces sublimation; on the other, aggression directed against the father strengthens the preexisting agency "called the superego" and also deepens repression (51 / 19). How the superego came to be established *before* the Oedipus complex will be dealt with in the next section.

Thus the child's confrontation with the Oedipal father, like the mirror-stage encounter with the sibling rival, both repeats and develops the situational dynamics of the weaning complex, of which it is a more fully differentiated version. The concept of the complex is therefore abyssal, as well as organic, because the later structures are contained within the originary one.

VI

Lacan's discussion of the stages of childhood development, all enmeshed in the familial-social environment that divides the nurturing experiences of human infants from those of animals, does not only differ from his own later formulations. His discussion broadly deviates on two levels from the premises of what in 1938 could already be termed canonical psychoanalysis.

On the ontogenetic level, his concept of *sevrage* subverts the preeminence accorded the Oedipus complex and the functions of the father, as well as the linkage between castration anxiety and male genitalia. On the phylogenetic level, Lacan challenges the Freudian explanation in *Totem and Taboo* (1913) of the rise of religious and societal organization. He briefly but decisively refutes the mythic father's role—"a phantom increasingly uncertain," as he puts it—in shaping the murderous inclinations and, subsequently, the acute (and culturally definitive) remorse of the horde of brothers. Lacan offers an alternative explanation of the origins of civilization: "[T]he universal traces and long survival of a matriarchal family structure which developed all basic cultural forms, especially a strong repression of sexuality, reveal that the structure of the human family has foundations far removed from male physical supremacy" (*CF*, 54–55 / 20).[14]

If the paternal sphere of influence is thus delimited, and the "repression of sexuality" traced back to the matriarchal group, it follows that the emergence of the superego should differ as well. Such, indeed, is Lacan's dissident thesis. It is necessary to recall at this point that the superego, as defined in *The Ego and the Id* (1923), is the psychical agency causally linked to repression. In Freud's reiterated designation, the superego is also the heir of the Oedipus complex (*SE*, 19: 36 and 22: 129); that is, when the little boy renounces his hostility toward his father-rival and begins to identify with him, the paternal prohibition of incest and other transgressions becomes internalized. The identification that facilitates the repression of desire for the mother and aggression toward the father brings about the installation of the superego in the child. Lacan proceeds to reorder this widely accepted chain of psychical events. However, because his version appears in the section of *Les complexes familiaux* entitled "Le complexe d'Oedipe," it might appear that he intends merely to confirm the Freudian correlation between the decline of the Oedipus complex and the ascent of the superego. In fact, the section heading may be read as a form of camouflage for the revisionist argument that follows.

Contra Freud (but without overt declaration of dissent), Lacan proposes that the superego is first formed in response to *maternal* authority. Disciplinary demands such as "weaning and sphincter control" ("disciplines du sevrage et des sphincters"), usually imposed by the mother or her substitutes, imprint the exigencies of outside reality on the nascent ego (*CF*, 62 / 21). In other words, the superegoic functions appear prior to the Oedipus complex and any paternal intervention.

Lacan's ideas converge at this point with Sándor Ferenczi's provocative proposal, in his "Psycho-Analysis of Sexual Habits" (1925), that a "sphincter-morality" precedes and paves the way for moral development. Ferenczi describes the early process of morality-building as follows: "[A]nal and ure-thral identification with the parents . . . appears to build up in the child's mind a sort of physiological forerunner of the ego-ideal or super-ego. . . . It is by no means improbable that this, as yet semi-physiological, morality forms the essential groundwork of later purely mental morality" (267). Citing Ferenczi, Klein claims to expand—"My findings lead rather further"—the suggestion of her former training analyst and mentor: "[T]he tyranny of a super-ego which devours, dismembers and castrates . . . is formed from the image of father and mother alike" ("Early Stages," 70, 75). Lacan integrates this notion of a semi-physiological superego into his own work. Unlike Ferenczi and Klein, however, he identifies the mother alone, and not the "father and mother alike," as the parental model who inculcates the first traces of morality in the child. The mother thereby acquires yet another formative capacity that, according to Freud, belongs mainly to the father. Lacan's "single-parent" focus is also consistent with his theorization of three complexes over which three different imagos sequentially preside.

More broadly viewed, Lacan's "return to Freud" throughout his early essay is highly systematic, however stylistically or in other ways obscure. The argument generally unfolds with a relentless, revisionary coherence. For instance, given his contention that the father and other authoritative figures do not provide the prototype for the superego, the correlative assumption should be that repression is not activated by the resolution of the Oedipus complex. Indeed, Lacan argues that both "the most archaic nucleus of the superego" and "the most massive repression" originate with the maternal imago (*CF*, 61 / 21). The reiterated "most" ("le plus archaïque . . . la plus massive") underscores the crucial formative functions attributed to the mother. But, for Freud (as Lacan well knew), the emergence of the superego and repression is linked to the decline of the Oedipal phase. When Freud writes in "The Dissolution of the Oedipus Complex" that he sees "no reason for denying the name of a 'repression' to the ego's turning away from the Oedipus complex," he also immediately specifies the causal relation among these movements: "[L]ater repressions come about for the most part with the participation of the super-ego . . . only just being formed" (*SE*, 19: 177). In the beginning was the Oedipus complex, and then the superego, and lastly repression. According to the Lacanian scheme of genesis, by contrast, in the beginning was *sevrage*. All the rest follows from this intrauterine rupture and its repetition when actual weaning from the maternal breast takes place.

To recast into the terms of Lacan's future teaching, the Name-of-the-Mother initiates the child into the realm of language, law, and culture. The "no" of the mother—as in: "Thou shalt not dwell in my womb" or "Thou shalt not incorporate my breast"—is decisive for the formation of the subject. This transposition is not fetched from afar. As formulated in *Les complexes familiaux*, although weaning interrupts the biological tie between mother and child, that vital relationship is embedded in social structures from its inception. Insofar as Lacan defines the weaning complex as a variable and contingent phenomenon for which, above all, cultural factors are decisive, his contribution to the *Encyclopédie française* anticipates his concept of the symbolic order. Still more specifically, in enumerating the ways whereby the family environment enables the transmission of culture, Lacan includes "early education, the repression of instincts, and the acquisition of language justly called maternal" (13).

It may therefore be argued (quite cogently, in my view) that Lacan's discussion of the superego and repression would be more appropriately placed in the first section of his essay, "Le complexe du sevrage," than in the third, "Le complexe d'Oedipe." The motive for this displacement—calculated defense or not?—is a matter of speculation. Be that as it may, Lacan soon demonstrates fealty to his paternal precursor (acceptance) and brackets the mother (refusal) by reiterating that the archaic origins of the superego must be surmounted:

> Even though the superego might have received some traces of reality solely from maternal repression (the disciplines of weaning and sphincter control), it is in the Oedipus complex that repression transcends its narcissistic form. (62 / 21; trans. modified)

> The structure of the Oedipal drama points to the father as giving the function of sublimation its pre-eminent and purest form ["la plus éminente . . . la plus pure"]. In the Oedipal identification the maternal imago betrays the contamination of primordial identifications. (64–65 / 22)

In adjudicating between the parents, Lacan finds in favor of the father. He is a source of endowment and transcendence; she, of contamination. The one parent gives; the (m)other betrays. Rhetorically, Lacan uses a parallel structure—the doubled superlative of "most eminent" and "most pure"—if not to cancel, then, at least to contain the formative effects—"most archaic nucleus of the superego" and "most massive repression"—of the maternal imago. Whereas previously the weaning complex was deemed the basis for psychical development, in the passages just quoted, the paternal function is paramount.

Such incompatibilities disappear in Lacan's formulations of the late 1940s and early 1950s. He no longer perceives separation from the mother as setting all individuals in the direction of their dialectical destinations. The crucial factor for mental life is the specular encounter: "This moment in which the mirror-stage comes to an end inaugurates, by the identification with the *imago* of the counterpart and the drama of primordial jealousy . . . the dialectic that will henceforth link the *I* to socially elaborated situations" (*Écrits*, 98 / 5). Lacan thus silently discards his earlier concept of a primordial ambivalence whose point of origin is the process of weaning. Correspondingly, he reassigns other subject-building functions formerly attributed to a maternal presence. In revising himself, he draws closer to Freud. At the same time, however, he modifies the Freudian connection that he upheld in 1938 between the real father (as opposed to the "phantom" or mythic father of the primal horde) and the socialization of the child. It is now "the *imago* of the counterpart" that introduces "the *I* to socially elaborated situations." Lacan thereby clears the stage (*stade*, as in "stadium") for the subject's aggressive competition with the other.

VII

Les complexes familiaux continually displays analogous patterns of hetero-orthodoxy. Compliance mingles with dissension, adherence with heresy, throughout the essay. The controversial concept of *Todestriebe*, a concept developed in *Beyond the Pleasure Principle* (1920) and sustained throughout Freud's writings,[15] provides an exemplary instance of Lacan's argumentative decorum. On the one hand, unlike many of Freud's disciples and colleagues,[16] Lacan expressly accepts the notion of a basic tendency to return to an inorganic state of quiescence: "The fact of man's inclination toward death as though it were a desirable object," he writes, "is a reality that analysis lays bare at all levels of the psyche." On the other, he proceeds to describe this desire for death as conditioned by the weaning complex, which is, in his definition, a culturally dependent formation. As manifested in human beings, the impulsion toward death is not organic or biologically encoded. "The attraction toward death," in his 1938 view, "can be satisfactorily explained by the idea that we are developing here, viz., the complex, a functional unit of the psyche" (*CF*, 33 / 15).

Drawing on clinical and anthropological evidence, Lacan attempts to reinforce the cultural connection between the imago of the breast and the death wish: "the hunger strike of the anorexic; slow poisoning through the ingestion of drugs; the starvation diets of gastric neuroses. . . . burial practices where certain customs clearly signify a psychological return to the maternal breast." In a rare moment of outright dissent, Lacan asserts that the central thesis of *Beyond the Pleasure Principle* exemplifies how "Freud's genius bowed to the biological prejudice which demands that all tendencies refer to an instinct" (33–34 / 15). Even as he agrees with Freud that the inclination toward death is "generic" and "not just morbid" in all human subjects, he also argues contra Freud that this regressive inclination is primarily determined by cultural phenomena (34 / 15).

Lacan returns to the same issue ten years later. In "Aggressivity in Psychoanalysis" (1948), he again argues that Freud's choice of the term *Todestriebe* (which in the highly ambiguous context of *Beyond the Pleasure Principle* generally does denote a phylogenetic trend that consists of an instinctual conservative impulse extending to all living organisms) discloses "the aporia that confronted this great mind in the most profound attempt so far made to formulate an experience of man in the register of biology" (*Écrits*, 101 / 8). The "experience of man" cannot be reduced to biological determinations or nature; the symbolic mediates all that pertains to the strictly human realm. It is not instincts as such that govern the psyche but, rather, what now may be termed the *inscription* of those instincts. The relationship between "man and his own body" is visibly exhibited in social practices: "from rites involving tattooing, incision, and circumcision in primitive societies to what, in advanced societies, might be called the Procrustean arbitrariness of fashion" (104–5 / 11). There is no dark realm of death-related desires beyond language. The metapsychological source of death's attraction is to be found in concrete discursive systems. In effect, as elsewhere in his writings, Lacan here advocates a reorientation of the very notion of materiality, shifting the medico-analytic focus from organic mechanisms to the actualities of verbal communication. While he still concurs with the psychical reality of the death tendency, he swerves from both his previous viewpoint—namely, that "the subject seeks to regain the maternal imago in his capitulation to death" (*CF*, 34 / 15)—and Freud's. "The unconscious," Lacan writes in "The Agency of the Letter" (1957), "is neither primordial nor instinctual; what it knows about the elementary is no more than the elements of the signifier" (522 / 170).

The question of the death tendency thus bears the complex mark of diverse stations in Lacan's analytic career. It also presages the complications of his future position in the psychoanalytic movement. Straining against the Freudian enclosure, he nevertheless strives to remain within its bounds.

To recapitulate the main trends presented in this chapter:

First, in relation to Freud, Lacan's essay on the family abounds in "returns" to the founding father. Lacan puts a considerable distance and yet creates proximities between his vision of psychoanalysis and Freud's. The paternal imago embodied in the work of Freud apparently represented from the outset a highly ambivalent object for Lacan. If the dynamic relation exemplified by the *Fort/Da* game indeed carries over into other stages (and Lacan says it does), it might not be too strained to suggest a structural analogy between Freud's texts as handled by Lacan and the famous bobbin cast back and forth by the child. As Lacan proposes in 1938, once established during the weaning complex, a dialectical tension marks the subject's reactions to all of the imagos.

Second, in relation to Lacan himself, multiple aspects of mental functioning—castration anxiety, ambivalence, the superego, and repression—are said to derive from primary separation in *Les complexes familiaux*. If the title "formative of the function of the *I* as revealed in the psychoanalytic experience" had been assigned in 1938, it would probably have been accorded the mother. From the late 1940s on, however, the mirror and then the letter (in)form the subject. In "The Mirror Stage," Lacan describes the gestalt, or total body image, as a form "more constituent than constituted"—that is, as determining rather than determined by the ego (*Écrits*, 95 / 2). And in his

"Seminar on 'The Purloined Letter'" (1955), he also claims that the symbolic order is "constitutive for the subject" (*Écrits*, 12 / 29). Interactions with the maternal imago become marginal to these processes of formation. The mirror stage and the Oedipus complex are no longer "new categories" that bear the archaic, indelible, and sometimes unendurable mark of the weaning complex (*CF*, 28 / 14). Summarily stated, Lacan revises his remapping of the psychical trajectory of the subject.

CHAPTER 3

"History Is Not the Past"

Lacan's Critique of Ferenczi

In the ten-year interval between the composition of *Les complexes familiaux* and "Le stade du miroir," Lacan's thinking about psychical causality and temporality changed greatly. He turned from a primarily genetic view that assumed a series of developmental stages and increasingly took into account the revision of the past from the vantage point of the present. Chronological or unidirectional progression gave way to the notion of *Nachträglichkeit*, a term usually translated as "deferred action" or "retroaction" (*après coup*).[1] This shift entailed the abandonment of his three-stage model of subjectivity.

By 1953, Lacan openly disparaged the "mythology of instinctual maturation" that other writers had "built out of selections from the works of Freud" (*Écrits*, 263 / 54). As indicated in Chapter 2, instead of a series of more or less sequential complexes (weaning—intrusion—the Oedipus complex), a dialectical structure (identification/alienation), which is set in motion by the confrontation with the specular image, becomes a constitutive feature of the subject's inner world and relation to outer reality. This subject would be no more than a "living marionette" were it not, as Lacan stipulates in "The Direction of the Treatment" (1958), that "language allows him to regard himself as the scene-shifter, or even the director of the entire imaginary capture" (*Écrits*, 637 / 272). Thus, the second complex (now exclusively called the "mirror stage") and the third complex continue to be elaborated in his writings, whereas the first complex—and the predominant imago of the maternal breast—virtually disappears. In this chapter I explore some implications of Lacan's reconceptualization of the clockwork that regulates mental life.[2]

I

In the introductory remarks to "The Signification of the Phallus" (1958), a lecture originally delivered at the Max-Planck Institute in Munich and subsequently published in *Écrits*, Lacan allows himself a moment of self-congratulation. Looking back briefly on his achievements, he notes that he was the first to rescue (*reprendre* is his word) Freud's concept of *Nachträglichkeit* from the neglect into which it had fallen in psychoanalytic circles: "[I]t should be known that they [these terms] were unheard of at that time" (685 / 281). Lacan again underscores his retrieval of this concept during his seminar on *The Four Fundamental Concepts of Psycho-Analysis* (1964): "When I said, at the beginning of these talks—*I do not seek, I find*, I meant that, in Freud's field, one has only to bend down and pick up what is to be found. The real implication of the *nachträglich*, for example, has been ignored, though it was there all the time and had only to be picked up" (*Seminar XI*, 197 / 216).

In echoing Christ's promissory injunction "Seek, and ye shall find," Lacan unhesitatingly distinguishes his rediscovery of the truth first revealed by Freud from those who have followed in Freud's path with a lesser degree of vision. The allusion to the Sermon on the Mount may also be intended to recall—and Lacan is often most invested where he is most allusive—the response that Christ's sayings elicited: "[T]he people were astonished at his doctrine. For he taught them as *one* having authority, and not as the scribes" (Matt. 7:7, 28–29). Priority is bound up here with the authority of a teaching, with its preeminence over that of other scribes or scribblers. Lacan's claim to have found "the real implication of the *nachträglich*" is part of the larger claim that would establish him as the foremost follower of Freud.

But the issue of priority has other ramifications for Lacan. As will be seen, it extends beyond the dialectics of conflict between fraternal counterparts for recognition and mastery. It also encompasses more than the competitive (Oedipal) tension between father and son, however well defended or concealed by the son's protestations of fidelity. At the furthest verge where indebtedness is (or is not) acknowledged, there emerges an anxiety about origins with a maternal presence at its core.

These several concerns notwithstanding, Lacan's critique of those who ignored what "was there all the time" is also based on historical grounds. Although Karl Abraham, Sándor Ferenczi, Carl Jung, and others chose to focus on the developmental suggestions in Freud's work, the idea of deferred action recurs throughout his writings. In a letter dated 6 December 1896, he tells Wilhelm Fliess: "I am working on the assumption, that our psychical mechanism has come about by a process of stratification: the material present in the shape of memory traces is from time to time subjected to a rearrangement in accordance with fresh circumstances—is, as it were, retranscribed" (Freud, *Origins*, 173). Freud himself never formulated a definitive and summary theory of *Nachträglichkeit*. However, in this early passage as in later ones, the Freudian conception entails the operation of the subject's current experiences on past events and impressions. Memory traces may be given new meaning as a result of maturation, or of specific situations in the present. As Jean Laplanche and J.-B. Pontalis observe, "Psycho-analysis is often rebuked for its alleged reduction of all human actions and desires to the level of the infantile past. . . . In actuality Freud has pointed out from the beginning that the subject revises past events at a later date (*nachträglich*), and it is this revision which invests them with significance" (112).

This idea of "rearrangement" or retranscription of the past has numerous implications, both clinical and theoretical, in Freud's writings. For instance, he analyzes the dream that resulted in the outbreak of neurosis in the "Wolf Man" case (1918) as a reconstruction of the primal scene. Paradoxically, the first event (witnessed at age one and a half) became the second event's traumatic cause (at age four) only after the later one had taken place (*SE*, 17: 7–122). And, in his famous description of mental life, Freud compares the psyche to the city of Rome, in which all the buildings ever built are still standing on the same site, layer upon layer: "On the Piazza of the Pantheon we should find not only the Pantheon of to-day, as it was bequeathed to us by Hadrian, but, on the same site, the original edifice erected by Agrippa; indeed, the same piece of ground would be supporting the church of Santa Maria sopra Minevera and the ancient temple over which it was built" (*SE*, 21: 70). Even though this analogy seems to draw on a notion of a fixed and stable stratification, Freud's archaeological metaphor is also a dynamic one. Deferred action does not rule out psychical causality and development but, rather, posits a reverse dynamic. It assumes an ongoing readjustment of the causal relations among past events and impressions, as if the ancient layers of Rome were periodically reshuffled.

The mythic Janus could also be invoked as a metaphoric analogue for this aspect of mental functioning. The double-faced Janus was the god of doorways: "of public gates (*jani*) through which all roads passed, and of private doors." The two faces of Janus (*Janus bifrons*) enabled him to watch over the exterior and the interior of houses, exits and entrances, departures from and returns to the city. He looked ahead even as he looked back. As scholars have noted, Janus is also unique in being an exclusively "Italic god or, more precisely, Roman" and cannot be found in the mythologies of other peoples (Guirand and Pierre, 200). It therefore seems hardly surprising that Freud (whose fascination with Italy and especially with Rome lasted a lifetime) added a Janus head to his collection of antiquities very early in his career. "The ancient gods still exist," he wrote to Fliess in 1899, "for I have bought one or two lately, among them a stone Janus, who looks down on me with his two faces in very superior fashion" (*Origins*, 286).[3] The antiquities that Freud took great pleasure in collecting, as Peter Gay suggests in *Freud, Jews and Other Germans*, "both freed him from his work and brought him back to it" (43). If it may be further allowed that these purchases occasionally had a direct bearing on his psychoanalytic interests,[4] the importance of the stone Janus for Freud lay in its reification of the duality of mind-time.

The concept of *Nachträglichkeit* became a central tenet in Lacan's teachings. In the yearlong seminar published as *Freud's Papers on Technique*, 1953–1954, Lacan distinguishes between "reliving"—"that the subject remembers something as truly belonging to him, as having truly been lived through . . . is not what is essential"—and "reconstructing" the past: "What is essential is reconstruction." Moreover, he insists that the distinction is not his own invention. Freud must be credited with giving precedence to the retroactive mode over the seeming chronometric certitude of reliving. Lacan repeatedly invokes the authority of the founding father in order to revoke the notion of psychical stages: "[W]e have the most explicit indication in Freud's writings. . . . it is less a matter of remembering [i.e., reliving] than of rewriting history"; and again, "I tell you what there is in Freud. . . . He never abandoned something which can only be put in the way I've found of saying it—*rewriting history*" (*Seminar I*, 20 / 14). There is a polemical point to this insistence. Lacan's acknowledgment of Freud's discovery implicitly inveighs against those theorists who (contra Freud, in his view) promote developmental models.

In "Function and Field of Speech and Language in Psychoanalysis" (1953), the manifesto more familiarly known as the "Rome Discourse," Lacan reiterates: "The point is that for Freud it is not a question of biological memory"; rather, it is "a question of recollection, that is, of history, balancing the scales, in which conjectures about the past are balanced against promises of the future." History, then, is to biological memory as culturally determined complexes are to instincts. Another word to note here is "conjectures." Shortly afterward, Lacan cites the "meanders of the research pursued by Freud into the case of the Wolf Man," giving particular emphasis to the highly conjectural status that the patient's childhood recollection of a primal scene takes on in Freud's analysis: "Freud demands a total objectification of proof so long as it is a question of dating the primal scene, but he no more than presupposes all the resubjectifications of the event that seem to him to be necessary to explain its effects at each turning-point where the subject restructures himself . . . *nachträglich*, at a later date [*après coup*]" (*Écrits*, 256 / 48). It is the significance attached to the recollected experience—for example, witnessing an act of parental intercourse—in the present, and not the presumed reality of this scene in the past, that may assist in reorienting the subject's relations to reality.

But already in the "Rome Discourse," crucial differences begin to emerge between Freud's concept of *Nachträglichkeit* and Lacan's. As developed by Freud, the concept has pertinence only in the field of sexual feelings. He consistently restricts the notion of deferred action to sexual causes or the awakening of sexual excitations in the individual. "Although it does not usually happen in psychical life," Freud writes in his *Project for a Scientific Psychology* (1895), "that a memory arouses an affect which it did not give rise to as an experience, this is nevertheless something quite usual in the case of a sexual idea, precisely because the retardation of puberty is a general characteristic of the organization. Every adolescent individual has memory-traces which can only be understood with the emergence of sexual feelings" (*SE*, 1: 356). The example of the Wolf Man is only one case in point. Freud also correlates his patient Emma's symptom, her "compulsion of not being able to go into shops *alone*," with two episodes from her past: "a memory from the time when she was twelve years old (shortly after puberty)" that activated a second, repressed memory of a scene when she was "a child of eight . . . and the shopkeeper had grabbed at her genitals through her clothes" (*SE*, 1: 353–54). The memory of age twelve endows the event experienced at age eight with pathogenic force and, retroactively, generates the current symptom: "If we ask ourselves what may be the cause of this interpolated pathological process, only one presents itself—the *sexual release*. . . . Here we have the case of a memory arousing an affect [of fright] which it did not arouse as an experience, because in the meantime the change in puberty had made possible a different understanding of what was remembered" (1: 356). As is further evident in Freud's clinical accounts, not every sexual experience is subject to this process. Specific traumatic events (such as a primal scene, or a shopkeeper's assault) give rise to the repression on which a later event may operate in a deferred fashion. "It is not lived experience in general that undergoes a deferred revision," as Laplanche and Pontalis explain, "but, specifically, whatever it has been impossible in the first instance to incorporate fully into a meaningful context" (112).

   In the course of refuting the supporters of evolutionary stages, Lacan once again cites the authoritative demonstration of deferred action in Freud's "History of an Infantile Neurosis": "The case of the Wolf Man shows us well enough the disdain in which he holds the constituted order of the libidinal stages" (*Écrits*, 264 / 54–55). However, Lacan simultaneously begins to alter the Freudian theory with his characteristic revisionism—that is, without overtly indicating that what he offers is a radical rearticulation of that theory.

   First, he does not limit retranscription, or the workings of later states on earlier ones, to traumatic events. Thus, "to say of psychoanalysis or of history" that they both are "sciences of the particular, does not mean . . . that their ultimate value is reducible to the brute aspect of the trauma" (260–61 / 51). Second, not only sexual life but every lived experience is inscribed in a nonlinear yet time-bound dimension that determines its assimilation by and effects on the subject: "[T]he instinctual stages, when they are being lived, are already organized in subjectivity. . . . the anal stage is no less purely historical when it is actually experienced than when it is reconstituted in thought." The young child who registers the "heroic chronicle of the training of his sphincters" already engages in an act of historicization. For the training of bodily functions takes place in an intersubjective realm marked by the resources of the symbolic order. Therefore,

> seeing it [the anal stage] as a mere stage in some instinctual maturation leads even the best minds straight off the track, to the point that there is seen in it the reproduction in ontogenesis of a stage . . . to be looked for among threadworms, even jellyfish. . . . Why, then, not look for the image of the ego in the shrimp, under the pretext that both acquire a new carapace after shedding the old? (262 / 52–53)

The irony of this rhetorical question underscores Lacan's revisionary proposition that human subjects live *nachträglich* perpetually, not extraordinarily. Malcolm Bowie most lucidly summarizes this difference between Freud's view of temporality and Lacan's expansionist version: "The principle of *Nachträglichkeit*, on the basis of which Freud had scanned and interconnected the widely separated epochs of the individual patient's emotional history, now reappears inside every moment of human time" (*Lacan*, 189). So Lacan does not merely find what he seeks but—as if finders indeed were keepers—appropriates and transforms it.

Third, and not least, for Freud deferred action primarily encompasses two temporal stations, the past and the present. Lacan takes three into account. He introduces an anticipatory dimension into the psychoanalytic process as "a question of recollection . . . in which conjectures about the past are balanced against promises of the future" and, even more emphatically, as having "for its goal only . . . the realization by the subject of his history in his relation to a future" (*Écrits*, 256 / 48, 302 / 88). In Lacan's usage, however, the future does not simply mean—as "promises" and "realization" might be taken to suggest—better or brighter things to come. Present time, as well as recollected time or history, "implies all sorts of presences," including "[i]n

Heideggerian language . . . types of recollection [that] constitute the subject as *gewesend*—that is to say, as being the one who thus has been" (*Écrits*, 255 / 47).

Lacan redefines the temporal condition of subjectivity in a sense that may therefore be specified, after Heidegger's *Sein und Zeit* (1927), as "futural." "By the term 'futural,'" Heidegger writes, "we do not here have in view a 'now' which has *not yet* become 'actual' and which sometime *will be* for the first time. We have in view the coming [*Kunft*] in which Dasein, in its own-most potentiality-for-Being, comes towards itself." The content of this future does not comprise the simple tense of what-will-be but, rather, the more complex yet delimited ("always only") future perfect of what-will-have-been:

> [A]nticipation itself is possible only in so far as Dasein, *as being*, is always coming towards itself. . . . Only in so far as Dasein *is* as an "I-*am*-as-having-been," can Dasein come towards itself futurally in such a way that it comes *back*. As authentically futural, Dasein *is* authentically as "*having been*". . . . Only so far as it is futural can Dasein *be* authentically as having been. The character of "having been" arises, in a certain way, from the future. (Heidegger, 373)

By way of analogy, Lacan transposes these philosophical formulae into a psycho-political drama: "the drama in which the original myths of the City State are produced before its assembled citizens." From such historical material—as from the recollections of dream material—"a nation today learns to read the symbols of a destiny on the march" (*Écrits*, 255 / 47). Rome, ancient and modern, as well as the Third Reich, might be equally on Lacan's mind in his "Discourse" of 1953. The future of a nation, like that of a person, inexorably marches toward the point where it catches up with its past. Interpolated into Freudian *Nachträglichkeit*, Heideggerian *Gewesenheit* (having been) and *Zu-kunft* (future as coming towards)[5] exchange the full panoply of human possibilities for a more restricted range of maneuvers. "The meaning of Dasein's Being," as Heidegger distinctly puts it in *Sein und Zeit*, "is not something free-floating" (372).

Four months after presenting his report to the Rome Congress, Lacan returns to the concept of deferred action in his seminar on Freud's psychoanalytic technique. Echoing the metaphor of multiple city layers, his reconfigurations serve to link the subject's discourse to "a score with several registers," "several longitudinal strata," and, most significant, "a stream of parallel words" (*Seminar I*, 30 / 22). Not only has the theoretical focus shifted from the orderly procession of phases to the overlapping of mind-time. The practice of psychoanalysis, as conducted by exegetes proficient in the arts of recuperation, could henceforth be called an "archae-logogical" investigation. For Lacan also increasingly insists on the indispensability of logos or the symbolic register for the "whole organisation of certainties, beliefs, of coordinates, of references"—in brief, for the "ideational system" explored in the analytic experience (31 / 23).

The notion of oral history thus takes on a special meaning closely intertwined with the temporality of the subject. Language enables the convergence of retroversion *and* anticipation effects in which "truth" or "full speech" (terms that become conflated in Lacan's text) sometimes emerges. The complete position statement excerpted above reads: "Analysis can have for its goal only the advent of a true speech and the realization by the subject of his history in his relation to a future" (*Écrits*, 302 / 88). It is only through "the speech addressed to the other," through the dimension of interlocution, that the assumption of the past and future might take place. "I might as well be categorical," Lacan says—and so he is:

> [I]t is not a question of reality, but of truth, because the effect of full speech is to reorder past contingencies by conferring on them the sense of necessities to come, such as they are constituted by the little freedom through which the subject makes them present. (256 / 48)

II

Previously, however, Lacan still tended to envisage a life cycle whose progress could be tracked and precisely relived. His discussion of the three complexes of early childhood is largely, although not exclusively, developmental. Moreover, as I have shown, Lacan grants not only chronological but formative priority to the weaning complex and the ensuing "primordial ambivalence" toward the imago of the maternal breast. According to *Les complexes familiaux*, the process of weaning provokes conflicting attitudes in the infant that regulate all subsequent stages of development: "[P]rimordial ambivalence *will resolve itself* [*se résoudra*] in psychic differentiations on an increasingly sophisticated and irreversible level" (27 / 14; emphasis added).

To borrow a literary distinction, Lacan initially reads for the story and not for the plot.[6] He reads forward more often than not. The complications of *Nachträglichkeit*, of rewriting the past from a present perspective, are not yet foregrounded in Lacan's thought. His classification of the family complexes draws on and reinforces the evolutionary arguments proposed in such influential works as Abraham's "Study of the Development of the Libido" (1924). Abraham surveys the three main phases of libidinal organization (oral, anal-sadistic, and genital), as well as the child's evolving ambivalent attitudes during each phase (see, e.g., 452–53, 496), within an overall framework that corresponds to Lacan's sequence of three complexes and dialectical differentiations in 1938.

By contrast, among the captions of the first session of his 1953–54 seminar are "Confusion in Analysis" and "History Is Not the Past." To be confused is to equate the subject's history with a developmental story. Lacan presents a short survey of the so-called "development" of the individual— "the stages of the evolution of the human mind"—in traditional psychoanalysis (*Seminar I*, 146 / 127). While he criticizes both Abraham and Ferenczi for introducing "falsely evolutionary notions" into Freudian theory, Ferenczi's role receives particularly negative notice: "Ferenczi is the one who started to put the famous stages into everyone's heads." Soon after, he castigates the conception of evolutionary stages as follows: "These ideas bring with them their power of confusion and disseminate their poison." Even though several psychoanalysts could be held accountable for promoting such ideas, Lacan reserves his severest criticism for Ferenczi's 1913 article on "Stages in the Development of the Sense of Reality": "Similarly, when some chap writes something truly stupid, it's not because no one reads it that it doesn't have consequences. Because, without having read it, everyone repeats it. Some inanities circulate like that" (146/127).

Evidently, the stakes of this debate are very high. The issues may be focused by asking what might be involved conceptually and politically—also personally, that is to say—for Lacan behind the notion of rewriting, rather than reliving, the past? Why does his advocacy of *Nachträglichkeit* seem at times to overstep the bounds of polemical decorum?

In the same passage accusing Ferenczi of disseminating "poison," Lacan excuses Freud, still in the early stages of his own theoretical development, for relying on Ferenczi's "very poor" 1913 article and thereby beginning an unfortunate psychoanalytic trend. According to Lacan, Freud extricated himself as best he could from the embarrassment caused by his disciple and, in time, came to the correct conclusion that "development is far from being that transparent." Lacan's own position—a position he claims to be consonant with the more fully considered views of Freud—emphasizes *structures* as opposed to *stages*: "It is a question, rather, of elucidating structural mechanisms, which are at work in our analytic experience." Such elucidation can only be attained *après coup*, by working back from the present moment and never losing sight of the tentative aspect of this exploration. The past is a place to which full access is never possible. "Retroactively, one may clarify what happens in children," Lacan explains to the clinicians in his audience, but only "in a hypothetical and more or less verifiable manner" (*Seminar I*, 147 / 127–28).

If my earlier literary analogy is recalled, a crucial difference now emerges. The story line that the reader extrapolates from a literary text usually provides the factual, chronological basis for the plot; that is, although all the textual "facts" are fiction, within the narrative framework certain events, circumstances, relations, et cetera, have the status of incontrovertible facts. By contrast, as Lacan conceives it, the narrative produced in the analytic situation is always a web of fictions. For the enabling uses of therapeutic treatment, the psychoanalyst extracts suspect, unstable, or, in a word, shifty accounts of the subject's experience. Lacan sums up his viewpoint in a single statement: "What is realized in my history is not the past definite of what was, since it is no more, or even the present perfect of what has been in what I am, but the future anterior of what I shall have been for what I am in the process of becoming" (*Écrits*, 300 / 86).

Lacan's convoluted sentence is mimetic. Rapid alterations of verb tense both reflect the structural complexity of mind-time and challenge the notion of an autonomous and stable identity based on the reliving of past events. In "The Subversion of the Subject" (1960), Lacan recaptures this psychical-syntactic structure via the image of "rear view" mirroring: "In this 'rear view' (*rétrovisée*), all that the subject can be certain of is the anticipated image coming to meet him that he catches of himself in his mirror" (*Écrits*, 808 / 306). The futural ("anticipated") image that comes up from behind in the rearview mirror renders into spatial terms the paradoxical compression of discrete temporal states that constitute human subjectivity. Lacan situates the *I* (which is largely a function of the eye) in the future of a far from perfect tense.

Samuel Weber aptly describes this condition as "the inconclusive futurity of what will-always-already-have-been [*Immer-schon-gewesen-sein-wird*]" (9). There is no bedrock, no fixed and unalterable substratum of the past; rather, the incremental layers of the psyche are ever-changing. Lacan elaborates a staging of the subject because (as he reiterated in 1964) "the very originality of psycho-analysis lies in the fact that it does not centre psychological onto-genesis on supposed *stages*" (*Seminar XI*, 61 / 63). Hence the act of retro-spection is continually submitted to reinspection and retranscription—or, so it should be when the real work of psychoanalysis gets under way.

I would like to pause for some qualifications in this account of Lacan's in-tellectual progress. To describe his straightforward movement from a ge-netic (developmental) to a structural (deferred action) position might satisfy the commentator's storytelling and ordering inclinations. Such satisfaction is not so easily wrested from Lacan's texts. And yet it also oversimplifies the path he actually followed. While the exposition of successive stages does provide a conceptual scaffolding for *Les complexes familiaux*, Lacan occasion-ally formulates a more intricate view of subjectivity in his essay:

> The contents of this [maternal] imago are produced by feelings specific to infancy. . . . They do represent themselves there, however, in the mental structures that shape, as we have said, subsequent psychic experiences. They will be reevoked [*Ils seront réévoqués*] through association when these [experi-ences] occur, but inseparably from the objective contents that they [the ar-chaic contents] will have *informed* [*ils auront* informés]. (*CF*, 28 / 14; trans. modified)

This passage encapsulates the to-ing and fro-ing of psychical activity. Ini-tially, Lacan seems to reaffirm ("avons-nous dit") an incremental process. Old contents give shape to new forms. His last sentence, however, reverses ("will be reevoked") the linear development described in the preceding one, until its final clause partly reinstates ("will have informed") the sequential order just abandoned. These complications exemplify at the level of syntax the phenomenon of retranscription more fully articulated in his later work.

During the 1950s, Lacan further integrated the idea of deferred action into his theory of subjectivity. It is likely that the post–World War II years accelerated the erosion of the Cartesian conception of a stable and centered self-consciousness. He pointedly opens his 1949 essay on the mirror stage with a declaration of opposition to "any philosophy issuing from the *Cogito*." It is also likely that the continual and close study of Freud's texts deepened his understanding of the relevance of *Nachträglichkeit* for his own work. Be that as it may, the importance of this concept cannot alone explain Lacan's vituperative attack on Ferenczi's 1913 article. The question of who was actually responsible for promoting the psychoanalytic doctrine of stages remains debatable. Gay observes, for instance, that Abraham's papers on libido development "served to redirect Freud's own thinking," and thus had far-reaching consequences for the history of psychoanalysis (*Freud: A Life*, 182). Similarly, John Forrester endorses the plausibility of the claim that "Abraham was the theoretical mainstay of this line of development of psychoanalytic theory" (363 n. 135). Nevertheless, Lacan insists on Ferenczi as the principal perpetrator. In imputing to Ferenczi's theories the dissemination of a poison, Lacan goes beyond direct disparagement—"very poor," "truly stupid," and "inane"—to convey a sense of invidious, possibly deadly contamination. I therefore want to propose another explanation for this surcharge of criticism.

Thirteen years after the essay on "Stages in the Development of the Sense of Reality," Ferenczi published a follow-up paper entitled "The Problem of Acceptance of Unpleasant Ideas—Advances in Knowledge of the Sense of Reality" (1926). This essay was soon translated into English and reprinted in his *Further Contributions to the Theory and Technique of Psycho-Analysis* (1927). Its central thesis anticipates the correlation developed in *Les complexes familiaux* between the weaning complex and the emergence of ambivalence. That is, a dozen years or so before Lacan, Ferenczi identified a dialectical process of mental adaptation whose inception he attributed to the infant's responses to the mother.

Drawing on Freud's recently published "Die Verneinung" ("Negation" [1925], in *SE*, 19: 235–39), Ferenczi argues that the defensive procedure termed "negation" constitutes for the infant "a transition-phase between ignoring and accepting reality" ("Problem of Acceptance," 367). An unpleasant or painful reality need no longer be completely ignored. It can be affirmed "as a negation" by the nascent ego. Ferenczi likens the opposition between acceptance and rejection of reality to "the positive and negative currents in an electrically inactive body"; *Verneinung* de-neutralizes these currents and prompts mental activity. These responses, in turn, enable advances in infantile mental life: "[W]e can in all seriousness assume that the mutual binding of attracting and repelling forces is a process of mental energy at work in every compromise-formation and in every objective observation" (372).

Ferenczi thus posits a binary configuration in very early childhood that precipitates a dialectical chain of reactions. Ambivalence is a first stepping-stone on the way toward the recognition of external reality. Among the ambivalent objects in the environment to which the infant soon attaches a special and separate significance is the maternal breast. The attitude toward this object constitutes the core of his theoretical innovation:

> When after long waiting and screaming the mother's breast is regained, this no longer has the effect of an indifferent thing which is always there when it is wanted, so that its existence does not need to be recognized; it has become *an object of love and hate.* . . . In any case it certainly becomes at the same time, although no doubt very obscurely, the subject of a "concrete idea." (370–71)

At the origin of the dialectical dynamics through which thought processes emerge is the mother-child relationship. Ferenczi extrapolates from Freud's essay on negation what is not *in* the text—except, perhaps, as a form of negation: "The first and immediate aim . . . of reality-testing," according to Freud, "is, not to *find* an object in real perception . . . but to *refind* such an object, to convince oneself that it is still there" (*SE*, 19: 237–38). Freud does not specify or name the object sought. The infant ego inhabits a rarefied and abstract landscape, tentatively "sampl[ing] the external stimuli" and then withdrawing into itself again. Even when Freud's formulations seem very close to identifying a maternal presence, the mother is nonetheless absent: "[A] precondition for the setting up of reality-testing is that objects shall have been lost which once brought real satisfaction" (19: 238). Yet the mother features among the first and possibly most famous examples of negation in the essay: "'You ask who this person in the dream can be. It's *not* my mother.' We emend this to: 'So it *is* his mother'" (19: 235).

Rhetorically, the psychoanalyst identifies an irony. The patient's pronouncement—"It's *not* my mother"—means the opposite of what it says. In context, I propose, there is a double irony. Freud's meditation on the genesis of intellectual activity omits the infantile ego's capacity to perceive and, then, re-present the maternal object. The image of the breast is negated (rather than repressed) by repeated circumlocutions that recall its presence without accepting it as such: "[T]he ego took things into itself or expelled them from itself" (19: 239). To highlight this irony—the essay on negation replicates the concept it defines—is to take up the critical position of the one who knows: "So it *is* his mother."

But Ferenczi abstains from assuming this position vis-à-vis Freud. The question is: how is it possible for him to affirm what Freud has implicitly discounted without adopting an oppositional stance? Ferenczi does so quite simply by asserting, without any intentional irony, that Freud means what *he* (that is, Ferenczi) says. Ferenczi insists that his own contribution is no more than the supplementary notion[7] of an ambivalence elicited by the mother as a precondition for ideational organization. He claims merely to underscore what Freud has already discovered. "When Freud tells us," Ferenczi interprets, "that a human being . . . observes his environment by 'feeling after,' 'handling' and 'tasting' little samples of it, *he clearly takes a baby's procedure when it misses and feels after its mother's breast as the prototype for all subsequent thought-processes*"; and therefore, his interlocutor need only bring out the function of ambivalence: "We are only tempted to add further that the ambivalence indicated above . . . is an absolutely necessary condition for the coming into existence of a concrete idea" ("Problem of Acceptance," 370–71; emphasis added).

To read Ferenczi's 1926 essay, with its frequent tributes to Freud, after reading Lacan elicits the strange sensation of recognition of the unfamiliar. Ferenczi defers to "Freud's discovery"—those are his words—even as he sets out to range beyond it: "Following in his footsteps, I shall attempt once more to deal with the problem of the sense of reality in the light of his discovery" (373, 367). It is not only the content of what he says but also his defensive mode of saying it that anticipates Lacan's first and future readings of Freud. Both theorists present some of their most unorthodox expansions of (in effect, departures from) psychoanalysis as if they were Freud's own tacit ideas and therefore acceptable or already accepted for years. "Like almost every innovation," Ferenczi begins his essay "Further Development of an Active Therapy" (1921), "'activity' on closer inspection is found to be an old acquaintance. . . . We are dealing here . . . with the formulation of a conception and of a technical expression for something which, even if unexpressed, has always *de facto* been in use" (198). Among the imponderables of such statements is to what extent Ferenczi and Lacan themselves were confounded by or aware of their rhetorical strategies of defense while advancing their revisionary positions.

III

If Lacan knew Ferenczi's essay on "The Problem of Acceptance of Unpleasant Ideas," and it is not implausible to assume he did, it may have generated its own problem of acceptance. Acknowledgment was often enough difficult for Lacan. Even though he borrowed liberally, he could be stinting in his distribution of credit.[8] But the motive in this instance, I want to propose, was neither a lack of generosity or intellectual probity on his part nor the result of an academic (French) style that allowed a more liberal appropriation of ideas than current scholarship approves. Rather, Lacan's diatribe against Ferenczi suggests that "history" is at stake in two senses. First, as already discussed here, it is a question of how to conceive and approach the past in psychoanalysis. Second, it involves a problematic of origins and priority.

The issue of priority is a particularly complicated one in the case of Ferenczi. He occupied a position in the early psychoanalytic movement into which Lacan eventually would catapult himself. As Lacan told his audience in a seminar session held several weeks after his (displaced, in my view) attack on the 1913 article,

> Ferenczi was to some extent considered, up to 1930, to be the *enfant terrible* of psychoanalysis. In relation to the analytic group in general, he remained a freewheeler ["il gardait une grande liberté d'allure"]. His way of raising questions showed no concern for couching itself in a manner which was, at that time, already *orthodox.* (*Seminar I,* 233 / 208)

Ferenczi emerges in such passages as a composite figure of precursor and semblable: the one-who-came-before who is also the one-like-me. It was not only in his alluringly maverick theories that he demonstrated an intuition that foreshadowed Lacan's understanding of dialectical mental functioning. Ferenczi's "active therapy" and other innovative techniques were, in some respects, forerunners of the variable-length sessions with which Lacan was to experiment. Ferenczi also raised a central question concerning analytic technique that Lacan himself, as will be seen, fully appreciated—namely, "whether the doctor is in the position to further the treatment *by his own behaviour in relation to the patient*" ("Further Development of an Active Therapy," 215). While Ferenczi's inventiveness and flexibility in response to his patients' needs enabled him to develop different methods over the years, his answer to this question remained fundamentally, unequivocally affirmative.[9] Moreover, Lacan was only too well aware, as his comments on the "*enfant terrible* of psychoanalysis" indicate, of another point of resemblance between himself and Ferenczi. The bitter warring over Lacan's "short sessions" in the 1950s and 1960s paralleled the reactions that Ferenczi's therapeutic activities aroused in the 1920s.[10]

Briefly to review this earlier outbreak of controversy: in 1924 Ferenczi and Rank published a book entitled *The Development of Psychoanalysis*, which was soon (along with *The Trauma of Birth*) strenuously disputed. Book title notwithstanding, their joint venture did not offer an account of the origins of psychoanalytic thought and how it evolved. Instead, the 1924 title may be glossed by a position statement from Ferenczi's 1928 essay on "The Elasticity of Psycho-Analytic Technique": "Analysis should be regarded as a process of fluid development unfolding itself before our eyes rather than as a structure with a design pre-imposed upon it by an architect" (90). Freud is, of course, the unnamed architect whose design is in imminent danger of congealing. Moreover, the word *Entwicklungsziele*—"development," or, more accurately, "developmental aims"—in the German title of the book implies goals to be achieved rather than those already gained (Bókay, 16). Drawing on clinical experience, Ferenczi and Rank outlined a set of flexible practices aimed at speeding up the treatment. Broadly defined by Michael Balint, active therapy required "abandoning the sympathetic passive objectivity [of the analyst] by responding to something in the patient in a specific way." These energetic interventions were intended to produce, according to Balint (who was in training analysis with Ferenczi), "a considerable increase of tension," leading to a breakthrough for the patient (124–25).

Active therapy not only modified the so-called "passive" techniques that had acquired a sanctity for many practitioners by the 1920s. It also tended to curtail the prolonged dwelling on childhood memories integral to Freud's theory and method. Freud was nonetheless inclined at first to welcome the proposals of Rank and Ferenczi, who showed him their work in progress: "The fresh daredevil initiative of your joint draft is really gratifying" (Freud to Rank, letter dated 8 September 1922; quoted in Gay, *Freud: A Life*, 472). However, under the influence of criticism from the heresy-hunters in his inner circle, Freud gradually became far less tolerant and benevolent. In a letter circulated among the "Committee" after the publication of *The Development of Psychoanalysis* in early 1924, Freud began to withdraw his approval and gave vent to "certain misgivings": "There are certainly many dangers attaching to this departure from our 'classical technique' as Ferenczi called it in Vienna. . . . Ferenczi's 'active therapy' is a risky temptation for ambitious beginners, and there is hardly any way of preventing them from making such experiments" (quoted in Jones, 3: 63). From the vantage point of hindsight, Freud's apprehension about the example of active therapy presages such risk-taking ventures as Lacan's "short" or variably punctuated sessions and the institutional schisms provoked a generation later.

In sum, Ferenczi provided a many-faceted model for Lacan. It is therefore necessary to read beyond Lacan's categorical, and sometimes contradictory, assertions about Ferenczi and balance them against each other. Thus he compliments—and devotes his first footnote in the "Rome Discourse" to—Ferenczi's visionary essay on "Confusion of Tongues Between Adults and the Child" (1933).[11] Of this essay, Lacan says in 1953: "[P]sychoanalysts who are also mothers, even those who give our loftiest deliberations a matriarchal air, are not exempt from that confusion of tongues by which Ferenczi designated the law of the relationship between the child and the adult" (*Écrits*, 243 / 36).[12] In his 1958 lecture on "The Direction of the Treatment," he further praises Ferenczi for posing "the question of the analyst's being . . . very early in the history of analysis" and thereby introducing "the problem of analytic action" almost fifty years before in an essay entitled "Introjection and Transference" (1909). According to Lacan, the essay "anticipated by a long way all the themes later developed about this topic" (*Écrits*, 613 / 250). Clearly, he appreciates Ferenczi's risk-taking methods and intellectual enterprise. He likes him whom he is like. However, he also charges him with expounding a doctrine of developmental stages for which Ferenczi was not solely responsible, while ignoring or "forgetting" to mention his insight into the cognitive gains of ambivalence—an insight that predates Lacan's thesis about the dialectical structure of human thought.

IV

Precursors provoke, on occasion, severe criticism, or silence on Lacan's part. Ferenczi's second (1926) essay on reality compounds the provocation. It not only analyzes the effects of infantile ambivalence but also, and perhaps even more disturbingly for Lacan, foregrounds the role of the mother. In this view, Lacan's quarrel with Ferenczi was triggered by an anxiety concerning genesis—with the powerful maternal imago at its core—that is not commensurate with an anxiety of influence. Harold Bloom portrays the anxiety of influence primarily as a manifestation of the Oedipal conflicts arising between paternal precursors and their disciples: "Battle between strong equals, father and son as mighty opposites" (11). Such a scenario may well describe the complexity of Lacan's interpretive stance toward Freud. As Bloom remarks, Lacan conceives his project as the "completing link" of Freud's work: the French son attempts "to persuade himself (and us) that the precursor's Word would be worn out if not redeemed as a newly fulfilled and enlarged Word" (67).

Yet a more archaic type of anxiety is also evident in Lacan's writings. The maternal imago of the weaning complex that generates both ambivalence and castration anxiety, according to his 1938 essay, is eliminated or marginalized in his subsequent formulations. The oscillation between identification/alienation that characterizes the mirror stage replaces the acceptance/refusal of weaning. For Lacan, a maternal presence no longer activates a dialectical tension that inaugurates the "coming-into-being" (*le devenir*) of the subject. Rather, the specular encounter, the recognition of the "*imago of one's own body*," takes on that decisive role (*Écrits*, 94, 95 / 2, 3). Furthermore, Lacan now adopts Freud's position, as opposed to Rank's, that anxiety owing to "separation from the womb at birth" goes into effect only retroactively, *nachträglich*, after "this idea of a loss has become connected with male genitals" and the castration complex has been established in relation to the father (*SE*, 19: 144). Therefore, when Françoise Dolto, Lacan's colleague and an eminent children's clinician in her own right, raises an objection to this retroactive view during his seminar of 1964:

> I don't see how, in describing the formation of intelligence up to the age of three or four, one can do without stages. I think that as far as . . . the phantasies of the castration veil are concerned, and also the threats of mutilation, one needs to refer to the stages,

Lacan immediately responds by dismissing the notion of developmental stages and then reaffirming the Freudian explanation for the retroactive effect of castration anxiety:

> The description of the stages . . . must not be referred to some natural process of pseudo-maturation, which always remains opaque. The stages are organized around the fear of castration. . . . The fear of castration is like a thread that perforates all the stages of development. It orients the relations that are anterior to its actual appearance—weaning, toilet training, etc. (*Seminar XI*, 62 / 64)

In such passages and others, Lacan disengages himself completely from his initial hypotheses concerning the effects of the maternal imago.

Nevertheless, even though the mother's inaugural role is elided in these later formulations, she continues to cause disturbances. The anxiety of genesis predates concerns with influence defined as a strictly Oedipal preoccupation. In the chapter entitled "Completion and Antithesis," Bloom twice quotes Kierkegaard's injunction: "he who is willing to work gives birth to his own father" (56, 73). That wishful thought may now be emended to read: "he who is willing to work gives birth to himself." Genesis is what Lacan's critique of Ferenczi is about.

CHAPTER 4

On Chimpanzees and Children in the Looking-Glass

Wallon's Mirror Experiments and Lacan's Theory of Reflexive Recognition

This offspring was begot without a Mother.

> CHARLES DE MONTESQUIEU, EPIGRAPH TO *The Spirit of Laws*

To live without mirrors is to live without the self.

> MARGARET ATWOOD, "MARRYING THE HANGMAN"

The publication history of "The Mirror Stage" is a curious and convoluted one. It involves a dramatic reversal of fortunes for Lacan: from loss to recovery and restitution, from near oblivion to worldwide renown. I therefore begin with a narrative of beginnings that is also a tale of two difficulties: the commonplace difficulty of beginning, of starting out and making one's own mark and the difficulty, peculiar to "The Mirror Stage," of finding out where the beginning began.[1] From the description of these professionally and textually obscure origins (sections I–II), I turn to the work of Henri Wallon, a major resource for Lacan's theory of the onset of subjectivity through reflexive recognition (sections III–VII). Even though more or less sequentially presented, these several points of origin are closely intertwined.

I

In the summer of 1936, Lacan presented a paper entitled "Le stade du miroir" at the fourteenth International Psychoanalytical Congress held at Marienbad under the chairmanship of Ernest Jones.[2] It was his debut address at a congress of the International Psychoanalytical Association (IPA). During Lacan's presentation, an incident took place that, in retrospect, presaged his troubled relations with that governing organization. Ten minutes into the address, Lacan was cut off by Jones. At the chairman's behest, the unknown delegate from France did not complete his lecture. It was possibly Lacan's initiatory experience of what would become the controversial hallmark of his own analytic technique—that is, a very short session.

Ten years later, in "Propos sur la causalité psychique" (Remarks on Psychic Causality), Lacan gave a highly ironic account of this incident just before discussing his theory of the mirror stage. This prefatory account, which includes an exact notation of the moment he was interrupted—"au quatrième top de la dixième minute"—recurred thirty years after the event, in 1966, with the inclusion of his "Remarks" in Écrits (184–85). Evidently, Jones's intervention still continued to reverberate. The immediate result, however, was that the "original" essay never appeared in print. Although it is indexed under the English title, "The Looking-Glass Phase," in the report published in the International Journal of Psychoanalysis of January 1937, all there is under the entry is the title itself, with no text or abstract.[3] Lacan publicly accounted for this empty entry many years later. In a footnote to "Of Our Antecedents," an introduction to the early works collected in Écrits, Lacan writes that he "neglected to deliver" his text for publication in the congress proceedings. He neglected or forgot little else connected with the Marienbad affair. The same footnote also gives the exact place and date (31 July 1936) of his lecture's aborted delivery and reaffirms that the mirror stage constitutes, in Lacan's own view, the "pivot" of his contribution to the psychoanalytic field (Écrits, 67 n. 1).

The inaugural version of Lacan's famous essay thus has the distinction of not being delivered on two separate occasions. Twice diverted from its destination, it did nonetheless arrive. It appeared in 1938 and the late 1940s in installments that are not only temporally but theoretically distinct from one another. A comparison of the "Le complexe de l'intrusion" section of Les *complexes familiaux* with Lacan's later texts on the mirror stage brings out the evolution in his thinking. As indicated in the preceding chapters, these alterations include: the reduction from three family complexes to a two-phase theory of specular and Oedipal identifications; the shift from a primarily genetic (developmental) emphasis to a structural (deferred action) view of psychical temporality; and the recasting of the maternal role. Thus elaborating the mirror stage as "an ontological structure of the human world" (*Écrits*, 94 / 2), Lacan departs from both his own earlier positions and established psychoanalytic theory.

After *Les complexes familiaux* appeared in volume 8 of the *Encyclopédie française*, World War II and the German occupation of France intervened. Lacan did not publish any new work until 1945. Thirteen years following the memorable intervention at Marienbad, Lacan presented an uninterrupted communication at the sixteenth International Psychoanalytical Congress in Zurich on 17 July 1949. "The Mirror Stage as Formative of the Function of the *I*" was published in the October–December 1949 issue of the *Revue française de psychanalyse* and subsequently reprinted in *Écrits*. In addition to "The Mirror Stage" essay itself, Lacan provided summaries of his theory in three papers written during this period: "Remarks on Psychic Causality" (1946), "Aggressivity in Psychoanalysis" (1948), and "Some Reflections on the Ego" (1953).

However, the conceptual changes introduced after 1945 did not prevent Lacan from drawing a close connection between the pre- and postwar versions of his essay. In "Remarks on Psychic Causality," just before summarizing the concept of specular recognition ("l'assomption triomphante de l'image"), he directs the reader to his encyclopedia article. "I did not give my paper to the congress proceedings," Lacan explains, "and you may find the essential in a few lines in my article on the family that appeared in 1938" (*Écrits* 185). The cue-word in this context is "essential": it signals not merely that the unpublished lecture of 1936 has been preserved but also that the content remains unchanged. No significant disparities exist between what "appeared in 1938" and what Lacan is about to present in 1946. The final state of "The Mirror Stage" was already present in the past.

II

It is no longer necessary to seek the "essential" in the pages of the *Ency-clopédie*. In recent years the convoluted publication history of "Le stade du miroir" has taken another surprising turn. Elisabeth Roudinesco, historian of the French psychoanalytic movement and biographer of Lacan, has re-covered the lost lecture in the archives of Françoise Dolto. Six weeks before the Marienbad conference, Lacan presented his "Looking-Glass" paper at a meeting of the Société Psychanalytique de Paris (SPP). Dolto, a clinician specializing in children, took careful and copious notes on that occasion. Ac-cording to Roudinesco, the archival notes dated 16 June 1936 corroborate Lacan's claim that the discussion of the mirror stage in 1938 reiterates the main ideas of his unpublished paper (*Esquisse*, 159). So the entry in the offi-cial conference records need not stay empty. Dolto's notes on the Paris lec-ture could be used to fill in the blank under the title, "The Looking-Glass Phase," in the IPA proceedings.

It is to these proceedings that Jacques-Alain Miller refers in the annotated bibliography compiled under his supervision:

Le stade du miroir.
Produit pour la première fois au XIVe Congrès psychanalytique interna-tional tenu à Marienbad du 2 au 8 août 1936 sous la présidence d'Ernest Jones. . . . Cf. *The International Journal of Psychoanalysis*, vol. 18, part. I, jan-vier 1937, p. 78, où cette communication est inscrite sous la rubrique 'The Looking-glass Phase.' (*Écrits*, 917)

A similar directive appears in the "Bibliographical note" attached to Alan Sheridan's translation of *Écrits*. Unlike the French edition, however, the translator's note refers to both an "earlier version" delivered at Marienbad in 1936 and a "much revised later version" presented in 1949. "The present translation is of the later version," Sheridan writes (xiii). In Miller's "Repères bibliographiques", however, there is no mention of "earlier," "later," or "much revised" versions of the essay. Two separate entries are given: the first points to the interrupted August 1936 lecture and the January 1937 congress report, and the second to the 1949 lecture and publication. Since the first en-try directs the reader to a nonexistent text, Miller's referral may well, as Jane Gallop remarks, be "not just ambiguous, but ironic" (*Reading Lacan*, 75).

The entry for the 1936 essay in *Écrits* produces or, rather, collaborates in the production of yet another ambiguity. It begins with the words "Produit pour la première fois au XIV Congrès . . . " (917). "Produced for the first time": in an age of mechanical reproduction, the phrase implies a series of reprints of the same work. Lacan does not revise or "return" to his own texts. He only repeats them. The bibliographer's formulation is comparable to the final sentiments expressed on the back cover of the 1984 edition of *Les complexes familiaux*: "One does not know what to admire more—the mastery of the whole, or that it did not present an obstacle to that which was to follow [qu'elle n'ait pas fait obstacle à ce qui devait suivre]." There is no impediment, no contradiction (among the synonyms for the French *obstacle* listed in *Le Grand Robert* is *contrariété* [6: 86]) between the work of 1938 and the rest of Lacan's teaching. Unlike the alarming hauteur (and humility) of Walt Whitman's: "Do I contradict myself? Very well then I contradict myself," the back-cover text provides this reassurance: Lacan could do no worse than repeat himself.

But to exclude the diachronic dimension of Lacan's work would seem to countermand his own instructions. Lacan thus cautions his eager readers in 1966: "It happens that our students delude themselves into finding 'already there' ['déjà là'] in our writings that to which our teaching has since brought us. Is it not enough that what is there has not barred the way [ce qui est là n'en ait pas barré le chemin]?" (*Écrits*, 67). He apparently resists the implication of an already-thereness, of a synecdochic reading of his writings that makes every part correspond with or adequate to the whole. There is a progression in the path he has pursued. And yet the back-cover panegyric— "One does not know what to admire more . . . "—does not get it entirely wrong. Lacan himself, in spite of his criticism of overzealous seekers, claims to find in Freud's texts an appeal to something that may be termed "always there" (*toujours là*): namely, the Name or Interdiction (*nom–non*) of the Father. The symbolic father designates an invariant, unconscious feature of the social group or community that elevates human subjects above mere brute, instinctual existence and simultaneously subjugates them to its signifying structures. Lacan's writings would transmit the universal law of the signifier discovered by Freud. Such a teaching, however, cannot be subject to the time-bound procession of "earlier" and "later" variants. Its meaning value is supra- or hyperlogical and not chronological.

In keeping with this domain of law and truth, Lacan concludes "Of Our Antecedents" with the acknowledgment that he finds himself placing the early texts now collected in *Écrits* in a "future anterior": "they will have preceded our insertion of the unconscious into language [ils auront dévancé notre insertion de l'inconscient dans le langage]" (71). He implants a future construction in the past tense to express a time that is already in the future, even when viewed through the prism of the past. His conclusion does not repeat the diachronic indication given in the rhetorical question ("Is it not enough that what is there has not barred the way?") posed earlier in "Of Our Antecedents," but rather controverts it. What emerges, then, from a reading of Lacan's several directives to his readers is the impasse of an ambiguity: is this work to be viewed in the incremental sense of "that to which our teaching has since brought us"? or, on the contrary, as that which is "always already there"?

Put another way, the retranscriptive movement that invests past events with later significations (in a word, *Nachträglichkeit*) may be no less central to the temporality of Lacan's teaching than to his teaching about the temporality of the subject. Although the discussion of the intrusion complex in 1938 diverges in certain basic respects from "The Mirror Stage" of 1949, Lacan tends to gloss over these differences when speaking of his fully developed theory. His mention of "the essential . . . in [his] article on the family" encourages the reader to consider the concept of reciprocal reflexivity first expounded in the 1930s, *après coup*, from the perspective of the subsequent meanings it acquires. Analogously, the use of the future perfect to present his early work in "Of Our Antecedents" achieves, or strives after a retrospective/anticipatory effect.

Lacan's inclination to rewrite his intellectual history ("it is less a matter of remembering than of rewriting history" [*Seminar I*, 20 / 14]) parallels another type of self-fashioning: the rupture he effected between his family ties—the devoutly Catholic and middle-bourgeois milieu of vinegar merchants into which he was born—and the socially upscale and *avant-gardiste* identity he forged for himself. He was intent on, and largely succeeded in, becoming "a grand bourgeois, a son of no one" (Roudinesco, *Esquisse*, 312). Lacan's reticence about his past, particularly his childhood and familial ancestry, contrasts with Freud's many autobiographical reminiscences and anecdotes. (There is nothing, for instance, comparable to the confessional mode of *The Interpretation of Dreams* in Lacan's writings.) This reticence may be traced to the tension between the need for a beginning, a point of departure that requires antecedents, and the need to cut one's self off from one's origins. The crux is: how can one begin to be without origins? If, in Freud's celebrated formulation, there is "one spot in every dream at which it is unplumbable—a navel, as it were, that is its point of contact with the unknown" (*SE*, 4: 111), for Lacan, the navel is a mark or image or reminder of what is too well known: the umbilical connection that cancels the dream of beginning entirely anew.

It is in keeping with this trend toward self-fashioning that Lacan, baptized Jacques-Marie Émile, eventually discarded two of his first names. Like his father Charles-Marie Alfred, his brother Marc-Marie, as well as other relatives, he bore the name of the Holy Mother, who was venerated as the "protective saint" of the family vinegar trade (Roudinesco, *Esquisse*, 23). Émile is, moreover, almost identical to the first of his mother's Christian names: Émilie Philippine Marie. The emergence of "Jacques Lacan" seems to have required, quite literally, an effacement of the names-of-the-mother. The correlative to this revisionary erasure in Lacan's later theory of ego formation is the absence of the mother's face in the mirror.

III

To recall for a third and last time the bibliographic note that begins "Produit pour la première fois au XIV Congrès . . . ," I would now propose that the "first time" mentioned in this note is as difficult to read as the entry blank, the communication meticulously but invisibly "inscribed" on page 78 of the *International Journal of Psychoanalysis* ("Cf. . . . vol. 18, part. I, janvier 1937") in an additional sense. The first presentation—the lecture that Jones interrupted at Marienbad turns out actually to be the second—after the SPP meeting that Dolto attended in Paris—or, by another count, even more belated. If Wallon's research on the mirror experiences of children and animals is included among the antecedents of Lacan's theory of the mirror stage, the question of beginnings and succession returns in a different guise. So our horizon of origins keeps changing.

Lacan became acquainted with Wallon, a fellow member of the Société de Psychiatrie, in the early 1930s. During this period, he read Wallon's book-length monograph, which cites and develops the studies of Charlotte Bühler, Charles Darwin, Paul Guillaume, Elsa Köhler, and W. T. Preyer. Wallon's work first appeared in the *Journal de Psychologie*, November–December 1931, and was soon after reprinted in *Les origines du caractère chez l'enfant* (The Origins of the Infant's Character) (1933). When Wallon was put in charge of volume 8 of the *Encyclopédie française*, on *La vie mentale* (Mental Life), he commissioned the article that came to be called "La Famille" from the young psychiatrist Lacan (Roudinesco, *Jacques Lacan & Co.*, 142–43). For the 1938 account of the mirror stage and throughout its later permutations, Lacan draws on the extensive data and observations gathered in Wallon's *Les origines*.

In "Aggressivity in Psychoanalysis," Lacan briefly acknowledges his debt to "Wallon's remarkable work" (18), a debt that remains otherwise unmentioned in his writings. Disclosing "a certain forgetfulness or a curious lapsus," Lacan consistently "skips over" Wallon, as Bertrand Ogilvie puts it (113 n. 1). Wallon is most noticeably absent from the 1949 essay on the mirror stage. Lacan also neglects to mention Wallon in "Some Reflections on the Ego," where he recapitulates *his* theory of the mirror stage for the British Psycho-Analytical Society: "I introduced the concept. . . . I returned to the subject two years ago. . . . The theory I there advanced, which I submitted long ago to French psychologists," and so forth (14). Furthermore, when he presents his "antecedents" in *Écrits*, Wallon's name is not among those singled out for recognition. Instead, Lacan speaks of his "invention" of the ideas of the *moi* and mirror stage (67). Whether the mirror stage is universally formative of the *I*-function or not, it would certainly seem to have been so in the case of Lacan.

However, a different perspective can be brought to bear on the scandal surrounding this silence. Lacan's recourse to Wallon is revisionary and, at times, antithetical. In this respect, it resembles his much-vaunted "return" to Freud. As I shall presently show, Lacan not only appropriates and assimilates but also transforms Wallon's observations to such an extent that, like the White Knight in Lewis Carroll's looking-glass world, he can proclaim, "It is my own invention" without egregious prevarication. Nonetheless, the discrepancy in Lacan's treatment of Freud and of Wallon raises the question: why this flagrant omission of Wallon's contribution? Why does Wallon only once receive due credit from Lacan, whereas reiterated tributes to Freud fully acknowledge the doctrine from which Lacan departs?

One motive for trumpeting certain influences while muting others may derive from the difference between the arenas of Oedipal and specular rivalry. Proclamations of fidelity to the Freudian discovery, amid often transgressive commentary, may be read as a defense against or cover-up for what (theoretically) Lacan understands very well: aggressivity in psychoanalysis. Viewed thus, Lacan's praise of Freud is also a preemptive strike. Frequent homage accompanies a revisionary reading that, at times, completely repudiates Freud's theories and, at others, makes them anticipate those of Lacan. He wants Freud—dead or alive—no longer behind him. He would put his precursor in the place of a follower.

Wallon occupies a different relational arena. In the strict chronological sense, Wallon (born 1879) belonged to the preceding generation: "But in his innovative position in the field of psychology, he was closer to Jacques Lacan . . . twenty years his junior" (Roudinesco, *Jacques Lacan & Co.*, 66). Like Rank (born 1884) and Ferenczi (born 1873), Wallon is a specular counterpart to Lacan. The adversarial relation with the (br)other, the fight for "pure prestige," in Alexandre Kojève's well-known phrase (7), mandates that only one survive and prosper. This type of struggle leads to a "slaying" of the fraternal rival rather than of the father. So while Lacan tends to present his own work as (a tribute to) Freud's, he presents Wallon's work as his own; that is, he translates himself into Freud, but translates Wallon into himself.

To characterize this rivalrous ratio in other terms, Wallon is the Red Knight to Lacan's White Knight. In contradistinction to the deadly seriousness of the dialectics of Master and Slave, and to the tragic outcome of the competition between Cain and Abel, Lewis Carroll offers a satiric version of the drama of fraternal feuding. Carroll's crimson-clad knight arrives first on the scene and, "brandishing a great club," claims proprietary rights over the startled Alice: "'You're my prisoner!' the Knight cried, as he tumbled off his horse." The pure display of the ego flourishes and, intermittently, falls under the banner of its aggression. The White Knight arrives next and confronts the Red Knight with an inverted symmetry: "He drew up at Alice's side, and tumbled off his horse just as the Red Knight had done; then he got on again, and the two Knights sat and looked at each other for some time without speaking."[4] On this rarefied imaginary plane, words are marginalized, hardly matter. The moment of recognition-cum-possession is what is fought for. "'She's *my* prisoner, you know!' the Red Knight said at last" (Carroll, 294).

Alice is an excuse for and not an actual cause of conflict. Carroll constructs a parody of epic warriors locked in mortal combat over an illusory trophy-object. In René Girard's lexicon (as in Lacan's), Alice is an object of "mimetic desire": "By making one man's desire into a replica of another man's desire, [mimetism] inevitably leads to rivalry; and rivalry in turn transforms desire into violence" (169). Both Girard's dictum—"the subject desires the object because the rival desires it"—and Lacan's—"the desire of man is the desire of the Other"—derive from the Kojèvian notion of aggression as an outcome of mimesis (Girard, 145; Lacan, *Seminar XI*, 105 / 115). "Desire is human," according to Kojève, "only if the one desires . . . the Desire of the other" (6).[5] In the exchange of blows between the knights, whose self-absorption completely defeats whatever gallantry their chivalric code defends, Alice represents no more than a function of their narcissistic and imitated desires. After the inconclusive battle is over ("'It was a glorious victory, wasn't it?' said the White Knight . . . "), the Red Knight mounts and gallops off. Even though the White Knight has appeared belatedly in the field of contest, he vaunts his possessive claim: "*I* came and rescued her!" He continues his journey for some distance with the looking-glass girl in tow.

In what follows I propose to explore the analogical relations between Wallon's ideas about the mirror-image and Lacan's. By means of this ideational dialogue, I shall try to present not only the singularity of Lacan's theory about the encounter with the specular image and its ramifications but also why and how this theory produces a specular effect.

IV

In the chapter of *Les origines* entitled "The Body Proper and Its Exteroceptive Image," Wallon introduces a zoo of creatures to demonstrate, first, the disparity between animal and human modes of cognition and, second, the series of intricate stages in which consciousness of reflexive reciprocity develops in the child. A dog or a cat or a bird can perceive the mirror image, but only the human infant, although still motorically uncoordinated, can grasp the reciprocal relation between the self and its reflection. Wallon cites the striking instance of a drake (*un canard de Turquie*) that acquired the habit, his partner being dead, of peering into a reflecting windowpane. "Without doubt his own reflection," Wallon writes, "could more or less fill in the void left by the absence of his companion" (218–19).[6] The drake found consolation only because it was unable to identify the image; that is, it did not see itself but rather an extension of its entourage in the glass. The animal, as opposed to the human infant, cannot grasp the relation between the virtual image seen in the mirror and the reality outside.

Wallon's text on mirror behavior vividly exemplifies the differences in the mental capacities among animal species, as well as among children at various developmental stages. Similarly, Lacan contrasts the behavior of the child and the chimp in his 1949 essay: "The child, at an age when he is for a time, however short, outdone by the chimpanzee in instrumental intelligence, can nevertheless already recognize as such his own image in a mirror" (*Écrits*, 93 / 1; see also 112 / 18 and 185). The motoric advantage of the animal is offset by the spark of early human intelligence. Like Wallon, Lacan also mentions the experiments of Elsa Köhler and other psychologists who published their observations in the 1930s. In further keeping with these empirical arguments, Lacan repeatedly refers to Leonard Harrison Matthews's study of ovulation in pigeons and Remy Chauvin's research on migratory locusts (*Écrits*, 95–96 / 3, 189–91; "Some Reflections," 14). Their studies demonstrate that visual stimulation links mental and physical processes in these animals; even seeing the reflected image of members of the same species can produce a physiological change. Matthews's experiments especially support the preeminence accorded the visual in Lacanian theory by proving that, for ovulation to occur in a female pigeon, either the sight of other (male or female) pigeons, or a mirror image of herself alone is sufficient.[7]

It is very odd, as David Macey points out, that Lacan with his "reputation for militant anti-biologism" should thus repeatedly invoke experimental psychology, ethology, and biology (99). But he had already done so earlier. Despite the polemical emphasis on culturally determined complexes as opposed to instinctual factors throughout *Les complexes familiaux*, Lacan had unhesitatingly recalled the "material base" of the complex in order to substantiate his idea of the enduring influence of separation from the maternal body (*sevrage*). "The organic connection," he contends in his encyclopedia essay, "accounts for the fact that the maternal imago possesses the very depths of the psyche" (32 / 15). Because the mirror stage now replaces the nursing dyad and weaning as the governing structure of the psyche, it is not unexpected to find Lacan's anti-biologism once again suspended.

Among others ideas specified in Wallon's work that resonate in Lacan's is the linkage between the child's acquisition of a unified body image and a preliminary understanding of symbolic representation. According to Wallon, the human infant, whose direct vision is limited to a partial body image ("only certain fragments and never assembled"), accedes to a coherent image of the "total body" through the mediation of the mirror (227). Simple though this unification of the self in space may appear to adults, it implies a cognitive subordination of "the givens of immediate experience to pure representation." The mirror experience is thus also the "prelude to symbolic activity," enabling a transition from partial, sensorial perceptions to what Wallon calls the "symbolic function" (230–31).

Wallon's detailed observations clearly established a conceptual paradigm for Lacan's understanding of the mirror stage. Yet Lacan decisively parts company with Wallon—and this departure is arguably the core of his theoretical innovation—on two points: the status of the mirror and the identity of the specular image.

V

What is the phenomenological status of the mirror? Is it a real or metaphorical reflector? In Wallon's numerous descriptions of attitudes before the looking glass—be it those of dogs, monkeys, infants in their cradles, or a little girl admiring the straw hat on her head—a real mirror is involved. Wallon placed a literal reflector before his subjects, as did the several researchers whose data are cited in the pages of *Les origines*. Lacan has a more complicated mirror in mind. It may (but need not) be a real one. Lacan does not rule out the perceiving subject's actual reduplication; yet the mirror is also a metaphor, and, as he remarks in another connection, "it is not a metaphor to say so" (*Écrits*, 528 / 175).

In Lacan's theory, the mirror stage or phase functions as a figurative designation for two temporal modalities: first, a sudden moment or flash of recognition—the "jubilant assumption of his specular image by the child"—in which assimilation to the image of the counterpart (sibling, playmate, or actual reflection) takes place; and second, a state of identification/alienation involving the other—"the mirror disposition"—that constitutes a permanent structure of the psyche (*Écrits*, 94, 95 / 2, 3). These modalities are implicated in each other but can nevertheless be elaborated separately. Whereas the first phase coincides with early childhood, the second characterizes a psychical tug-of-war, a dialectical tension ranging over the life span of the subject. The first specifies a moment of genesis in which the ego begins its formation. In this respect, Lacan adheres to Freud's supposition in the essay "On Narcissism: An Introduction" that "a unity comparable to the ego cannot exist in the individual from the start; the ego has to be developed" (*SE*, 14: 77). The second phase entails an ongoing narcissistic, imaginary relationship based on aggressive alienation/erotic attraction between the ego and the other.

This second phase in particular bears the mark of another major influence on Lacan's thought. As Miller recapitulated in a 1989 interview (eight years after the death of Lacan, his father-in-law): "Lacan reorganized the Freudian discovery from a point of view that was foreign to [Freud], the mirror-stage . . . which comes from Henri Wallon for its empirical basis and from Hegel revised by Kojève for its theory" (quoted in Borch-Jacobsen, 249 n. 11). Lacan's familiarity with Hegelian philosophy and, especially, with Kojève's influential commentary on *The Phenomenology of Spirit* is evident in *Les complexes familiaux* and his later writings. Kojève began what was to become a legendary six-year series of lectures on Hegel at the École des Hautes Études in 1933. Lacan was among the Parisian avant-gardists (including Georges Bataille, André Breton, Maurice Merleau-Ponty, Raymond Queneau, and many others) who attended these lectures and discovered the key terms of Hegel's phenomenology via Kojève's teaching (Roudinesco, *Jacques Lacan & Co.*, 134–35, 140; see also Borch-Jacobsen, 4–5; Casey and Woody, 76–77; and Macey, 57–58, 95–98).

"Hegel speculated," Lacan writes in *Les complexes familiaux*, "that the individual who does not fight to be recognized outside the family group will never attain autonomy before death" (35 / 16). The dark, agonistic aspect of the mirror stage (which cancels or mitigates the jubilation it brings) derives from a Hegelian-Kojèvian version of the encounter between the subject and the other as a fight for "pure prestige," a life-and-death struggle for recognition on which independent self-consciousness is predicated. More needs to be said about this influence; but, for the purposes of the present comparison, it is noteworthy that Lacan transforms the real mirror that confronted Wallon's experimental subjects into a metaphor for a metapsychological concept of human genesis.[8]

To trace further this skein of similarities and dissimilarities, D. W. Winnicott, in his "Mirror-Role of Mother and Family in Child Development" (1967), discloses an interest in the constitution of selfhood analogous to Lacan's. At the very outset of this essay, Winnicott acknowledges Lacan's influential ideas on "the mirror in each individual's ego development" (130), and, in his concluding statements, he also makes quite clear the metaphoric status of the mirror, a status that is implicitly (but not consistently) upheld in Lacan's writings. Thus, although it is possible to "include in all this [reflecting activity] the actual mirrors that exist in the house," Winnicott still insists, "[i]t should be understood . . . that the actual mirror has significance mainly in its figurative sense" (138). For Winnicott, too, a real mirror is not prerequisite for the maturational process of mirroring to ensue. In opting for a figural approach, Winnicott is closer to Lacan's views than Lacan is to Wallon's.

Yet whose face appears *as* the mirror? What body forms or attitudes can function in reflexive relation to the perceiver? Winnicott designates a range of individual forms and even entire familial attitudes: "[W]hen a family is intact . . . each child derives benefit from being able to see himself or herself in the attitude of the individual members or in the attitudes of the family as a whole." But, as his essay title suggests, he gives precedence to the mother's role. Under normal circumstances, her responsiveness to the child ("giving back to the baby the baby's own self") confers a positive experience of formation (138). Winnicott thus draws on Lacan's mirror-stage theory but also indicates where his own stance differs. As he notes in his mirror-role essay, "Lacan does not think of the mirror in terms of the mother's face in the way that I wish to do" (130). The mirror remains a metaphorical concept. However, in the terminological alteration from "stage" (*stade*) to "role," an abstract setting becomes an actual habitation: a familial setting in which the mother's face serves as primary reflector for the young child.[9]

This distinction carries over into the rhetoric that Lacan and Winnicott use to conceptualize what occurs during the analytic situation. Winnicott, in his 1967 essay and throughout his work, develops an analogy between the infant-mother and the analysand-analyst relationships.[10] That is, in exploring what analysts actually do, the "holding" environment they provide for those under their care, Winnicott alludes to aspects of maternal care. Psychotherapy, according to Winnicott, "is a complex derivative of the face that reflects what is there to be seen": "I like to think of my work this way, and to think that if I do this well enough the patient will find his or her own self" (137–38). Doing it "well enough" casts the analyst in the mirror-role of the mother. Lacan, too, in his "Direction of the Treatment and the Principles of Its Power" (1958) and other writings, draws analogies between the "metaphor of the mirror" and the analyst's task; however, he typically evokes the "smooth surface [*surface unie*] that the analyst presents to the patient" (*Écrits*, 589 / 229). Lacan stresses the element of "abnegation," or self-imposed absence—"an impassive face and sealed lips" instead of the resilient, affective reciprocity suggested in Winnicott's recourse to the mirror analogy. Whereas Lacan describes the analyst as bringing to the session "what in bridge is called the dummy (*le mort*)" (589 / 229), Winnicott envisages the mommy (*la mère*) in the analysis.

The connections sketched here (Wallon-Lacan-Winnicott) constitute a line of disrupted continuities in more ways than one. Whereas mimetic rivalry arguably determines Lacan's relations with Wallon, Winnicott does not engage Lacan either as a precursor (paternal) or as a contemporary (fraternal) adversary. Rather, after forthrightly acknowledging Lacan's influence, Winnicott moves on and proposes an alternative mode of understanding the child's formation. Furthermore, given Lacan's sustained reticence about Wallon and the general obscurity of the latter's work outside of France (*Les origines* has not been translated into English), it is unlikely that Winnicott was directly acquainted with Wallon's research. And yet despite the distance between Wallon's literal and Winnicott's figural notions about the mirror, their views converge in two respects that differ from Lacan's formulations.

The first can be compared to the divergent inflections of rising and falling tones. Wallon evokes the child's triumph at the resolution of the mirror "ordeal" (*épreuve*), and Winnicott the potential for growth and self-enrichment as a result of maternal mirroring. By contrast, Lacan describes a short-lived moment of jubilation. A sense of radical, unalterable alienation pervades his account. He envisions the ego whose formation is precipitated by the visual image of the counterpart in terms of a negativity derived from Kojève's reading of Hegel: "The dialectic which supports our experience . . . obliges us to understand the ego as being constituted from top to bottom within the movement of progressive alienation in which self-consciousness is constituted in Hegel's phenomenology" (*Écrits*, 374; trans. quoted in Macey, 97–98). Both Michael Eigen, in a comparison of Winnicott and Lacan, and Roudinesco, in a more recent comparison of Wallon and Lacan, comment on the negativistic aspect of the Lacanian vision (Eigen, 421–22; Roudinesco, *Jacques Lacan & Co.*, 143). Significant though this aspect may well be, I would propose that the second point of divergence discussed below is the more fundamental to Lacan's conception of subject formation. It enables or seems to enable an exorcism of the powerful maternal presence.

VI

Where the question "Who's in the mirror?" is concerned, Lacan provides a Hegelian-based determination. Unlike Wallon, for whom the identity of the triggering image is indifferent, and most unlike Winnicott, for whom the image is usually—and preferably—an average devoted ("good-enough") mother, Lacan posits the conjunction between the ego and its antagonist-double as a necessary precondition for the moment of recognition. The self sees the *self-same* image in the dialectical encounter. A sharp contrast in content as well as in tone thus sets apart Lacan's theoretical formulations.

In particular, Wallon's text about the origins of the child's character becomes an origin that is also a point of new beginning (or departure) for Lacan's definition of the specular image. According to Wallon, the reflected body of the perceiving subject need not be the one to activate the mental integration of model and image. Other bodies may serve the same purpose. Wallon gives the example of a little boy, still in an intermediate stage of development, who smiles at his own and his father's images in the mirror but turns in surprise upon hearing his father's voice behind him. The child has not as yet grasped the connection between the reflection and the real presence of the father (223). In Wallon's analysis, the difficulty seems to lie in a spatial realism that prevents the child from linking the actual figure with the virtual one. The pre-mirror-stage child does not yet understand that the two bodies located at two points in space—the tactile body here and the visual body there—constitute only one body. The child attributes an independent reality to each object or person occupying a different space (225).

Yet after the child has grasped the distinction between reality and its symbols or representations, a ludic element can enter into these relations. If asked, "Where is Mommy?" a post-mirror-stage child may point to her image in the mirror and then turn toward her laughing. The child now plays with the duality. "Slyly, he pretends to grant preponderance to the image," Wallon writes, "precisely because he has just clearly recognized its unreality and purely symbolic character" (232).

For Wallon, then, the essential factor is the recognition of spatial values, or, more precisely, the coordination of what was perceived as two bodies in two distinct places. The child's behavior suddenly demonstrates a comprehension of the reciprocity between model and image. The realization of their subordinate rather than independent relation is the turning point. Wallon does devote separate sections in his work to children's specular relations with others ("L'enfant devant l'image speculaire d'autrui") and with their own bodies ("L'enfant devant sa propre image speculaire"); and he also discusses the different mental operations involved in withdrawing reality from the images of other bodies and from the self-image. More crucial, however, than the identity of the person seen in the mirror is the elimination of the schism between the felt "me" and the visual "me."

In "The Child's Relations with Others" (1960), Maurice Merleau-Ponty comments on the Lacanian extension of the ideas found in *Les origines*:

> In reading Wallon one often has the feeling that in acquiring the specular image it is a question of a labor of understanding, of a synthesis of certain visual perceptions with certain introceptive perceptions. For psychoanalysts the visual is not simply one type of sensibility among others. . . . With the visual experience of the self, there is . . . the advent of a new mode of relatedness to self. . . . The sensory functions themselves are thus redefined in proportion to the contribution they can make to the existence of the subject

and the structures they can offer for the development of that existence. (137–38)

For Lacan, Merleau-Ponty suggests, the perceptual synthesis achieved during the mirror stage is a first stepping-stone in a far more complicated process of maturation. This process involves unconscious as well as conscious mental activities. Moreover, as I have already indicated, the identity of the specular image is not an indifferent one. The reflected body belongs neither to the mother nor to any adult caretaker. On the contrary, Lacan's formulations repeatedly underscore the ego's captivation by its own image: "[T]he mirror-image would seem to be the threshold of the visible world, if we go by the mirror disposition that the *imago of one's own body* presents in hallucinations or dreams" (*Écrits*, 95 / 3). This emphasis recurs in his work during this period. He speaks of "the autonomy of the *image of the body proper* in the psyche" and of the infant's jubilant interest in "his own image in a mirror" (*Écrits*, 185; "Some Reflections," 14). The figure in the glass is none other than the counterpart of the self.

Adopting the stance of an objective or external focus, Lacan describes an observer's reaction to this drama of reflexive identification: "[O]ne is all the more impressed when one realizes" (and I take the impersonal "one" as a sign of special investment on his part) "that this behaviour occurs either in a babe in arms or in a child who is holding himself upright by one of those contrivances to help one to learn to walk without serious falls" ("Some Reflections," 15). At this juncture, then, the question of the subject—"Which dreamed it?" to borrow Carroll's looking-glass conundrum—might arise: how can one see what the child sees without putting one's self in the frame? Lacan's description conjures the child before the mirror in such a way that the presence of other persons is minimized ("arms") or eliminated ("holding himself"). Likewise, in "The Mirror Stage," he renders the mother or caretaker a virtually invisible factor:

> Unable as yet to walk, or even to stand up, and held tightly as he [the child] is by some support, human or artificial (what, in France, we call a "*trotte-bébé*"), he nevertheless overcomes, in a flutter of jubilant activity, the obstructions of his support and, fixing his attitude in a slightly leaning-forward position, in order to hold it in his gaze, brings back an instantaneous aspect of the image. (*Écrits*, 94 / 1–2)

Thus the hand that proverbially rocks the cradle and, more ominously, rules the world is whisked away. What remains is some contraption—a baby walker or a pair of disembodied arms—holding the infant. Lacan makes it abundantly clear that the image in the mirror is *not* the mother's. He reiterates this cardinal point in "Aggressivity in Psychoanalysis": it is the "*imago* of one's own body" (*Écrits*, 120 / 25; also 95 / 3). Even when an adult holds the infant before the mirror, Lacan asserts that the crucial formative identification occurs only between the self and its semblable. If such repetition may be considered a symptom (or a symbol), then Lacan's evocations of an infant overcoming the actual obstruction of various supporting agents, however literally intended, acquire an added resonance. His insistence brings me, at the risk of a certain implausibility, to offer the following interpretation: in the small world of the infantile ego striving to surmount its supports, the venerable injunction "Thou shalt have no other images before me" has a revisionary, projective meaning. The ego (*moi*) receives a message from the big Other (*le grand Autre*) that originally emanated from itself.

Some commentators, however, refuse to allow the radical absence of the mother in the mirror-stage theory. Hence there is a tendency to reintroduce her. Mario Rendon, for example, cites Lacan's 1949 essay as a source for the observation that "the image of the self is originally constructed around the perceived image of the mother" (350). Elizabeth Grosz writes of "the (m)other/mirror-image" (32), making the mother integral to the Lacanian concept of reflexive identification. These readings fail to grasp both the literal meaning of the mirror stage and its doctrinal significance. As described in *Les complexes familiaux*, the intrusion complex already entails a scene of ego formation through the mirroring of the child's own body. From the very outset, Lacan thus posits a psychical mechanism—"narcissistic intrusion" as he calls it—that requires "the subject's recognition of his image in a mirror" (*CF*, 45 / 18, 42 / 17).

VII

Critical differences notwithstanding, Lacan and Wallon both maintain that the unity of the specular image, the total bodily form, or gestalt, is an indispensable part of the maturation process. According to Lacan, "[w]hat the subject welcomes in [the image] is its inherent mental *unity*; . . . what he applauds in it is the triumph of its *integrative power*" (*CF*, 18 / 44; emphasis added). Lacan's statement here does provide grounds for finding that which is to come already there (*déjà là*), anticipating his later formulation of the mirror stage as a drama involving self-reflection and self-integration: a perception of one's-*own*-body and of one's-*whole*-body.

Lacan singled out both of these factors in 1948: "What I have called the *mirror stage* is interesting in that it manifests the affective dynamism by which the subject originally identifies himself with the visual *Gestalt* of his own body: in relation to the still very profound lack of coordination of his own motility, it represents an ideal unity, a salutary *imago*" (*Écrits*, 113 / 18–19). Appropriately enough, "ideal [that is, unreal or imaginary] unity" is endowed by a reflected totality. The celebratory sense of the *I* is a function of the formal constellation of parts in the mirror. The term "affective dynamism" in this passage should be glossed by the "triumphant jubilation" frequently associated with the child's identification of the image: "[W]hat demonstrates [*sic*] the phenomenon of recognition, which involves subjectivity, are the signs of triumphant jubilation and playful discovery that characterize, from the sixth month, the child's encounter with his image in the mirror" (*Écrits*, 112 / 18). For Lacan (as for Wallon), the behavioral evidence for the child's momentous insight is a joyous kind of playfulness.

The question arises: why joy? Why indeed does recognition of the specular other initially bring with it such jubilation? It is after all also accompanied, in Lacan's agonistic view, by an inevitable estrangement, or "assumption of an armour of an alienating identity" (*Écrits*, 97 / 4). Lacan accounts for the child's joyful antics before the mirror as follows: the good gestalt equips the child with a unitary mental image. This image ("the total form of the body") allows some compensation for the malaise ("the fragmented body-image") that persists in the psyche after the prematurity and discordances of birth. Hence he calls the totality glimpsed in the glass "orthopaedic" (97 / 4). The specular counterpart puts Humpty Dumpty together again, however temporarily and phantasmatically.

One source of the widespread appeal of the mirror-stage theory, I therefore suggest, derives from this account of human genesis that, painful and fraught with psychical dangers (fantasies of fragmentation, acute narcissism, alienation) though it might be, takes place without mediation: sans mother and sans father. To a largely secular and skeptical readership, Lacan's mirror stage presents a new myth of genesis. It is a powerful creation myth whose passion and investment is overlaid by the dignity that an abstract and "scientific" terminology confers upon conjecture.[11] Unlike the myth of the goddess Athena (Freud's favorite artifact in his large collection) who sprang forth from Zeus's forehead, in Lacanian theory, the function of the *I* does not emerge as a result of any parental intervention. The birth of the ego takes place in and through the looking glass. In Lacan's view, the mirror is the mother of the ego. But the mother is not in the mirror.

In effect, "The Mirror Stage" as theory and text marks another complex moment of separation for Lacan. First and foremost, identification with the semblable, or self-same, prepares the way for identification with the figure of the father. Reflexive recognition displaces the Oedipal conflict as the linchpin or turning point in the constitution of the subject. Next, in orienting the psychoanalytic focus toward the fraternal (and, only secondarily, the paternal) function, Lacan furthers the challenge, only summarily presented in his essay on the family, to the growing influence of Melanie Klein and the inclination since the 1930s to view the mother as the center of the child's world. As Lisa Appignanesi and John Forrester observe, "[T]he Lacanian scheme guaranteed that psychoanalysis was removed from the ambiguously *ewige mutterliche*, or eternally maternal, tendencies that British Kleinian and other object-relations theories were encouraging" (462). With these two revisionary moments, Lacan could be said to put himself in place of the (Freudian) father and the (Kleinian) mother. Thus Lacan (re)constitutes himself. The mirror stage of the late 1940s represents his emergence as an embattled but full-fledged contender for theoretical preeminence in the Freudian field.

Briefly to pursue these speculations, critics and historians such as Mikkel Borch-Jacobsen, Wilfried Ver Eecke, Ogilvie, and Roudinesco have traced the mirror stage to numerous sources. The theory presents a stunning synthesis of several strands of thought in psychoanalysis, philosophy, and experimental psychology. Although Lacan would cast aside most precursors or supports, these same neglected ones merely wait to be recalled. They seem to impose, or at least contribute to, the alienation that curtails Lacan's jubilant assumption of his own invention. He thus tells the truth when he says that the sense of fragmentation is never fully overcome, even in those pleasurable moments in which an image of totality is glimpsed. His famous theory is itself a kind of body-in-pieces, a dream composed of diverse concepts. The vision of the self-constituted individual, or what might be called "the good-enough gestalt" indeed turns out to be a mirage. Humpty Dumpty, the seemingly complacent but ever-fragile ego (*hommelette* in Lacan's wordplay),[12] is what the idea of the mirror stage defends against.

CHAPTER 5

Topographies of Conflict

The Machia *in the Mirror Stage*

The idea of a dual relationship with a conflict at its core is a constant feature of Lacan's ways of formulating the human experience throughout his long and active career. Without a struggle between opposing attitudes, without an ambivalence generating dialectical structures of mental organization, Lacan cannot conceptualize the advent of the subject. But while a formative conflict remains central to his theoretical concerns, fundamental changes occur in his conception of its participants as well as in the modes he uses to describe it.[1]

To recapitulate the trajectory of the participants, in *Les complexes familiaux*, Lacan charts three stages of childhood development that predicate a dialectical engagement with three different imagos: the weaning complex engages the maternal imago, the intrusion complex the fraternal, and the Oedipus complex the paternal. The primordial ambivalence or "basic tension" provoked during weaning persists and presides over all later stages of psychical differentiation (27 / 14). Thus, while seeming to uphold the

Freudian view that "a unity comparable to the ego cannot exist in the individual from the start" (*SE*, 14: 77), from the very outset and despite the changes to follow, Lacan does not adopt the paradigm of Oedipal rivalry as the primary arena of confrontation in which the ego is constituted. The infant's first ambivalent object (which causes, and becomes the target of, contradictory feelings) is the imago of the maternal breast.

In the series of essays written approximately ten years later, Lacan rearticulates not the dynamic process but, rather, the dyadic basis of this conflicted relation. It is the initial encounter with the counterpart—be it sibling, or playmate, or actual mirror image—that activates the subject's oscillation between fusional identification and aggressive alienation. Perceived in a sudden moment of jubilant reflexivity, the *"imago of one's own body"* soon takes on the role of provoking-depriving agent formerly consigned to the maternal imago: "[T]his captation by the *imago* of the human form . . . dominates the entire dialectic of the child's behaviour" (*Écrits*, 95 / 3, 113 / 19). In "Aggressivity in Psychoanalysis," "The Mirror Stage," and other writings, the concept of specular "captation" does not denote merely a scene of self-idolatry or narcissism. The self is also the agent of its own production as radically other.

Nevertheless, with the installation of the mirror apparatus as the primary source of conflict and competition, the mother does not entirely disappear from Lacan's theory of the process of ego formation. Traces of her presence, or what he calls the "humoral residues of the maternal organism" (*Écrits*, 96 / 4), need to be overcome through identification with the form of body totality: the gestalt given at the mirror stage. Although the infant is "still sunk in his motor incapacity and nursling dependence," the moment of self-assumption mediated through this unitary form is said to raise him above the maternal element and to reverse, if only "in a mirage," the images of the body-in-pieces, of fragmented corporeality that derive from a "real *specific prematurity of birth*" (95 / 2, 96 / 4). Lacan continues in "The Mirror Stage," as he had done in his earlier work, to attribute a profound psychical importance to these inauspicious physical beginnings. However, the fact that the human infant is dispatched into the world in an adamic state of unpreparedness, lacking the anatomical self-sufficiency of an infant chimpanzee, is not the only material concern of his later writings. Formerly, verbal resonances had linked Lacan's idea of the paradisal "prenatal habitat" with Rank's (see Chapter 2), whereas now the analogies between intrauterine existence and utopian states no longer hold for him. The "very essence of Anxiety," Lacan argues, invoking the figure of the mother as *prima materia*, as formless substance, "entails a constant danger of sliding back again into the chaos from which [the infant] started" ("Some Reflections," 15). "To the *Urbild* of this [specular] formation, alienating as it is . . . corresponds a peculiar satisfaction deriving from the integration of an original organic disarray," he similarly proposes in his essay on "Aggressivity" (*Écrits*, 116 / 21). Mental "integration" is an effect of the visual image or form (*Urbild*); "organic disarray," of the maternal body. The child's journey is from the chaos of beginning and darkly dwelling in the mother to the let-there-be-light of the mirror stage.

Together with these attempts to reformulate the functions of the mother and the mirror, Lacan's conception of how the subject comes into being takes another turn. Rhetorically, as I shall endeavor to show, this transformation involves a "genre shift." Whereas in *Les complexes familiaux*, Lacan delineates the child's continuous growth within a generally realistic configuration of familial relations, a descriptive mode whose generic literary affiliation is psychological realism, in "The Mirror Stage," he gives an account of human consciousness that, in several respects, bears a marked resemblance to allegory. In other words, while still engaged in formulating a model for the ambivalent relations that structure the psyche, Lacan moves to a different level of description. His late 1940s presentation of the mirror stage, although not completely allegorical in format, has recourse to distinctive allegorical procedures. Lacan thereby departs—sets out and also diverges—from another psychoanalytic precedent. Given Freud's marked predilection for myths to instantiate as well as provide the terminology for some of his foundational concepts, it does not seem random that Lacan's "return to Freud" should proceed via the retelling of ancient tales.

In section I of this chapter, I discuss an aspect of the Hegelian-Kojèvian dialectics, the deadly fight for "pure prestige" between self-conscious individuals, as a paradigm for one type of conflict elaborated by Lacan. In section II, I explore the parallelisms between Lacan's concept of intrapsychic conflict and the Christian *psychomachia*; and in section III, his renarrativization of "classical psychoanalysis" (a term coined by Ferenczi in another connection)[2] as embodied in the myths of Narcissus and Oedipus. However, these various lines of argument—philosophical, theological, and psychoanalytic—which, for the purposes of my analysis, will be considered as separate and distinct are, in fact, complexly interwoven in Lacan's own synthesizing formulations.

I

As indicated in Chapter 4, in spite of an early and sustained emphasis on cultural (symbolic) factors, Lacan does not hesitate to use biological data in order to reinforce the roles of visual imprinting and the body-image. His empirical resources include Elsa Köhler's observations on patterns of mimicry among children, Remy Chauvin's study of migratory locusts, and Leonard Harrison Matthews's research on the ovulation of pigeons (see *Écrits*, 93 / 1, 95–96 / 3, 189–91).[3] These data are clearly intended to accord the prestige of a scientific register to a quasi-mythic rebirth that takes place before a mirror: "Unable as yet to walk, or even to stand up, and held tightly as [the infant] is by some support, . . . he nevertheless overcomes, in a flutter of jubilant activity, the obstructions of his support and, fixing his attitude in a slightly leaning-forward position, in order to hold it in his gaze, brings back an instantaneous aspect of the image" (93 / 1–2). This early childhood event, however remarkable or startling (*saisissant*), might appear to be arbitrarily singled out and privileged in Lacan's writings. For instance, the moment when an infant suddenly flips over from stomach to back without assistance and then repeats this action in reverse, whether or not emitting a triumphant gurgle that appears to be self-directed as much as directed at the (alarmed) caretaker, could also be accounted a primary occasion for the constitution of that infant subjectivity.[4] The mirror stage would not have the singular importance that it undoubtedly possesses for Lacanian theory, and for postmodern discourses on the subject, without some additional level or levels of signification.

For Lacan, the cognitive drama of the mirror stage indeed provides an exemplum of a broader relational experience: "This jubilant assumption of his specular image by the child at the *infans* stage," he writes, "would seem to exhibit in an *exemplary situation* the symbolic matrix in which the *I* is precipitated in a primordial form" (*Écrits*, 94 / 2; emphasis added). How a subject comes into being also enacts the ways of being a subject in the world. Lacan's just-so story of the formation of the *I*—one day an infant arrives in front of a mirror and instantaneously grasps the contingent relations between this body right here and its image over there—serves as the highly particularized foundation for a universal structure of human existence. Lacan explicates that structure through its exhibition by two concrete entities (a child and a mirror) and the situations (recognition-identification-alienation-aggression) he composes around them.

Thus the conceptualization of the mirror stage has correspondences with a literary tradition familiar from the world of Greek and Roman allegory to, say, the psychological allegory of Kafka's "Metamorphosis" and "The Hunger Artist." As Northrop Frye explains, allegory is "a contrapuntal technique": "A writer is being allegorical whenever it is clear that he is saying 'by this I *also* (*allos*) mean that'" (90). The elements of ancient mysteries, for example, often conjoin or are brought into correspondence with something else for the purpose of making them less perplexing and more widely acceptable. Walter Burkert illustrates these proceedings in his discussion of nature allegory in pre-Hellenistic times: "[M]ysteries easily offered themselves to allegorizing in terms of nature, and it was not only officious outsiders who indulged in the method but often the insiders themselves." These insiders, "priests and priestesses" who apparently wanted to account for what they were doing, found it "no problem to recognize Mother Earth in Demeter, and Persephone consequently became grain"; moreover, "if golden ears of grain are buried with the dead, allegory seems to turn into faith" (Burkert, 80–81). That is, in addition to the specific mythic event or detail plausibly described in terms of its *physica ratio*, these ritual practices and narratives may invite, and even seem to require, a further level of metaphysical explanation: "[W]hatever elements of pagan mysteries show up are modified by the filter of a religious system" (67). With varying degrees of explicitness, allegorical or potentially allegorical components in Greco-Roman and Christian interpretations entail such an ulterior intention. The allegorist seeks a revelatory or supratemporal dimension: "The Christian interpreter of the Bible and the Stoic interpreter of Homer both want to discover their versions of the truth" (Rollinson, 19).

Likewise, Lacan, in reconceiving his theory more than a decade after he introduced it at Marienbad (1936) and in *Les complexes familiaux* (1938), would expound "the light it sheds"—his turning to a rhetoric of revelation is consonant with the genre shift—on "psychical realities, however heterogeneous": "I think it worthwhile to bring it again to your attention . . . " (*Écrits*, 93 / 1, 95 / 3). But, while the idea of the specular encounter between child and counterpart remains constant, it has evolved during the ten-year interim into a way of presenting a supervalent model or meta-narrative of the human world. Although the later work extends the "essential" preserved in the earlier work on the family, the two installments of Lacan's theory of the mirror stage are not coextensive (185).

In a quite different context, Jacques Derrida makes a comparable claim about the allegorical purpose (or, he might say, pretension) of Lacan's seminar on Edgar Allan Poe's "The Purloined Letter" (in *Écrits*, 11–61). The Derridean critique, succinctly stated, is that by "reading 'The Purloined Letter' as an allegory of the signifier, Lacan . . . has made the 'signifier' into the story's truth" (Johnson, 232).[5] The details of this famous debate and the numerous responses it has produced do not require rehearsal here. More pertinent to this discussion, the truth—"as revealed in psychoanalytic experience"—that Lacan reshapes in his 1949 essay could be distinguished from his 1956 seminar on Poe's story as follows: what takes place in the case of "The Mirror Stage" is the practice of allegorical *composition*. Lacan constructs an allegorical text of his own rather than an allegorical *interpretation* or extraction of meaning from the text written by another author.[6] The "light" or truth purveyed by his text is not purloined from another.

The validity of this distinction is, however, problematic. As already seen, the intrusion complex of 1938 (which evolves out of the weaning complex and relationship to the maternal imago) is not the same as the "startling spectacle" celebrated in 1949. Lacan silently, even surreptitiously—insofar as he neglects to mention basic differences and debts—"returns" to his own pre-texts on the mirror experience as well as to Wallon's *Les origines du caractère chez l'enfant* and other sources. "The Mirror Stage" as an act of allegorical composition cannot be strictly delimited or separated from these acts of interpretive appropriation. Yet a different perspective on the same proceedings would be to point out that, in attempting to track the transformations of the mirror-stage theory, I engage in an allegorical (or confrontational) interpretation of Lacan's allegorical composition; in other words, as Frye reminds us, "all commentary is allegorical interpretation" (89). But even with these various frames of reference in view, the commentator does not necessarily lack or lose conviction.

In Lacan's later formulations about the mirror stage, the allegorical mode asserts itself in two immediate ways. First, the child who sees the semblable is not just any child or a typical child but also a type of psychical structure. The figure of the child incarnates the Lacanian concept of the ego (*moi*). The mirror-image itself is also a metaphor for a relational position. It is a depository for the dialectical irresolutions of the imaginary order. Both the actual infant and the virtual one thus take on the quality of conceptual paradigms. If, as Lacan contends, the "*mirror stage* is a drama," then its dramatis personae embody abstract ideas (*Écrits*, 97 / 4). Second, one of the designations of the French *stade* is "stadium"—a place set aside for competitive events and defensive exercises. Battle is a basic pattern of allegory. This pattern, as Angus Fletcher writes in his study of the genre, probably dates in Western literature from Hesiod's gigantomachia, in which titanic adversaries fight for mastery of the world (151). However, whether the stakes be control over the whole world, or only over the little world of man, a deadly clash characterizes the meeting of the rivals. Two competing forces vie for complete victory.

The life-and-death struggle between personified abstractions such as "virtue" and "vice," or any pair of symmetrically inverted concepts, may be read as a figural means to conjure up the dual topographies of human aggression: the "internal conflictual tension" that swiftly develops into "aggressive competitiveness" in the social environment (*Écrits*, 113 / 19). Correspondingly, the discordance between the child and the specular counterpart serves as a concrete realization of the aggressive tendencies found in both *inter*human relations and *intra*psychical operations of individuated egos. Speaking from clinical experience, Lacan offers a symbolic equivalent of the psyche's geographical agitation: "[T]he formation of the *I* is symbolized in dreams by a fortress, or a stadium—its inner arena and enclosure, surrounded by marshes and rubbish-tips, dividing it into two opposed fields of contest" (97 / 5). Rather than a single-centered arena as might be supposed, the narcissistic structure of selfhood generates, as it were, two war zones: the *Umwelt*, or outer world, and the *Innenwelt*, or inner world.

The intersubjective dimension of this configuration primarily derives from Hegel's idea of a "trial by death" between opposing forces. As noted in

Chapter 4, Lacan's familiarity with the work of Hegel, and particularly with *The Phenomenology of Spirit*, was mediated by Kojève's lectures at the École des Hautes-Études in the 1930s. According to Kojève, the Hegelian notion of self-realization and identity—"the why or the how of the birth of the word 'I,' and consequently of self-consciousness"—stresses a struggle with a socially constituted other (3). In order to "attain autonomy before death," Lacan writes in 1938, reiterating the Kojèvian reading of Hegel, the individual must be prepared to "fight to be recognized outside the family group" (*CF*, 35 / 16). In "The Mirror Stage" and related essays, Lacan's description of the specular encounter also draws on a Hegelian-Kojèvian conception: "It is this moment that decisively tips the whole of human knowledge into mediatization through the desire of the other" (*Écrits*, 98 / 5). When speaking of "the desire of the other," Lacan intentionally recalls Kojève's dictum: "Human Desire must be directed toward another Desire" (5). The rival whose desire enables consciousness to come into "Being-for-itself," and to acquire its independent value, is found in the outer world. Thus "man can appear on earth only within a herd," Kojève asserts; and, "the human reality can only be social" (6). The autonomous *I* is constructed through its adversarial relations. For "its essential being," Hegel writes, "is present to it in the form of an 'other,' [and] it is outside of itself and must rid itself of its self-externality." By this account, it takes two to make one. As Kojève paradoxically puts it, "this object, i.e., the I, is absolute mediation, and its essential constituent-element is abiding autonomy" (Hegel, 114; Kojève, 15).

Taking up the terms of Hegel's phenomenology as transmitted through Kojève's teaching, Lacan begins to submit them to further revision. Prior to any social or cultural mediation, the human subject is riven, split, or barred by a psychical phenomenon predicated on reflexive recognition. Reciprocal reflexivity enables intersubjectivity. In Lacan's formulation, "This moment in which the mirror-stage comes to an end inaugurates, by the identification with the *imago* of the counterpart . . . the dialectic that will henceforth link the *I* to socially elaborated situations" (*Écrits*, 98 / 5). The "moment" in this key statement, just like the titular term *stade*, is poised between two temporal modalities.

In the one instance, to speak of the "moment" seems to imply a chronological succession—*stade* as evolutionary stage, a movement from the imaginary, dyadically enclosed situation in which the ego is held in thrall by its double to the symbolic, socially interactive state of desired desires. As the mirror moment "comes to an end," in Lacan's stop-watch phrase, the next phase of differentiation begins. The alienating image within moves out, as it were; the other is projected and thereafter found in the external world. This developmental viewpoint restricts the text to a literal, nonallegorical level of meaning, and its "genre" or rhetorical mode to that of a psychological essay. In the other instance, the word "moment" suggests a trans- or atemporal *structure* of the psyche—*stade* as stadium. There is no getting beyond the imaginary of human experience until death. To the extent that the mirror stage exemplifies a universal mental mechanism, the "moment" is a metaphor for a systemic formation that defies the categories of succession. Moreover, not only temporal (before/after) but spatial (inside/outside) polarities are suspended. The other is neither strictly in-here nor out-there. Despite the apparent opposition of the *Innenwelt* and the *Umwelt*, a continual interplay goes on between them. (Hence the spatial dispositions of our adversaries are not always easily determined.) The structural viewpoint also entails a different rhetorical register. Lacan translates a psychical situation into a physical spectacle, a condition of what was formerly called the "soul" into an allegorical configuration of the child and the mirror.

Even though what Lacan means by the "moment in which the mirror-stage comes to an end" remains ambiguous, his modification of the Kojèvian tenet of social relations as prerequisite for autonomous self-consciousness ("man can appear on earth only within a herd") is explicit and clear. In Lacan's view, "the structural effect of identification with the rival is not self-evident"; rather, it is conceivable only "if the way is prepared for it by a primary identification that structures the subject as a rival with himself" (*Écrits*, 117 / 22). Just as we are constrained to put down one foot after another, so the self-reflexive dimension of rivalry must predate the discovery of the rival other in the outer world. Yet while seeming to reassert a classifiable set of evolutionary stages, the same statement may be read, and was probably intended to be read, otherwise.

Lacan conceives the mirror stage not as a proleptic encounter, or figure of things to come, but rather as a figure of speech. The fight for recognition and ascendancy between rival entities is a correlated level of meaning of the child's encounter with the counterpart.[7] The relationship between these confrontational "moments" is one of correspondence and not of chronological sequence. (This structural distinction is analogous to the difference between a double-decker bus and a two-car bus in which the hind part trails after the front.) Lacan himself expressly describes "[t]he notion of aggressivity as a *correlative tension* of the narcissistic structure in the coming-into-being (*devenir*) of the subject" (*Écrits*, 116 / 22; emphasis added). The child before the mirror provides a figural representation (or ground deck) for another doctrinal interest and abstract idea. The analytic discursive mode and empirical evidence brought to bear on "The Mirror Stage" of 1949 should not be allowed to obscure Lacan's invitation to regard the description of how the ego is constructed as a vehicle for conveying that structure itself.

II

No less important for Lacan's conception of subjectivity, although a less familiar or expected resource than the Hegelian-Kojèvian dialectics, is his assimilation of the tropes of Christian theology into his writings. In describing the self's relation to the specular image, Lacan implements a rhetorical as well as a structural synthesis of Christian thought about the motions of the typical soul. The question that arises at this point thus concerns not only the location of conflict but also its locution: what do certain verbal configurations in the Lacanian text imply about the topological relations of the ego and its adversaries?

But before turning to this question, I would recall a key trope that suggests a purposive intermingling of religious and secular allusions in Lacan's writings—"the passion of the signifier":

> [I]t is Freud's discovery that gives to the signifier/signified opposition the full extent of its implications: namely, that the signifier has an active function in determining certain effects in which the signifiable appears as submitting to its mark, by becoming through that passion the signified.
>
> This passion of the signifier now becomes a new dimension of the human condition in that it is not only man who speaks, but that in man and through man *it* speaks (*ça parle*), that his nature is woven by effects in which is to be found the structure of language, of which he becomes the material. (*Écrits*, 688–89 / 284)

In this passage from "The Signification of the Phallus" (1958), the terminology of Saussurian linguistics becomes complexly bound up with a world of Christian reference. Placed in a religious context, the word "passion" (derived from the Latin *passio*, meaning suffering) refers to Christ's suffering, especially during the days before his crucifixion, for the redemption of humanity. Thus the possessive "of"-genitive in the phrase "passion of Christ" unambiguously designates the one who suffered: Christ who spoke for and in defense of humanity through his suffering. In the excerpt just quoted, Lacan does not simply alter the semantic principle ("Christ") through substitution ("signifier") but also revises the syntactical functioning of the genitive. Bearing in mind his often unconventional use of prepositions,[8] the *du* in "la passion du signifiant" may be read as "by means of" or "from" rather than as "belonging to" or "pertaining to." This passion derives *from* the signifier, which inflicts it on something or someone else.[9]

The same phrase recurs in Lacan's definition of the singular factor that distinguishes the human collectivity in "its fullest possible dimension"—namely, "the subject insofar as he suffers from the signifier. It is in this passion of the signifier that the critical point emerges" (*Seminar VII*, 172 / 143). This reference even more explicitly points to a metonymic reversal: a new coinage that replaces an old one by overturning its established semantic valence. Lacan takes the figure of the suffering savior out of its context and invests it with an antithetical meaning. The passion that derives from the signifier is not modeled after the pattern by which Logos descends from a divine realm for the salvation of humankind. It holds out no such redemptive hope for the language user. Rather, Lacan repeatedly evokes the signifying chain in its constraining and subjugating effects. The signifier does not speak "in man and through man" with the passion of Christ. The Lacanian "subject" is a trope—an irony, to be precise—because the speaking being is always subjected to and by the enclosure of speech. The *I* is the hostage rather than the keeper of the Word: "Periphrasis, hyperbaton, ellipsis, suspension, anticipation, retraction, negation, digression, irony. . . . Can one really see these as mere figures of speech when it is the figures themselves that are the active principle of the rhetoric of the discourse that the analysand in fact utters?" (*Écrits*, 521 / 169). With a single turn of phrase—"the passion of the signifier," Lacan simultaneously hybridizes Christian and Saussurian terminology and summarizes the existential predicament whereby individual autonomy is continually deferred by its dependency on language and speech.

Similarly enmeshing diverse realms of discourse, Lacan's meditation on the mirror stage, one of the landmarks of postmodern theory, may be considered a late variant of Prudentius's early Christian *Psychomachia*. The two texts comprise a part of the same analogical-rhetorical system. As C. S. Lewis remarks in a perspicacious footnote in *The Allegory of Love* (1936), an "obvious parallel" to the Christian allegory of the soul in conflict is "modern psycho-analysis and its shadowy personages such as the 'censor'. . . . [I]t might be argued that the application of psychological terms *at all* to the unconscious is itself a species of allegory" (61 n. 1). It might also be helpful to underscore that the sources of allegory in classical Western literature are theological as well as philosophical and literary. Allegorical narratives not only appear, for example, in the dialogues of Plato and in the *Golden Ass* of Lucius Apuleius, but also were part of the Neoplatonic elaboration of mystery cults in which divinities, ritual, and the details of myth received some kind of allegorizing interpretation: "Following Plutarch, many Platonic writers invoked the mysteries for confirmation of the basic tenets of their philosophy, for illustration, or for the addition of a religious dimension to the exercises of philosophical dialectic" (Burkert, 85). The allegorical treatment of the mysteries as possessing a spiritual value (which is both hidden and revealed in the myths themselves and in related rituals) established a dynamic and diversified generic pattern. Accordingly, the typological method of scriptural interpretation uses events and persons in the Hebrew Bible as prophetic "types" or figures of events and persons in the Christian Scriptures. Every passage in the Bible, Saint Augustine writes, "asserts nothing except the catholic faith as it pertains to things past, future, and present"; and therefore, "whatever appears in the divine Word that does not literally pertain to virtuous behavior or to the truth of faith you must take to be figurative" (*On Christian Doctrine*, 88).

In the *Psychomachia* (ca. C.E. 405), Prudentius syncretizes two Greco-Roman traditions—the epic theme of heroic warfare and religious allegory—with Church doctrine by relocating the battle within the individual.[10] Transported from an exteriority to an interiority, the battlefield as the locus of allegorical action becomes, as Fletcher summarily puts it, "psychologized"

(151). Highly influential throughout the Middle Ages, Prudentius's *Psychomachia* was assimilated into the cultures of Christianity. Of course, despite the pious Catholic environment in which Lacan was raised, he might not have read it. What I am suggesting is that the tropes of the Christian soul-struggle are interwoven with the other discourses of conflict in his writings. Lacan's analysis of the tensions that govern the psyche succeeds in articulating the old battle with the double, the *bellum intestinum* or divided will described as "the root of all allegory" (Lewis, 68),[11] in new ways that partially, and perhaps unintentionally, demonstrate his complex indebtedness to Christian sources.

First and most elementary, a basic aspect of human experience links the poet's religious epic with the apostate's psychoanalytic essay. Different generic forms notwithstanding, both writers envision a scene of interiorized conflict. As early as 1938, in the section of *Les complexes familiaux* devoted to the mirror stage, Lacan proposes: "Even though two partners are on stage, their communication reveals not a conflict between two persons but *a conflict within each subject*" (37 / 16; emphasis added). Analogously, images of inner strife frame the opening and closing lines of Prudentius's allegory: "[T]here is disorder among our thoughts and rebellion arises within us, . . . the strife of our evil passions vexes the spirit"; "We know that in the darkness of our heart conflicting affections fight hard in successive combats"; and "Light and darkness with their opposing spirits are at war, and our two-fold being inspires powers at variance with each other" (ll. 7–8, 893–94, 908–9). The *Psychomachia* primarily consists of vividly realized scenes of intrapsychic battle between twinned rivals. The central insight of the poem—"non simplex natura hominis" (l. 904)—thus has its actualization in the narrative device of doubling. Every positive egoic aspect (Virtue) contains its negative or alterity (Vice). Just as the identity of light emerges against darkness, so these polarities are inseparable from each other.

This doubling constitutes a second point of analogy between poem and essay. In the killing fields of the *Psychomachia*, bitter adversaries gather together in inverted symmetry: Faith and Worship-of-the-Old-Gods are followed by Chastity and Lust the Sodomite, Long-Suffering and Wrath, Lowliness and Pride, Soberness and Indulgence, and so forth. In "The Mirror Stage," the warring parties are no longer invoked as Spirit and Flesh, or Virtue and Vice. Rather, Lacan names them the Ego and the Double: "[W]e observe the role of the mirror apparatus in the appearances of the *double*" (*Écrits*, 95 / 3). Now duplication usually entails sameness. However, what binds these two psychical entities in their mirrored relationship, as it does, say, Soberness and Indulgence, is an inversion. Lacan insists on the diametric opposition between the carbon copy (image) and the original (subject):

> [T]he total form of the body by which the subject anticipates in a mirage the maturation of his power is given to him only as *Gestalt*, that is to say, in an exteriority in which this form . . . appears to him above all in *a contrasting size* (un relief de stature) that fixes it and in *a symmetry that inverts* it, *in contrast with* the turbulent movements that the subject feels are animating him. (*Écrits*, 94–95 / 2; emphases added)

Imagine an enlarged photograph of one's self awakening to life. The duplicate becomes a replicant, a monster wanting to be master. The mirror image—or, condensed into a word, the "mirage"—is not only whole and nonhuman as opposed to fragmented, turbulent, and human; it is an "exteriority," an outside that is also inside. The ego experiences a perpetual rift that is modeled on the child's dual relations with its specular counterpart. Thus, the mirror stage presages (the genetic view) or, alternatively, presents (the structural view) through dramatic exemplification "a certain level of rupture . . . between man's organization and his *Umwelt*," that is, between inwardly lived and external realities (111 / 17). However, the child's assumption of the image also anticipates or, alternatively, enacts the ego's capacity to be self-different, to live at variance within the stadium—or fortress—symbols of its dreams. By visibly incarnating an alterity, "a symmetry that inverts," the semblable shatters the very unity (the gestalt) it offers to the gaze of the jubilant beholder. What is held out is also, alas, withheld.

The simultaneity of fatal aggression and attraction, of desirous intent to destroy, constitutes a third major point of analogy. In the *Psychomachia*, the life-and-death struggle between two combatants is predicated upon a hatred that often approaches its opposite. Prudentius portrays successive martial confrontations in which an erotics of destructiveness comes to the fore. Thus Faith arrives in seductive disarray to engage her idolatrous rival:

> Faith first takes the field . . . , her rough dress disordered, her shoulders bare, her hair untrimmed, her arm exposed; for the sudden glow of ambition, burning to enter fresh contests, takes no thought to gird on arms or

armour, but trusting in a stout heart and unprotected limbs challenges the
hazards of furious warfare. . . . Lo, Worship-of-the-Old-Gods ventures to
match her strength against Faith's challenge and strike at her. But she, rising
higher, smites her foe's head down . . . lays in the dust that mouth. . . . The
throat is choked and the scant breath confined by the stopping of its passage, and long gasps make a hard and agonising death. (ll. 21–35)

In comparable oneiric scenes of ferocious violence, bodies embrace one another and sink into combat. The division of the soul is envisioned here as a
nightmare of consummation-in-death. The intermingling between making
love and making war that apparently unintentionally marks the *Psychomachia*'s rhetorical machinery tends to undermine the hostilities it stages.
Does Chastity ("Pudicitia"), for instance, secretly love the harlot Lust ("Libido"), into whose throat she thrusts her sword? It is, as Jon Whitman aptly
points out, "a rather lusty thing for modest Chastity to do": "one of the illuminating failures of the *Psychomachia* is the constant anomaly between the
behavior of a personification and its very meaning" (85, 90).

The continuities just drawn between the allegorical procedures of Prudentius and Lacan repeatedly evokes the libidinal dynamics attending the aggressive relationships of "the slave . . . with the despot" and, in a
parallel phrase, of "the seduced with the seducer." However, the correlation
between these characters-in-conflict and their antithetical activities is not a
failure of Lacan's vision but, rather, a complication. There is neither confusion nor inadvertence in his discussion of the captivation (*captation*)—in both
senses of subjugation and of seduction—that the mirror stage imposes on
the perceiving subject: "this erotic relation, in which the human individual
fixes upon himself an image that alienates him from himself" (*Écrits*, 113 /
19). In such dialectical formulations, the ego defines itself against the specular image, with which it also merges.

The continuities just drawn between the allegorical procedures of Prudentius and Lacan do not cancel the fundamental discontinuities in their
subject matter. One major disparity between the *Psychomachia* and "The
Mirror Stage" is the marked presence, in the former, of an ethical-didactic
dimension in the foreground of the action. The *Psychomachia* "participates in
universal-salvation history" and, pragmatically, is meant "to aid in the salvation of its Christian audience" (Smith, 4). In Prudentius's text, there is warfare and worship; in Lacan's, only warfare. Nor does it unequivocally emerge
from Lacan's writings that the aims of psychoanalysis are, and should be, cu-

rative. The "passion of the signifier," as we have seen, is not a trope to salve the soul.

Another difference lies in the perception of the *psyche*, the "life" or "soul," whose typical state is characterized by *machia*, a "fight." Prudentius belongs to a long tradition of Western thought for which the idea of an essential self or identity is above all a given reality. The diverse applications of allegory found in mystery religions, classical philosophic writings, and scriptural exegesis nonetheless have something in common. Their ontological presupposition is "I am"—and the investigation proceeds from there. For Prudentius, the major questions are therefore epistemological and ethical: what is the nature (good or evil?) of the soul? The author of the *Psychomachia* does not ask "Am I?" but rather "What or who am I?" Although the Christian soul may be riven between warring internal tendencies, its being *qua* being is not called into question.

For Lacan, the basic question is "Am I?" and it has, in a sense, already been answered. The "I" is an optical effect, a mir(or-im)age, a trick done with mirrors. In short and rapid order, Lacan speaks of: "an ontological structure of the human world" inseparable from "paranoiac knowledge"; "phantoms that dominate" the functions of the ego; and the "lure of spatial identifications" and the "succession of phantasies" that determine mental orientations (*Écrits*, 94–97 / 2–4). So while his presentation of intrapsychic conflict resembles that of Prudentius in some strategic respects, the battleground greatly differs. The terrain of the Christian *psychomachia* is a substantial, albeit sinful, individual soul. The *I* formed in and through the specular encounter is not just illusory but radically unstable, split, divided, ex-centric to itself. The Lacanian subject does not possess a unitary soul composed of warring but (e)mendable parts. Yet, by virtue of being differentially placed in relation to other subjects in the symbolic universe, this subject exists: "existence is here synonymous," as Slavoj Žižek cogently puts it, "with symbolization, integration into the symbolic order—only what is symbolized fully 'exists'" (136). Such existence requires the qualification of quotation marks or reinscription as *ex-sistence* to convey the situation of the subject not only as located or locked in the imaginary dimension of phantoms and fantasies but also as constituted in and captured by the symbolic ("*cette prise du* symbolique").[12] Thus "the *insistence* of the signifying chain," Lacan writes at the outset of his seminar on "The Purloined Letter," is "a correlate of the *ex-sistence* (or: eccentric place)" of the human organism (*Écrits*, 11 / 28).

In sum, Lacan imports specific features of the "fight for mansoul" into his theory, while discarding or ignoring others. The interest and irony lie in the ways in which he contravenes the secularism of Freud, a militant secularism raised to the level of dogma, by drawing on rhetoric and imagery from the religious domain. In so doing, Lacan effects a synthesis between the Hegelian phenomenology that posits conflicted *inter*subjective relations— "the social reality," in Kojève's phrase—as paramount to subject formation and the theological outlook that envisions the psyche as an *intra*subjective battlefield. I would pause here to observe that by integrating these two viewpoints, Lacan elaborates a virilocal image of self and social functioning in which aggression immediately accompanies identificatory bonding, in which hostility rather than connection is normative. He envisions human individuals and groups primarily as sites of division and strife. The tension between violent and cohesive forces often modulates in his writings into an all-pervading situation of aggression. This inclination to put the emphasis on negative social interaction, on splitting, on passion as suffering inflicted on the speaking subject may further explain why he found Kojève's reading of Hegel and other (male) cultural correlates, such as the Christian concept of the soul at war, so congenial to his own way of thinking about human realities.

III

Nevertheless, war alone is not enough. The psychoanalytic categories of "libido" and "eros" also become conjoined with the "aggressivity" of the specular encounter. Upon grasping the reciprocal relations with the visual image, the child's ecstatic behavior "discloses a libidinal dynamism" (*Écrits*, 94 / 2). Similarly, when Lacan presented the mirror-stage theory to the British Psycho-Analytical Society, he specified "an essential libidinal relationship with the body-image": "[T]he child seems to be in endless ecstasy when it sees that movements in the mirror correspond to its own movements" ("Some Reflections," 14). The notion of "endless ecstasy" may be understood to imply that the model for this experience is the figure of Narcissus trapped in the pool of his own reflection. Lacan does not, however, view the child's captivation by the reflected image as wholly negative. It is not frequently enough noted that the imaginary is alloyed with benefits in his thought.[13] Lacan envisions the infant before the mirror in a situation of discovery, exploring the relations between "this virtual complex and the reality it reduplicates" (*Écrits*, 93 / 1).

Contrastively, the traditional Narcissus refuses the attachments of social or objectal bonds. His rejection of the love of many women, including the nymph Echo (or, in another version, his lover Ameinius), brings upon him the retribution of the gods. In an Olympian display of justice, they turn his favorite entertainment into a deadly containment. Distracted and consumed by love for his own image, the beautiful youth pines away in (ec)static and stagnant self-contemplation. The cautionary moral is that too much looking into mirrors, too much erotic self-fascination, or what Lacan might call the repudiation of intersubjectivity, can congeal into intrasubjectivity. In brief, the subject can get stuck in the imaginary.

But Lacanian theory concedes—in fact, insists—that the narcissistic dimension of ego formation also includes a different trajectory. The new Narcissus enters into society and acquires knowledge of the outer reality via the looking glass. The child's ludic activities before the mirror are "rounded off by attempts to explore the things seen in the mirror and the nearby objects they reflect" ("Some Reflections," 14). Far from closing down or narrowing the outer world, far from representing an impasse, the mirror apparatus opens up new paths for experiencing both "the child's own body, and the persons and things, around him." The child begins to perceive and react to objects or persons in the environment as separate and apart. According to Lacan, the mirror stage therefore can, and often does, lead from the "specular *I*" to the "social *I*" (*Écrits*, 93 / 1, 98 / 5). Thus reconceived, the story of Narcissus need not end in calamity but rather in comedy—that is, with the hero's integration into the community and cultural milieu. The narcissistic structure of selfhood enables the libidinal normalization of the subject. Under these circumstances, the question of the proper name arises. Is the subject of this narrative still to be called "Narcissus"?

These remarks are intended to prepare for what is arguably one of the most innovative passages in Lacan's articulation of the mirror mechanism:

> There is a sort of structural crossroads [*carrefour*] here to which we must accommodate our thinking if we are to understand the nature of aggressivity

in man and its relation with the formalism of his ego and its objects. It is in this erotic relation, in which the human individual fixes upon himself an image that alienates him from himself, that are to be found the energy and the form on which this organization of the passions that he will call his ego is based. (*Écrits*, 113 / 19)

The crucial word is "crossroads." Where is the subject introduced to desire? At a crossroads, Lacan answers. In the Sophoclean tragedy of Oedipus, the crossroads is a meeting place where two destinies diverge: the father marked for death; the son, for a brief reprieve. What happens at the crossroads is a fatal act, a point after which there is no turning back. Metaphorically transposed, this juncture occurs in Shakespeare's *Hamlet* when the prince of Denmark suspends his sword and fails to kill the king at prayer; or, alternatively, it occurs when he fails to hold back his sword and kills the king's importunate adviser. Shakespeare, grand master of ambiguities, locates the "crossroads" in so indeterminate a place (was it the act of omission, the act of commission, or did it happen elsewhere?) that only in retrospect does it become evident that the tragic hero has passed it. However, be it Sophocles's or Shakespeare's or Freud's rendition of the tale, one narrative component remains invariable. A father and his son confront each other. The French *carrefour*, sometimes known in English dialect as a "four-cross-road," thus seems more accurately to denote this point of intersection: the two roads taken after the confrontation are not the same as the two roads traveled before.

Using the term "crossroads" as a metaphor for a transitional stage, like a frontier or a threshold, Lacan exhorts us to alter our thinking ("nous devons accommoder notre pensée") about it. New accommodations are indeed required in several respects. First, Lacan displaces or relocates the "crossroads" from the Oedipal phase to an anterior structural, if not temporal, moment in the subject's life-journey. In a manner of speaking, the place and the time of the encounter have changed. Second, in this restaging of the fight for "pure prestige," it is not only the setting that changes: the brother, and not the father, turns up at the crossroads. Instead of a paternal representative of the law and societal custom, this turning point involves a less-than-harmonious identification with a semblable, as in: "The child who strikes another says that he has been struck" (*Écrits*, 113 / 19). Lacan imagines the future king of Thebes encountering what might be termed a "similiar"; he meets a stranger who is uncannily familiar. Third, the figure of the adversary is not the sole change in central casting. If you are what you meet, then Narcissus rather than Oedipus comes to the crossroads.

Viewed metacritically, Lacan's exegesis freely borrows and superimposes motifs from the classical myths of Narcissus and of Oedipus. To paraphrase the formula of Philo, the fictions that Freud adopted and imported into the clinic become the "handmaid" to a different philosophy.[14] Lacan constructs a composite scenario of the confrontation that brings about the formation of the *I*. He again advocates a "return to our crossroads" in his seminar of 1955–56 and explains what such a return would entail: "Desire is at first sight [*au premier abord*] understood as an essentially imaginary relation. Setting out from here, we set about cataloguing instincts, their equivalences and interconnections" (*Seminar III*, 222 / 197). If the first contact that elicits desire belongs to the encounter with the specular image, neither the maternal imago (of the weaning complex) nor the paternal imago (of the Oedipus complex) is the individual's primary object of erotic fascination. By introducing the crossroads, a metaphor for radical transition, into the static enclosure of the imaginary dyad, Lacan refuses the restrictions of fictional boundaries (Narcissus's story as distinct from Oedipus's) and of orthodox psychoanalytic terminology. In his inventive rendition, two textual-psychical situations become condensed into one. The question is: what does he gain from this condensation or isomorphic graphing of the one narrative onto the other?

In thus mixing stories and metaphors, Lacan presents a conception of human conflicts and desires that profoundly differs from Freud's theory. Specifically, by deploying the word "crossroads" to mark the inaugural moment of "misrecognition" (*méconnaissance*) when the infant suddenly assumes an image, Lacan announces his second reorganization of the Oedipus complex. Following *Les complexes familiaux*, the 1949 essay on the mirror stage is foremost among the places, in a manner of speaking, where Lacan deliberately crosses the father of psychoanalysis and goes his own way. Again in "Aggressivity in Psychoanalysis," Lacan enacts the "aggressive competitiveness" he describes by defining the resolution of the Oedipus complex as an "identificatory *reshaping* of the subject": the basis for further egoic maturation is "a *primary* identification which structures the subject as rival of himself." (I take up this concept of primary identification and its linkage to the subject's "capture" by the specular [br]other in the next two chapters.) In sum, identification with the father situates the subject in relation to the laws, prohibitions, and exchanges that comprise the symbolic order only *if* and *after* the encounter with a reflected rivalrous image has taken place: "[T]he Oedipal identification is that by which the subject transcends the aggressivity that is constitutive of the *primary* subjective individuation" (*Écrits*, 117 / 22–23; emphases added).

Whereas previously the paternal imago occupied a tertiary position in Lacan's view—after the maternal and fraternal imagos had done their developmental work—it now becomes secondary. But this transposition of the Oedipus complex into a belated, subordinate position only supplies further evidence of an ineluctable generational conflict. In the very act of second placing or preempting the Oedipus complex, Lacan corroborates the validity of the Freudian insight. He cannot help but reinforce his psychoanalytic patrimony.

Mixing stories in a manner studied from Lacan, I want therefore to conclude this chapter by proposing that the son's feet are already tied at the very moment when he seems to overcome the "obstructions of his support." He must stumble even as he surmounts the blocking agents that impede him. The attempt to upstage the Oedipal father (and the powerful author of *Totem and Taboo*) by means of the mirror stage demonstrates the paramount significance of the paternal function in the regulation of human affairs. Hence Shakespeare's *Hamlet* may well provide a more perfect dramatic example of the Freudian theory than Sophocles's *Oedipus Rex*. The Oedipal father is indeed a ghost. Even when one has situated one's self before or beyond the figure of the father, one hears his footsteps stalking close at hand. Even when contemplating one's own reflection in a pool, one is haunted by his voice welling up from below.

CHAPTER 6

"Lacannibalism"

The Return to Freud's Idea of Identification

We are not following Freud, we are accompanying him. The fact that an idea occurs somewhere in Freud's work doesn't, for all that, guarantee that it is being handled in the spirit of the Freudian researches. As for us, we are trying to conform to the spirit, to the watchword, to the style of this research.

JACQUES LACAN, *Seminar I*

During the late 1940s and early 1950s, Lacan redefined the term "identification" in ways that implicate two conceptual systems. First, in relation to the primal horde's murder and incorporation of the father—which Lacan tellingly describes as Freud's "ultimate horizon of the problem of origins" ("Desire," 42)—the revision mainly concerns the paternal function. Second, Lacan's reworking of the weaning complex presented in *Les complexes familiaux* brings in its wake changes that extend from major category shifts ("narcissism" rather than "affection," for example, becomes coterminous with "identification") to the reassignment of terminology or functions associated with the mother ("pregnancy" and "matrix" are among the more striking examples) to the image of the subject's own body. Identification with the semblable effectively brackets the formative agency of both parents. Like the proverbially efficient one stone that kills two birds, this reformulation not only delimits the influence of the Oedipal father (Freud's view) but also vir-

tually eliminates the agency of the mother in the construction of a dialecti-
cally determined subject (Lacan's 1930s view).

The revised theory of identificatory processes and its rhetorical inflections thus further demonstrate an anxiety about the parental role in the genesis of subjectivity and an accompanying fantasy about birth untainted by the
maternal body.[1] The Lacanian subject appropriates (self-)reproductive powers through the mediation of the specular image. This corrective wish or
fantasy does not, however, preclude other motivations. Lacan's early emphasis on the maternal imago put him in a position uncomfortably close to such
innovative dissenters as Otto Rank and Melanie Klein.[2] While the conceptualization of separation from the mother at birth and actual weaning in *Les
complexes familiaux* effectively distanced Lacan from Freudian doctrine, it
also restricted his assumption of the status of originator in the psychoanalytic field. In transforming the notion of primary identification into an outcome of the mirror stage, he was able to elaborate the work of Freud in ways
that were quite uniquely his own and yet remain, at the very same time, af-
filiated with Freud's foundational concerns. Once again, even as Lacan
vaunts his return to Freud, he also sometimes quietly returns to Lacan.

In effect, the vicissitudes of the term "identification" comprise more than
an exemplary instance of Lacan's return to—which is, of course, also a departure from—Freud and himself. Self-corrective tendencies are apparent in
Freud's writings as well. This chapter has therefore a threefold focus. As in
previous chapters, I shall try to present Lacan's continual repair of his own
work ("Lacan against Lacan") and the conjunctions/disjunctions that emerge
in his reading of Freud ("Lacan against Freud"). In addition to these com-
ings and goings, I take into account the directions in which Freud's early
ideas about identification evolved ("Freud against Freud").

I

In *The Language of Psycho-Analysis*, Jean Laplanche and J.-B. Pontalis give a
concise definition of the term "identification." Their explanation is followed
by a three-page commentary that outlines the origins, evolution, and main
structural features of the term in Freud's thought. This is the definition:

Psychological process whereby the subject assimilates an aspect, property or attribute of the other and is transformed, wholly or partially, after the model the other provides. It is by means of a series of identifications that the personality is constituted and specified. (205)

According to Laplanche and Pontalis's foreword, the preliminary definition of each entry in their compilation "seeks to sum up the concept's accepted meaning as it emerges from its strict usage in psycho-analytic theory" (xii). In the case of "identification," however, such a summation is particularly problematic. As Laplanche and Pontalis briefly mention, Freud himself did not provide a definitive and systematic description of this mental operation in his writings. Quite the contrary, his usage over the years is richly nuanced and also abounds in inconsistencies. By singling out the constitutive aspect of identification—namely, its relation to how the personality is built up, Laplanche and Pontalis's definition (in bold-face type) foregrounds a signification that is highly relevant for Lacanian theory.[3] To designate the "accepted meaning" in this instance is to display an inclination toward a specific meaning.

As variously described by Freud, identification could be any of the following: primary (the earliest form of emotional tie), regressive (the object-choice is introjected back into the ego), narcissistic (the self is taken as a model), and hysterical (the patient's symptom expresses an unconscious assimilation of the experiences, usually sexual, of other people). Lacan's elaborations add, on the one hand, complexity to an already complicated and sometimes contradictory concept and, on the other, specificity where Freud ranges widely. But before turning to the evolution of Freud's and Lacan's ideas about the workings of identification in the psyche, I first want to show what it might mean for Lacan to be "accompanying" rather than "following" the Freudian concept in another respect (*Seminar I*, 139 / 120).

From the several definitions given in *The Interpretation of Dreams* (1900) to the partial recapitulation in *Group Psychology and the Analysis of the Ego* (1921), Freud generally, albeit implicitly, distinguishes between two types of identification. He uses the term in reference to psychosexual disturbances or pathologies and to normative modes of mental functioning. In *The Interpretation of Dreams*, for instance, identification appears at one point as a factor in the formation of hysterical symptoms ("A hysterical woman identifies her-

self in her symptoms . . . with people with whom she has had sexual relations" [*SE*, 4: 150]); and at another point, as a representational feature of the
dream-work, specifically as condensation ("[I]dentification or the construction of composite figures serves various purposes in dreams" [4: 322]).

For Lacan's model of ego formation, however, neither hysterical identification nor the assimilation of people to one another in dreams has relevance. Moreover, his theory of the mirror stage also undoes the differentiation between pathological and normative identifications. The basis of all
interhuman relations, according to Lacan, is a paranoid identification with
the specular counterpart.[4] "All human knowledge stems from the dialectic
of jealousy, which is a primordial manifestation of communication"; and
further, "paranoid knowledge is knowledge founded on the rivalry of jealousy, over the course of the primary identification I have tried to define by
means of the mirror stage" (*Seminar III*, 49–50 / 39). Insofar as the gener-
ality of human individuals experience or, rather, submit to the drama of
identification/alienation, the mirror stage may be regarded as common and
normal. But insofar as the seesaw relation to the reflected image bears the
symptomatic markings of paranoia, it exhibits the psychical dis-ease or
pathology that characterizes everyday life. "Observe the fortunate opportu-
nity," Lacan proposes with some irony—it is to be hoped, "that the signifier
offers us in French, with the different ways of understanding *tu es* ['thou art'
and 'kill']." His wordplay gives expression to a deadly serious worldview:
"This is the foundation of the relationship with the other. In all imaginary
identification, the *tu es, thou art*, ends in the destruction of the other, and
vice versa, because this destruction is simply there . . . in what we shall call
thouness" (341 / 303).

One conclusion, then, may already be drawn about Lacan's reformulation
of the Freudian idea of identification. Whereas Freud can contemplate the
possibility of a successful or benign resolution to the Oedipal crisis, a resolution that results in the son identifying with the father, Lacan views the
alienating effects of narcissistic identification with the (br)other as in-
escapable. Put another way, whereas neurosis can (but need not) be an outcome of the Oedipus complex, paranoia is the certain outcome of the mirror
stage. A kind of madness is the basic ground for the emergence of consciousness as socially defined and socially constructed. In Lacan's words,
"The [symbolic] domain of knowledge is fundamentally inserted into the

primitive paranoid dialectic of identification with the counterpart" (*Seminar III*, 200 / 177–78). Imaginary identification thus puts the subject in a double bind. To bypass the mirror stage (as possibly happens in the flower-doll cases described in section VI below) is to refuse the human dimension of existence; however, to enter into the mirror stage is to acquiesce in a permanent condition of psychical estrangement and derangement.

II

Some aspects of Lacan's divergence from his earlier conception of identification as well as from Freud's views are signaled in his texts, but others are not. Furthermore, Freud himself does not adhere unswervingly to his own ideas about identification. At the hub of these revisionary movements, the figure of the mother may often be discerned. To substantiate this central but spectral presence[5] requires a description of the divergent trajectories of two related concepts—oral incorporation and narcissism—in Freud's and Lacan's writings. I begin here with Freud.

Although Freud investigates several types of identification in the course of his work, the son's identificatory tie with the father occupies a preeminent position. The father initially appears as the primary object of identification in *Totem and Taboo* (1912–13). Freud upholds and develops this notion in three essays: *Group Psychology and the Analysis of the Ego* (1921), *The Ego and the Id* (1923), and "The Dissolution of the Oedipus Complex" (1924). Despite the differently inflected meanings of the term "father-identification" (*Vateridentifizierung*) in these texts,[6] Freud repeatedly stipulates a primal form of *emotional* attachment: "Identification is known to psycho-analysis as the earliest expression of an emotional tie. . . . A little boy will exhibit a special interest in his father; he would like to grow like him and be like him" (*SE*, 18: 105; also *SE*, 13: 131).

In *Totem and Taboo*, evidence for identification with the father that is an affective and, therefore, immeasurable bond is adduced from a variety of ritualized behaviors. These rituals may be broadly differentiated as modes of "imitation" and of "incorporation." Imitation is the less radical expression of identification: "[T]he clansman seeks to emphasize his kinship with the totem by making himself resemble it externally, by dressing in the skin of the animal, by incising a picture of the totem upon his own body, and so on" (*SE*, 13: 105). Freud famously reverses the clansman's supposed substitution of the totem for the father. That is, in asserting an equivalence between the father and the sacred animal or object, Freud endows the tribal symbol in its varied and complex manifestations with a single originary meaning. He thereby arrives at his boldest reduction—the scenario of identification through incorporation. The sons of the primal horde, who literally take the father into themselves, thereby appropriate his qualities; or, more plainly put, they become what they eat: "Cannibal savages as they were, it goes without saying that they devoured their victim. . . . [I]n the act of devouring him they accomplished their identification with him, and each one of them acquired a portion of his strength" (13: 142). For Freud, cannibalism or oral incorporation is coextensive with a specific type of identification: *Vateridentifizierung*.

A different possibility emerges in "On Narcissism: An Introduction," an essay published shortly after Freud's 1914 study of totemism. Here Freud presents the concept of *Anlehnungstypus der Objektwahl*, a term translated in the *Standard Edition* as an "anaclictic type of object-choice."[7] The anaclictic or attachment type designates a formative relation based on nurturance and protection at the beginning of infant life. Individuals take the mother or other caretakers—and not only the self, as Lacan contends later—"as a model" (*SE*, 14: 88) for their erotic choices. According to Freud, "the persons who are concerned with a child's feeding, care, and protection become his earliest sexual objects: that is to say, in the first instance his mother or a substitute for her" (14: 87). Even though he does not use the word "identification" in this essay, the dynamics of the mother-child relationship suggest that both collective rituals and individual fantasies of oral incorporation could be traced to a maternal agency. Matricide is, Kenneth Burke observes, at least as likely as patricide to be a component of rebirth rituals and identity formation: "Totemism, as Freud himself reminds us, was a magical device whereby members of a group were identified with one another by the sharing of the same substance. . . . And it is to the mother that the basic informative experiences of eating are related" ("Freud," 274). Citing the anthropologist Bronislaw Malinowski's work on variants of the Oedipus complex in matriarchal societies, Burke proposes that, even in predominantly patriarchal societies, "the phenomena of identity revealed in totemism might require the introduction of matricidal ingredients also" (274 n. 6). Nevertheless, although Freud briefly acknowledges his embarrassment concerning the role of mother-goddesses in prehistory ("I cannot suggest at what point . . . a place is to be found for the great mother-goddesses, who may perhaps in general have preceded the father-gods" [*SE*, 13: 149]), the mother is not a participant in the totemic festivities conjured up in *Totem and Taboo*. Her absence is in keeping with her subcultural presence in Freud's speculation about the origins of social organization and, especially, religion: "[W]hat constitutes the root of every form of religion [is] a longing for the father" (13: 148).[8]

The connection between oral incorporation and identification recurs in several works written within the span of a few years: the 1915 edition of *Three Essays on the Theory of Sexuality* (1905), "Mourning and Melancholia" ([1915] 1917),[9] and *Group Psychology and the Analysis of the Ego* (1921). Freud's attention shifts in these texts from phylogeny to ontogeny, particularly from the prehistory of social groups to that of individuals, but different emphases and discrepancies also begin to appear. In *Three Essays*, for example, Freud refers to "cannibalistic pregenital sexual organization" as a normative feature of childhood development: "the prototype of a process which, in the form of identification, is later to play such an important psychological part" (*SE*, 7: 198). The incorporated object remains unspecified in this text. Similarly, in *Group Psychology*, the term "identification" designates a mental mechanism normatively linked to ingestion: "It [identification] behaves like a derivative of the first, *oral* phase of the organization of the libido, in which the object that we long for and prize is assimilated by eating. . . . The cannibal, as we know, has remained at this standpoint" (*SE*, 18: 105). The object-choice, however, has undergone an alteration.

Whereas formerly the question *"Who's for dinner?"* was left vague or suspended, Freud now specifies that the child's first appetitive choice falls upon the father: "We may simply say that he takes his father as his ideal." This modest proposal is apparently intended to forestall objections to his reevocation of cannibalism. Yet, even while Freud's "cannibalistic" (*kannibalisch*) component designates a figurative appropriation of the exemplary paternal object's properties or qualities, it also recalls the archaic and literal origins of identification as oral consumption. Freud clearly believes that the "devouring affection" for the father in the individual's prehistory bears the stamp of the prehistory of the human race (18: 105). Primitivism and perversion are among the connotations usually attached to cannibal activities. As presented in *Three Essays*, *Group Psychology*, and *The Ego and the Id*, however, the linkage between oral incorporation and the earliest phases of identification is more than just nondeviant.

In the seventh chapter ("Identification") of *Group Psychology* and, two years later, in *The Ego and the Id*, Freud discusses identification with the father as universally constitutive for little boys—a kind of first building block for the character under construction. The German *Vorbild*, in the sense of paragon and model, appears frequently in his analysis of the paternal function: "[I]dentification endeavours to mould a person's own ego after the fashion of the one [i.e., the father] that has been taken as a model [*Vorbild*]." And likewise: "The super-ego arises . . . from an identification with the father taken as a model [*Vatervorbild*]" (*SE*, 18: 106; *GW*, 13: 116 and *SE*, 19: 54; *GW*, 13: 284). Deviance is not, the reader may safely presume, a part of the individual's self-fashioning after the *Vorbild* of the father.

But in "Mourning and Melancholia," which was written only a few months after the passage on infantile cannibalistic aims in *Three Essays* ("Editor's Note," *SE*, 14: 241), Freud draws an altogether different type of linkage between ingestion and identification. His theoretical interest shifts from broad phylogenic patterns and the ritual practices of "primitive" groups to the pathological vagaries of his patients. He turns from the cave, as it were, to the clinic. What occurs during the pathological state of mourning designated "melancholia" is a rigid assimilation of the loved person into the ego. Melancholia recasts a well-worn aphorism: it is sometimes better not to have loved and lost than never to have loved at all.[10] In the melancholic condition, the ego wishes "to incorporate this [lost] object into itself, and, in accordance with the oral or cannibalistic phase of libidinal development in which it is, it wants to do so by devouring it" (14: 249–50). Thus the melancholic patient exhibits two regressive trends. In the manner of the primal horde who killed and hungrily devoured their totem-father, so the ambivalence always inherent in the love bond manifests itself through a resurgence of the archaic urge to cannibalize the object. Furthermore, by withdrawing the emotions formerly cathected (invested) in the beloved into the ego, the adult reverts to the infantile, narcissistic type of object-choice: "[T]he object-cathexis, when obstacles come in its way, can regress to narcissism" (14: 249). The bereft self re-takes itself as an object of erotic interest.

The evolution of Freud's thought on this issue may be summarized as follows: the innovations introduced in two distinctive essays, *Totem and Taboo* and "On Narcissism," converge in his analysis of melancholia. In addition to the incorporation of an ambivalent external object, Freud also links the notion of a universal tendency to take the self as a love-object presented in his essay on narcissism ("[W]e are postulating a primary narcissism in everyone" [*SE*, 14: 88]) to melancholic states. In deviant or acute instances of mourning, a cannibalistic-narcissistic-regressive identification goes into effect and replaces the libidinal tie with another person. "The narcissistic identification with the object then [in melancholia] becomes a substitute for the erotic cathexis. . . . It represents, of course, a *regression* from one type of object-choice to original narcissism" (14: 249). He thereby conjoins the terms "narcissism" and "identification"—a conjunction that becomes crucial for the Lacanian lexicon—in order to elucidate a pathological condition of loss.

III

Whatever might be obscure or variable about the Freudian view of "identification," one aspect of it is clear and constant. Freud never yields ground about the desire for identification through oral ingestion—in a word, cannibalism as an early expression of the relation toward the *father*. So when Lacan initially links cannibalism to the child's emotional tie to the *mother*, he is already moving fast and far in a renegade direction. His first theory of identification as expounded in the *Encyclopédie française* in 1938 also instantiates one of his first radical swerves away from Freud. Lacan speaks of the "maternal embrace" that instills an abiding wish for oral fusion with an other. The conflation of aggression with desire, of hunger and food with love, is the lifelong result of the infant's relation to the mother:

> [T]he creature who is absorbing is completely absorbed and the archaic complex resonates in the maternal embrace. [We shall not speak here with Freud of auto-erotism, . . . still less of oral erotism, since the longing for the nurturing breast, over which the psychoanalytic movement has equivocated,

arises again from the weaning complex only through its restoration by the Oedipus complex.][11] "Cannibalism" in the sense of fusional cannibalism, inexpressible, active and passive at the same time, continues to survive in the symbolic words and games which in the most highly sophisticated form of love-making, recall the desire of the new-born. (*CF*, 29–30 / 15; trans. modified)

"Oral erotism," first generated during weaning and resurgent during the Oedipus complex, is not to be correlated here with "fusional cannibalism." Although a libidinal component prevails in both trends, Lacan seems to be differentiating between a desire for identificatory fusion, in which the longed-for object is devoured, ingested, and absorbed, and a desire in which the object is not so much annihilated as possessed. In the more primordial instance (fusional cannibalism), the mother or her surrogate is removed from an outside into an inside; in the second instance (oral erotism), which acquires psychical reality only during the Oedipal crisis, the mother remains on the outside. In fact, if she were not on the outside—in her function as a desired object of rival others—there would be no Oedipus complex. If she were not on the outside, our erotic lives would be considerably impoverished or, at best, simplified.

The usage of "fusional cannibalism" and "oral erotism" in *Les complexes familiaux* thus bears a resemblance to the Freudian distinction between "identification with the father" (eating) and "choice of the father as an object" (having) in *Group Psychology* (*SE*, 18: 106). However, one notable difference marks these two sets of terms: in place of the father, Lacan evokes the maternal imago. So Lacan's "We will not speak here with Freud" in the passage just quoted may be understood in two ways. While ostensively meaning to say: "We will not speak here with Freud of auto-erotism nor of oral erotism but, rather, of fusional cannibalism," what he says also means: "We will not speak here with but against Freud."

In detaching the concept of cannibalism from the child's relation to the father, Lacan also necessarily inflects the Oedipus complex in a different way. According to *Les complexes familiaux*, "the play of tendencies arising from weaning," that is, the initial ambivalence experienced by the nursling, provides a paradigm for subsequent dialecticized attitudes. During the Oedipal crisis, the young child (whose recent specular encounter ratified the boundaries and unity of its own body) is suddenly overwhelmed, not so much by an eruption of genital desire for the mother, as by the imago of the maternal breast inextricably associated with the primordial desire for, and fear of, oral incorporation:

> The Oedipus complex is set in motion by a triangular conflict in the subject; we have already seen that the play of tendencies arising from weaning produces a similar formation; it is also the mother, first object of these tendencies, as nourishment to be absorbed and even as the breast where one is reabsorbed, that initially offers herself to Oedipal desire [c'est aussi la mère, objet premier de ces tendances, comme nourriture à absorber et même comme sein où se résorber, qui se propose d'abord au désir oedipien]. (*CF*, 56 / 20; trans. modified)

If any body part predominates here, it is the mouth and not the eye. Nevertheless, Carolyn Asp's translation diverges from the French edition at this point. The translator introduces a visual reference where none exists in Lacan's text: "There also the mother, first object of the desires to feed from the breast and to merge with it, is what Oedipal desire first gazes upon."[12] In the light of Lacan's later formulations, to recall his own metaphor of illumination, it would be accurate to speak of an Oedipal gaze of desire. But Lacan does not yet grant predominance to visuality and spectacle in 1938. On the contrary, in detailing the infant's responses to the mother, he writes: "[S]ensations of sucking and gripping obviously form the foundation of that experiential ambivalence and have their source in the same situation: the creature who is absorbing is completely absorbed [l'être qui absorbe est tout absorbé]" (*CF*, 29 / 15).

Lacan's assertion here doubly differs from his later theory: first, in its contention that kinesthetic sensations and contacts *prior* to visual images determine the infant's perception of the environment; and second, in its designation of the bipolar forces at play during the weaning complex. Swings between desiring to devour / to be devoured, between keeping something inside one's self / being kept inside someone, characterize the "experiential ambivalence," the motion of to be or not to be at this stage. For the *infans*, the mother simultaneously represents "nourishment to be absorbed" and "the breast where one is reabsorbed." Lacan's description of these conflicted feelings explains and reinforces the bipolar interplay—"active and passive at the same time" (30 / 15)—attributed to fusional cannibalism earlier in his encyclopedia essay.

IV

Although in 1938 the idea of a primary emotional tie to the mother served to contain the formidable Oedipal father as represented in (and by) Freud's work, in Lacan's subsequent writings the concept of the specular image takes over that function of containment. In what I propose be called "Lacan's second theory of identification," the ground for the formation of the ego or self and its dialectical relations to the other is "the primitive libido, whose object is the subject's own image": "That is a crucial phenomenon" (*Seminar I*, 203 / 180). In brief, Lacan revises his former revision of Freud.

These revisionary movements are perhaps nowhere more vividly dramatized than in the sessions that Lacan devoted to a close reading of "On Narcissism" during his seminar of 1953–54. In the following excerpt, Serge Leclaire (who underwent his training analysis with Lacan) presents a key passage in Freud's essay and then directly quotes Freud:

> *He thereby comes to the distinction between two types of choice which one may translate as anaclitic and narcissistic, and he studies their genesis. He is led to putting it as follows*—A human being has originally two sexual objects—himself and the woman who takes care of him. *We might start from there.*

Lacan quickly intervenes:

> Himself, that's to say his image. It's absolutely clear. (*Seminar I*, 151 / 131)

Freud was, it would seem, already talking about the mirror stage in 1914. The singular stress in Lacan's intervention here (as elsewhere) is: "First of all, within the field of fixation in love, there is *Verliebtheit*, the narcissistic type"; and also, "each object's attachment to the other is produced by the narcissistic fixation on this image, because it is this image, and it alone, that it was expecting" (152 / 132, 158 / 137). So our capacity to fall in love, to respond to the lure of the other, is solely a result of our narcissistic identifications.

And yet, as Leclaire observes in his presentation, Freud himself distinguishes between mother-oriented (anaclitic) and self-oriented (narcissistic) types of object-choice. In the German text: "Wir sagen, der Mensch habe zwei ursprüngliche Sexualobjekte: sich selbst und das pflegende Weib" (*GW*, 10: 154; see *SE*, 14: 87–88). It could also be noted that these two types are not opposed but generally concurrent in Freud's account; that is, "both kinds of object-choice are open to each individual, though he may show a preference for one or the other." Nevertheless, the child's early attachment to those persons who offer "feeding, care, and protection . . . in the first instance his mother or a substitute for her" is not brought out in Lacan's reading. He also deviates from his source text in another critical respect. Although Freud does indicate that certain individuals tend to take "as a model not their mother but their own selves," the term "model" (*Vorbild*) is not obviously or necessarily restricted to the visual field (14: 87–88). It could mean "image" but, in context, also denotes "standard," "pattern," and "example": "ihr späteres Liebesobjekt nicht nach dem Vorbild der Mutter wählen, sondern nach dem ihrer eigenen Person" (*GW*, 10: 154). Freud's formulation does not clearly lead to—"Himself, that's to say his image." Lacan selects and rearranges the textual milieu that authenticates his own theory.

It might be helpful to pause and enumerate the several turns and returns already taken. Lacan revises the Freudian notion of cannibalism as the prototype for identification with the father twice: in *Les complexes familiaux*, by substituting the imago of the maternal breast for the paternal presence, and later, in "The Mirror Stage as Formative of the Function of the *I*," by redirecting the child's libidinal and aggressive energies toward the specular image. By way of further contrast, he contends in 1938 that the range of affective reactions and, specifically, the "experiential ambivalence" related to ingestion are essential for further cognitive development. He thus traces the fantasies of castration that appear during the Oedipal phase back to the infant's mother-oriented cannibalism.[13] "The examination of such fantasies reveals that their sequence is inscribed in a destructive and probing form of penetration, which seeks the secret of the maternal breast" (*CF*, 60 / 20). So close is the interlinking between oral and mental organization, between digestive and dialectical processes, that Lacan's thesis here may be paraphrased without undue vulgarization as: "I eat / or not; therefore I think." The later elaborations of the mirror stage and the symbolic register in his writings may therefore be read as a sustained correction of his preliminary "neo-Cartesian" position. It's what comes out of the mouth (words) and not what goes in (food) that really matters.

"It is not a question of knowing," Lacan writes in "The Agency of the Letter" (1957), "whether I speak of myself in a way that conforms to what I am, but rather of knowing whether I am the same as that of which I speak"

(*Écrits*, 517 / 165). This assertion instantiates his breakaway from the autonomous subject of Cartesian tradition, fully identical with its own consciousness ("what I am" [ce que je suis]) to the symbolically mediated subject ("that of which I speak" [celui dont je parle]).[14] Lacan rings these several parodic changes on Descartes's proposition: "I think where I am not, therefore I am where I do not think. . . . I am not wherever I am the plaything of my thought; I think of what I am where I do not think to think." However, despite his critique of systems of knowledge or so-called truth grounded in the phenomenology of a unified, self-knowing subjectivity, he also claims in the same essay: "It is nonetheless true that the philosophical *cogito* is at the centre of the mirage that renders modern man so sure of being himself even in his uncertainties about himself" (517–18 / 165–66). In the same vein, the opening paragraph of "The Mirror Stage" concludes with a truth claim: "It [the mirror stage] is an experience that leads us to oppose any philosophy directly issuing from the *Cogito*."

In "The Agency of the Letter," Lacan primarily defines the functions of the symbolic dimension, and in "The Mirror Stage," those of the imaginary. But the remarkable mouth-mind continuum of his earlier work is interrupted and transformed in both essays: on the imaginary level, the mechanism of this transformation is a substitution (mirror for mother); on the symbolic level, an inversion (what comes out of rather than what enters into the mouth). Sight and speech are the co-determinants of human subjectivity. "Speech is in fact a gift of language," Lacan announced in his 1953 report to the Rome Congress, "and language is not immaterial. It is a subtle body, but body it is. Words are trapped in all the corporeal images that captivate the subject" (*Écrits*, 301 / 87). Words as body, images as body: a double transferal removes the subject in all but the strictly literal, biological sense from any maternal moorings.

As Lacan elaborates his theory of the ego's formation, his definitional statements bear the stamp of a twofold reformation. He would discard the phenomenological viewpoint implicit throughout *Les complexes familiaux*, with its emphasis on affective experience, as well as appropriate the Freudian concept of primary father-identification for the mirror stage. These two trends are bound up with each other; for the purposes of analysis, however, it is useful to bear their distinction in mind. In the following pages, I first examine the alterations in Lacan's own theoretical orientation (sections V–VII) and then the issues involved in his redefinition of Freud's idea of primary identification (section VIII).

V

In *Les complexes familiaux*, Lacan describes both weaning and intrusion (the mirror stage) as eliciting modes of *affective* reaction. Feelings are essential to the formative identifications at each stage of development:

> *Affective identification* is a psychic function whose originality has been established by psychoanalysis, especially in connection with the Oedipus complex. But the use of this term at the stage we are studying remains ill-defined in psychoanalytic literature. We have tried to fill this gap by offering a theory of this identification whose genetic appearance we define by the term: mirror stage. (41 / 17; emphasis added)

What the translator renders as "literature" in English is termed *la doctrine* in French. Lacan openly disengages himself here from established psychoanalytic doctrine. In fact, this disengagement is not the first in his essay. Previously, in the "Le complexe du sevrage" section, he had broadened "affective identification"—a term explicitly associated with the father-child relationship in Freud's writings (as in *SE*, 18: 105)—to include the infant's experience of the mother. He spoke of the "feelings specific to infancy," "first affective interests," and "affective adaptation" that characterize the weaning period (*CF*, 28–29 / 14–15). In the passage just quoted from the "Le complexe de l'intrusion" section, Lacan posits the continuity of such emotions, expanded to "family feeling," during the mirror stage as well (35 / 16). Hence references to *felt* identifications recur in this section: "As long as the mirror image plays only its primary role, which is limited to the function of expressivity, it evokes identical emotions and movements in the subject" (45 / 18).[15] By extending the idea of affective identification, Lacan includes not only the two parental imagos but the "ideal of the double's imago" within its purview (44 / 18). Thus the affective value of identification accrues to all three imagos that successively dominate the infant psyche.

However, while stressing the developmental significance of affect, Lacan also already notes the "predominance of visual functions" during the intrusion complex. Both feeling and seeing are vital causes whose joint consequence is the identity-effect of the mirror stage: "If the search for affective unity promotes in the subject the forms though which he represents his identity for himself, the most intuitive form at this phase is provided by the specular image [Si la recherche de son unité affective promeut chez le sujet les formes où il se représente son identité, la forme la plus intuitive en est donnée, à cette phase, par l'image spéculaire]." Lacan immediately adds: "What the subject welcomes in [the image] is its inherent mental unity . . . the triumph of its integrative power" (*CF*, 44 / 18; trans. modified). The conjunction of "affective unity" and "intuitive form" would be startling in his later formulations. However, the idea of the specular image as an "affective"—and not solely perceptual—"unity" is fully congruent with the phenomenological framework of his essay on the family. Primary apprehensions (imagos) and emotions inform the child's visual perceptions of the environment.

Mikkel Borch-Jacobsen similarly comments on Lacan's position in 1938 that "'formative' identification, well before it is a question of vision and ideal modeling, is first and essentially a matter of *affection* of the 'ego' by the 'other'" (69). He then poses the difficult question: "Why did Lacan forget that so quickly?" The question is followed by a volley of rhetorical questions that contain his strong but, in my view, limited answer:

> Was it because this spec(tac)ular staging was the only way of objectifying a mimesis that otherwise would have been untheorizable, ineffable, and unrepresentable? No doubt; but who says that the stakes for the actor are knowledge, self-knowledge via (the gaze of) the other that freezes him into a statue, an idol? . . . And why, after all, should true life always be elsewhere, in front of me, in that double who augurs my death? (70–71)

Borch-Jacobsen's first two rhetorical questions challenge the arbitrary, preferential status accorded to visual representation in Lacan's later theory of subjectivity. The third question implicitly links the insistence on visual objectifications to Kojèvian negativity. In Kojève's reading of Hegel, the negated subject, a site of irreparable void or lack, searches for self-validation in visible forms and figures.[16] Although these answers to "Why did Lacan forget that so quickly?" might well be compelling, they do not address the motive—and the gain—of maternal marginalization that accompanies Lacan's forgetting of affection and foregrounding of visual values.

Just as sight preempts other sensibilities, so what Lacan calls the "similar" or "counterpart" now takes over the dialecticizing functions of the maternal imago. (That near-antithetical words should designate the specular image is entirely appropriate to these functions.) The two preemptions are contingent "moments" in his second theory of identification:

> It is this captation by the *imago* of the human form, rather than an *Einfüh-lung* the absence of which is made abundantly clear in early infancy, which, between the ages of six months and two and a half years, dominates the entire dialectic of the child's behaviour in the presence of his similars. . . . it is by means of an identification with the other than [*sic*] he sees the whole gamut of reactions of bearing and display, whose structural ambivalence is clearly revealed in his behaviour. (*Écrits*, 113 / 19)

In this passage from "Aggressivity in Psychoanalysis," Lacan rules out the possibility of any empathy and affective response (*Einfühlung*) as a constitutive factor. Five years later, in his "Rome Discourse," he likewise asserts: "The subject goes well beyond what is experienced 'subjectively' by the individual" (265 / 55)—and a disparaging tone marks that "'subjectively,'" set apart as it is by inverted commas. While retaining certain psychoanalytic terms, Lacan signals a change in their signification as well as a departure from his genetic-phenomenological viewpoint via different rhetorical pairings. He no longer refers to "experiential ambivalence" (*ambivalence du vécu*) but, rather, to a "structural ambivalence" directed toward the other (*CF*, 29 / 15; *Écrits*, 113 / 19). The term "narcissistic," and not "affective," now premodifies "identification." Where feelings were formerly considered instrumental in generating the visual functions, visual images and especially processes of reflexive recognition are said to give rise to diverse emotional responses such as "triumphant jubilation" and "the child who sees another fall, cries" (*Écrits*, 112–13 / 18–19). In sum, affect is now an effect of vision.

In keeping with this reversal of psychical causality, Lacan precisely delimits the mirror stage: "We have only to understand the mirror stage *as an identification*, in the full sense that analysis gives to the term: namely, the transformation that takes place in the subject when he assumes an image" (*Écrits*, 94 / 2). This "full sense," however, is no longer the inclusive sense that had encompassed the infant's lived experience of the maternal imago. Moreover, to the extent that the word "analysis" presumably stands for "Freudian psychoanalysis" in this statement, the "full sense" Lacan proceeded to expound from the late 1940s on is, in fact, only a partial and programmatic rendering of the multiple processes of identification encountered in Freud's works. By singling out "narcissistic identification" defined as "the reflected image of himself, which is the *Urich*, the original form of the *Ich-ideal* as well as that of the relation to the other," Lacan casts the *eye* in the role of preeminent organ (*Seminar I*, 145 / 126).

Some implications of this emphasis on "specularization" as well as on the visibility of sexual difference in psychoanalytic discourse are taken up in Luce Irigaray's *Speculum of the Other Woman* (1974). In a close critique over 100 pages in length of Freud's "Femininity" and other essays on female sexuality,[17] Irigaray also dissects the biases of Lacan's presuppositions. She does so with the deconstructive energy and intensity that is the hallmark of her writing—and without once mentioning the name of Lacan. Obliquity here may well be quid pro quo. Irigaray's omission of explicit reference to Lacan suggests a retaliatory strategy paralleling the exclusion of female sexuality and maternity from his theory of ego formation:

> [A] dominant *specular* economy does not tally with female sexuality. The specular organization leaves, in no doubt different ways, both the female sexual function and the female maternal function in an amorphous suspension of their instinctual economy and/or shapes them in ways quite heteronomous to that economy. Their "economy" will be governed by the demands of drives . . . that only men can actually put into practice. Governed above all by the need to maintain the primacy of the Phallus. (102)

The regime of the privileged signifier constructs the female sexual organ as invisible, as the lack of the penile form and, therefore, as outside symbolic representation. It also refuses representation to the originary matrix within which the child was first formed and held. Irigaray's mimetic commentary, in turn, substitutes a gap for a gap. Her text constructs a hole in the place of the proper name "Lacan." The absence of this identity tag may be glossed by the numerous absences tallied in her analysis: for instance, "the hole, the lack, the fault, the 'castration' that greets the little girl as she enters as a subject into representative systems." What these systems require and inculcate for their perpetuation is the myth of an original maternal flaw: the castrated mother who gave birth to a castrated child—"even though she prefers (to herself) those who bear the penis" (83).

To Irigaray's analysis of this economy of psychoanalytic representation, I want now to add a dynamic consideration. Visuality is *antithetically* linked to maternity in Lacan's texts.[18] The more the one is valued, the more the other is diminished. As the visual-fraternal component gains ascendancy, the oral-maternal component is eclipsed. To be sure, the issue here is also the primacy of the "ambivalent father-complexes" (*SE*, 13: 143). In Freud's writings, the earliest stages of identification with the father, at both individual and collective levels, are inseparable from incorporation; by contrast, in Lacan's second theory of identification, the oral is largely absent. Lacan would sever the linkage of primary incorporation (cannibalism) and identification with the Oedipal father.

One of his most overt critiques of the Freudian position appears during the session devoted to "Le maître châtré" (The Castrated Master) in *Seminar XVII*. At the outset, Lacan briefly refers to Freud's "very strange" assertion in *Group Psychology* that affective identification primarily pertains to the father, an assertion that contradicts the prevailing psychoanalytic persuasion that the child's relation to the mother is primary. What, then, leads Freud so strongly to affirm an originary love bond with the father? Lacan returns to this problematic at the end of the same session, arguing:

> [W]hat Freud preserves, in fact if not in intention, is very precisely that which he designates the most substantial aspect in religion . . . that is to say, the idea of an all-loving father [*un père tout-amour*]. And it is indeed what is designated the primary form of identification . . . —the father is love. What there is first to love in this world is the father. Strange vestige. Freud believes that that is going to make religion vanish, when it is truly its very substance that he conserves with this bizarrely composed myth of the [murdered] father. (*Seminar XVII*, 100)

Paradoxically, Freud, who strains so mightily to depose the Heavenly Father, reinstates Him in *Totem and Taboo*: "Yes, this recourse to the myth of Oedipus is really something sensational" (*Seminar XVII*, 114).

But no less important than this challenge to the concept of primary paternal identification, I suggest, is another investment. Lacan would also eliminate the alimentary basis for identification. Formerly—in the very early history of his own intellectual development—the mother and the mouth were deemed an integral part of the subject's dialectical formation. Now the mirror stage replaces the archaic imago of the breast; and the eye, the mouth; and visual forms, the functions of feeling (that is, both tactile and affective sensation).

VI

In 1949, the same year in which Lacan delivered "The Mirror Stage as Formative of the Function of the *I*" at the IPA Congress in Zurich, Françoise Dolto published an article entitled "Cure psychanalytique à l'aide de la poupée-fleur."[19] Dolto was to become Lacan's friend and associate for many years. At a session of the Société Psychanalytique de Paris (SPP) on 18 October 1949, she reported on and expanded her recent work. Lacan's intervention on that occasion, as will be seen, gives another indication of the psychical groupings that were pitted against each other in his thought.[20]

Dolto, a highly skilled child analyst, had used a flower-doll in the treatment of two little girls and drawn them out of their psychotic states. The object was made of a stem wrapped in green cloth and a head fashioned in the shape of a daisy. At the analyst's specification, it had no limbs and no facial features. In the discussion held after Dolto's presentation at the SPP, Lacan expressed his appreciation of her work and said that he hoped someday to contribute a theoretical commentary to it. The record of their exchange appears in the "Interventions de Lacan à la Société Psychanalytique de Paris" compiled by Jacques-Alain Miller: "Dr. Lacan has an increasingly keen feeling that Mme. Dolto's flower-doll fits in with his personal research on the imago of the body proper, the mirror stage, and the fragmented body. He finds it important that the flower-doll has no mouth." While agreeing with Lacan's view that the doll elicited some reactions commensurate with the mirror stage, Dolto nonetheless had a strong reservation: "[I]t is necessary to understand the idea of the mirror as an object of reflection not only of the visible, but of the audible, the palpable, the intentional. The doll has no face, neither hands nor feet, neither front nor back, no articulations, no neck" (21–22). Dolto briefly but pointedly calls into question the privileged status given to visuality in both Lacan's specific intervention and general theory. She proposes here (as does Julia Kristeva in a different context)[21] that kinesthetic and other factors need to be taken into consideration. Her reply also implicitly asks of Lacan: Why "no mouth"? Why specify the absence of one feature in a faceless doll? As Dolto observes in her published accounts, the flower-doll served as a *bouc émissaire* for her young patients: a kind of scapegoat that was held responsible for—even if not guilty of—their ill-adapted attitudes and aggressive tendencies (169). The blank-faced and limbless doll elicited a variety of projections from the little girls. Yet Lacan singles out the absence of the mouth.

One explanation for his special notice might concern an aspect of each girl's symptoms. Bernadette could only express herself through unmodulated screams and screeching; Nicole, mainly through monosyllables or silence (Dolto, 133, 150). Both girls could be said to exhibit a "foreclosure" (*Verwerfung*) of the Name-of-the-Father, a repudiation of speech and language. The doll with no mouth may have enabled a narcissistic identification on their parts. It initiated them into the imaginary and, then, into the symbolic registers. In other words, to effect their transition into the world of verbal communication and social exchange, it was necessary for them first to go through a hall of mirrors. The absence of the mouth thus corroborates the importance of the eye.[22] However, an alternative explanation for the success of the flower-doll experiments might take into account, as Dolto certainly does, what is left out of Lacan's singular emphasis. Her reply suggests a multisensory reflexive object corresponding to a more complex system of symptoms than only the emptiness or disturbance of speech.

Over thirty years after the publication of the "flower-doll cure" and the exchange with Lacan at the SPP, Dolto republished her clinical observations, together with a series of newly revised comments. Dolto's reflections on her own work may be read as a continuation of her debate with Lacan. Without expressly referring to Lacan, one passage particularly recalls and reinforces her reservations in 1949:

> But, it is also necessary to observe that the head of the doll had no eyes, no nose, no mouth, no orifices of communication, and that it had no feet, no hands, no front, no back. I believe it is extremely important if one thinks that the very young nursling does not know it has a face: the face experienced is that of the mother. Here, too, there is no face. Children who have already seen themselves in the mirror are encouraged, on the other hand, not to project onto the flower-doll their present-day personality: they can project onto it a wholly archaic feeling. (161)

After noting that the type of transference activated by the flower-doll was highly distinctive in each case, Dolto proposes here a common ground for the efficacy of her clinical innovation. Although Nicole's conduct was in some ways diametrically opposed to Bernadette's (mutism versus screaming), their overall comportment suggested to the analyst an identical diagnosis:

"hysterical behavior, following a narcissistic wound at the oral stage, having prevented the integration of the rules common to human beings in our society" (159). Dolto repeatedly traces her patients' symptoms back to what she calls the "wounded narcissistic affects" of the oral stage, in which the primary caretaker was unusually defective: "The materialization of this imaginary object [i.e., the doll] allowed to discharge onto it, in reality, the anguish of the mother-nursling dyad" (148, 165; see also 153). Such diagnostic statements implicitly corroborate Freud's designation, in "On Narcissism," of the mother or her surrogates—and not only the self—as a model for subsequent object-choices.

Dolto is arguing, then, with Lacan's position on maternal agency. Feeding and feelings related to pre- or nonverbal experiences emerge as crucial in her theory and clinical practice. For example, one of the little girls exhibited a "thirst perversion": Nicole refused to drink clean water from a glass or bowl and would hide herself in order to lap up machine oil, urine, dishwater, or laundry water (150). The doll facilitated a "[l]iberation of tender-sadistic emotions belonging to the cannibalistic ethic of the oral stage" and, therefore, allowed her patient to recuperate "a narcissism without anguish" (171). That the liberating object was in each case a doll fashioned by the girl's mother, after a design recommended by the analyst (who herself was a mother of young children, as both girls knew), is also arguably important for the identificatory processes leading to the successful outcome of the treatment. The "bad" mother could be spewed out, discarded, eliminated; the "good" mother, assimilated. Nicole need no longer take into herself machine oil, instead of, say, milk. But maternal involvement in *producing* the doll does not enter into Lacan's specular considerations: "the imago of the body proper, the mirror stage, and the fragmented body" is what he sees in the efficacious flower-doll.

VII

A question of production and reproduction, of origins, is at the origin of Lacan's commentary on the flower-doll cases. In his second theory of the subject's first identifications, pregnancy becomes associated with visual perception. This association is not only a metaphoric analogy. Lacan draws a correlation between gestation and the gestalt given in the mirror on both the literal (physiological) and figurative (psychological) levels.

Empirical data on animal behavior thus enter into his discussion of the mirror stage: "That a *Gestalt* should be capable of formative effects in the organism is attested by a piece of biological experimentation" (*Écrits*, 95 / 3). In particular, as mentioned earlier, he finds corroboration in Leonard Harrison Matthews's research on "Visual Stimulation and Ovulation in Pigeons,"[23] which demonstrates how the act of seeing another pigeon or a mirror-image can stimulate ovulation. For Lacan, the significant fact is that a female pigeon who only saw the reflected image of itself could start laying eggs. As he stresses, "so sufficient in itself is this condition that the desired effect may be obtained merely by placing the individual within the reach of the field of reflection of a mirror" (*Écrits*, 95 / 3; see also 189–90, and "Some Reflections," 14). It is noteworthy that the "desired effect" is not modeled on acts of mating and of maternity. What Lacan specifies is an autogenic parturition: a kind of immaculate conception in which the entity represents and reproduces itself. The notion of womb envy, of the "boy's intense envy of motherhood," which Karen Horney introduced in 1926, does not encompass the full extension of this desire (60).[24]

However, if Matthews's empirical study of ovulating pigeons is compared to an invented scene of reproduction, its importance for Lacan may be more fully appreciated. In Freud's "Analysis of a Phobia in a Five-Year-Old Boy" (1909), little Hans recounts a creation scene in which he produces an egg out of himself. Here is the little boy's myth-in-embryo:

> At Gmunden I lay down in the grass—no, I knelt down—and the children didn't look on at me, and all at once in the morning I said: "Look for it, children; I laid an egg yesterday." And all at once they looked, and all at once they saw an egg, and out of it there came a little Hans. . . . all at once I laid an egg, and all at once it was there. (*SE*, 10: 85–86)

The passage follows a conversation between Hans and his father about how chickens are born. Even though the father insists that "boys can't have children," the child responds with solemn conviction: "Well, yes. But I believe they can, all the same." This daydream of rebirth and duplication brings into clearer focus the fantasies of self-generation evoked by the facts of reproduction among certain nonhuman species. Put another way, little Hans's "*I* once laid an egg, and a chicken came hopping out" is the analogue of Lacan's "so sufficient in itself is this condition" (*SE*, 10: 95, 85; *Écrits*, 95 / 3).

In an often quoted passage from the mirror-stage essay of 1949, a passage directly preceding the exemplum of fertile pigeons, Lacan uses terms of gestation to describe the effects of the gestalt or total body-image on the human subject:

> Thus, this *Gestalt*—whose pregnancy should be regarded as bound up with the species, though its motor style remains scarcely recognizable—by these two aspects [i.e., "a contrasting size" (*un relief de stature*) and "a symmetry that inverts"] of its appearance, symbolizes the mental permanence of the *I*, at the same time as it prefigures its alienating destination; it is still pregnant [elle est grosse encore] with the correspondences that unite the *I* with the statue in which man projects himself, with the phantoms that dominate him. (*Écrits*, 95 / 2–3)

To speak of *la prégnance* in this context is, as Freud might say, overdetermined. Figuratively, in French, as in English, the word "pregnant" denotes weighty or rich in significance, having possibilities of development or consequence. Linguistically, it signifies a construction whose meaning or realization is anticipated: "valeur prégnant . . . dont le sens n'est pas complètement énoncé; sens de l'attribut proleptique" (*Grande Larousse*, 5: 4566). Applied to the statement just quoted, these meanings suggest the following paraphrase: although the gestalt seems to be full, teeming with a promise of unity and integration that would mitigate or even obliterate the fragmented body-image of the subject, what it delivers, in actuality, is an unalterable estrangement—"the armour of an alienating identity" (*Écrits*, 97 / 4).

Technically, as used in the school of Gestalt psychology, the word *prégnance* has a specialized sense, to which Lacan also alludes in his essay. From Gestalt theory and the laws of *Prägnanz*, he derives the idea of sensory perceptions (most especially visuality) as a mode of mental functioning that tends to the formation of "good forms," that is, of cogent patterns: "[G]ood forms are pregnant because they are simple, regular, symmetrical" (Piaget, 24). The receptor does not register the physical world and its impinging stimuli in piecemeal fashion. What is registered is an entire field, a gestalt with discrete parts.[25] For such organization to be produced, according to the Gestaltist argument, requires an *illusion* of totality and simplicity. That the latter idea left its mark on Lacan's theory is evident in his many references to the phantasmatic aspects of the mirror stage: "the lure of spatial identification," "the illusion of autonomy to which [the ego] entrusts itself," and "[t]his illusion of unity, in which a human being is always looking forward to self-mastery" (*Écrits*, 97 / 4; 99 / 6; "Some Reflections," 15).

But illusory unity is only one of the effects of "good forms" on the Lacanian subject. *Prägnanz*, in Gestalt psychology, also designates the force and stability of a privileged field or structure. This field impinges more strongly than other fields upon the sensory organs. In Lacan's elaboration of the concept, the privileged structure comes to mean, specifically, a reflected image: "[T]he subject originally identifies himself with the visual *Gestalt* of his own body" (*Écrits*, 113 / 18). The ego is put together, placed, *gestellt* by the recognition of the semblable. However illusory and ultimately alienating, the visual perception of a unitary bodily form produces a primary ideational formation: "I am (like) that one" leads to "I am one" and "I am other." In a manner comparable to the stimulation of a pigeon's ovaries through its own reflection, the specular image generates the ego.

Although Lacan's applications of the term *prégnance* are chiefly figurative and technical, the literal-anatomical meaning associated with childbearing nonetheless resonates in his usage. The human subject, in his view, is the product of a double matrix. Therefore, when describing the narcissistic drama before the mirror that constitutes the infant's primary identification, Lacan also immediately mentions a related order of gestation: "the symbolic matrix in which the *I* is precipitated" (*Écrits*, 94 / 2). Added to the imaginary enclosure in which the ego is said to be formed, this notion of the matrix assimilates the uterine space of the mother into the symbolic domain.

Matrix, denoting "womb" in late Latin or "pregnant animal" in early Latin, derives from *mater* or mother by "changing the ending into the suffix of feminine agent-nouns" (*OED*, 9: 476). In *Les complexes familiaux*, the terms "mother" and "matrix" are synonymous and interchangeable, as in "Strictly defined, weaning provides the first and most adequate psychic expression for the very obscure imago of a primordial weaning which separates the infant at birth from its matrix [celui qui, à la naissance, sépare l'enfant de la matrice]" (31 / 15). In the later work, the organ of reproductive agency is a factor of the specular and the symbolic dimensions: the mirror and the signifier. "The subject is born," Lacan argues in his *Four Fundamental Concepts of Psycho-Analysis*, "in so far as the signifier emerges in the field of the Other" (*Seminar XI*, 181 / 199). In the actual event of human birth, Lacan does not refer to a separation from the maternal body or matrix but, quite remarkably, to a process of hatching: "[T]he membranes of the egg in which the foetus emerges on its way to becoming a new-born are broken" (179 / 197). Of course, this last statement is part of a joke. Lacan is stressing what he calls the "joky side" of the birth process and also extending a Joycean pun on "hommelette."[26] And yet Lacan's description of birth as a kind of hatching could also be interpolated into a signifying chain made up of these disparate but interlinked parts: a gestalt that is pregnant with correspondences between itself and "good forms" in the outer world; a pigeon that spontaneously sets to laying eggs; and a little boy kneeling in the grass at Gmunden and engendering himself.

Even as the matrix disappears from the world of the mothers and enters into that of mirrors and signifiers, so the notion of imprinting as formation (*Bildung*) also undergoes a category shift in Lacan's work. As he explained to a meeting of the British Psycho-Analytical Society in 1953: "It is the stability of the standing posture, the prestige of stature, the impressiveness of statues, which set the style for the identification in which the ego finds its starting-point and leave their imprint in it for ever" ("Some Reflections," 15). *Le style*, stylus, pen, tool of imprimatur: the upright or erected counterpart engraves a lasting image upon the ego. The terminology of this paper echoes the passage on the gestalt quoted above. The ego comes into being solely on the basis of its narcissistic identifications. A visible structure or "statue" impinges itself on the subject-in-process and, likewise, the total form glimpsed in the mirror is also presumed to "unite the *I* with the statue in which man projects himself" (*Écrits*, 95 / 2). The *Urbild*—"a unity comparable to the ego"—is born in a vast hall of statues (*Seminar I*, 133 / 115).

According to *Les complexes familiaux*, however, imprinting is a function of the imago of the maternal breast. The weaning complex "leaves a permanent trace in the human psyche of the biological relationship it interrupted" (27 / 14). In concluding the section on weaning, Lacan reevokes the image of an indelible mother-scripture, an archaic writing that remains legible throughout later life: "The overflowing quality of the [weaning] complex establishes maternal feeling; . . . its discharge leaves traces we can recognize"

(35 / 16). Furthermore, he himself draws out the impact of the social institutions and systems that distinguishes *sevrage* in the human as opposed to
animal species: "Whereas instinct has an organic substructure and is limited
to regulating this substructure in a vital function, a complex . . . makes up
for an inadequacy of existence through the regulation of a social function.
Such is the case with the weaning complex" (32 / 15). The *infans*, by definition, is incapable of speech and therefore not yet fully evolved into a social
being; nevertheless, the primary affective experience of the maternal imago
comprises a complex or "social function" rather than merely an instinct or
"vital function."

By contrast, in Lacan's accounts of the subject in the late 1940s and early
1950s, the mother is a corporeal and not a culturally mediated presence. He
speaks of the "extreme archaism of the subjectification of a *kakon*," thereby
suggesting that the child is borne along or within an unformed and, possibly,
excremental substance (*Écrits*, 115 / 21). The neonate who is immersed in
the mother—or, in another one of Lacan's revealing phrases, "the child [*le
petit homme*] at the *infans* stage, still sunk in his motor incapacity [*impuissance
motrice*] and nursling dependence"—needs to surmount this condition in order to attain the "motor style" (*style moteur*) and autonomous unity endowed
at the mirror stage (94–95 / 2). Lacan assigns to every (male) subject a pre-
carious transition from the impotence of infantile dependency to the prestige of upright stature.

Hence the anxiety of genesis—the "very essence of Anxiety"—linked to
the maternal body: the fear of falling back into the mother. As Lacan vividly
puts it, "This illusion of unity, in which a human being is always looking forward to self-mastery, entails a constant danger of sliding back again into the
chaos from which he started" ("Some Reflections," 15). The mother as primordial matter lacks the addition of stature and erectile form. She is therefore precluded as a matter of course from setting the identificatory style for
any future imprintings of the ego.

VIII

The linkage between the terms "primary" and "identification" in the discourses of Freud and Lacan is far from simple. It remains now to be seen in

what ways Lacan accompanies and conforms to the spirit, if not to the letter, of Freud's research concerning the conjunction of these terms.

On the few occasions when Freud speaks of "primary identification" or its cognates, he expressly links the concept to the two periods that occur before and after the dissolution of the Oedipus complex. He writes of the first period: "Identification is . . . the earliest expression of an emotional tie with another person. It plays a part in the early history of the Oedipus complex. A little boy will exhibit a special interest in his father. . . . he takes his father as his ideal" (*SE*, 18: 105; also 18: 107). This acquisition, however, is neither simple nor straightforward. For Freud further specifies in *The Ego and the Id* that the boy's initial identificatory tie with the father predates all of his object-cathexes. Added to the notion of chronological priority (first), another signification (foremost) accrues to the concept of primary identification:

> [T]he effects of the first identifications made in earliest childhood will be general and lasting. This leads us back to the origin of the ego ideal; for behind it there lies hidden an individual's first and most important identification, his identification with the father. . . . it is a direct and immediate identification and takes place earlier than any object-cathexis. (*SE*, 19: 31)

The constitutive identification that Freud designates "the primary one" thus both precedes and governs the relations to all others. During the second period, following "the demolition of the Oedipus complex" (*SE*, 19: 32), a process of surrender and substitution goes into effect. The mother as desired object is given up and replaced by identification with the father: "[T]he child's ego turns away from the Oedipus complex." This phase famously brings about the installation of paternal authority and its institutional representatives within the psyche, resulting in the supervisory agency known as the "super-ego" (*SE*, 19: 176).

Lacan's conception of what represents the "most important identification" basically differs from Freud's. In his revision of the ego-building process, the term "primary identification" defines the relation to the specular fraternal image or, in a word, the (br)other; the father no longer embodies the child's original ideal or model. The image of the sibling rival first acts upon the subject and only then, the father. (The Augustinian anecdote about infant jealousy discussed in Chapters 7 and 8 further clarifies the fraternal function in this psychical structure.) Thus Lacan reminded his followers in the mid 1950s: "[P]aranoid knowledge is knowledge founded on the rivalry of jealousy, over the course of the primary identification I have tried to define by means of the mirror stage" (*Seminar III*, 50 / 39). Moreover, as indicated in Chapter 5, this identificatory tie to the semblable simultaneously encompasses libidinal and aggressive inclinations. The ambivalence toward paternal figures follows the relational pattern of bipolarity already established during the mirror stage. "Lacan invites us to look back," as Malcolm Bowie acutely comments, "beyond the play of rivalries and aliases that the Oedipal phase invites, and to behold an anterior world in which the individual has only one object of desire and only one alias—himself" (*Lacan*, 32).

Initially, the conjunction of the term "secondary" with "identification" or "narcissism" appears in Lacan's work as designating the attitude toward the Oedipal father. This combination, however, gradually acquires a broader meaning. In 1948, "a primary identification . . . structures the subject as a rival with himself," while the Oedipus complex is "a *secondary identification* by introjection of the *imago* of the parent of the same sex" (*Écrits*, 117 / 22; Lacan's emphasis). Primary identification clearly belongs to the imaginary, and secondary identification—insofar as it manages the subject's entry into the social realm—to the symbolic. That is, in describing the Oedipal complex as "an identificatory *re*shaping" (*remaniement*) of the subject, Lacan does not repudiate the paternal function; on the contrary, he insists that "the Oedipal identification is that by which the subject transcends the aggressivity . . . constitutive of the *primary* subjective individuation" (117 / 22, 23; emphasis added). Such formulations nonetheless serve to undermine the psychoanalytic regime of the father(s). They violate a venerable commandment, as it were, by putting another image before him. For the statues said to "set the style for the identification in which the ego finds its starting-point" are engraving images that impinge themselves and forever "leave their imprint" on the psyche ("Some Reflections," 15).

From the mid 1950s on, the terms "secondary narcissism" and "secondary identification" no longer denote the interactions between father and child but, more generally, come to mean interhuman relations at large. "Narcissistic identification"—and Lacan expressly indicates, "that of the second narcissism"—"is identification with the other which . . . enables man to locate precisely his imaginary and libidinal relation to the world in general." Falling in love is an extension of the capacity to recognize one's own reflection. "That's what love is. It's one's own ego that one loves in love" (*Seminar I*,

144 / 125, 163 / 142). Similarly disabusing the courtly notion of love as self-transcendence, Lacan also asserts: "*Verliebtheit* is fundamentally narcissistic. On the libidinal level, the object is only ever apprehended through the grid of the narcissistic relation" (*Seminar II*, 199 / 167).

In the early 1960s, the term "primary identification" underwent yet another transformation in Lacan's thought. I offer here a very rapid summary of a complicated evolution in order to bring out one of its conceptual mainsprings: namely, another point of departure from Freud. Lacan argues in his seminar of 1961–62 that identification is linked to neither biological nor psychological processes but, rather, to the structure of the signifier and its effects in the unconscious. Identification occurs only because there is the signifier and not because of any person or object. The subject is constituted as an effect of the signifier. Symbolic identification becomes the primary one. The first identification is with a primordial and unitary trait (*trait unaire*) whose defining characteristic is, in the terminology derived from Saussure, pure difference. The first signifier (S_1) has no positive value and cannot be identified in terms of itself (that is, it is not self-identical) but only in terms of its differential relations with other systems of signifiers.[27]

Lacan thus redefines primary identification as a linguistic operation of exclusion or negation. For what does it mean, for instance, to call a cat a cat? It is not "/k/ is /k/" but "/k/ is not /m/" that endows the fabled cat-on-the-mat with an existence.[28] The unitary trait (also translated as the "single stroke") of the subject's primary identification marks the place of nothing, an absence, a lack, and becomes accessible only retroactively, *après coup*, through secondary identifications (S_2). As Lacan further explained in 1964, the subject

> is marked off by the single stroke, and first he marks himself as a tattoo, the first of the signifiers. When this signifier, this *one*, is established—the reckoning is *one* one. It is at the level, not of the one, but of the *one* one . . . that the subject has to situate himself as such. In this respect, the two ones are already distinguished. Thus is marked the first split that makes the subject as such distinguish himself from the sign in relation to which, at first, he has been able to constitute himself as subject. (*Seminar XI*, 129–30 / 141)

What Lacan is reprising in this passage needs to be annotated by his innovative recourse to a hitherto unremarkable term, the *einziger Zug* (single trait). In Chapter 7 of *Group Psychology*, Freud describes a type of identification in which the person develops a symptom identical to that of another person: "[T]he identification is a partial and extremely limited one and only borrows a single trait from the person who is its object" ("die Identifizierung eine partielle, höchst beschränkte ist, nur einen einzigen Zug von der Objecktperson entlehnt" [*SE*, 18: 107; *GW*, 13: 117]). Given the notion of singularity expressed through the identificatory symptom, it bears emphasizing that the single trait could be translated as "le trait unique." Lacan, however, chooses to call it "le trait unaire." He thereby reintroduces the function of the *einziger Zug* into the psychoanalytic framework not as a unique or unifying trait, not as a special case, but as a countable one within a signifying chain. The subject is established, in Lacan's precise formula, "at the level, not of the one, but of the *one* one."

So Lacan picks up the *einziger Zug* from Freud's chapter on identification in order to find in it or "detach from it," as he himself writes, "the single stroke, the foundation, the kernel" that may be altered to uphold his revised theory of identification. "The single stroke, insofar as the subject clings to it, is in the field of desire"—or, in the field of lack, of pure difference—"which cannot in any sense be constituted other than in the reign of the signifier" (*Seminar XI*, 231 / 256).

To say that Lacan cannibalizes Freud's idea of *Vateridentifizierung* is, in a sense, to congratulate him. The compliment is an ambiguous one, to be sure, but nonetheless a compliment. By taking parts of the Freudian corpus into his own conceptual system, Lacan's cannibalistic activity—or, in short, "Lacannibalism"—sustains his claim to affiliation. As Freud had occasion to observe: "[O]ne's father is what one would like to *be*" (*SE*, 18: 106); yet, bearing in mind the ambivalent attitudes inherent in the father-son relationship, it is also possible to turn the observation around: "One would like one's father to be like one."

Lacan puts his own words into Freud's mouth, even while contending that he is merely mouthing the words of Freud:

> If Freud's [whose?] theory, in which narcissism structures all of man's relations with the external world, has a meaning, . . . it does so in a manner which clearly is in harmony with everything which the so-called *Gestaltist* line of enquiry has given us in the course of the last few years concerning the apprehension of the world by the living organism. (*Seminar II*, 198 / 165)

In another exemplary scene of instruction, the final session of the 1953–54 seminar on *Freud's Papers on Technique*, Lacan offers this rapid summary of his theory:

> There is another way of approaching the problem of transference, which is to place it on the level of th[e] imaginary. . . . this dimension has certainly been named as such in Freud's [again, whose?] text—*imaginaire*. How could he have avoided it? You have seen as much this year in "On Narcissism: An Introduction," the relation of the living organism to the objects that it desires is linked to the conditions of the *Gestalt* which locate the function of the imaginary as such. (*Seminar I*, 310 / 281)

At the same time as Lacan appropriates psychoanalytic terms and gives them a cast of his own unmistakable making, he typically (one might say, ritually) attributes his articulations to Freud. Lacan's tributes—and attributions—to Freud serve the economy of his own ambivalence. In the act of incorporating his precursor's properties, he also accomplishes his identification with him. "I am like Father" reverses into "Father is like me."

Nevertheless, in an even more obscure and roundabout sense, Lacan does adhere to the legacy of Freud. In "On Narcissism," as previously discussed, Freud describes an *Anlehnung*, an "original attachment" related to the oral stage and mother (*SE*, 14: 87). However, seven years later in *Group Psychology*, he stresses an identification with an ideal, the father, as "the earliest and original form of emotional tie" (18: 107). That is, whereas in 1914, Freud assimilated all types of identification to sexual choice and accorded primacy to the mother-child bond, in 1921, he contended that identification with the father is both primary and *pre*sexual. According to his later metapsychology of family ties, the father occupies the position initially assigned the mother—with one reiterated stipulation: the boy's identification with the same-sex parent occurs "before any sexual object-choice has been made" (18: 106; see also 19: 31). The crucial word is "before." Freud would avoid the logical ramification of a universal and normative homosexuality for men. This timing ("before") enables him to dissociate the libidinal component ("sexual object-choice") from male identificatory attachments. Put another way, "By extracting identification from desire, insisting that a subject cannot identify with another person and desire that person at the same time, Freud is able to conceptualize homosexuality and homosociality as absolutely distinct categories" (Fuss, 45; see also 47, 67–69).

In the course of Lacan's work, it is the image of the subject's own body that takes over the functions formerly attributed to the mother: "[A]ll the objects of [man's] world are always structured around the wandering shadow [*l'ombre errante*] of his own ego" (*Seminar II*, 198 / 166). As this thesis takes hold in his writings, the powerful imago of the weaning complex sinks silently from sight. The primary erotic-aggressive relationship of every individual is *intra*subjective. So despite the fundamental differences between Freud's idea of primary identification and Lacan's, an identical pattern emerges in their texts. The mother's role becomes peripheral to their psychoanalytic narratives of the birth of the *I*.

Described schematically, Lacan's project in relation to the father is threefold: to be fatherless, or, rather, the father of himself (the *causa-sui* fantasy);[29] still more expansively, to father himself and his father, to transform his precursor into his own progeny; and breaking the revisionary mode, to let go of the burden of self-creation, of self-fashioning, and yield himself up to an exalted surrogate father's name and providence. If the latter fantasy is reminiscent of the Freudian family romance, that romance now needs to be recounted. It is a single-parent castle in the air. Mother does not live there anymore. For while Lacan's early recognition of her formative role may have stemmed from and served a desire to separate himself from Freud, it also strongly bound him to the influence of her archaic imago. His subsequent work put him beyond the maternal principle as well. With the fully developed theory of the mirror stage, Lacan was "liberated" unto himself.

Augustine in Contexts (Part 1)

The Riddle of a Repetition

Where could such a living creature come from if not from you, O Lord? Can it be that any man has skill to fabricate himself?

AUGUSTINE, Confessions

In book 1, chapter 7, of the *Confessions*, Saint Augustine briefly describes the following scenario:

> I have myself seen jealousy in a baby and know what it means. He was not old enough to talk, but, whenever he saw his foster-brother at the breast, he would grow pale with envy.
>
> *Vidi ego et expertus sum zelantem parvulum: nondum loquebatur, et intuebatur pallidus amaro aspectu conlactaneum suum.* (1.7.28)[1]

Lacan never seems to exhaust the full significance of this anecdote. A first citation appears in the section entitled "Le complexe de l'intrusion" in his essay on the family: "'I have myself seen,' says Saint Augustine . . . " (*CF*, 36). Lacan mentions the "classic theme" of jealousy illustrated by Augustine a few pages later and, shortly after, again alludes to the "sight of the unweaned sibling" (40, 41 / 17). References to the anecdote appear in his writings from *Les complexes familiaux* (1938) to *Encore*, 1972–1973 (1975). He repeatedly asserts its exemplary representation of the emergence of human consciousness. The encounter with the sibling rival delineates the contours of the *I*.

Lacan's repetition of this passage nonetheless presents a riddle. Augustine's brief vignette is unremarkable as a depiction of fraternal rivalry. Lacan might have singled out, for instance, the story of Cain and Abel, or Claudius and King Hamlet, or other compelling examples drawn from the clinic. Why, then, did Augustine's "Vidi ego . . . " elicit and sustain his attention over so many years? In exploring the privileged status of this anecdote, I propose to take several factors into account: the specific content of the passage, its wider context in the *Confessions*, and its changing contexts in Lacan's writings. Moreover, in addition to the theoretical relevance of Augustine's exemplum, it may also be read as a substitutive screen memory that resonates with diverse personal significances.[2] Lacan borrowed, as it were, someone else's childhood scenario. For his general inclination was not to draw on his own past experiences and impressions. "Few men have displayed as clearly as he," Roudinesco remarks, "a desire to keep secret (if not intact) the part of his life relating to his childhood and family origins" (*Jacques Lacan & Co.*, 101). François Roustang similarly observes: "Whereas Freud revealed himself through his dreams, his correspondence, or his case histories, Lacan did everything possible to avoid leaving any trace of his subjectivity" (8). That a scene of fraternal rivalry from a devout confessional narrative composed at the end of the fourth century holds such a singular place in his work signposts the extratheoretical territories on which it might encroach.

I

I shall begin, however, with the less speculative aspect of this investigation. First, the anecdote of the jealous child does exemplify the reflexive mental construct designated the "intrusion complex" in *Les complexes familiaux* and developed in Lacan's later work. "The intrusion complex," he explains just prior to his 1938 citation of Augustine, "represents the experience of an immature subject especially when he sees one or several of his own kind participating with him in a domestic relationship" (35–36 / 16). Second, the repeated citation of the passage helps to generate and reinforce an impression of conceptual continuity. Thus Lacan comments on his reiterative emphasis when reinvoking the anecdote in 1954—and his embellishment of Augustine's description through overstatement ("all-consuming, uncontrollable") is also noteworthy: "Saint Augustine, for example, notes, in a phrase I've often repeated, this all-consuming, uncontrollable jealousy which the small child feels for his fellow being" (*Seminar I*, 193 / 171). As demonstrated in previous chapters, Lacan has a predilection for blurring or, at times, obliterating his revisions of his own work. In tandem with the "total form of the body" so central to his idea of the mirror stage (*Écrits*, 94 / 2), he cultivates an effect of doctrinal totality, of an ahistorical theoretical corpus. The anecdote has, therefore, both an actual function definable by means of specific coordinates and an imaginary function in his teachings.

In actuality, the passage from the *Confessions* contains several features that characterize Lacan's early and later views of subjectivity. A rapid survey of these features would include:

1. A rivalrous encounter with a double during the *infans* stage, even before the child can speak

2. An anguished yearning, attributed in *Les complexes familiaux* to the loss of the first nurturing relationship, and, subsequently, to the lack of something unknown and unknowable, represented by the term *objet petit a*

3. A gap between the human infant's motoric prematurity and intellectual capacity that has far-reaching (albeit different) ramifications for both authors: it is not the mind of infants that is innocent, Augustine argues, but rather the weakness of their infant limbs ("ita imbecillitas membrorum infantilium innocens est, non animus infantium")—and, analogously, Lacan underscores the infant's capacity to grasp the specular image in a jubilant moment of self-assumption, although still unable to walk or even stand up without assistance

4. Directly after the description of fraternal rivalry, a motif corresponding to the Lacanian concept of desire appears in Augustine's text: "but surely it cannot be called innocence, when the milk flows in such abundance from its source, to object to a rival desperately in need."

Augustine depicts a child who is well-fed and yet cannot endure the sight of another's satisfaction. Translated into Lacan's formula, subtract need (*besoin*)—in this instance, actual hunger or thirst—from the child's demand (*demande*), and desire (*désir*) is the remainder: "[D]esire is neither the appetite for satisfaction, nor the demand for love, but the difference that results from the subtraction of the first from the second" (*Écrits*, 691 / 287). Hunger produces the particularity of a need or, in Augustine's phrase, a child "depending for his life on this one form of nourishment," whereas the jealous child is not in want of actual food (1.7.28). The satiated child casts toward a counterpart the pallid stare of an unappeasable desire: the desire constituted by the desire of the other.

Several analogies thus obtain between the observation recorded in the *Confessions* and key concepts elaborated in Lacan's writings. These analogies notwithstanding, the exemplum serves a different doctrinal purpose in each instance. For Augustine, the image of the *infans*, already jealous and needlessly so, illustrates the Christian tenet of the Fall—"How wicked are the sins of men!" (*Confessions* 1.7.27)—and provides a response to a difficult ethical query: How can one who has not yet learned to speak be immersed in sin? What does it mean to expound, as he does, the sins of infancy? In context, Augustine implies a typological kinship between the little child and the fallen Adam, both longing for forbidden fruits and straying from the path of God. For the psychoanalyst, the same anecdotal image also has a metaphoric or allegorical dimension. However, instead of the tension between man and God, it symbolizes the inauguration of a dialectical conflict between subject and other. As cited by Lacan, the anecdote becomes an Ur-text and model for the mirror stage. This usage is consistent with Lacan's lifelong practice of borrowing concepts and phrases from Christian literature (his coinage of "the passion of the signifier" is one striking instance, as noted in Chapter 5) in order to integrate and secularize their meaning in his texts. Just as Augustine did not hesitate, according to Eric Ziolkowski, "to draw figuratively upon the *Aeneid* for his own theological purposes in the *Confessions*" (4), so Lacan never hesitates to employ a passage from the *Confessions* to advance his own theoretical arguments. His recourse to Augustine is not an act of explication, or what Derrida ironically calls the "respectful doubling of commentary," but rather an act of incorporation and transformation (*Of Grammatology*, 158).[3] Lacan assimilates into his own system what he purports merely to repeat.

Put a different way, Lacan "returns" to Augustine in a manner comparable to his complex and sometimes quite contrary "return" to Freud. Augustine provides a primal scene for the relations of the mirror stage. For Lacan, what Freud identified as primal—an actually witnessed or imagined scene of parental intercourse—is secondary to the ego's formative apprehension of the counterpart. Desire is inseparably conjoined to the emergence of the narcissistic dimension of human experience and not to the Oedipus complex: "Each time the subject apprehends himself as form and as ego, each time that he constitutes himself in his status, in his stature . . . his desire is projected outside" (*Seminar I*, 193 / 171). At times, Lacan explicitly defines the Oedipal crisis (which he calls a "quasi fraternal rivalry with the father") as a subsidiary formation of the mirror stage: "[T]he aggression involved is of the same type as that which enters into play in the specular relation, in which the *either me or the other* [ou moi ou l'autre] is always the fundamental impulse" (*Seminar IV*, 207). Lacan's tenacious interest in the Augustinian passage may thus be understood partly in terms of his theory of reflexive recognition and its decisive role in the shaping of human consciousness.

Added to the several points of analogy already mentioned, both the immediate and the wider contexts in which the anecdote appears might also account for its recurrence in Lacan's texts. In the chapter directly following the scenario of infant jealousy, Saint Augustine records the processes of his self-initiation into language: "I ceased to be a baby unable to talk," he recalls, noting the etymology of the word *infans*, "and was now a boy with the power of speech." The acquisition of power over language is linked in chapter 8 of the *Confessions* to the genetic moment of entry into the social realm. Augustine describes how sounds became transformed for him into a system of self-expression and communication:

> I noticed that people would name some object and then turn towards whatever it was that they had named. I watched them and understood that the sound they made when they wanted to indicate that particular thing was the name which they gave to it, and their actions clearly showed what they meant, for there is a kind of universal language, consisting of expressions of the face and eyes, gestures and tones of voice. . . . So, by hearing words arranged in various phrases and constantly repeated, I gradually pieced together what they stood for, and when my tongue had mastered the pronunciation, I began to express my wishes by means of them. In this way I made my wants known to my family and they made theirs known to me, and I took a further step into the stormy life of human society, although I was still subject to the authority of my parents and the will of my elders. (1.8.29)

Ludwig Wittgenstein opens his *Philosophical Investigations* by quoting from this (rite of) passage and singling it out for analysis as a "particular picture of the essence of human language" (§1). According to Wittgenstein, Augustine's description gives a "primitive idea of the way language functions" and is, therefore, only appropriate to a "narrowly circumscribed region" of verbal usage (§§2–3). It exemplifies an "ostensive teaching of words" that presupposes an adequation or correlation between the word and the thing in the world (§6). But a more complex language-learning process may be discerned in the quoted passage. Young Augustine not only grasps the one-to-one correspondence between objects and sounds. He also begins to build relational or extension bridges ("hearing words arranged in various phrases") between the nouns and the proper names that he apprehends, presumably acquiring sentential and social skills at the same time. "I began to express my wishes," as he says—and thus embarks on "the stormy life of human society."[4]

It need not, then, be the theme of jealousy alone that elicited Lacan's attention and re-citation. The internecine tension portrayed in one chapter of the *Confessions* is followed in the next by the accession to language and interhuman relations. Augustine's trajectory from the preverbal to the verbal parallels the odyssey of mirror-stage child from the specular *I* to the social *I*, from the narcissistic conflict with a fraternal double to the symbolic order where the paternal law ("the will of my elders") prevails. Yet, despite occasional ambiguities in Lacan's own formulations, the mirror stage does not chiefly designate a moment or event in the progress (developmental) narrative of the child. Rather, it involves a psychical structure that is also an existential situation. The ongoing tensions between the ego and its counterpart dominate both the symbolic and the imaginary spheres. Although each of these spheres is associated with distinctive mental processes, they hardly ever function separately.

In the wider context of the *Confessions*, Augustine traces a gradual pilgrim's progress from inner waywardness and malaise to the steadfast, divinely inspired attainment of truth. Language plays a critical role in this theological or "therapeutic" process.[5] Various techniques of verbalization, or "technologies of the self," in Michel Foucault's phrase, enable Augustine (who was trained as a rhetorician and taught language and philosophy for many years) to manage and understand his spiritual transformation.[6] He primarily acts upon himself through practices of self-examination, disclosure or

confession, and constant writing about himself. The outcome of his quest after extended introspection is a movement "from the secular profession of
words by the rhetor to the Christian profession of the Word" (Sturrock, 40).
In effect, Augustine's self-portraiture as a whole—from its transitional childhood phases to the actual moment of conversion prompted by the voice of a
child repeating the chant "Take it and read" (*Tolle, lege*)—dramatizes the determining role of speech and language. Interpreting the child's refrain as a
"divine command to open my book of Scripture and read the first passage on
which my eyes should fall," Augustine finally attains the Christian spiritual-
ity that has long eluded him (8.12.177). Thus the story of his conversion
demonstrates the Lacanian notion of "signifying dependence": namely, the
preeminence of the symbolic order in human affairs (*Seminar XI*, 73 / 77).

Contra these explanations, it could be argued that Lacan did not introduce structural linguistics into his theory until the mid 1940s. In the 1930s,
he had neither begun to elaborate his concept of the symbolic, nor yet read
the work of Ferdinand de Saussure at the instigation of his friend Claude
Lévi-Strauss (Roudinesco, *Jacques Lacan & Co.*, 144). Nevertheless, I would
count the proximity between the image of fraternal rivals (chapter 7) and
the acquisition of language and entry into society (chapter 8) among the
motives for Lacan's citation of the *Confessions* as early as 1938. Jealousy, he
writes in *Les complexes familiaux*, is "the archetype of all *social* feelings" (46
/ 18; emphasis added). His later insistence on the cultural construction of
subjectivity is already evident in the consistent use of the term "complexes"
(as opposed to "instincts") in order to designate the sociocultural factors
that distinguish human from animal groups. In defining the family in the
opening pages of his 1938 essay—"la famille humaine est une institution"
(13)—Lacan begins his elaboration of the strictly human organization he
would call the symbolic order.

Briefly to recapitulate my argument thus far, Lacan quotes Augustine for
three principal reasons: as an exemplary instance of the mirror stage; as evi-
dentiary support of his own theoretical continuity; and, implicitly, for the association in the *Confessions* between the preverbal aggression provoked by
the sight of a fraternal intruder and the accession to language and society.

II

Augustine's text is not only conceptually important for Lacan, however; it also has a strong bearing on his self-conception. As Freud observes in his analysis of screen memories, the specific image that stands out vividly while so many others vanish or fade away often turns out to stand for "impressions and thoughts . . . whose content is connected with its own by symbolic or similar links" (*SE*, 3: 316). Even though grounded in the facts of Lacan's biography, the connections I shall now draw between the anecdotal image of jealousy and other contents or configurations in his history are necessarily tentative. Unlike Augustine, Lacan does not offer the reader a "manifesto of [his] inner world," or a "study of the evolution of his will" (Brown, 168, 172). Nevertheless, his repetition of a borrowed childhood scene may provide a trace of his unwritten autobiography.

The first and possibly least speculative connection involves the fraternal relation. The nursing child or "milk brother," object of another child's envious look, may well represent a composite figure. Two brothers converge in a single image: the first lost in early childhood through illness, and the second in young adulthood through religious conversion. The facts are as follows: within a year after Jacques's birth in 1901, his brother Raymond was born, only to die of hepatitis two years later. The effects of this (devoutly wished-for and guilt-inducing?) death on young Jacques remain unrecorded. Yet the brothers were certainly close enough in age for the seesaw of identification/alienation to have been set in motion. The more well-documented relationship between Jacques and his second younger brother reenacts and, retrospectively, reinforces the dialectical pattern possibly established with the first. Born on Christmas day in 1908, Marc Lacan was given the same middle name as his older brother: "Marie," in honor of the Virgin Mary, patron saint of the family vinegar trade. His date of birth ("What's in a date?"), as later developments suggest, was no less significant than his name. Jacques-Marie and Marc-Marie also shared the same young governess. Although employed soon after the birth of Jacques, this governess demonstrated a clear preference for little "Marco," her more recent charge. Jacques, called "Jacquot," grew quite jealous of this preference, even though he was his mother's favorite child (Roudinesco, *Esquisse*, 25).

If two divergent destinies may be presaged in one word, "Marie" is a good

proof case for the preeminence of the signifier in determining human sub-
jectivities. The Lacan brothers, in a gesture that belies the implied answer to
Juliet Capulet's poignant question, both eventually dropped their middle
names. When Marc took the vows of the Benedictine order in 1931, he replaced "Marie" with "François," in honor of Saint Francis of Assisi. Henceforth known as "Marc-François," he symbolically reassigned to himself a
new identity and vocation through affiliation with a holy paternal precursor.
In contrast to Marc's act of substitution, his older brother renamed himself
through an act of twofold severance. He excised not only "Marie" but also
"Émile": the first name of his much disliked paternal grandfather—"the ex-
ecrable petit-bourgeois . . . thanks to whom I started cursing God at a very
precocious age" (quoted in Marini, 96; also in Roudinesco, *Esquisse*, 373)—
that was almost identical to the name of his mother, Émilie. "Jacques"
henceforth stood alone.

The two brothers' lives parted in other ways as well. In 1926, Roudinesco
writes, "while Jacques was causing scandal in the midst of his family because
of his taste for libertine doctrine and adherence to the theses of the An-
tichrist, Marc-Marie made the definitive decision to become a monk" (*Esquisse*, 32). Thus both brothers, although notably different in their chosen
vocations, effected a profound alteration in their family ties. One winter day
in 1929, Jacques stood at the train station and watched his younger brother
leave for the isolated Abbaye de Hautecombe, where he would eventually
take religious orders. The departure of Marc was an "intolerable abandonment" for Jacques, compounded by his parents' incomprehension of his intellectual evolution (190). The distance between the brothers was to remain
pronounced throughout their adult lives. And yet, as symmetrical inversions
of each other or, in analogous terms, as type and antitype, Marc-François
and Jacques Lacan were also always close enough: the one devout and the
other agnostic, if not atheist; the one abstinent and the other dedicated to
libertinage and the accumulation of lucre; the one garbed in the plain cowl
of his religious order and the other a dandy.

These mirror relations were further complicated—at least on Jacques's
part. From among the points of contact he maintained with his brother, I
would suggest two interrelated, albeit seemingly heterogeneous, examples.
First, in numerous photographs dating from the 1970s and in the interview
aired on French television in 1973, Lacan looks out at his viewers wearing a

dark suit and white shirt with a distinctive band-like collar. Is this sartorial preference to be understood simply as a fashion statement? Or is it a sign of solidarity with, or a parody of, ecumenical authority? The choice of collar, with its indubitable clerical associations, like the repeated citation of the *Confessions*, appears to be both deliberate and symptomatic.[7] Second, the Lacanian concept of the name of the father (*nom du père*) was at first, in the early 1950s, a metaphoric, secularized reference to the societal laws that restrict human speech and desire. It also suggested, as Malcolm Bowie notes, a "semi-facetious allusion to the Christian liturgy and its celebrated triad" (*Lacan*, 108). However, the concept gradually evolved into the Name-of-the-Father: "an imperious metaphysical force that could no longer simply be described in terms of family, society and sexual conduct and that was not so much an observable feature of speech as the origin and ubiquitous condition of human language" (13). Is the Name-of-the-Father, in its later designation, to be read as a sign of rapprochement with his brother's faith? Or does it rather indicate a consistently and ironically kept distance from it? It could have served in both capacities. The Name-of-the-Father belongs to the category of antinomies that allowed Lacan to sustain a dialectical relationship with the lost companion of his childhood games.

Whereas the preceding example would seem to indicate that Lacan's fraternal ties became more complexly inflected over time, the dedication of his doctoral thesis to his brother at two nodal points (in 1932 and 1975) may indicate a different turn—that is, a simplification. The 1932 dedication reads: "To the Reverend Father Marc-François Lacan, Benedictine of the Congregation of France, my brother in religion." For Michel de Certeau who quotes this "strange dedication," the phrase "'brother in religion' points to a brotherhood based not on blood but on a common sharing in the Order," while the statement as a whole "highlights 'Benedictine' characteristics" in the Lacanian discourse that he had not hitherto remarked.[8] Among the parallelisms de Certeau proposes are: "Lacan's conception of the 'master' (according to the rules which characterize 'spiritual guidance'); the definition of a 'work' which is essentially 'speech' (like the Benedictine *opus Dei*); . . . and the very idea of a school of truth where membership is determined by an experience involving the subjects and where the *abbas* (elected) holds both the authority of discourse and the power of management" (59). In 1932, however, Lacan was not yet "Lacan." Moreover, after he assumed the position that may indeed be likened to "the founder of a 'congregation' in a desert" (59), he altered his dedicatory phrasing. The 1975 dedication of the second edition of his thesis reads: "To my brother, the Reverend Father Marc-François Lacan, Benedictine of the Congregation of France" (quoted in de Certeau, 242 n. 47). The familial connection, the symbolics of blood (being of the same parentage) is acknowledged, but the notion of brotherhood, of spiritual consanguinity (belonging to the same parish) has been suspended. The removal of "in religion" delimits Lacan's later dedication to his brother.

A second motivational factor involves the maternal relation. In Augustine's text, the mother appears as a "part-object" toward which basic infantile feelings are directed or, rhetorically speaking, as a synecdoche in which the component represents the whole: "[W]henever he saw his foster-brother at the breast, he would grow pale with envy." William Watts's 1631 translation renders the maternal body with even greater discretion: "[W]hat an angry and bitter look it would cast at another child that sucked away its milk from it." This synecdochical portrayal of the mother works very well for Lacan. At times, he chooses to bring the whole figure into his discussion; at others, he focuses only on the maternal breast or its product, milk; and he also relegates the mother to the background—or completely erases her from the scene. The maternal figure in his texts is comparable to Lewis Carroll's Cheshire cat, who fades away and reappears at different intervals. But these altered states are a function of the beholder's (and not the mother's) desire. The Lacanian gaze takes possession of what it takes in.

However tenuous the maternal element is in the anecdote, she is more than amply represented throughout the *Confessions*. "What Augustine remembered in the *Confessions* was his inner life," his biographer Peter Brown writes, "and this inner life is dominated by one figure—his mother, Monica" (29). The significance of the anecdote for Lacan therefore could also derive from the general context in which Augustine describes his mother's role in his spiritual-intellectual formation. What compelled Lacan's interest was not just the theoretical adaptations enabled by the metaphoric representation of maternity in the specific passage but also, in all likelihood, the full portrait of Monica in the *Confessions*. Although actual information about the relationship between Émilie Lacan and her son, especially during his infant years, is sparse, a few verifiable details suggest a resemblance to the patterns of Augustine's childhood.

Like Monica, who was a devout Catholic with a mystical tendency, Émilie was "heir to an elaborate Christian culture and an ardent streak of mysticism" (Roudinesco, *Jacques Lacan & Co.*, 103). Monica's upbringing by her Christian parents had been austere—"my mother was brought up in modesty and temperance" (*Confessions* 9.9.194)—and Émilie, too, was raised by pious parents and acquired "a taste for austerity": "Always dressed in black, she was thin, with somber eyes, and seemed imbued with a Christian ideal" (Roudinesco, *Esquisse*, 24). And, like Monica, Émilie brought up two sons, one of whom chose a priest's vocation. Other family constellations were also similar. Augustine's father Patricius converted to Christianity only during the last days of his life (*Confessions* 9.9.196), and Alfred Lacan, although a Catholic, did not share his wife's intense religious piety. Marc-François, recalling differences between his parents, observed that his mother was "a true Christian, which my father wasn't. . . . she was very happy about my decision [to take holy orders], whereas my father showed hostility" (*Esquisse*, 31). Clearly, Jacques did not possess the religious sensibility that pervaded his brother's life. However, their dual relationship, as well as the domestic tensions that were a part of his childhood, apparently contributed to his long-term fascination with the passage from the *Confessions*.

Augustine's frequent praise of his mother's piety, while comparable to Marc-François's appreciation of Émilie, seems to contrast sharply with Jacques's overall silence. Here again surprising parallels emerge. Together with many expressions of loving devotion and admiration for Monica, there is evidence of a strong ambivalence. In the early life described in the first eight books of the *Confessions*, Saint Augustine portrays an "obstinate" and "all-absorbing" mother whose inordinate love for her gifted son was matched by her determination to see him dedicate his life to God (O'Connell, 107; Brown, 30). "For as mothers do, and far more than most, she loved to have me with her," Augustine writes, in the same chapter that relates how he tricked the woman who so loved him and abandoned her at Carthage.[9] Slipping away at night to sail for Rome, he left a Dido-like Monica to mourn his departure with "her tears and her prayers" (*Confessions* 5.8.101). Monica's grief at abandonment did not lead her to suicide, however. She followed her son to Italy and gradually weaned him from his worldly ways to her faith.[10] For Augustine, a chief obstacle was his profound, often-mentioned reluctance to renounce the pleasures of the flesh—the "chain" he dragged along but felt "afraid to be freed from" (6.12.128), were he to comply with his mother's tireless campaign for his conversion. In persuading Augustine to render his body and his soul to the service of "our Catholic mother the Church" (9.13.205), did Monica also wish to ensure that her son would have no other woman before her?[11] Be that as it may, shortly after his completed conversion, she informed him during their visionary conversation at a cottage window in Ostia: "There was one reason, and one alone, why I wished to remain a little longer in this life, and that was to see you a Catholic Christian before I died. God has granted my wish and more besides. . . . What is left for me to do in this world?" (9.10.198–99). Monica fell ill with fever five days later and died on the ninth day of her illness. In Augustine's Neoplatonic-Christian description of her death, "[W]hen she was fifty-six and I was thirty-three, her pious and devoted soul was set free from the body" (9.11.200).

Monica's final "liberation" has been interpreted as the ultimate act of maternal sacrifice. In dying two weeks after Augustine's conversion, Ziolkowski suggests, she prevented her newly baptized son "from having to confront the moral dilemma posed by the teaching of Luke" (13). At Luke 14:26, Jesus says: "If any *man* come to me, and hate not his father, and mother, and wife, and children, and brethren, and sisters, yea, and his own life also, he cannot be my disciple." Likewise, the spiritual example set by Jesus's public rejection of his mother in the Gospels according to St. Mark and St. John[12] would have been difficult to reconcile with Augustine's ardent feelings for Monica: "[H]ow could there be any comparison between the honour which I showed to her and the devoted service she had given me? . . . her life and mine had been as one" (*Confessions* 9.12.201).

But even if the deaths of both parents averted the actual need to "hate" them and sever family ties, Augustine did complexly adhere to this injunction in his autobiographical narrative. He did so verbally, symbolically, using imagery that simultaneously commemorates and alters his filial relationships. The *Confessions* dramatizes the rhetorical art of double negotiation. On the one hand, Augustine's panegyric presentation of Monica did result in her canonization as a "patron of widows" and her reverential status as a "paragon of Catholic piety and Christian motherhood" (Ziolkowski, 3); on the other, he delimits his filial bonds on several occasions.[13] In encouraging Augustine to turn from his father Patricius and adopt a new patrimony, his mother had done "all that she could to see that you, my God, should be a Father to me rather than he." But, in so doing, she also showed him the way to alter his view of her role as progenitor and caretaker: "You, O Lord my God, gave me my life and my body when I was born. . . . you implanted in it all the instincts necessary for the welfare and safety of a living creature" (*Confessions* 1.11.32; 1.7.28). Similarly, when Augustine depicts his mother as the "good servant in whose womb you created me, O God, my Mercy" (9.9.195), he uses a conventional religious trope that nonetheless attenuates the agency of both parents. Looking back on his relations with Monica, the converted Augustine also reflects that "perhaps I was guilty of too much worldly affection [*carnalis affectus*]" (9.13.203). He thus repeats the complicated separation adumbrated by his setting sail for Rome. He carries out Jesus's teaching in his acts of speech, even though the deaths of both parents removed the need to do so in the language of his acts.

In psychoanalytic terms, the Name-of-the-Father assumes a decisive function for Augustine and leads him to reconstruct his personal history, *nachträglich*, in the light of his present convictions. In fashioning a new identity for himself, he reconfigures his ancestral and spiritual lineage. His parents, quite extraordinarily, become his siblings, his brothers, in his newfound relations with the Heavenly Father and Lawgiver and with the Mother Church:

> O my Lord, my God, inspire your servants my brothers . . . inspire those of them who read this book to remember Monica, your servant, at your altar and with her Patricius . . . by whose bodies you brought me into this life. . . . With pious hearts let them remember those who were not only my parents in this light that fails, but were also my brother and sister, subject to you, our Father, in our Catholic mother the Church, and will be my fellow citizens in the eternal Jerusalem. (*Confessions* 9.13.204–5)

Augustine's revised familial construction has been interpreted as a "story of oedipal separation" analogous to a male coming-of-age myth: "Just as a conversion narrative suggests a separation between the sinner and the saint who tells his story, . . . so the myth of male maturation is represented as a separation from the parents" (Freccero, 19).[14] However, in recasting Patricius and Monica as "my brother and sister" and "my fellow citizens," Augustine does not leave the parental position open or unfilled. Separation finds expression through surrogation in the *Confessions*. It is therefore helpful to recall the parameters of the "family romance": a fantasy or daydream in which the child replaces the real parents with other parents of better, nobler birth.[15] According to Freud, "The technique used in developing phantasies like this . . . depends upon the ingenuity and the material which the child has at his disposal" (*SE*, 9: 239). Augustine not only substitutes for his earthly, sinning parents an incomparably elevated parentage. He also speaks of a nurturing *and* paternal divinity. The "comfort of woman's milk" and the law are not opposite but composite or overlapping in the matrix he invokes as "you, my God": "But neither my mother nor my nurses filled their breasts of their own accord, for it was you who used them, as your law prescribes, to give me infant's food" (*Confessions* 1.6.25).

In a detailed analysis of "Verbal Action in St. Augustine's *Confessions*," Kenneth Burke calls attention to the verb "fill" in the passage just cited. First used in Augustine's opening invocation to God ("in His plenitude filling all Creation"), it reappears here, "applied literally to the milk that filled the breasts (*ubera implebant*) of the women who had nursed him." Burke lists other instances in which ideas of God are conjoined with ideas of nourishment, especially by means of milk, in the *Confessions*. This pattern includes: Augustine's explicit parallel between "the 'consolations' of God's mercies (*consolationes miserationum tuarum*) and the 'consolations' of human milk (*consolationes lactis humani*)"; his reference to God as "a mount, fertile and flowing with milk (*in monte incaseato, monte tuo, monte uberi*)"; his self-description in the opening invocation of book 4 as "sucking God's milk and eating of Him as a food that does not perish"; and likewise, when citing "the Word was made flesh" (John 1:14), Augustine compares it to "a food whereby God's Wisdom (*sapienta*) might give milk (*lactesceret*) to our infancy" (Burke, 66). Even earlier, and possibly more striking, examples of this Christian assimilation of maternity to the Godhead occur in the apocryphal Odes of Solomon.[16] There Christ speaks of his intimate knowledge of his faithful servants thus: "I fashioned their members; My own breasts I prepared for them; That they might drink my holy milk and live thereby." In another verse, Christ is spoken of as a "cup of milk" offered to the Odist: "The Son is the cup, and He who is milked is the Father; and He who milked Him is the Holy Spirit. Because his breasts were full; And it was not desirable that His milk should be spilt to no purpose" (Harris and Mingana, 2: 254, 298).[17] Such passages ignore primary biological restrictions with what Marina

Warner aptly describes as a "rare flexibility," overleaping the "barrier of sexual polarity until God himself becomes a nursing mother" (196).

Early Christian symbolism notwithstanding, Augustine's insistent linkage between God and maternal milkiness raises the issue of motivational significance. In Burke's view, the imagery should not be ascribed merely to Augustine's "artful use" of a religious tradition: "[T]he motive fits well with the strongly *oral* nature of his speciality as a rhetorician, ranging from his feel for words as such ('select as precious vessels') to thoughts of Christ the Word as 'the goblet of our ransom'" (66–67). Yet these recurrent tropes, I propose, also signify more than the oral associations that words hold for the classical Christian rhetor. Monica dominated her son's life both before *and* after his baptism in late April of 387, as the autobiography begun ten years later vividly shows (Brown, 74, 184). Invoking Monica as a theological figure, Augustine describes how her "daily tears" constrained God himself to heed her prayers: "But *you* . . . rescued my soul from the depths of this darkness because my mother, your faithful servant, wept to you for me. . . . tears which streamed down and watered the earth in every place where she bowed her head in prayer" (*Confessions* 3.11.68). Nevertheless, Augustine did try to contain her influence, the effluvia of milk and tears that seeped into all aspects of his life. The figural identification of God with lactation does not only transform a powerful maternal agency into a passive vessel. The emblems of motherhood, the womb and the breast, do not only become the conduits through which God the Father engenders and sustains the life of his dedicated servant. Augustine's "verbal action" also transposes the maternal body as a real object in the world of human creatures into a property of God.[18]

Hence the oral fulfillment associated with a divine paternal essence ("Unseen by us you plant [your gifts] like seeds in the hearts of your faithful and they grow to bear wonderful fruits" [9.11.199]) enables a remarkable variant of the family romance. For Augustine is not content to substitute a better mother for the actual one. His rhetoric subsumes the maternal breast into an idealized paternal function. Moreover, this symbolism may be extended to Augustine himself. As his biographer notes, Augustine's conception of his basic role as a preacher and a bishop was to distribute spiritual food, to break bread among his congregation by expounding the Bible: "'I go to feed so that I can give you to eat. I am the servant, the bringer of food, not the master of the house'" (quoted in Brown, 252).

What Lacan could apprehend in the Augustinian anecdote of the jealous child, then, was a two-stage development: the initial exposure to maternal loss and its relation to the process of self-transfiguration. Yet, where Augustine invokes the divine (or symbolic) father in order to implement his passage from malaise to rebirth, Lacan does not in the first specular instance call upon or for paternal intervention. If one cannot *have* the maternal object—that is, the object irretrievably lost from the moment it is recognized as such, the object first constituted through separation—then one will *be* without it. There is perhaps a dimension of revenge and retaliation in any achieved conversion. An analogous imperative to qualify, reassign, or erase the functions of the mother appears in the textual configurations of Augustine and Lacan. Particularly, a parallelism may be drawn between Augustine's images of the transcendent God who subsumes not only the nutrient of milk but His subjects' very conception in the womb of time and Lacan's idea of the total form or image that enables the advent of the human subject: "This form would have to be called the Ideal-I" (*Écrits*, 94 / 2). For Lacan, the contours of a subjectivity cannot emerge without the mediation of a mirror.

III

To reiterate some earlier suggestions, Lacan's turnings to Augustine at the metaphysical level are comparable to his many returns to Freud. He retraces a famous pilgrim's spiritual progress at his own secular pace. That is, unlike Augustine, Lacan has no theological intentions. His Catholicism is nevertheless part of his theoretical formation and formulations. In examining Lacan's movements from the mother to the mirror to *das Ding*, a concept to be delineated in this section, it is therefore important to remember Augustine and the major role played by Monica in his gradual transition and conversion to the True Word, which is the only way of access to the Ineffable who is God.

In *Seminar VII: The Ethics of Psychoanalysis, 1959–1960* (1986), Lacan introduces the idea of *das Ding*. Before marking the distance of the "Ideal-I" of his mirror-stage theory from what comes after, *das Ding*, I would underscore a dual connection. First, the reflected totality that activates the infant's "libidinal dynamism" (*Écrits*, 94 / 2) and *das Ding* (also called *la chose*) both function at different periods in Lacan's teaching as supervalent terms for that which generates and organizes human desire. It takes two for desire to appear in the one: "Man's desire is the desire of the Other." Desire is born, as it were, through the dialectical reciprocity that the mirror stage instills in the perceiving subject. But if it is "at the level of the desire of the Other that the subject's desire is constituted" (*Seminar XI*, 213 / 235), that desire is also always the product of a lack, of something irrevocably missing. "What is desire?" Lacan asks in *Seminar VII*, and replies, "I can only remind you of what I have articulated in the past: realizing one's desire is necessarily always raised from the point of view of an absolute condition. . . . [A]ll that exists lives only in the lack of being" (340–41 / 294). Second, the conceptual constructs of the mirror stage and *das Ding* are interlinked through their elaboration of a constitutive and distinctive phenomenon—the desire of the Other's desire—that is emphatically unrelated to the parental imagos. In other words, like the mirror model of relations, the concept of *das Ding* developed in this seminar, a concept closely related to the *objet petit a* in Lacan's later work, is also integral to a *causa sui* project: a creation or rebirth of the self that entails an imperative to eliminate the determining influence of both parents.

But while the dual relation between the ego and its semblables belongs to the realm of the imaginary, *das Ding* pertains (because it cannot properly be said to "belong") to the real, to the order that cannot be comprehended by any imaginary and symbolic coordinates of human existence. In contrast to a given signifier located at points in the signifying chain, this Thing cannot be situated: "*Das Ding* is that which I will call the beyond-of-the-signified" (*Seminar VII*, 67 / 54). Unlike things in the world of persons, places, objects, *das Ding* is nowhere and everywhere. In a structural sense, to the God of Saint Augustine, Lacan holds up *das Ding*.

By way of figural approximation, it may be described as an ex-centric centrality or, in similarly oxymoronic terms, as an excluded interior. The difficulty of articulating such a Thing is graphically demonstrated at the blackboard: "Simply by writing it on the board and putting *das Ding* at the center," Lacan tells his seminar audience, "with the subjective world of the unconscious organized in a series of signifying relations around it, you can see the difficulty of topographical representation. The reason is that *das Ding* is at the center only in the sense that it is excluded." *Das Ding* elicits a primary affect that partakes of the uncanny. It recalls "something *entfremdet*, something strange to me, although it is at the heart of me" (*Seminar VII*, 87 / 71). Statements elaborating the concept occasionally acquire a transcendent tonality—"at the heart of man's destiny is the *Ding*, the *causa*" (116 / 97). It might be argued that in this instance and others throughout *The Ethics of Psychoanalysis*, an alternative term such as "Divinity" or "Deity" could fit into the slot of "*das Ding*." What Lacan envisions, however, is an eradicable void, an emptiness rather than a plenitude of being. Every life may be compared to a vase made from clay whose center, so to speak, is a gap or a hole: "[T]he potter, just like you to whom I am speaking, creates the vase with his hand around this emptiness, creates it, just like a mythical creator, *ex nihilo*, starting with a hole" (146 / 121).

Even though Lacan repeatedly insists that *das Ding* cannot be equated with any experiential forms of human reality and also presents numerous examples of sublimatory avoidance, the efforts to correlate it with a particular signified continue. Thus, offering an explication of the concept in *An Introductory Dictionary of Lacanian Psychoanalysis*, Dylan Evans identifies it with "the lost object which must be continually refound . . . in other words, the forbidden object of incestuous desire, the mother (S7, 67)" (205). At the textual point designated, Lacan himself does not posit an equivalence between the mother and *das Ding*. His formulation is: "[T]he whole development at the level of the mother/child interpsychology . . . is nothing more than an immense development of the essential character of the maternal thing, of the mother, insofar as she occupies the place of that thing, *das Ding* [la mère, en tant qu'elle occupe la place de cette chose, de *das Ding*]" (*Seminar VII*, 82 / 67). The qualifying phrase here—"insofar as she occupies the place"—is crucial to an understanding of the Lacanian concept. The mother is in a metaphoric or substitutive relation to the Thing. She is not the real Thing. The term *das Ding* is no more (but also no less) than a way of marking the place of an absence, of a void that invites but also eludes our discursive efforts to fill it with symbols. *Das Ding*, like the *objet a* or an unknowable x, is an empty signifier. There is nothing, no signified beneath or behind it. The equation of *das Ding* with a fixed and material object, say, with the maternal object of incestuous (Oedipal) desire, is comparable to putting a cover on top of what is commonly called a "manhole" so that passersby will not fall in.

The object of desire as structured in the narcissistic interaction—for example, between sibling rivals who covet the maternal breast—is also not co-extensive with *das Ding*: "[T]here is a difference, and it is precisely on the slope of that difference that the problem of sublimation is situated" (*Seminar VII*, 117 / 98). Sublimation, in Lacan's general definition, "raises an object . . . to the dignity of the Thing" (133 / 112). Attempts to evade the void, and Lacan classifies all such attempts under the defensive category of sublimation, assume a variety of forms. The desired object is the function of an imaginary, sometimes collective phantasm that overlays and sublimates a fundamental, nonbinary absence. The social collectivity constructs such "useful" objects in order to generate a space "where it may in a way delude itself on the subject of *das Ding*, colonize the field of *das Ding* with imaginary schemes." Already looking ahead to the elaboration of the *objet petit a*, what Lacan designates the "*a* elements" assume historically and socially particularized forms (he gives an example of designer dresses and hats at this point) that serve to delude as well as to comfort the subject at the very juncture where *das Ding* enters (118–19 / 99).

Das Ding, defined as "whatever is open, lacking, or gaping at the center of our desire," continually elicits attempts to curtail its abyssal dominance by means of figural transformations. By way of further example, the lady, "our Lady" who becomes the focus of courtly love is put in the position of *das Ding*: "I would say—you will forgive the play on words—that we need to know what we can do to transform the dam-age into our 'dame' in the archaic French sense, our lady" (*Seminar VII*, 102 / 84). In French usage, the word *dam* denoting detriment, prejudice is closely linked to the word "damnation," eternal deprivation of the Lord, the heavenly Father, but is also a morphological variant of "dame," a lady of nobility. The idealized focus of the courtly lover's passion—"object of praise, of service, of devotion, and all kinds of sentimental, stereotyped behavior"—enables Lacan to demonstrate how it becomes possible "to give an object, which in this case is called the Lady, the value of representing the Thing" (151–52 / 126). As Žižek puts it, recalling and adjusting the "notorious wisdom" of King Lear: "[I]n the movement of desire, 'something comes from nothing.' Although it is true that the object-cause of desire is pure semblance, this does not prevent it from triggering a whole chain of consequences that regulate our 'material,' 'effective' life and deeds" (12).

Another variant of the lady-love, *la dame de coeur*, has surfaced, according to Lacan, in the work of Melanie Klein. He therefore proposes the "whole of Kleinian theory" be reconsidered with a certain "key": "namely, Kleinian theory depends on its having situated the mythic body of the mother at the central place of *das Ding*" (*Seminar VII*, 127 / 106). The success of the Kleinian school, which "polarizes and orients the whole development of analytic thought" derives from its attempt to approach something primordial and unapproachable in the subject's relations to the field of *das Ding*. The "Kleinian myth," in Lacan's phrase, allows those who subscribe to it to achieve a socially recognized sublimation of *das Ding*, a symbolic repair of the rent or hole, by naming it. However, of the maternal body in Klein's influential work, as of the lady in the Provençal troubadour's love song, he would say: "[I]t is a thing that is not, of course, the Thing" (142 / 118).

These sites of reparation or sublimation try to take *das Ding* out of the real and endow a constitutive obscurity with a transparent content. "You have to admit," Lacan asserts in *Seminar VII*, "that to place in this beyond a creature such as woman is a truly incredible idea" (253 / 214). But his rejection of all attempts to place the father in such a position should be noted as well. Contra the Freudian speculation that social, religious, and cultural institutions are an outcome of the slaying of the primal father, Lacan posits *das Ding* as the empty gravitational center around which civilization comes into existence. "All art is characterized by a certain mode of organization around this emptiness. . . . Religion in all its forms consists of avoiding this emptiness" (155 / 130).

So although essentially extra-worldly or asymbolic, the Thing is operational in reality. In Lacan's precise wording, "This *Ding* is not fully elucidated, even if we make use of it" (*Seminar VII*, 125 / 104). His elevation of the Thing to an ineffable realm beyond, and implicitly above, the relations to the heavenly Father, or to the mythic symbolic father of *Totem and Taboo*, or to "our Lady" as object of religious and/or courtly veneration is analogous to devotional discourse. As absence is to presence and dark to light, so the empty Thing that Lacan finds at the heart of human life is inversely symmetrical to the full Thing ("O God, you are the Light of my heart") that Augustine discovers in his priestly vocation (*Confessions* 1.13.34). Opposites are often close enough; and yet, where Augustine reaffirms "the saving name of Christ" (5.14.108), Lacan would counter that the idea of God is an effect of *das Ding*. Moreover, when he repudiates the "favored image of Christ on the cross," he does so with a rhetorical flourish whose irony does not cancel a bitter, even scathing inflection. He thus recalls the historical consequences of a too-vehement insistence on the truth of the image of the crucified Saviour: "Need I go further and add that in connection with that image Christianity has been crucifying man in holiness for centuries? In holiness" (*Seminar VII*, 304 / 262). In the conflicts that inform his self-conception, Lacan is aligned with Augustine; in his secular vision, he stands apart.

CHAPTER 8

Augustine in Contexts (Part 2)

Three Variations on a Scene from the Confessions

In examining Lacan's repeated citation of a passage from the *Confessions*, I have so far considered two types of context: the relevance of the image of infantile jealousy to his theoretical work, as well as the personal associations and childhood experiences that arguably led to the substitutive function of this passage as a screen memory. Yet whatever the private resonances generated by the anecdote, it appears in Lacan's carefully deliberated teachings— occasional lectures, seminars, and essays—over a period of forty years. Turning from issues of motivation to actual instances of its citation, I would like now to clarify (or to confess) my own critical presupposition: Lacan's successive readings of Augustine are rereadings. The significance of the anecdote as cited in 1938 profoundly changes when Lacan re-sites it in his later writings.[1] As demonstrated by Menard's great, unfinished lifework—the composition of "*the Quixote itself*"—in Jorge Luis Borges's "Pierre Menard, Author of the *Quixote*," identical words in different contexts are no longer identical. "It is not in vain that three hundred years have gone by, filled with exceedingly complex events" (Borges, 39, 41–42). In what follows I therefore try to trace the progress of an anecdote in Lacan's texts.

Scene I

Lacan first cites Augustine in the second paragraph of the "Le complexe de l'intrusion" section of *Les complexes familiaux*. The quotation is preceded by the evocative closing paragraph of the "Le complexe du sevrage" section, in which he describes the residues of primary fusion with the mother in the lives of individuals and communities:

> The overflowing quality of the [weaning] complex establishes maternal feeling; its sublimation contributes to family feeling; its discharge leaves traces we can recognize. . . . If we were to sketch out the most abstract form in which one refinds it [i.e., the structure of the maternal imago], we might characterize it thus: it is the perfect assimilation of the totality to being [*de la totalité à l'être*]. We can recognize the longing of humanity in this somewhat philosophical formula, a longing that shapes the metaphysical mirage of universal harmony, the mystic abyss of affective fusion, the social utopia of totalitarian guardianship—all derived from man's preoccupation with a paradise lost before birth and with a dark longing for death. (*CF*, 35 / 16; trans. modified)

The movement from "totality to being" here is not to be confused with the later articulation of the "form of . . . totality" that extends the fragmented body-image and produces the ego's illusory syntheses (*Écrits*, 97 / 4). The term *totalité* has quite different meanings in 1938 and 1949. Whereas in "The Mirror Stage as Formative of the Function of the *I*," the term dignifies the relation to the visual form of the counterpart, in the earlier usage it denotes an affective experience (akin to the "oceanic feeling" described in Freud's *Civilization and Its Discontents*)[2] in which weaning has not yet taken place. According to Les *complexes familiaux*, the infant's primary fusion or totality ("the perfect assimilation . . . to being") tends to recur in a variety of metaphysical-mystical experiences. The source of all these experiences is the archaic tie to the maternal body.

The next paragraph opens the section on sibling intrusion. Lacan first notes the young child's widening circle of awareness: "[H]e sees one or sev-

eral of his own kind [*semblables*] participating with him in a domestic relationship; . . . he becomes acquainted with his brothers [il se connaît des
frères]" (35–36 / 16; trans. modified). He then presents Augustine's scenario—which is omitted in the English translation—with these introductory
words: "Infantile jealousy has long struck its observer. . . . " The anecdote is
intended to instantiate a very particular concept of jealousy, which, according to Lacan, "in its fundamental form, represents not a deep-seated rivalry
but a mental identification [la jalousie, dans son fonds, représente non pas
une rivalité vitale mais une identification mentale]" (36 / 16; trans. modified).

To redefine jealousy as a representation of "mental identification" might
appear completely counterintuitive. Perhaps that is why the translator renders Lacan's statement as "jealousy . . . represents *not so much* a deep-seated
rivalry *as* a mental identification" (16; emphasis added). The problem is: how
to conceive the hostile disposition fundamental to jealousy without a rival
who is believed to enjoy an advantage? Can jealousy be a self-reflexive attitude or feeling? Were the question put to Lacan, I suggest, his answer would
be affirmative. His discussion of jealousy and identification is most subtly,
complexly argued in an essay whose theoretical sophistication harbingers
coming developments. In drawing a causal connection between these psychical mechanisms, Lacan assembles and synthesizes three main lines of
thought: psychoanalysis (primarily Freud), experimental psychology (Wallon), and phenomenology (Hegel-Kojève).

From the psychoanalytic viewpoint, Lacan implies a prolongation of the
mother-infant dyad during the second phase that is, at one and the same
time, a transformation: "If children between six months and two years are
brought together in pairs and left to their own playful spontaneity, the following fact can be observed: diverse reactions occur . . . which seems to indicate a kind of communication." This communication involves a blurring of
self-boundaries: "[E]ach partner confuses the part of the other with his own
and identifies with it" (*CF*, 36, 38 / 16). However, while implicitly extending
the infant's range of affective identifications, it also retriggers the distress
that accompanies the fusional bliss lost through separation (*sevrage*) from the
mother. Hence among the reactions observed between two children at play
is a patterning into "provocations and ripostes"—that is, into displays of aggressive activity. Although such aggression might be regarded as an outcome

of differentiation and rivalry, in Lacan's view it results from a process of convergence (identification) of the playmates. Close in age and in size, each subject experiences a reflexive reciprocity: a putting of one's self in the proverbial shoes (or mind) of another. The word that recurs in these pages of *Les complexes familiaux* is "similarity" (*similitude*). The mirror stage goes into effect only when there is "a similarity between subjects"; and also, "the imago of the other is linked to the structure of the subject's own body . . . by a certain objective similarity" (37–38 / 16–17; trans. modified).

Identification, then, provides the ground for the emergence of internecine violence. According to Lacan, "it is especially in the primitive fraternal situation that aggression proves to be secondary to identification" (*CF*, 39). "Secondary" here designates both temporal and causal factors. Lacan elaborates this psychical succession (identification-aggression) and also introduces another reactive mechanism into his exposition of the intrusion complex—namely, sadomasochism: "[P]sychoanalytic doctrine, in characterizing the typical libidinal tendency at this [infant] stage as sado-masochistic, certainly underscores the aggressiveness that then dominates the affective economy, but also that it is always at the same time . . . upheld by an identification with the other, the object of violence" (40). Just as aggression is "upheld by" and not "opposed to" identification, so sadism is predicated upon masochism. Seemingly the obverse sides of each other, or the Tweedledee and Tweedledum of psychoanalysis, these two trends (masochism-sadism) are as rigorously and unalterably ordered as the aggression that follows hard upon identification.

It is after the mention of the sadomasochistic tendency characteristic of the reactive relations called "intrusion" that Lacan recalls Augustine's anecdote via the evocation of an "unweaned brother." Of the several concepts brought into play in the passage, partly cited earlier (in Chapter 2) in connection with the enduring effects of *sevrage*, "primary masochism" is the key term for understanding this allusion:

> If we agree that . . . the distress of human weaning is the source of the death wish, we will recognize in primary masochism the dialectical moment when the subject assumes, by his first playful acts, the reenactment of this same malaise and, by that means, sublimates and overcomes it. . . . [The Fort/Da game] clearly signifies that the subject reinflicts on himself the pathos of

weaning, as he suffered it, but he triumphs over it now that he is active in its reproduction.

The identification with the brother permits the completion of the split-ting [*dédoublement*] thus begun in the subject: it provides the image that grounds one of the poles of primary masochism. Thus the non-violence of primordial suicide engenders the violence of the imaginary murder of the sibling. . . . The sight of the unweaned brother provokes a special aggres-sion only because it repeats for the subject the imago of the maternal situa-tion and, together with it, the desire for death. (*CF*, 40–41 / 17; trans. modified)

Lacan traces the motives for the jealousy exhibited during this developmen-tal stage back to the masochism that arises after maternal deprivation (the weaning complex) and its most radical effect—the wish not to be. Augus-tine's scenario supplies a paradigm for this psychical connection: both re-evoking the "pathos of weaning" (or maternal relation) and representing the pathos of dialectical battle (or fraternal relation). Identification with the double, symbolized by "l'image du frère non sevré" of the anecdote, reacti-vates the weaning crisis. Primary masochism, at times expressed through "the non-violence of primordial suicide," is a consequence of the originary experience of maternal loss. Its alternative and belated mode of expression is a murderous aggression directed against the counterpart.

In short, no mother, no other: fratricidal hostility is a later formation based on an affective identification in which the ego is represented in or by the other, bringing to such identification the surcharge of primary masochism. This surcharge is intensified by the mirror-stage consciousness that someone else is taking one's place, that someone else is benefiting from somebody or something still and, to a certain extent, always felt as belong-ing exclusively to one's own person. The violence aimed at the brother is the intertwined result of the violence aimed at the self.

Lacan summarily articulates these genetic processes when he explicitly mentions Augustine for a second time in *Les complexes familiaux*:

The emergence of jealousy in connection with nurturance, according to the classical theme illustrated above by a citation from Saint Augustine, must be interpreted prudently. In fact, jealousy can manifest itself in cases where the subject, long since weaned, is not in a situation of vital competition with his brother. The phenomenon thus seems to require as a preliminary condition a certain identification with the status of the sibling. (40)

Again jealousy is not a matter of difference but of sameness, not of rivalry ("competition") but of identification. The mention of the "connection with nurturance," however subsequently attenuated ("long since weaned"), underscores that even when sublimated, "the imago of the maternal breast continues to play an important psychic role" (34 / 16). Furthermore, Lacan argues that the first home in which the infant is formed, the environment "least accessible . . . to consciousness, the prenatal habitat," continues to resonate at later stages through varied symbolic correlates, "dwellings and thresholds, especially in their primitive forms, the cave and the hut." Not only the breast but also the womb are thus at the origin of necessary primal separation as well as of identification. "Any return to these [prenatal] securities, even partial, can precipitate a regression within the psyche which is out of proportion to any practical benefits of this return" (34 / 16).

The second perspective brought to bear on sibling jealousy derives from Wallon's *Les origines du caractère chez l'enfant*. Although no direct reference to Wallon appears in *Les complexes familiaux*, Lacan does broadly credit behavioral psychology at the outset of his section on sibling intrusion: "[E]xperimental observations of the child as well as psychoanalytic investigations reveal its role in the genesis of sociability, and through that, of human consciousness itself." Lacan immediately emphasizes what he regards as the main contribution of this research: "The critical point discovered by these projects is that jealousy, in its fundamental form, represents . . . a mental identification" (36 / 16). The reference to "experimental observations," which are partly credited with the discovery of the connection between identification and jealousy, indicates to the alerted reader that a return to Wallon's empirical work might be involved.[3]

Indeed, in the third chapter of *Les origines du caractère chez l'enfant*, a chapter subtitled "La jalousie," Wallon describes the etiology and consequences of jealousy, primarily in young children, anticipating Lacan's 1938 analysis of jealousy and masochism in several crucial respects. Wallon opens by stipulating that affective reactions such as jealousy and sympathy in children do not imply, as is widely thought, a notion of distinct personalities; on the contrary, these reactions derive from a primitive bipolar situation that he calls

"contemplation-parade." Their appearance initially indicates "regression toward a stage of relative nondifferentiation." Contemplation and parade are
not, however, polar positions situated or apportioned between two individuals. They co-occur within the same individual. Parade—that is, the wish to be
the one who acts and shows off before the other—complicates the relative
passivity of contemplation. In this connection, Wallon introduces another
concept, "participation," and how it functions in young children. Participation designates a reactive phenomenon in which proximity (*rapprochement*)
between two children also brings out their opposition: "Participation still, but
contrastive participation that announces the moment of individuation" (*Les
origines*, 257). Jealousy arises when the subject, still pulled between the internal polarities of contemplation-parade, begins to crystallize around a similar
(but not identical) subject. According to Wallon, children will want all the
sooner to displace, replace, or substitute themselves for those who most resemble them, "other children close . . . in age or in condition." When such
jealousy persists in some adults, it appears to indicate "a confusion between
self and other that rivalry cannot succeed in dissolving and replacing" (*Les
origines*, 258–59).

For Wallon, then, jealousy is not jealousy in the common acceptation of
this term. As in Lacan's definitional statements, rivalry is not its cause or origin; rather, the precipitating factor is an obfuscation or even an absence of
psychical boundaries (a condition resembling what Kristeva calls "abjection")[4] that is normative only in very young children. Wallon describes how
an insufficiently differentiated jealousy feeds (on) itself in the afflicted adult:
"Self-enclosed in his spectatorial attitude, the authentically jealous type
nourishes himself on mortifying spectacles with bitter greed. His very existence is invaded, ravaged, by the success of the other; he does not know how
to detach himself from the image; he confounds it with his own substance"
(*Les Origines*, 259). Metaphors of feeding and, most strikingly, of a hunger
that nourishes itself ("se nourrit . . . avec une âpre avidité") characterize this
regressive condition. The consummation devoutly wished in such a state is
to consume the self.

Although Wallon cites "real-life" evidence, both anecdotal (relating to his
two pet dogs) and empirical (Paul Guillaume's research on infant jealousy),
in support of his theoretical arguments, he also mentions the figure of
Shakespeare's Othello in the closing paragraphs of his chapter: "For every

Othello, how many secret 'magnificent Cuckolds!'" (260). In cases of pure jealousy, according to Wallon, masochism reigns. Indulging in acute agony, the individual punishes that part of himself he has (mis)placed in the desired object. By contrast, in the rarer instances of jealousy embodied in Othello's annihilating power, the pursuit of suffering in the other wins out over the infliction of suffering on the self. To Wallon's commentary on the sadism of Othello, I would add that murder is swiftly followed by self-immolation in this tragedy. Othello's violent suicide represents a reversion to the other pole—masochism—in which he seeks not only to punish himself but also to regain Desdemona (or that part of himself buried with her) through his own capitulation to death. Identification thus may propel the individual along the radical trajectory termed, after Freud, the death drive.

Hegelian doctrine is a third point of reference brought to bear on the importance of jealousy, "in its fundamental form . . . as a mental identification," for the genesis of subjectivity and sociability. Lacan first refers to Hegel in connection with another type of weaning or separation: the need to renounce the securities of the familial situation. "Completion of the personality demands this new weaning. Hegel speculated that the individual who does not fight to be recognized outside the family group will never attain autonomy before death" (*CF*, 35 / 16).[5] In delineating the onset of the intrusion complex, Lacan implicitly reevokes Hegel via the terms "recognition" and "rival": "[T]he recognition of a rival, that is, of an 'other' as object [la reconnaissance d'un rival, c'est-à-dire d'un 'autre' comme objet] begins from this stage" (37 / 16; trans. modified). In order to achieve a personal autonomy and dignity, the renunciation of family ties is not enough; the individual must also recognize the selfsame as the rival other. Lacan once again integrates Hegel's thought as transmitted by Kojève into his own teaching.

These comments lead me to pause at this point and readdress briefly the controversial issue of Lacan's debts. Roudinesco proposes that in addition to specific ideas (such as the "beautiful soul" and the "dialectic of Master and Slave") what Lacan more generally learned from attending Kojève's lectures was no less than "how to make Freud's text say what it does not say." Furthermore, it was through Kojève's innovative revision of Hegel that Lacan acquired "the wherewithal to effect a new interpretation of an original body of thought" (*Jacques Lacan & Co.*, 138).[6] By implication, Lacan's most significant contribution to psychoanalysis, namely, "the return to Freud" was not, at bottom, original. Reinterpretation, however, is an activity that goes on continually and not only among philosophers. Roudinesco's statement also begs the question of Lacan's vast erudition. He had many models—Rank, Ferenczi, and Klein immediately come to mind—from whom he may have studied, if such lessons were at all required, how to return to Freud. The issue of appropriation and imitation does nevertheless arise on occasion. Some further acknowledgment of Wallon, for instance, would have been no more than fair, not even generous, on his part. Nonetheless, Lacan's lifelong practice of integrating ideas from different fields into his work, a practice already evident in his early analysis of infantile jealousy and identification, amounts to an intellectual operation that is innovative in scope as well as in complexity. As Shoshana Felman aptly puts it, "one of the consequences of Lacan's originality is, precisely, a displacement of the very concept of originality" ("Originality of Jacques Lacan," 45). To speak of his originality is not, then, to say that Lacan did not learn from Kojève's lessons on Hegel. But it is to suggest that a limit may be put to the accounting of his debts.

As a case in point, the presentation of sibling intrusion (the mirror stage) in *Les complexes familiaux* certainly draws on the Hegelian-Kojèvian conception of how self-consciousness is formed. Yet Lacan also reformulates this conception and goes a different way. Hegel writes in the first section of chapter 4, "Independence and Dependence of Self-Consciousness: Lordship and Bondage," in *Phenomenology of Spirit*: "Self-consciousness exists in and for itself when, and by the fact that, it so exists for another; that is, it exists only in being acknowledged" (111). This "historical 'dialectic' is," Kojève comments in his *Introduction to the Reading of Hegel*, "the 'dialectic' of Master and Slave" (9). Only an inaugural conflict that determines the one as Master and the other as Slave enables the achievement of autonomy. Lacan's 1938 formulations diverge from this account in several respects. First, in respect of its temporality, the Lacanian "self-consciousness" has a prior history shaped by the human preoccupation with an archaic nurturing imago: "[T]he imago of the maternal breast dominates all of man's life" (*CF*, 32 / 15). The subject, while engaged in dialectical battle with the other or others, carries over affective identification and aggression from the stage of *sevrage* into the later relationships. Second, in respect of its situatedness, the conflict between rivals—the "play of Forces," in Hegel's phrase (112)—is not experienced as entirely outside the subject: "Even though two partners are on stage, their communication reveals not a conflict between two persons but a conflict within each subject" (*CF*, 37 / 16). Weaning has already inculcated feelings of ambivalence, a tension between acceptance/refusal, in the individual. In Lacan's later writings, the sign designating the barred subject, the slashed *S*, correlates to this conception of *psychomachia*, or war-within-the-soul. The bar is the cross borne by the Lacanian subject. Thrust into a world where lack prevails, the subject assumes an internal rift, a self-division analogous to the Hegelian "moment of splitting" (114). For Lacan (as for Hegel) that essential moment confers the dignity as well as the distress of an autonomous subjectivity. But for Lacan (and not for Hegel) splitting begins with the separation from the mother.

A third distinction may demonstrate yet more clearly what Felman calls the "irreducibly, radically dialogic" component in Lacan's recourse to his precursors ("Originality of Jacques Lacan," 47). Directly after speaking of the child's sudden encounter with the rival other, Lacan poses a series of rhetorical questions:

> Let us examine the most frequent reactions between two children: showing off, seduction and tyranny. . . . To understand this structure, let us pause a moment before the child who shows off and the child whose gaze follows him: who is the more intense spectator? Or again, observe the child who lavishes his seductive efforts on an other: who is the seducer? Finally, when watching the child who enjoys the trappings of power which he exercises and the one who delights in submission, one asks, who is more enslaved? (*CF*, 37–38 / 16).

Kojève, following Hegel, would answer: "The master is the more enslaved." The irony of the struggle for pure prestige is revealed here. Mastery, for which life itself was risked, leads to an impasse for the victor. The master becomes the spoil of the war he has won. As Hegel contends, "the *truth* of autonomous Consciousness is *slavish Consciousness*," a statement that Kojève unravels by describing the varieties of enslavement-in-mastery.

While the details of Kojève's exposition are not pertinent to the present analysis, it may be recalled that, according to his *Introduction*, "all slavish work realizes not the Master's will, but the will—at first unconscious—of the Slave, who—finally—succeeds where the Master—necessarily—fails" (30). By contrast, Lacan's response to the question of "who is the seducer? . . . who is the more enslaved?"—a response implicit in the very questions he poses—is to refuse a final determination. "This is the paradox," he announces in *Les complexes familiaux*, "each partner confuses the part of the other with his own and identifies with it" (38 / 16). If, as he maintains in his early and later writings, all social relations proceed from intrapsychic (narcissistic) conflict, that conflict derives from a reflexive reciprocity that disallows the possibility of saying, "One is more enslaved than the Other." So again, who is the seducer? "Both" and "neither" would be equally correct replies.

Among the behavioral paradigms for the existential confusion between "master" and "slave," as well as for the reciprocity manifested in identification with the other, is the phenomenon of transitivism between young children. The one child falls, and the other cries; the one child is fed, and the other is content. Neither the tears nor the contentment is a sign of sympathy for the other *qua* other, but rather for the self as represented in the other. Jealousy appears with the dawning recognition that the pleasure attributed to the self is not, in fact, one's own. In *Encore*, 1972–1973, Lacan would invent the portmanteau word *jalouissance* to convey the baffled mixture of "jealous hatred" (*haine jalouse*) and *jouissance* of the little child who pales "in observing the *conlactaneum suum* hanging on the nipple" (*Seminar XX*, 91 / 100). Another consequence of this situation is a redirection or, more precisely, a reversal of primary masochism.

In *Les complexes familiaux*, the aggression directed at others (sadism) derives from a prior experience of loss and aggression directed at the self (masochism). "The sight of the unweaned sibling," Lacan writes in the passage on primary masochism previously quoted, "provokes a special aggression only because it repeats for the subject the imago of the maternal situation and, together with it, the desire for death" (41 / 17; trans. modified). He again alludes to Augustine's image of the satiated child who presumably imagines the slaying of the sibling rival. Contra the Darwinian idea that aggression arises from the struggle for food per se, Lacan insists in his essay on the family that "this violence has no connection with the battle for survival" (41 / 17). The willingness to risk all in the life-and-death fight for mastery is predicated upon a retrograde movement whose source is "dark longing" for the mother. This struggle is not for survival but, on the contrary, for cessation: "[T]he subject seeks to regain the maternal imago in his capitulation [*abandon*] to death" (34 / 15). Lacan's *abandon* has connotations of an erotic as well as a suicidal capitulation to the mother. Analogously, Hegel's "trial by death" could also be read another way: not only as a struggle to achieve autonomous self-consciousness but also as a permutation of the desire born in birth for ultimate reunification, the desire that strives against the necessity of separation. Drawing on anthropological evidence, Lacan observes how this desire is displayed "in burial practices where certain customs clearly signify a psychological return to the maternal breast." In the clinical situation, "the hunger strike of the anorexic; slow poisoning through the ingestion of drugs; the starvation diets of gastric neuroses"—all of these food-related disturbances embody the oral component of the death drive (34 / 15).

More schematically phrased, ingestion is unalterably linked to aggression. In the lurid world Kojève describes, violence flares up intermittently between two entities. Images of food exemplify the relations between the master and the other whom he treats as his slave. "Since all the effort is made by the Slave," Kojève writes, "the Master has only to enjoy the thing that the Slave has prepared for him, and to enjoy 'negating' it, destroying it, by 'consuming' it. (For example, he eats food that is completely prepared)" (18). Food is not the focus here for food's sake. Beyond any need, the desire to consume represents the subject's darker, unconscious cravings. These cravings may take the destructive form of withholding food from one's own mouth. They may also emerge as a wish to be master of the world, a small world at first, but its boundaries steadily expand. "I took a further step," says Saint Augustine of the sinful child he was, "into the stormy life of human society" (*Confessions* 1.8.29). Hence the image of the well-fed child who suffers to see another being fed cogently denotes the complex feelings surrounding the formation of an autonomous consciousness. It is hardly surprising that the image reappears in Lacan's texts.

Scene II

Lacan re-cites Augustine's anecdote about sibling jealousy in three essays written between 1946 and 1953 that contain summaries of his theory of reflexive recognition ("Remarks on Psychical Causality," "Aggressivity in Psychoanalysis," and "Some Reflections on the Ego"), although not in the 1949 essay devoted to the mirror stage itself. In two instances, "Aggressivity in

Psychoanalysis" and "Some Reflections on the Ego," he directly quotes Augustine in Latin and in translation. Yet what he extracts from the privileged passage after his wartime "years of silence" is not the same as what he found in it before.[7]

In the 1946 essay "Psychical Causality" (which is not included in the English version of *Écrits*), Lacan mentions the anecdote at a point where he is advancing a twofold argument. First, "paranoid knowledge" characterizes the fundamental structure of the ego; this argument reappears in "Aggressivity in Psychoanalysis": "What I have called paranoiac knowledge is shown . . . to correspond in its more or less archaic forms to certain critical moments that mark the history of man's mental genesis" (*Écrits*, 111 / 17; see also 114 / 20). Second, a close resemblance is said to link paranoia with transitivism, the mode of relating to the world studied by Charlotte Bühler, Elsa Köhler, and other psychologists. Thus, without intending to lie, a child will impute a blow he has himself delivered to the companion who received it (180). The implied connection between such transitivism and the "paranoid alienation, which dates from the deflection of the specular *I* into the social *I*," is mental identification (98 / 5). Both in paranoia and in the transitivism observed in young children, facts such as "I hit him" (or "I hate him") become indistinguishable from the phantasmic accusation "He hit me" (or "He hates me") precisely because an identification is at work.

But the basic terms of Lacan's definition of identification have changed. Whereas in his 1936 essay "Beyond the 'Reality Principle,'" the identificatory process correlates to an "affective communication, essential to social grouping" (as in *Les complexes familiaux*, published two years later), in 1946, the word *spectaculaire* modifies identification (*Écrits*, 87, 181). According to his revised account of ego formation, a series of visually related phenomena—from spec(tac)ular identification to mimetic suggestivity to seductive comportment—are interconnected through dynamic mental operations. With the addition of jealousy to this series, Saint Augustine reenters the discussion:

> All are included . . . in the dialectic that ranges from jealousy (this jealousy of which Saint Augustine already glimpsed the inaugural value in an illuminating manner) to the first forms of sympathy. They are inscribed in a primordial ambivalence that appears to us . . . *en miroir*, in this sense that the subject identifies himself in his feeling of Self with the image of the other

and that the image of the other comes to captivate this feeling in him.
(*Écrits*, 181)

The very phrase used to designate the supervening mechanism that encompasses all of the enumerated phenomena, namely, primordial ambivalence, signals the change in Lacan's theoretical orientation. Viewed metacritically, "ambivalence" serves as a kind of weather-vane word. Compare its earlier attribution:

> This acceptance or refusal [of weaning] cannot be thought of as a choice, since in the absence of an ego which affirms or denies, they are not contradictory. Co-existent and contrary poles, they cause an essentially *ambivalent attitude* even though one of them will triumph. During these crises which guarantee continuing development, this *primordial ambivalence* will resolve itself in psychic differentiations on an increasingly sophisticated and irreversible dialectical level. (*CF*, 27 / 14; emphasis added)

Lacan initially posits a linkage between the relation to the maternal imago, especially during and after the weaning period, and the dialectical processes to be repeated with variations throughout the individual's life cycle. "It is without a doubt the first crisis," as he writes in this connection, "whose resolution will have a dialectical structure" (27 / 14). Primordial ambivalence, however, emerges *en miroir* in his later work. The emphasis is Lacan's. He detaches the concept of ambivalence from its prior linkage to the mother. Whatever primal cord or attachment—except for the biological, umbilical one—tied the infant to a maternal presence is now undone: "[T]his [ambivalent] reaction can only be elicited under one condition, that the difference in age between the partners remains below a certain limit that, at the outset of the phase studied, should not exceed one year" (*Écrits*, 181). Someone close in age must precipitate the reactive attitudes that lead to dialectical mentation. The mother is clearly out of the picture; in other words, Lacan effects a separation from *sevrage*.

It is helpful to step back for a moment from these shifting bearings of primordial ambivalence and recall little Hans's story of spontaneous self-generation. In Freud's 1909 case history, the boy recounts how he laid an egg in the grass and out of it hopped another little Hans. The latent wish is perhaps less charming than the dream itself. For the desire to clear the field not so much of competitors but of progenitors may be included among the generative factors of Hans's fantasy—and of Lacan's specular theory. The father had persisted in presenting the facts: "Only women, only Mummies have children" (*SE*, 10: 87). It is also striking that both Hans's egg and Lacan's mirror contain a double. The question of how and why the double came to be in those imaginary parameters leads to an entangled motivational milieu.

Hans's wishful "all at once I laid an egg" points to a structure of conflict in which the mother herself is his rival and not the object of rivalry between father and son. If the mother occupies an adversarial position for the child, it might seem that the father's affections constitute the contested object. At stake, however, is neither the father as the child's object-choice nor the mother as rival other (see Freud's "negative" Oedipus complex [*SE*, 19: 33]). What, then, does this child want? Hans expressly desires to be in the place of the mother: "But only woman have children," "But you can't," says the father. "Oh yes," and "why shouldn't I?" says the child (*SE*, 10: 85–87). Hans's insistence on "his children" elicits from Freud a footnote in defense of his young patient's masculinity: "There is no necessity on this account to assume in Hans the presence of a feminine strain of desire for having children." Yet, on several occasions duly reported to the Professor by the child's father, Hans states his wish to give birth and "do everything" for his own children (10: 97). Freud's footnote concludes with this explanation: "It was with his mother that Hans had had his most blissful experience as a child, and he was now repeating them [*sic*], and himself playing the active part, which was thus necessarily that of mother" (10: 93 n. 1). The clarification of the particular point—Hans has no "feminine strain of desire for having children"—turns out to defend a major psychoanalytic premise. The Oedipus complex, according to Freud, remains the motivating factor in this case history. Proof lies in the death wish directed at the father, from whom the boy would like to prise away his beautiful mother, and the fear of violent reprisal, symbolically represented by the phobic dread of horses that bite.

Even more complexly, Lacan's theory of the birth of the ego posits a *struggle* with the double. This struggle paves the way for the conflict with the parental blocking agent. Put another way, no sooner did the other Hans come out of the egg than the two little Hanses became locked in a battle for pure prestige. Lacan's remodeled theory of ego formation requires a life-and-death struggle between subject and (br)other to preempt the (allegedly) anterior conflict between father and son. Ironically, however, as discussed in the conclusion to Chapter 5, hostility toward the specular rival cannot help but reinforce the keystone it seeks to remove. Instead of dislodging Freud's foundational complex from its preeminent position, Lacan seems only to provide further evidence in its support. The idea of the mirror stage, *comme formateur*, discloses a desire for the place of the father. In a word, Freud wins.

And yet in a manner analogous to little Hans's fable of self-creation, Freud's and Lacan's formulations might also be regarded as defensive constructs. Autobiographical factors enter into the elaboration of their theoretical work, just as they do in dreams. Thus, when Lacan reallocates primordial ambivalence to the subject's encounter with the image or "Phantom Double" ("Some Reflections," 15), he is relegating the mother to the margins of a field from which she had already been distanced via the Freudian priority granted to the struggle between father and son. Both the Oedipus complex and the mirror stage exhibit an anxiety of genesis. The familial tableau is one of disorder and violence for some and of disfranchisement for (m)others. In a word, everybody loses.

From a third and different perspective that will bring us back to Augustine's anecdote, Lacan's revised attribution of ambivalence may be deemed a more benign vision of the maternal function. The German *Ambivalenz*, in the specialized sense coined by the psychiatrist Eugen Bleuler, is far from being a positive mechanism. It is identified as a symptom of schizophrenic thinking and disorder, as in this excerpt from the *American Journal of Insanity* (1913): "This ambivalency leads, even with normal people, to difficulties of decision and inner conflict" (quoted in *OED*, 1: 388). So it is not a great boon to be the mother of ambivalence. Lacan, however, reverses the valence of this psychiatric concept. The simultaneity of opposing attitudes or emotions enables mental organization and processes of socialization: "[W]e must try to correlate with the development of the organism and the establishment of its relations with the Socius those images whose dialectical connexions are brought home to us in our [clinical] experience" ("Some Reflections," 15). As expanded by Lacan, ambivalence is not merely a symptom of psychical disturbance but also an essential feature of the subject's inner reality and adaptation to the community.

Although the values associated with the terms "ambivalence" and "dialectic" are consistently upheld in Lacan's work, his conception of their trigger-

ing mechanism changes radically. When in 1946, for example, Lacan parenthetically refers to "this jealousy of which Saint Augustine already glimpsed
. . . the inaugural value," he is not simply restating an earlier thesis; the anecdote no longer exemplifies the conflict or dialectical movement activated by
the weaning crisis. *L'image est le maître.* The specular image schools the subject in the ways of the world. In contrast to the question "Who is the more
enslaved?" (a question that remained, effectively, unanswered and unan-
swerable in *Les complexes familiaux*), Lacan now insists on the priority of visual forms. He speaks of "a first captation [*première captation*] by the image in
which the first stage [*premier moment*] of the dialectic of identifications can
be discerned"; and similarly, he equates the mirror stage with "a stage where
the earliest formation of the ego can be observed" (*Écrits*, 112 / 18; "Some
Reflections," 14). The specular counterpart subjugates as well as seduces the
subject. In Lacan's own phrasing, "[L]'image de l'autre vient à captiver en lui
ce sentiment [de Soi]" (*Écrits*, 181).

Captiver and *captation* are conspicuously poised between negative and positive poles of meaning. Literally denoting "hold captive," "imprison," "en-
chain," "subordinate," et cetera, the words figuratively belong to the chain
of "charm," "enchant," "seduce," "enthrall," "win over," et cetera. Thus a
single signifier that oscillates between enchainment and enchantment comes
to represent a splitting or division of the subject. The interplay between
identification and aggression henceforth marks the imaginary realms that
the *I* inhabits.

In addition to the concept of ambivalence, Lacan brings the theory of the
mirror stage into a new alignment with the death drive in his essays on "Aggressivity in Psychoanalysis" and "Some Reflections on the Ego." Accordingly, Lacan's citations of Augustine in these two essays acquire a different
tonality, darker and more ominous, even while his expository style becomes
increasingly allusive and densely textured. In the following pages I want
closely to read the passage from each essay in which Lacan's interpolation
of the scenario of sibling jealousy instantiates and reinforces his evolving
theory.

> The libidinal tension that shackles the subject to the constant pursuit of an
> illusory unity which is always luring him away from himself, is surely related
> to that agony of dereliction which is Man's particular and tragic destiny.
> Here we see how Freud was led to his deviant concept of a death instinct.

The signs of the lasting damage this negative libido causes can be read in the face of a small child torn by the pangs of jealousy, where St. Augustine recognized original evil. "Myself have seen and known even a baby envious; it could not speak, yet it turned pale and looked bitterly on its foster-brother" (. . . *nondum loquebatur, et intuebatur pallidus amaro aspectu conlactaneum suum*).

Moreover, the whole development of consciousness leads only to the re-discovery of the antinomy by Hegel as the starting-point of the ego. As Hegel's well-known doctrine puts it, the conflict arising from the co-exis-tence of two consciousnesses can only be resolved by the destruction of one of them. ("Some Reflections," 16)

To read Lacan's reading of "the face of a small child" mentioned by Augus-tine in this context requires some backtracking. For Wallon, and subse-quently for Lacan, the mirror experience constitutes the beginning of the self-differentiation necessary for various cognitive processes. Wallon rapidly retraces, in the conclusion to his chapter on the body proper and its reflected image, the child's progress from mere sentience to the imaginary and, then, to the symbolic: "[T]he development of the infant demonstrates by what de-grees [1] immediate experience, the undifferentiated, dispersed, and transi-tory impressions of brute sensibility must become dissociated, fixed by [2] images initially concrete and seemingly coextensive with their object, [and] then give way to [3] symbolic transmutations of pure and stable representa-tion" (237). The progress described in Wallon's *Les origines* is a triumphal one, loosely corresponding to the three complexes of *Les complexes familiaux*.

In the late 1940s and 1950s, Lacan continues to remark on the "jubilant interest" shown at the moment of specular recognition. But he increasingly turns his attention to the alienation and struggle that swiftly follow. In the passage just quoted from "Some Reflections on the Ego," he characteristi-cally stresses the negative and regressive aspects of the libidinal relations be-tween the ego and its mirror image. He also calls upon and synthesizes two distinct theories—Freud's "deviant" or controversial concept of death and Hegel's dialectical category of Master/Slave—in order to explain rather than to exorcise the "agony of dereliction" accompanying the assumption of self-consciousness.

In the first explanatory instance (Freud), the promise of "an illusory unity," a promise held out by the total bodily form in the mirror, lures the subject "away from himself" into the night of nonbeing. Beyond the reality of duality, of split and suffering human existence, lies the pleasure principle of final cessation. In the second instance (Hegel), the conflict provoked by the realization of the "co-existence of two consciousnesses" may be alleviated, albeit not ultimately eliminated, by destroying the image of one's self as incarnated in one's enemy. However, these seemingly disjunctive aims— that is, the death of the self and the destruction of the other—are not, strictly speaking, separable. "The aggressiveness involved in the ego's fundamental relationship to other people is [based]," Lacan observes, "upon the intra-psychic tension we sense in the warning of the ascetic that 'a blow at your enemy is a blow at yourself'" ("Some Reflections," 16). If, at the core of being, *I* and the other occupy the same psychical space, any death blow dealt to the one cannot but annihilate the other. Or, as Edgar Allan Poe's dying William Wilson whispers to his double and destroyer, William Wilson, "*In me didst thou exist—and, in my death, see by this image, which is thine own, how utterly thou hast murdered thyself.*"

Formerly, however, Lacan claimed not only that "the source of the death wish is the distress of weaning" but further added that, at a later developmental stage, the image of an infant-rival at the breast, precisely because it recalls "the imago of the maternal situation and, together with it, the desire for death," elicits a murderous aggression in the subject (*CF*, 40 / 17). This connection between primary masochism and its derivative, sadism, no longer holds in his reformulation of the subject's derelict destiny. The articulation of the "maternal situation" and its effects is replaced by a different process that pervades all levels of his theory. Just as the etiology of primordial ambivalence is shifted forward to the confrontation with the specular image, so the death wish is now an outcome of the paranoiac alienation characteristic of the imaginary order. Same strokes, different folks: although primordial ambivalence and the death drive both remain crucial to the formation of the *I*, the fraternal factor replaces the maternal. Severing the tie between death and the mother might seem a favorable theoretical development. The pattern of Lacan's revision, however, entails a divestment of the mother as the properties formerly attributed to her are removed one by one.

The connection between death and the mirror stage is also intimated in "Aggressivity in Psychoanalysis." Lacan first proposes:

Subjective experience must be fully enabled to recognize the central nucleus of ambivalent aggressivity, which in the present stage of our culture is given to us under the dominant species of *resentment*, even in its earliest aspects in the child;

and then, interpolates his favored exemplum:

St Augustine foreshadowed psychoanalysis when he expressed such behaviour in the following exemplary image: "*Vidi ego. . . .* " (I have seen with my own eyes and known very well an infant in the grip of jealousy: he could not yet speak, and already he observed his foster-brother, pale and with an envenomed stare). Thus, with the *infans* (pre-verbal) stage of early childhood, the situation of spectacular absorption is permanently tied: the child observed, the emotional reaction (pale), and this reactivation of images . . . that are the psychical and somatic co-ordinates of original aggressivity. (*Écrits*, 114–15 / 20)

The implications of this generous tribute are noteworthy: "Augustine foreshadowed psychoanalysis," no less, by describing an event whose details correspond to "the situation of spectacular absorption." In praising the prescient image and drawing a point-by-point analogy with the recognition of the reflected other, Lacan posits an equivalence between his theory and psychoanalysis itself. The primal scene of psychoanalysis is to be found in an episode of sibling jealousy at the *infans* stage and not in the agonistic encounter between father and son at the Oedipal crossroads. The verbal indicators of Lacan's dislocation—or relocation—of psychoanalysis in this passage are twofold: "ambivalent aggressivity" and "spectacular absorption."

By drawing a correlation between ambivalence and the specular counterpart, Lacan is not only readjusting his own earlier emphasis (closely related to Rank's and Klein's) on the mother as both origin and object of the individual's internal conflicts. Freud repeatedly associates feelings of ambivalence with the Oedipal crisis. In *Totem and Taboo* and other works, the primal figure who first provokes both love and hatred is the father: "[W]e need only suppose that the tumultuous mob of brothers were filled with the same contradictory feeling . . . at work in the ambivalent father-complexes of our children and of our neurotic patients. They hated their father, who presented such a formidable obstacle to their craving for power and their sexual desires; but they loved and admired him too" (*SE*, 13: 143). Freud does not, of course, leave the argument at the level of the murderous horde and tyrannical father. Seeking a similar dynamic in recorded history, he aligns ambivalence with such institutional developments as religion and monarchy: "[T]he first phases of the dominance of the two new father-surrogates—gods and kings—show the most energetic signs of the ambivalence that remains a characteristic of religion" (13: 151).

In *The Ego and the Id* and *Inhibitions, Symptoms and Anxiety*, Freud complicates the link between a specific type of conflict and ambivalence. He first focuses on the dual attitude toward the father that constitutes the "simple positive Oedipus complex in a boy" and then turns his attention to the bifurcation of ambivalence. This bifurcation corresponds to the "more complete Oedipus complex" and the "bisexuality originally present in children": "[A] boy has not merely an ambivalent attitude towards his father and an affectionate object-choice towards his mother, but at the same time he also behaves like a girl and displays an affectionate feminine attitude to his father and a corresponding jealousy and hostility towards his mother" (*SE*, 19: 33). However, in reviewing the 1909 case of little Hans, Freud reiterated in 1926 that the boy's anxiety symptoms primarily derived from "the jealous and hostile Oedipal attitude towards his father, whom nevertheless . . . he dearly loved. Here, then, we have a conflict due to ambivalence" (*SE*, 20: 101–2).

To take in the full measure of Lacan's radical departure from this thoroughly familiar position, a qualification needs to be appended to the Freudian connection between ambivalence and the father. Although Freud uses the concept to denote conflicted feelings toward a paternal figure, he also tends to apply it more broadly to account for a variety of psychical phenomena and pathological conditions. Even in the same text in which ambivalence is linked to Oedipal conflict in one chapter, it reappears in varied senses in the next: for example, as "ordinary ambivalence, which is so often unusually strong in the constitutional disposition to neurosis"; as love in the range of human relationships that is "with unexpected regularity accompanied by hate (ambivalence)"; and as "another possible mechanism" in the reactive processes of paranoia where an "ambivalent attitude is present from the outset" (*SE*, 19: 42–43). So while Freud explicitly identifies ambivalence with a paternal agency, he also applies the term loosely, even impressionistically at times, to designate an affective dualism whose model could be, as he observes, "physiological processes running in opposite directions"—namely, erotic instincts and death instincts (19: 43).

The comparison with Lacan's conceptualization of ambivalence, then, is complex. For where the Freudian concept is sometimes imprecise or general, Lacan is systematic and almost rigorously consistent in his applications; where the term has mainly clinical and descriptive significations in Freud's texts, it acquires the urgency of an ontological imperative in Lacan's; and where Freud on several occasions specifies the Oedipal father as the person toward whom ambivalence is directed, Lacan at first designates the maternal imago and, approximately ten years later, "the situation of spectacular absorption" as the causal factor (*Écrits*, 115 / 20). Lacan's own conceptual evolution is encapsulated in this wordplay on "spectacular": the spectacle (derived from the Latin *spectaculum*, view, aspect) and the specular (from *speculum*, mirror). A child who observes is being observed. The Augustinian scenario supplies a paradigmatic instance of the reciprocity—to be called "the gaze and the gazed at" in 1964 (*Seminar XI*, 74 / 77)—that characterizes visual apprehension. In fact, there is a *mise en abîme*, or serial replication of the scopic impulse, here. Lacan looks at (and identifies with) Augustine, who looks at (and identifies with) an infant who is looking at another who looks back at him.

Nevertheless, the maternal element is still operative. Shortly after Lacan's 1948 citation of Augustine, the mother materializes, in a literal sense, as the organic base of the subject. Lacan evokes a subterranean uterine region from which the subject arises to assume his place under the sun. Thus, when envisioning the "imaginary primordial enclosure formed by the *imago* of the mother's body," he proceeds to fill in that enclosure—"the cartography . . . of the mother's internal empire"—with a near surrealistic portrayal of the maternal organs as a backdrop for the activities of embattled (male) subjects: "[T]he intestinal divisions in which the *imagos* of the father and brothers (real or virtual), in which the voracious aggression of the subject himself, dispute their deleterious dominance over her sacred regions" (*Écrits*, 115 / 20–21). On the one hand, Lacan presents the maternal topos as sacerdotal and indispensable; on the other, his mode of figuration is relentlessly synecdochical. He thereby delimits, while apparently acknowledging, the mother's role in early childhood: "[L]ack of sensory and motor co-ordination does not prevent the new-born baby from being fascinated by the human face . . . nor from showing in the clearest possible way that from all the people around him he singles out his mother" ("Some Reflections," 15). But what the sight of the mother's *face* cannot grant is "the gestalt of the vision of the whole body image." The neonate may be drawn especially to the human face and even to the mother's face above all others; however, the gestalt essential to the "elusive process of Becoming" does not prevail until the confrontation with the (br)other. The mother gives the biological basis for life, or what Lacan calls the "background of organic disturbance and discord" (15), but not the capacity for ego formation through "spectacular" encounters.

Scene III

Lacan had the good fortune—or foresight, and the link between these words is of course more than phonological, to select an exemplum in 1938 that was eminently reusable for his evolving purposes. Even when different theoretical concerns become uppermost, the passage from the *Confessions* continues to reinforce the implications of his work. The final section of this chapter focuses on a reference written approximately ten years after the essay on the ego.

At the close of a four-chapter analysis entitled "Of the Gaze as *Objet Petit a*," in *The Four Fundamental Concepts of Psycho-Analysis* (1964),[8] Lacan cites Augustine once again. This citation is quite possibly the most complex of all his recyclings. The anecdote of the jealous child functions as a kind of hub or nodal point in which various lines of argument converge. It is therefore helpful to review the cardinal connections leading up to the renewed citation. Lacan establishes the contingency of several concepts in these densely argued chapters: the gaze ("[I]n my existence I am looked at from all sides"); lack (*manque*); castration ("The gaze is . . . symbolic of . . . the thrust of our experience, namely, the lack that constitutes castration anxiety"), and the deliberately untranslated, algebraic *objet petit a* (*Seminar XI*, 69–70 / 72–73). He continually defines and refines these terms in relation to one another. Thus the "gaze may contain in itself the *objet a* of the Lacanian algebra"; and, the "gaze, *qua objet a*, may come to symbolize this central lack expressed in the phenomenon of castration" (73 / 76–77). Insofar as the gaze has the character or capacity of the *objet a*, it is also coextensive with the concepts of lack and castration and, as will be seen, with phallic emblems of castration.

The idea repeatedly brought to bear on the gaze and its coordinates is desire. As Lacan's English translator points out, *désir* is unlike the one-time or specific Freudian *Wunsch* (wish): "[T]he German and English words are limited to individual, isolated acts of wishing, while the French has the much stronger implication of a continuous force" (*Seminar XI*, 278; also *Écrits*, viii). In the relations of subject to subject, the structure of desire depends primarily on visual effects. It is "in the domain of seeing," as Lacan states, that "desire is established" (*Seminar XI*, 80 / 85). What you see is what you want. And therefore, the "geometral dimension of vision"—which organizes and maps out space—is far from exhausting "what the field of vision as such offers us as the original subjectifying relation" (81 / 87). When Lacan explains to an interlocutor, "If one does not stress the dialectic of desire one does not understand why the gaze of others should disorganize the field of perception" (83 / 89), it also becomes clear why he seeks exemplarity in the obscure phallomorphic structure that floats across the floor of Hans Holbein's otherwise precise, geometrically delineated *The Ambassadors* (1533). For Lacan, this object "which from some angles appears to be flying through the air, at others to be tilted," is no less than the "imaged embodiment of the *minus-phi* $[(-\phi)]$ of castration, which for us, centres the whole organization of the desires" (82–83 / 88–89). The linkage that Lacan invites us to contemplate here draws on—and also transfigures—the corporal reality of the male sex organ through its visual assimilation to Holbein's pictorial object and the abstract symbol *minus-phi*.

Thus, Holbein's oblique memento mori, the stretched-out skull that may be perceived as such only from a particular position, has a twofold symbolic value in Lacan's text. Its distortion illustrates the domain of the gaze as (dis)-organized by desire. It is a reminder not merely of mortality but of misrecognition, of all that escapes from the field of geometral vision.[9] What you see is rarely what is out there. Moreover, the figure of the skull suggests to Lacan (and he grants that it could represent, say, a "cuttlebone" for another author) the concept of the phallus. It brings to mind or, rather, to his mind's eye, Salvador Dali's "soft watches, whose signification is obviously less phallic than that of the object depicted in a flying position in the foreground of this picture" (*Seminar XI*, 83 / 88). This association between skull and soft watches is not as wild as it might appear—if one remembers that time, too, is said to fly.

Yet how Holbein's and Dali's variously distorted emblems of mortality lead back to Augustine's image of jealousy is not patently obvious. In the four chapters devoted to the gaze as *objet a*, Lacan's preference for paths of indirection is more than usually evident. The overall movement of his argument may therefore be better tracked if its point of departure is identified: the Freudian text to which Lacan implicitly returns throughout these chapters is "The 'Uncanny.'" Freud famously posits a "substitutive relation between the eye and the male organ" in his essay. These organs remain closely aligned, however, with their anatomical functions (*SE*, 17: 231). Conversely, although structures of substitution and juxtaposition also characterize Lacan's analysis in *The Four Fundamental Concepts*, actual body parts do not enter as such into his presentation of the gaze and the phallus. As he explains, "It is not a question of the relation to sexuality, or even to the sex [of the subject]" (94 / 102). Instead, "the eye may function as *objet a*, that is to say, at the level of lack," which, in turn, is represented by the phallus "in so far as it is lacking" (96 / 104, 95 / 103).

The Lacanian idea of the gaze, with all of its nonanatomical correlatives, could also be read in a different way as a figure of intersubjectivity. If, on the one hand, Lacan delimits the subject as "annihilated" and "imaged" in the varied forms of castration, on the other, he refers to the subject as "sustaining himself in a function of desire" that presupposes the gaze of the other (*Seminar XI*, 83 / 88–89, 80 / 85). The gaze partakes of the properties of being-in-difference (the symbolic or signifying network) as well as of nothingness. Acknowledging Sartre, Lacan contends: "The gaze in question is certainly the presence of others as such" (80 / 84). Freud's initial "substitutive relation" thus complexly extends into different registers. The signifying functions of the eye and the male organ come into conjunction with several coordinated concepts. Together these concepts form a chain (phallus = lack = *objet a* = gaze = others) that maps and traps the subject within the scopic field.

Lacan foregrounds the place that is also the predicament of the fractured subject—the subject caught up in the lure of the imaginary and constituted through differential relations with others—by means of a fragmented word in italics: "I am *photo-graphed* [*je suis* photo-graphié]."[10] As the portrait of *The Ambassadors* illustrates, the fact of external focalization, of being looked at and re-presented to one's self is crucial for the skein of reflexive consciousness that delimits subjectivity. In the scopic field, the *I* becomes the product of such representation, submitted to or "under" the gaze of the other whose locus is the *Umwelt*. Through the instrumentality of what may be called an otherworldly gaze, the contours of the subject receive a shape and local definition: "What determines me, at the most profound level, in the visible, is *the gaze that is outside*." One answer to the question posed in Lacan's chapter title "What Is a Picture?" is then, "I am looked at . . . I am a picture" (*Seminar XI*, 98 / 106; emphasis added). The magisterial certainty of "I think, therefore I am" is not so much controverted here as transformed. In situating the emergence of subjectivity in the lived and looked-at body, Lacan's formulations undermine the mutual exclusivity of traditional metaphysical categories: mind/matter, spirit/flesh, contained/container, and so forth. The split he imagines lies elsewhere. Even if implicitly or inadvertently, his distance from the Cartesian *cogito* is pronounced. "I have introduced painting into our field of exploration by the narrow door offered us by Roger Caillois—everyone noticed last time that I made a slip of the tongue in calling him René, heaven knows why" (100 / 109).

It is via painting that Lacan arrives at the notion of showing, *le donner-à-voir* ("literally, 'to give to be seen' and, therefore, 'to offer to the view'" [*Seminar XI*, 105 n. 2]), and via showing that unexpectedly and yet somehow predictably, he turns to Augustine's anecdote. In so doing, he discards the materiality of deprivation at the oral level in favor of a metaphoricity of the ravenous eye; more precisely, the figural linkage of seeing and appetite, of food for the eye, verges on literal application in the final paragraphs of his discussion. Properties of the mouth are transferred to the eye, just as the functions of the maternal imago were previously relegated to the specular counterpart. In short, the eye becomes a kind of mouth. Here is how it happens:

> Modifying the formula I have of desire as unconscious—*man's desire is the desire of the Other*—I would say that it is a question of a sort of desire *on the part of* the Other, at the end of which is the *showing* (*le donner-à-voir*).
>
> How could this *showing* satisfy something, if there is not some appetite of the eye on the part of the person looking? (105 / 115)

Lacan now attaches to his familiar adaptation of Kojève's formula—"Desire is human only if the one desires . . . the Desire of the other"—the following entailment: "the appetite of the eye that must be fed." This appetite is restricted but not selective. The eye feeds itself on those objects for which someone else displays desire. The desire shown and the showing seen generate the vagaries of human perception. The value of the object, indeed, its very existence in the world of desired objects, is mitigated (as well as heightened) by its vulnerability. The eye diminishes, destroys, or poisons what it hungers after and cannot obtain.

For this reason, Lacan announces: "[T]he true function of the organ of the eye, the eye filled with voracity, [is] the evil eye." With the mention of the eye's voracity, from the Latin *vorare*, to devour, the associative leap to the little child looking at his nursing brother "*amare conspectu*, with a bitter look" seems almost inevitable (*Seminar XI*, 105 / 115–16). In describing the small-town environment in which Saint Augustine was raised, Peter Brown observes in his biography, "It is not surprising that 'envy' should be one of the emotions which Augustine understood most deeply. We can appreciate its power among his fellow-Africans through scores of amulets against the evil eye" (32). Whether this detail of Augustine's life was available to Lacan or not is difficult to say. Before recalling the anecdote, however, he takes a brief detour through a persuasion that has existed for millennia in diverse cultures around the world: the belief in the malevolent powers of the eye.

I would point out that the line of Lacan's argumentation being traced here is, at the same time, freely associative, even poetic, and also profoundly coherent and logically ordered.[11] Showing leads to envy leads to the evil eye: "*Invidia*," Lacan explains in *The Four Fundamental Concepts*, "comes from *videre*" (105 / 115), the Latin word for "envy" deriving from the verb "to see." Envy, as anthropological evidence shows, is linked to the evil eye throughout the Indo-European and Semitic worlds (see, e.g., Roberts, 229, 234). The phenomenon is widespread both historically and geographically. Amulets against the evil eye are not only to be found in Augustine's Africa and in remedies dating from the ancient Greeks and Romans. Its effects already appear in a 5,000-year-old Sumerian text that opens with this litany of injuries: "The eye afflicting man with evil, the *ad-gir*. Unto heaven it approached and the storm sent no rain; unto earth it approached and the fresh verdure sprang not forth. . . . Unto the stalls it approached, and milk . . . was no longer plentiful" (Langdon, 40). A form of witchcraft that causes a variety of misfortunes or calamities, the evil eye is predisposed to drying up milk and water. It is nonetheless noteworthy that among the many disasters in-

flicted by the evil eye, Lacan selects for emphasis "[t]he powers that are attributed to it, of drying up the milk of an animal on which it falls—a belief
as widespread in our time as in any other, and in the most civilized coun-
tries." The word "milk" supplies the link that brings Lacan back to his favored citation. "The most exemplary *invidia*, for us analysts," he argues, "is
the one I found long ago in Augustine" (*Seminar XI*, 105 / 115–16).

But of course the contenders for such exemplary status are numerous and
far-ranging. Especially striking is the frequent association of lactation (liquid) with dryness in the evil eye belief.[12] To cite one example, the anthropologist Clarence Maloney reports on the evil eye in South Asia: "A family in
Kerala had a goat with a big udder. Someone came and commented on it,
and the next day that goat gave bloody milk. Soon the milk decreased to the
point where the goat had to be sold" (107). Hence the strict observance of
protective injunctions: "Milk behind a palm-leaf screen or out of sight of
passersby, for if someone notices that the milk is abundant the next day it
will diminish" (117). One of the most common prophylactic measures taken
to ward off the evil eye is spitting. (The sound "pfut, pfut" uttered before ex-
pressing admiration is a derivative of this remedial practice.) Presumably,
spitting works because it counteracts the drying-up effects caused by casting
an evil eye.[13] However, the types of sorcery attributed to the evil eye can be
far worse than the ruination of a milk or water supply. A look can kill. As a
field study of Slovak and Slovak-American rituals reveals, anything said "ad-
miringly (without spitting first, thereby breaking the spell) will cause immediate destruction to what is admired. . . . An inadvertent compliment or stare
will kill an infant." The "preventative medicine" of spitting is therefore required to contain the damage of the evil eye (Stein, 201, 209). Clearly, the
nursing child in Augustine's vignette is endangered because his slightly older
brother knows how to stare but still must learn to spit.

Observations of this belief and ritual activity extend from Pliny's *Natural
History* ("the right course on the arrival of a stranger, or if a sleeping baby is
looked at, is for the nurse to spit three times at her charge") to Giuseppe
Pitrè's late nineteenth-century reports from Sicily and Italy ("one sees mothers who catch some dubious woman kissing their babies, spit energetically in
her direction as soon as they see her turn her back") to the psychoanalytic
folklorist Géza Róheim's 1952 analysis of Hungarian peasant customs: "In
the evening any careful mother or loving aunt will lick the child's eyes three

times. Each time she spits right, left, backwards" (Pliny 28.39; Pitrè, 137; Róheim, 354). And while performing these nightly rites, she utters a protective incantation that enumerates all the people who might have seen the child during the day. Mischief is unpredictable and may come from unexpected directions: "'Auntie Borcsa, Auntie Sára, all that have seen you, may they not harm you.'" The "key to the whole evil eye belief," according to Róheim, is oral jealousy and oral aggression. This "key" leads to a distinction between the roles of child-victim and parental-protector. In those who fear the evil eye, the "aggression of the sucking infant is projected" onto the figure of a "hostile devouring" witch-mother. In those who have recourse to countermagical remedies, mainly mothers and midwives, "it reveals that they themselves are identified with the evil one and they are now spitting the child out, instead of devouring him" (Róheim, 356, 358).

Spitting is not only, then, intended to protect the young child from ill-wishers. It also deflects the aggression experienced by family members or caretakers and projects it onto others in their environment. Without expressly mentioning Freud, Róheim's "The Evil Eye" apparently takes up another suggestion made in "The 'Uncanny'"—namely, that "dread of the evil eye" derives from fear of envy compounded by mechanisms of projection: "Whoever possesses something that is at once valuable and fragile is afraid of other people's envy, in so far as he projects on to them the envy he would have felt in their place" (*SE*, 17: 240). Although the eye is the prime instrument of injury, orality or a cannibalistic component is also crucial in this belief complex. Other anthropological investigations have corroborated Róheim's psychoanalytic emphasis on the oral. For example, villagers in rural Greece, in describing their competitive jealousy and hostility toward any achievement and happiness of other villagers, repeatedly use phrases of incorporation to express their feelings: "'We eat each other,' or 'They eat the bride,' [or] 'They eat the newborn infant'" (Blum and Blum, 128). In these communities, the effects of the evil eye are numerous, "disabling targets as diverse as humans and locomotives" (132).

Lacan bridges the gap between the cultural-folkloric beliefs observed in an ethnographic frame of reference and psychoanalytic explanation in a different way. He connects the evil eye phenomenon to the reflexive dynamics of the mirror stage and to the concept of the gaze. The child, "seeing his

brother at his mother's breast," stares at him with deadly intent, "with a bitter look, which seems to tear him [the brother] to pieces and has on himself
the effect of a poison" (*Seminar XI*, 105 / 116). The evil he wishes on the
other rebounds on himself. The poisoner himself is not poisoned because
Lacan would uphold a belief in "poetic justice" or divine retribution; rather,
it is due to a doubling in which the separated form or image is also a part of
one's self. The operative mechanism is reflexivity, or a kind of projection *in-
ward* to the other who inhabits the subject. The Lacanian connection between the evil eye and the spec(tac)ular may therefore be glossed by another
citational allusion. In "Aggressivity in Psychoanalysis," Lacan quotes and
compliments the "truth" of this insight: "'I is an other,'" describing it as "an
observation that is less astonishing to the intuition of the poet than obvious
to the gaze of the psychoanalyst" (*Écrits*, 23 / 118). Arthur Rimbaud's "Je est
un autre" appears after his statement, in a letter dated 13 May 1871, that
"C'est faux de dire: Je pense. On devrait dire: On me pense [It is false to say:
I think. One ought to say: People think me]" (302–3). Both Rimbaud's "I is
an other" and Lacan's "I am *photo-graphed*" intentionally unsettle the ontological assumption that anything concerned with human subjectivity might
be as self-contained and self-enclosed as Descartes's *cogito*. The poet's perception of the self's extraneousness to itself, like the situation in the Augustinian vignette, serves to reinforce Lacan's quarrel with the Cartesian subject
of certainty.

No less important for the integration of anthropology and psychoanalysis is Lacan's distinction between jealousy and envy. "In order to understand
what *invidia* is in its function as gaze," he writes, "it must not be confused
with jealousy. What the small child, or whoever, *envies* is not at all necessarily what he might want—*avoir envie*, as one improperly puts it" (*Seminar XI*,
106 / 116). Jealousy, however, as defined in *Les complexes familiaux*, represents a form of mental identification that precedes differentiation from and
rivalry with the double. The definition offered almost thirty years later in
The Four Fundamental Concepts is, by comparison, conventional. Jealousy apparently addresses a specific need or demand ("what he might want"),
whereas envy is a far more pervasive craving for possession. Jealousy can
characterize both animal and human subjects, whereas envy is a strictly human disposition. Jealousy, it may further be inferred, is to *Wunsch* as envy is

to *désir*. "Who can say that the child who looks at his younger brother still needs to be at the breast?" (106 / 16). That he still needs the breast at which his unweaned rival sucks is doubtful. But that he desires it is not in question.

The attempt to define or circumscribe envy yields yet another assertion on Lacan's part: "Everyone knows that envy is usually aroused by the possession of goods which would be of no use to the person who is envious of them, and about the true nature of which he does not have the least idea." The idea of a coveted object that is not just unneeded but also fundamentally unknown is a major adjustment. The imago of the maternal breast no longer exists in correlation to the final reference point of desire. In the ego's narcissistic experience of the other, every object of envy, including the maternal object, is a surrogate or a symbol for something that cannot be properly named. The term *objet a* stands in place of a gap. It marks the void, the lack, the ever-receding cause of the serial substitutions that organize the human drives: "Such is true envy—the envy that makes the subject pale before the image of a completeness closed upon itself, before the idea that the *petit a*, the separated *a* from which he is hanging, may be for another the possession that gives satisfaction, *Befriedigung*" (*Seminar XI*, 106 / 116).

Two folk ideas may serve to connect this allusion to Augustine's rival brothers with the evil eye phenomenon. First, as Lacan observes, the child pales before an *image*—that is, before an illusory perception or mirage of the completeness and satisfaction belonging to the other. In proverbial terms, the grass is always greener elsewhere. Hence the remedies resorted to in Pakistan: "Hang up a black rag in the field," and in Maharashtra: "Tie a coconut shell or an old shoe on a choice fruit tree or vine." The rag, or coconut shell, or shoe will, it may be hoped, attract the attention of passersby "so they will not look at the crops" (Maloney, 116). And in fourth-century Spain, the Council of Elvira passed a canon law that "forbade Jews to stand among ripening crops belonging to Christians lest they cause the crops to rot and wither with their malevolent glances" (Moss and Cappannari, 8).[14] Because the evil eye is rampant, great care must be taken to tame or avoid it. Nothing here is out of keeping with Lacan's understanding of the workings of human perception and the gaze. "One thinks it is a question of the geometral eye-point," as he explains, "whereas it is a question of a quite different eye" (*Seminar XI*, 83 / 89).

The second idea, however, is not easily reconciled with Lacanian theory.

It is a self-evident truth to many peoples that twice-weaned infants are highly susceptible to the evil eye. A few statements about the dangers of double weaning gathered during interviews with Slovak-Americans mothers in Pennsylvania vividly display this belief. The word *oči* means "eyes" in Slovak, and *počorič*, "to cast a spell" (Stein, 196):

> They say baby get evil eye if mother go back nurse the child after she take him off the breast. . . . You never say: "That's nice" [about the baby], because it will turn bad. . . . Spit first and then say what you want. When you wean your baby, *don't ever go back! Finished! Done!*
>
> No more breast. Quite final. Nine months, one year, 14–15 months breast feed. Once you stopped, you never go back. Evil eye: *počorič*.
>
> If she puts the baby back . . . —something about the eyes. *Oči* —strangers shouldn't stare at babies. Stop once feeding baby breast—giving back causes *oči* . . . . Baby could even die from it. . . . She [a two-month-old baby] doesn't sleep—cries. My husband lit three matches. Drop them in water. They sink—somebody must have stared. (Stein, 198–99)

Likewise, in locales ranging from Greece to Romania to Sweden, it is self-evident that being weaned twice might bring the evil eye and even death upon the child (Blum and Blum, 186; Murgoci, 125; Róheim, 356). Yet why renewed weaning should be thus linked to the evil eye is not apparent. According to the folklorist Alan Dundes, Melanie Klein's theory of the maternal breast as the primary object of infantile envy serves to explain popular beliefs about the harmful effects of weaning reversal (Dundes, 271). Reciprocally, I suggest, anthropological evidence corroborates Klein's clinical findings, such as those reported in her 1956 lecture "A Study of Envy and Gratitude": "My work has shown me that the first object to be envied is the feeding breast, for the infant feels that it possesses everything that he [*sic*] desires and that it has an unlimited flow of milk and love which it keeps for its own gratification" (213). Returning an infant to the breast after weaning reinforces greedy behavior and possibly deprives a younger sibling. Double weaning thus produces a person who in later life either inflicts the evil eye on others by always craving for more, or deservedly suffers from the evil eye for displaying excessive envy. Greed, in this view, is dangerously enhanced by maternal gratification and indulgence.

Lacan similarly describes an inextricable connection between the process of weaning and later interhuman relations in his 1938 essay on the family.

This elaboration no longer holds in the 1964 reference to Augustine. Lacan's formulation replaces or erases the functions of the maternal breast and weaning through the abstraction of the "separated *a*"—a symbol removed as far as language will allow from the realm of actual objects or persons: "Such is true envy . . . the idea that the *petit a*, the separated *a* from which he is hanging, may be for another the possession that gives satisfaction." Relatedly, in a very brief citation of the same scene in 1973, Lacan provides a series of terminological equivalents, all intended to suggest that what is at stake in the jealous child's observation of the sibling—"hanging on the nipple [*tétine*]," as he puts it—is beyond the mere corporeality of maternal nurture: "the *a*," "the first substitute jouissance," "the desire evoked on the basis of a metonymy," "what I called *Ding* . . . namely, the Freudian Thing." In a further effacement of the agency that is already reduced to something akin to the nipple of a bottle or an animal teat, Lacan punningly writes: "L'enfant regardé lui l'a, le *a*" (*Seminar XX*, 91 / 100). The infant who is looked at, he is the one who has it, the *a*. Possession is (like beauty) a function of perception.

Yet, although Lacan traduces the maternal into a representation of the *objet a*, a residual presence haunts his symbolic scenario. It is as if the mouth that was banished returns; the effaced is reconfigured. For surely he could have picked up or "found" (*relevée*) (*Seminar XI*, 105 / 16) an image less imbued with literal attachment to the mother, and a consciousness less demonstrably, less ambiguously aware of its debts to a maternal agent than that displayed throughout the *Confessions*. Following the specular example of Saint Augustine, Lacan strives to divest himself of, to transcend his "garments of flesh" (*Confessions* 8.11.175). However, in his many citations of the exemplary anecdote, something remains unassimilable to his systemic incorporation and conversion. Something remains resistant to his removal of the embodied figure of the mother nursing her child onto the rarefied, algebraic plane of the *objet a*.

CHAPTER 9

"Grandma, what a dreadfully big mouth you have!"

Lacan's Parables of the Maternal Object

From the mid 1940s on, Lacan conceived of visuality and the eye as the primary psycho-physical organ in the formation of the *I*. This emphasis on the function of the eye is antithetically linked, as argued in Chapter 5, to a "forgetting" or neglect of the mouth, the sensory organ that, in Lacan's 1938 view, predominates during the weaning complex. However, beginning with his seminar on *La relation d'objet, 1956–1957*, the mouth, in a manner of speaking, returns. It is neither the infant mouth "sucking and gripping" at the maternal breast nor the "fusional cannibalism" of the nursling he had previously described (*CF*, 29–30 / 15). Rather, it is the mouth of the mother that becomes paramount in his revised formulations. At the same time, Lacan elaborates the Freudian theory of the Oedipus complex by introducing the "paternal metaphor," a concept also designated by terms such as symbolic father, paternal function, phallic signifier, and Name-of-the-Father. The father's role is to extricate and protect the child from a very dangerous place whose metaphoric analogue is the workings of the mother's mouth.

In what follows, I present Lacan's theoretical revisions via a series of narratives, including the fable of a child and a crocodile, the case histories of an obsessional man ("Philo") and a phobic boy ("Little Hans"), Victor Hugo's retelling of the biblical encounter of Ruth and Boaz, and Hesiod's descriptions of family violence among the ancient gods. Added to these exemplary narratives, I propose to recall several folkloric, fairy-tale, and psychoanalytic accounts of a little girl who meets a wolf. Her story provides a kind of linking or metatext for the others presented here.

I

In a passage from the seminar entitled *L'envers de la psychanalyse*, 1969–1970, Lacan addresses the mother-child relation and its restructuration during the Oedipal crisis:

> The mother's role is her desire. That is of capital importance. Her desire is not something you can bear easily, as if it were a matter of indifference to you. It always leads to problems. The mother is a big crocodile, and you find yourself in her mouth. You never know what may set her off suddenly, making those jaws clamp down. That is the mother's desire.
>
> So I tried to explain that there was something reassuring. I am telling you simple things—indeed, I am improvising. There is a roller, made of stone, of course, which is potentially there at the level of the trap and which holds and jams it open. That is what we call the phallus. It is a roller which protects you, should the jaws suddenly close. (*Seminar XVII*, 129; trans. in Fink, 56–57)

The Oedipal process necessitates a movement from an all-consuming dyadic unity (mother-child) to a triangulated dimension of human relations (father-mother-child). The symbolic element represented by the phallic signifier, that is, the father's name or interdiction ("le nom-non du père") intervenes and produces a space in which the child may attain libidinal normalization. In these paragraphs, as Bruce Fink observes, "Lacan sums up in very schematic terms what he had been saying for years" (56).

The dual relationship of mother and child, however, is also triadic. From the outset, what Lacan ambiguously calls the "désir de la mère" (the child's desire for the mother and the mother's own desire) implicates an imaginary term—the phallus: "[T]he notion that the mother lacks this phallus, that she is herself desiring . . . will be for the subject most decisive of all" (*Seminar IV*, 71). In this view, the Oedipus complex involves the transformation of a preoedipal triangulated unity into another type of construct: the imaginary triad of mother-infant-phallus serves as a "prelude" to the symbolic relations that can only go into effect with the "fourth function, that of the father, introduced by the Oedipal dimension." The fourth term, "le quatuor," which constitutes itself with the appearance of the paternal function reforms or, rather, annuls the initial mother-child constellation: "The triangle is in itself preoedipal" (81). With such definitional statements, Lacan radically alters the very shape of Freud's conception of the Oedipus complex. The Oedipal is in itself a quadrangle.

The example of the crocodile and the roller may also be reprised another formulaic arrangement:

$$\frac{\text{Name-of-the-Father}}{\text{Desire of the Mother}}$$

This formula brings out the figural dimension of the father's name; that is, it clearly shows the substitution of the paternal signifier for the mother's desire (see *Écrits*, 557 / 200) . Lacan further condenses this substitutive process into a single phrase—the paternal metaphor: "[T]he paternal function seems to us to be, for the subject, of the order of a metaphoric experience" (*Seminar IV*, 376). Insofar as the paternal metaphor is operative, it need not coincide with a biological father. It may take the shape of any person or object or interest that for the mother is not coextensive with her child. In representing the object of the mother's desire, the symbolic father constitutes a rival phallus that opposes the imaginary phallus with which the infant identifies in the preoedipal situation. The intrusion of this rival detaches the infant from the psychical dangers of fusional identification, from wanting to be the mother's phallus, from striving to fill completely the place of her lack. The renunciation of this position is prerequisite for the accession to the dimension of language and law where the symbolic phallus prevails.

But if the paternal metaphor does not enter and break up the mother-child enclosure, if for any reason she refuses to allow the substitutive function of the father, the following devastation might result:

The efficacity proper to this aggressive intention is manifest: we constantly observe it in the formative action of an individual on those dependent on him; intended aggressivity gnaws away, undermines, disintegrates; it castrates; it leads to death: "And I thought you were impotent!" growled a mother, suddenly transformed into a tigress, to her son, who, with great difficulty, had admitted to her his homosexual tendencies. And one could see that her permanent aggressivity as a virile woman had had its effect. (*Écrits*, 104 / 10–11)

Whether or not a real father was part of this family setting is immaterial. The father's absence (*carence paternelle*) at the symbolic level, his deficiency or non-intercession, owing in all likelihood to the man-eating or "virile" woman, precipitated the son's homosexuality. The perverse structure of this subject (Lacan classifies homosexuality as a perversion), irrespective of the sexual acts in which he engages, entails his atypical position vis-à-vis the paternal signifier in the Oedipus complex (*Seminar IV*, 201).

Furthermore, on the basis of the mother's response to her son, it is also reasonable to assume that before she set about gnawing at, undermining, and castrating him, she had feasted on his father. In other words, this woman rendered "the signifier of the Father, as author of the Law" inoperative (*Écrits*, 556 / 199); or, symbolically speaking, the phallus became totally dysfunctional. Hence her assumption might be slightly rephrased: "And I thought you were impotent *too!*" Under these circumstances, the Name-of-the-Father could not take up its superordinate position in the formula of Oedipal substitution.

From the atypical we may learn, as Freud repeatedly reminds us, about the normative and typical. From the examples of the crocodile and the tigress, we may also extract a moral lesson. It is incumbent upon the mother to turn to the fourth term, to signal that she is lacking and dependent, to affirm that she desires for herself something other than the child-phallus. The paternal signifier only appears on the scene with this maternal concession. "The advent of the *symbolic Father* as Name-of-the Father," Joël Dor writes in his highly informative account, "attests to the infant's recognition of a *castrator Father*, not only owing to the phallic attribute accorded him, but even more to the very fact that the mother is supposed to find in him the desired object that she does not have" (64). Dor's precise wording—"la mère est supposée trouver"—indicates what should but, unhappily, does not always happen. Whereas for Freud the father's prohibition of incest and accompanying castration threats enable the dissolution of the Oedipus complex, for Lacan the mother's acknowledgment of her castration and desire for the symbolic phallus is essential. As Lacan reconstructs the Oedipal situation, the emphasis falls on the mother's relation to the father and how her "formative action" impinges on the child who is dependent on her (*Écrits*, 104 / 10).

This reformulation of the maternal role involves a partly paradoxical, threefold consequence: added to the imperative of subordination to the Name-of-the-Father, a formidable power is relegated to the mother as well as an endless responsibility for the (mal)formation of her child. For should the paternal metaphor not assume its proper position in the Oedipal configuration, the explicit cause is often the mother's desire: "[O]ne could see that her permanent aggressivity as a virile woman had had its effect." When she does not concede her desire for the symbolic phallus, her refusal is manifest in the child. Thus the mother as "matrix" in Lacan's 1938 essay on the family evolves into the mother as "mediatrix" in the mid 1950s—unless she is otherwise intent or, more precisely, bent on becoming a tigress.

II

In 1959, Serge Leclaire, whose attempt to present Freud's text on narcissism was discussed in Chapter 6, published an essay, "Philo, or the Obsessional and His Desire," that both explicates Lacan's thesis and exemplifies it by means of a case history. Leclaire distinguishes three phases in the crucial process that *"substitutes for the mother, taken as the central and primordial character, the father, as principal and ultimate reference."* During the first phase the child, whether girl or boy, seems to believe in a simple formula: "'To please mother, it is necessary and sufficient to be the phallus'" (121). The child identifies with the imaginary object of the mother's desire. The wish to fill up the whole space of her lack seems an achievable consummation. In this closed amatory circle, the child hardly dissociates from the mother.

The next stage is the most dangerous and delicate of all. "It is at this stage," Leclaire cautions, "that most of the accidents that generate neurosis occur." The infant soon realizes the mother's desire is directed elsewhere: "[A] reference or a symbol that has captured the mother's desire appears in the child's life, even before its nature is specified. In this way a *third person* presents himself to experience." Although analytic treatment demonstrates that "this third person, this father, appears especially *as a being to whom one refers* (to honor or to scorn) and to whom one refers as to a law," it is only through what Leclaire calls "the mediation of the mother's desire" that such recognition actually takes place. During the phase of Oedipal quadrangulation, the child "should gain access to the father's law, defined as the place of the *symbolic* phallus" (121–22). Like Dor's "is supposed to," the modality of Leclaire's "should gain access to" indicates the difficulty that arises when a mother fails to reveal her subordinate relation to the father's name. She does not suffer the infant object to be separated from herself. She blankets it, suffocates it, consumes it with her all-inclusive love.

However, if and when the second stage is successfully traversed, then the father not only becomes the symbolic referent of the law: "[H]e also possesses a *real* penis. In a word, the father is one who has the phallus and not the one who *is* it." During the third phase, boys and girls alike discover that the father is "the real possessor, and not merely the symbolic place, of a penis"; and so they renounce their earlier desire to be the "'phallus that pleases Mama'" (122). Leclaire's formulations closely follow both Freud and Lacan at this particular juncture. Just as the term "phallus" tends to slide in their discursive usage between the symbolic and the anatomical registers, so it eludes, at times, definitive placement in his essay.[1] But no ambiguity exists about the mother's position in the formulaic resolution of the Oedipus complex: "Thus the father, as the place of the phallus, replaces the mother as the principal and normative subject in the evolution. The mother, no longer the central character she was, takes on the role of mediator" (122). Recapitulation here is not far removed from recommendation.

Yet what happens if the mother resists the role of mediator? What if instead of a caterer to the paternal function, she is, for instance, a "crocodile"? Both father and child do not seem to stand a chance. In Leclaire's clinical example, the motif of mother-blame receives full expression. Close to thirty and unmarried, the alias "Philo" apparently never got beyond the preliminary phase. The father was excluded and the son fixated at stage one:

> If [Philo] does not say, "To please my mother it is necessary and sufficient
> that I be the phallus," he is not very far off when he says, "My unique goal is

to be the only thing necessary to my mother." All that matters is to please her, and that is how he finds his own pleasure. . . .

What happened, then, during the second stage, when he ought to have been opened to desire and the law through his mother's mediation? . . . [I]nstead of a dissatisfaction that could drive him to look at the relation between his mother and the enigma of the father, Philo encountered his mother's satisfaction.

Why? Very simply because his mother shifted her desire over to him, with all the unconscious and disturbing tenderness of a woman neurotically unsatisfied. . . . Philo summarized with these words: "It is as though she had found in me the satisfaction that she did not find in my father." (122–23)

The mother who "ought to have been" filling, and fulfilled in, her mediatory role imposed herself as "goal and object." Philo's desire, according to Leclaire, became the captive of her "unendingly sterile and exhausting" world: "Since then he has lived as though he were in a prison and as though he loved the prison" (123). Put another way, this mother neurotically, incestuously embedded her son within herself, not allowing him to cross over into the Oedipal dimension. Her passion was for control, for containing and holding, so that she could possess the child herself. Better to destroy, she said, than to lose or share him with another.

Leclaire recalls a pun of his obsessional, compulsively indecisive patient: "At the tenderest age, [Philo] tells me, wanting to appear witty, he already did not know which breast [*sein*, pronounced like *saint* in French] to choose. Matters have not changed: . . . the priesthood or marriage—it does not matter as long as someone else makes the decision" (115). Had Mama only been a gracious mediator, a devotee instead of a devourer of the paternal phallus, things might have worked out differently for Philo. He was kept too long inside a gravid monster.

III

By way of further reflection, Lacan's interesting menagerie might be held up to another figure of rapacious hunger: the wolf in the story of Little Red Riding Hood. I want to approach this wolf cautiously, metacritically, via a series of psychoanalytic essays on the Grimms' "Little Red Cap" ("Rotkäppchen") and then, to compare the disparate endings in other versions. This detour will facilitate a return to the crocodile of *Seminar XVII*, although with an altered perspective, given by looking, so to speak, through different glasses.

In two essays on denial and the story of *Rotkäppchen*, Rivka Eifermann, a practicing psychoanalyst and teacher at the Hebrew University, raises the question of why the little girl fails to perceive at once that the wolf is not her grandmother. "In the large variety of drawings of 'grandmother' in bed," Eifermann remarks, "it is the wolf that lies there, quite unmistakably. And children who look at these drawings unhesitatingly recognize him for what he is" ("Varieties of Denial," 159). Indeed, if one rules out the possibility that Little Red Cap suffers from mental retardation, temporary derangement, or a tendency to hallucination—and the child appears to be quite normal, nonpsychotic—then her denial of the traumatic reality before her is no less peculiar than the creature she sees in the bed: "The grandmother had her cap pulled way down over her face, and looked very very strange" (Grimm and Grimm, 100).

On the level of aesthetic motivation, denial is a prerequisite of the fairy-tale plot. Little Red Cap's misrecognition of the wolf leads to the unholy catechism for which the story is famous: "Oh, grandmother, what big ears you have!" "The better to hear you with," and so forth until the climactic moment when the wolf "bound[s] out of bed and gobble[s] up poor Little Red Cap" (100). Plot requirements, however, do not seem adequately to account for her denial. That the wolf has cross-dressed in grandmother's night clothes provides a flimsy excuse. "It may seem pedantic to demand logic from a genre that traffics in the supernatural," Maria Tatar observes, "but even fairy tales have their ground rules" (36).

Drawing on personal experiences as a child raised by parents of German-Jewish origin, Eifermann interprets Little Red Cap's denial as a result of overregulation: "To me she was extremely obedient to her mother, *had* to see things through her mother's eyes, and that, therefore, since mother had instructed her to go to *grandmother* (and did not mention any wolf), it *had* to be grandmother lying in the bed in her cottage" ("Interactions," 42). In contrast to the customary stress on the child's disobedience and transgression ("So she left the path and went into the wood . . . "), Eifermann brings out the component of docility in her behavior. To translate this insight into Lacanian terms, Little Red Cap was so well installed in the symbolic regime of which her mother was a premier exponent that she could not recognize the reality of the wolf. Her mother *said*: Go to your *grandmother*'s house. The sway of the signifier, the word "grandmother," constituted for her what she saw in the bed. She therefore, quite illogically, sought "help and reassurance from the very source of her terror" ("Varieties of Denial," 159).

In a third essay on the fairy tale, Eifermann explores her sustained, unconscious conflation between her own internalized mother who, on a certain occasion, had sent her off from home—*"trusting and unprepared"* and *"too small, hardly able to cope"*—and the idea of "the Germans" and "Germany." As a very young child, Eifermann was expelled from her birth country: "My family had left Germany when I was less than 3 (late in 1935)." The family left because, as she usually adds when explaining her background, "my father had lost his job, luckily" ("'Germany,'" 250, 249). Fifty years after this early leave-taking, Eifermann revisited Germany. The return of 1985, undertaken for what seemed to be solely professional reasons, generated initially baffling, symptomatic behavior that was followed by a period of intensive self-analysis. A chain of connections gradually unfolded: Eifermann's "feelings of anger and vengefulness" toward Little Red Cap's mother were linked to her relations with her internalized mother, as well as to the signifiers "Germany" and "Germans." That the analyst first heard "Rotkäppchen" and other Grimms' tales from her mother, in German, in Germany, is a significant feature of this signifying chain. After the trip to Germany, Eifermann also discovered another verbal trace or symptom of her history: "I had somehow always avoided calling the German language my 'mother tongue'—although that is the term used in both Hebrew and German—using 'first language' instead. Although I had never said it to myself explicitly, I had the vague feeling that 'German' did not 'deserve' to be so named" (250).

Eifermann's analytic exploration further clarifies the impasse of an always-to-be-defeated expectation. On the one hand, mothers are expected to privilege the paternal signifier so that their children will learn to honor and obey the ruling order: "[W]alk properly like a good little girl, and don't leave the path." Step like a goose, she might have said, and don't gander about. On the other, mothers are also supposed to protect their children from the depredations of the phallic function they uphold in their role as mediators. Thus the mother's admonition in the fairy tale—"[W]hen you get to her house, don't forget to say good morning, and don't go looking in all the corners" (Grimm and Grimm, 99)—is incompatible with the child's taking a close, hard look at the wolf and seeing him as he really is.

In Lacan's Sartrean formulation, "the existence of others as looking at me"—that is to say, "not a seen gaze, but a gaze imagined by me in the field of the Other"—overwhelms and distorts the subject's actual perception (*Seminar XI*, 79–80 / 84).[2] When the little girl encounters the wolf in her grandmother's bed, she does not perceive something that concerns her organ of sight. Her morning walk in the woods and flower-picking, albeit mildly transgressive, have not at all changed her scopic field. "From the moment that this gaze appears," Lacan explains, "the subject tries to adapt himself to it" (79 / 83). Little Red Riding Hood's gaze is policed by language and law, by the decorum of docility, by the habit of obeying the paternal order mediated by her mother. The litany of "Oh, grandmother!" that leads to her being gobbled up is not conducted in an interrogative mode. Her exclamatory miscallings are couched in the "mother tongue" of the fathers. She will submit to a great deal of devastation without admitting it even to herself, let alone crying out loud, "Wolf!"

Her response, however, may be read otherwise. In "Confusion of Tongues Between Adults and the Child" (1933), a prescient essay that challenges Freud's theory of the seduction fantasy, Sándor Ferenczi describes a reactive mechanism triggered by extreme violence and sexual abuse. Ferenczi observes that some children become "paralyzed by enormous anxiety":

> These children feel physically and morally helpless, their personalities are not sufficiently consolidated in order to be able to protest, even if only in thought, for the overpowering force and authority of the adult makes them dumb and can rob them of their senses. *The same anxiety . . . compels them to subordinate themselves like automata to the will of the aggressor, to divine each one of his desires and to gratify these; completely oblivious of themselves they identify themselves with the aggressor.* (162)

In keeping with Ferenczi's hypothesis, Little Red Riding Hood's perceptual confusion and related inability to defend herself against attack do not result from misidentification but, rather, from total identification with and introjection of the wolf. The aggressor "disappears as part of the external reality" and becomes part of her intra- instead of extra-psychic reality. The victim experiences both the menace and the violence intrapsychically in a trance, dream, or automaton-like state. Under the pressure of being destroyed from without, the ego (which is a proponent of the reality principle) falls to pieces within; or, as Ferenczi puts it, "the attack as a rigid external reality ceases to exist" (162). What the misused child feels as she mechanically says, "Oh, grandmother, what big ears, eyes, hands, and dreadfully big mouth you have . . . " is: "This is not really happening to me."

But whether Little Red Riding Hood's behavior is understood as an outcome of misidentification or identification with her aggressor, whether as stemming from too much contact with a certain reality or too little, one determiner of her destiny is clear. The jaws snap shut with the aid of the phallus. It is neither because her mother resisted the role of mediator nor because she refused the phallic insignia of the law that Little Red Riding Hood is swallowed up and, afterward, luckily—to borrow Eifermann's nuanced word—rescued.

IV

There was a time when the story of Little Red Riding Hood ended without a sojourn inside the belly of the wolf. Recorded in France at the end of the nineteenth century, this tale probably dates back to the late Middle Ages (Zipes, "Epilogue," 346). It remains, according to Tatar, "[o]ne of the fullest available texts faithful to oral, peasant versions" (37).[3] In the early folkloric version entitled "The Story of Grandmother," a woman sends her daughter to visit her granny with a freshly baked loaf of bread and a bottle of milk. Warnings and admonitions as well as the concupiscence of the red velvet hood do not appear. This daughter does not disobey her mother. She displays no self-indulgence and lack of caution on the way to her grandmother's house. Still, when she arrives with her gifts, the beast is in the bed.

"'Undress yourself, my child,' the werewolf said, 'and come lie down beside me.'" Even more overtly than the literary fairy tale, the folktale provides grounds for Susan Brownmiller's contention, in *Against Our Will*, that Little Red Riding Hood's story is to be read as "a parable of rape" (344). At the wolf's behest, the girl removes all her clothes. She does so slowly, item by item, in a striptease that could also be, as this encounter turns out, a strategy of delay. Each time she asks where to put her garments, "the bodice, the dress, the petticoat, and the long stockings," the wolf replies: "Throw them into the fire, my child, you won't be needing them anymore." When she finally lies down beside him, the famous exchange begins. But it is not at all evident that she fails to recognize the wolf: "Oh, Granny, how hairy you are!" and "what big nails you have!" is followed in some variants by "Oh, Granny, what big nostrils you have!"—to which close observation the wolf is constrained to reply, "The better to snuff my tobacco with, my child!" (quoted in Zipes, "Epilogue," 347–48). Is this girl in a state of extrapsychic denial? Or cleverly stalling in order the better to manage her defense? Is she deceiving her would-be deceiver in the very bed in which he would destroy her? That the girl may be no less calculating than the wolf is not merely the expression of a readerly wish. What happens next diverges remarkably from the tale as told by the Brothers Grimm:

> "Oh, Granny, what a big mouth you have!"
> "The better to eat you with, my child!"
> "Oh, Granny, I've got to go badly. Let me go outside."
> "Do it in bed, my child!"
> "Oh, no, Granny, I want to go outside."
> "All right, but make it quick."
> The werewolf attached a woollen rope to her foot and let her go outside.
> When the little girl was outside, she tied the end of the rope to a plum tree in the courtyard. The werewolf became impatient and said: "Are you making a load out there? Are you making a load?" (348)[4]

By the time he realizes nobody is answering, the girl has run away. She has made him lower his guard only to slip through it. He tries to recapture his dinner but arrives just in time to see her crossing over the threshold into safety.

Far from being a typical cautionary tale, the folk version does not deal with transgression and punishment. Instead of peddling what Tatar calls the "pedagogy of fear" that characterizes so many fairy tales, it entertains, even titillates the audience with a plot of near rape and narrow escape. In addition, the French tale might have served another social purpose. Folkloric studies suggest that oral narratives such as "The Story of Grandmother" were, literally, old wives' tales. As Karen E. Rowe observes, "To have the antiquarian Grimm brothers regarded as the fathers of modern folklore is perhaps to forget the maternal lineage, the 'mothers' who in the French *veillées* and English nurseries, in court salons and the German *Spinnstube* . . . passed on their wisdom" (68). Ruth Bottigheimer also remarks that "German folk tales were assumed to have originated in or to have passed through in many cases the *Spinnstube*, for it was there that women gathered in the evening and told tales to keep themselves and their company awake" (143). The genitive "of" in the story's title thus points to a double designation: the tale-topic (a story about grandmother) and the tale-teller (a story told by grandmother) are named. Because if the principal spinners of "The Story of Grandmother" were indeed "mothers" or "old gossips," then the events may be regarded as a narrative symbolization and fulfillment of a communally shared wish: the mothers' wish for their daughters, and no less for themselves, that, when faced with great danger and violence, they would react with patience, cunning, and courage.[5]

In the interval that separates the folk narrative from the Grimms' "Rotkäppchen," Charles Perrault published "Le Petit Chaperon Rouge" (1697). Perrault's fairy tale, the immediate literary precedent for the Grimms' well-known version,[6] ends in abrupt calamity for the child: "*Grandmamma, what great teeth you have got!* It is to eat thee up. And upon saying these words, this wicked Wolfe fell upon the *little Red Riding-Hood*, and eat her up" (97). The mother in this tale utters no cautionary instructions to the little girl before sending her off. The rhythm of obey-or-pay is nonetheless unmistakable. The child is spoiled ("Her mother was beyond reason excessively fond of her"), ignorant ("The poor child . . . did not know how dangerous a thing it is to stay and hear a Wolfe talk"), and also pleasure-seeking ("[T]he little girl . . . divert[ed] her self in gathering nuts, running after butterflies, and making nose-gays"). Clearly, the mother has done something wrong here. The brave little victor of "The Story of Grandmother" turns into a hapless victim, and the quick and clever wolf who ran "as fast as he was able, the shortest way" gets his just dessert (95–96).

Perrault attaches a *moralité* for the benefit of his elite young readership:

From this story one learns that children,
Especially young lasses,
Pretty, courteous and well-bred,
Do very wrong to listen to strangers,
And it is not an unheard thing
If the Wolf is thereby provided with his dinner.

What Perrault provides for the wolf is an apologetics for aggression; and for the little girl, a lesson in *civilité* and victim mentality.[7] The Grimms not only introduce the unheeded warnings of the mother but also add the dramatic rescue episode to Perrault's drastic ending. It is therefore given to the child herself to pronounce the lesson in obedience and self-mastery: "Never again will I leave the path and run off into the wood when my mother tells me not to" (Grimm and Grimm, 101). Little Red Cap's conclusion does not differ vastly from the moral coda appended to Perrault's tale. The narrative voice is that of the little girl; the narrative values, of the paternal symbolic order.

Bruno Bettelheim, in *The Uses of Enchantment*, proposes that the father is featured as both wolf and hunter in the Grimms' fairy-tale version. His reading of this paternal duality entails yet another transformation of the daughterly character: from victor ("The Story of Grandmother") to victim ("Le Petit Chaperon Rouge") to victimizer. She becomes the seducer in the tale of her own seduction. "What is meant here by 'seduction'," as Bettelheim expounds it, "is the girl's desire and efforts to induce her father to love her more than anybody else, and her wish that he should make all efforts to induce her to love him more than anybody else." Hence he is split into the "bad" and the "good" paternal *object* of the appetitive child. The wolf as object is "an externalization of the dangers of overwhelming oedipal feelings," as opposed to the hunter, who symbolizes the father "in his protective and rescuing function" (178). Bettelheim's analysis implicitly raises the question: who most needs to be rescued? From a conservationist (or speciesist?) perspective, the wolf is the more endangered. He might well plead for protection from his nymphet-daughter. He will be sorry forever after for the feckless, tumescent pursuit through the woods—"I let my hand rest on her warm auburn head. . . . We sped through the striped and speckled forest"—that led him to the fateful seclusion of The Enchanted Hunters and, then, down Grimm Road. In a retrospective view of his own unhappy end, the wolf could also say: "And my only regret today is that I did not quietly . . . leave the town, the country, the continent, the hemisphere,—indeed, the globe—that very same night" (Nabokov, 103, 114).[8]

However, in keeping with classical Freudian theory, Bettelheim describes the family plot from the perspective of the Oedipal child. His discussion presupposes that Little Red Cap's experience focalizes the entire narrative. The splitting into wolf/hunter, however, need not (only) incarnate the daughter's ambivalent feelings toward the paternal object. The perspectival orientation may also be patterned after the world of the fathers. The famous tale has passed, after all, through the complex collation and editorial processing of Jacob and Wilhelm Grimm, two dedicated preservers of Germanic folklore and tradition. As Bottigheimer comments in a different connection, not only the Grimms' texts themselves but historical evidence often suggest that their *Household Tales* "can be seen to consist of interpenetrating layers of narrative," in which submerged voices—"probably quite unintentionally"—commingle with a more conventional and overt message (141–42).

As soon as the mother sends the daughter off on her errand, the action is generated by the metamorphic figure of the father. His desire is as subject to change as his form. A powerful and protean symbol, he appears in various guises: as the friendly and sympathetic companion of Little Red Cap's forest walk; as the pretender knocking on grandmother's door with a promise of cake and wine; as the wolf who assumes a virtue, grandmother's clothes and nightcap, yet lies in bed and out; and as the hunter, "just passing" with a musket. The last of these several parts requires no less contriving and good timing than the others. The father slips into grandmother's house as a wolf and steps back in again as a hunter. He returns to the scene and rescues the victims from the devastation that his alter ego, the wolf-double, has visited upon them. In short, he saves those whom he has just swallowed.

Contra Bettelheim, I am suggesting here that the splitting in the Grimms' fairy tale is of the paternal *subject*. The father's fantasy enacts competing and incompatible wishes: he would seduce and yet safeguard the child from the deviant abomination of his own desires. Moreover, he returns in another doubled guise at the story's close. As midwife to his own cannibal labors, "he took a pair of scissors and started cutting the sleeping wolf's belly open" (Grimm and Grimm, 100). The hunter delivers the grandmother and Little Red Cap from the womb of the wolf. As Ann Sexton reimagines this deliverance, it resembles "a kind of caesarian section" performed with an highly invested instrument: "It was a carnal knife that let / Red Riding Hood out like a poppy / quite alive from the kingdom of the belly" (77). That the wolf dies shortly after, stone heavy, due to an unnaturally difficult second pregnancy, does not detract from the fulfillment of this barely concealed wish. The paternal representative usurps not only the place of midwife-deliverer, a place held by the girl herself in the folktale, but also the place of mother-container. The text symbolically discloses the father's phantasmatic attempts to alter an unsatisfying reality, a uterine deficiency or lack—if you allow, through its transposition into a fable of phallic self-sufficiency and heroism.

At the end of the Grimm brothers' story, the hunter goes happily home with the wolf's skin, which, presumably, he will have occasion to wear again. In the tale told by the old wives, he is identified from the beginning as a werewolf.

V

To come back to the big crocodile in Lacan's *Seminar XVII*, what is remarkable about the fable is its insistence on the negative elementary character of the mother.[9] Although Lacan omits the adjective "bad," it is understood that she is the dangerous, potentially destructive pole in the Oedipal constellation. Even before any barring, splitting, cleavage takes place at the mirror stage, the subject is barred behind the deathly *dentata*, the tooth-studded mouth of the mother. Should the phallic roller not be in its appointed place, she is likely to shut her trap: "refermer son clapet" is Lacan's somewhat coarse way of putting it. Insofar as the passage about the crocodile "sums up . . . what he had been saying for years" (Fink, 56), it describes the maternal function through its malfunction.

Typically, however, the mother—when she leaves the bed of her labored deliveries—assumes the task of the mediator who surrenders her central place to the master signifier, who subordinates her desires to his name and law, and who settles down to living in the universe of signs. The admonishing mother of Little Red Cap seems a more appropriate representation of Lacan's later theory than the monster-mother in *Seminar XVII*. The figure of the mother in the Grimms' tale, "with a raised finger addressing her daughter," is one of the "major scenes which almost invariably accompany the text" in the illustrated books produced over the past two centuries in both Europe and the United States (Zipes, "Epilogue," 355). Such a mother would not tolerate any deviance in herself, or in her daughter, from the prescribed social order. Lacan's improvised description of the mother's role, supposedly a straightforward rendering of reality ("I am telling you simple things"), invests a negativity, a pathology in maternity that invites investigation.

One possible reading would point to a reversal. He says the creature in his fable is the mother. So it is *not* the mother.[10] In this view, the image of the devouring maternal mouth serves as a projective defense. When Lacan imagines the mother as a crocodile, he is deflecting the father's share. But the paternal phallus as representative of the law, the police, the state is binarily, and perhaps necessarily, congruent with the signifying functions of predator-aggressor/protector-defender. The Germanic tale makes visible the split positionality of the father: "[D]er Jäger zog dem Wolf den Pelz ab und ging damit heim" (*Kinder- und Hausmärchen*, 178–79). The *Jäger* (hunter), a word associated with the police,[11] goes home with an alternative identity, literally, another skin in his possession. Olga Broumas, in her poem "Little Red Riding Hood," re-creates this splitting from the perspective of the newly (re)born daughter: "Dressed in my red hood, howling, I went— / evading / the white-clad doctor and his fancy claims: microscope, / stethoscope, scalpel, all / the better to see with, to hear, / and to eat—straight from your hollowed basket. . . . I grew up / good at evading" (67–68). The paternal "scalpel" is the verbal pivot of this passage into extrauterine reality. Someone else's hunter can easily turn into your wolf. And you find yourself in his mouth.

A corroborating image for what the crocodile veils may be found on the front cover chosen for Lacan's 1956–57 seminar, *La relation d'objet*: Francisco Goya's *Saturn Devouring His Son* (1819–23). The scene emerges against a tenebrous background, an abandonment of color and light. A small, partially eaten, bloodied, naked figure is gripped tightly in the hands of an enormous ogre-god, with dark gaping mouth and mad bulging eyes. No rod or roller has spared this child. Yet one of them was finally saved.

To unravel the implications of Goya's image for Lacanian theory, I want briefly to recall why and how Saturn became well practiced in the engorgement of his sons. Saturn, for the Romans, was identical with the Greek or pre-Greek god Cronos (Cronus, Kronos). Upon being warned that one of his own children would overthrow him, Cronos began swallowing his progeny as fast as they were born to his consort, Rhea. As Hesiod tells it, "His purpose was that none but he of the lordly Celestials should have the royal station among the immortals." So it came to pass that the grieving Rhea, after she bore her son Zeus, hid him well away and presented his father with a large stone wrapped up in swaddling clothes. He promptly and indiscriminately gulped it down. "[T]hereafter not a stone but his son remained, secure and invincible, who before long was to defeat him . . . and drive him from his high station." Great Cronos was thus undone by his wife's stratagem and son's strength (Hesiod, 16–17).

But it was the scene of ingestion, of terror and anguish, and not of the son's salvation that compelled Goya's and, later, Lacan's attention. "Goya was not groping towards God," André Malraux writes in his extraordinary study *Saturn: An Essay on Goya*, "but towards a power older and beyond salvation, the everlasting Saturn" (90). Anthony Cascardi similarly observes that "Goya characteristically takes the salvational moment as the occasion of an encounter with a kind of evil that neither religion nor reason had the power to uproot"; on the contrary, in many of Goya's "dark" paintings, evil "returns, like the Freudian repressed, as a reminder of the ways in which all that is 'earlier' in culture continues to hold us bound" (203–4).[12] If Goya is indeed the "greatest poet of blood," his appeal to darkness and nightmare is no less a spectacle; obsessed by an awareness of the dreadful, the negative aspect of the sacred, he chooses "moments, real or imaginary, when our relationships are overturned" (Malraux, 111, 155). A father's teeth tear into the flesh of his own flesh. In a pencil drawing simply entitled "Saturn," one child is already in the mouth and another in the hand of the demonic father. Goya depicts, and Malraux enumerates, "the carnival, madness, the corrida, monsters, horror, tortures, and darkness. Not love, and certainly not motherhood" (158).[13]

Lacan demonstrates an analogous occupation with ethical extremities, with moments when the overturning of human relationships occurs. Particularly, if motherhood may be deemed part of the sacred, then Lacan inclines toward the portrayal of its dark pole. He refers to the Saturnian scene toward the close of his seminar on object relations. In the midst of a discussion of Freud's case history of little Hans, he suddenly mentions the maternal role in the dramas played out "between Cronos and Ouranos, between Zeus and Cronos" (*Seminar IV*, 379). I shall return to this twofold reference shortly. But first, in cross-textual juxtaposition, the image of *Saturn Devouring His Son* may be compared to the fable of crocodile and roller. The two images, I propose, constitute symmetrical inversions of each other. In the Greco-

Roman myth of succession, the mother rescues the child from his father by the very means, a stone, that the symbolic father uses to save the child from the unappeasable maw in Lacan's later illustration. Briefly to recall: "There is a roller, made of stone, of course. . . . That is what we call the phallus. It is a roller which protects you, should the jaws suddenly close" (*Seminar XVII*, 129). The inverted images are close enough in this instance to suggest that the one has displaced the other. In other words, the mother *qua* crocodile has a metonymic or contiguous relation to the father *qua* cannibal of ancient myth. The connection between these parental signifiers instantiates the deferral of meaning along the "horizontal signifying chain" that, according to Lacan, characterizes metonymic mental functioning: "In the case of *Verschiebung*, 'displacement,' the German term is closer to the idea of that veering off of signification that we see in metonymy, and which from its first appearance in Freud is represented as the most appropriate means used by the unconscious to foil censorship" (*Écrits*, 515 / 164, 511 / 160).

To retrace, then, the historical transmutations that possibly generated the Lacanian formula "The mother is a big crocodile":

I don't want to eat, despoil, destroy the child.
She wants to eat, despoil, destroy the child.
A child is being eaten.

This sequence involves a double substitution: a denial and reapportioning of blame, the substitution of *She* for *I*, followed by a defensive reversal, the substitution of a passive fantasy for the activity of the first two phases.[14] Furthermore, given the mutability of the "sound image" or what Saussure designates "the principle of change [that] is based on the principle of continuity" (74), it may not be too strained to hear in the name of the mythic father, in "Cronos" itself, the alliterative transmission that selected the signifier "crocodile" from the many permutations of the animal-monster chain.

VI

An alternative reading of Lacan's fable of maternity, and I do not pretend to exhaust all the possibilities, is that the terror inspired by the mother is *not* deflected from the father. It is indeed the mother. Thus in *Seminar IV*, at the close of a chapter entitled "The Phallus and the Insatiable Mother" ("Le phallus et la mère inassouvie"), Lacan describes the real, unsatisfied mother ("c'est quelqu'un de réel, elle est là") as someone who continually seeks that which she will suck in and devour ("quaerens quem devoret"), who possibly appears before the child like an open mouth or muzzle ("comme une gueule ouverte") and who, in another image of unappeasable hunger, resembles the petrifying Gorgon. He correlates the maternal mouth with the phantom counterpart of the life-giving womb: "The gaping hole of the Medusa's head is a devouring figure that the infant encounters as a possible outcome in his pursuit of the mother's satisfaction" (195).

The psychoanalytic precedent for this mythic reference is, of course, Freud's commentary on the "horrifying decapitated head of Medusa":

> To decapitate = to castrate. The terror of Medusa is thus a terror of castration that is linked to the sight of something. Numerous analyses have made us familiar with the occasion for this: it occurs when a boy, who has hitherto been unwilling to believe in the threat of castration, catches sight of the female genitals, probably those of an adult, surrounded by hair, and essentially those of his mother. (*SE*, 18: 273)

Lacan's redescription not only effects a displacement upwards of the Medusa image from the female genitals ("the absence . . . which is the cause of the horror" [18: 273]) to the gaping mouth. It also expresses a concern with cannibalization, with reincorporation by the mother, no less intense or primal than the castration anxiety that, according to Freud, the Medusa's head elicits in the male spectator.[15]

The Lacanian imaging of the mother's open mouth, ready to desiccate and swallow the infant, suggests an animosity that also screens great anguish. Is that maw the representation of a birth anxiety or a death anxiety? a dread of the original abode or the final resting place? The two unalterable facts of all life are condensed and relegated to the single feature. In this view, the crocodile is not a metonymy, a displacement that masks the oral-sadistic aspect of the father; rather, it is a metaphoric composite of divergent traits. The monster-mother belongs to the category of condensation (*Verdichtung*), that is, to "the structure of the superimposition of the signifiers, which metaphor takes as its field" (*Écrits*, 511 / 160).

A corroborating image may be found in the concluding line of Victor Hugo's "Booz endormi" ("Boaz Asleep") (1859), "This sickle of gold in the field of stars" ("Cette faucille d'or dans le champ des étoiles"), which Lacan quotes directly before alluding to the mythic pairs, Ouranos-Cronos and Cronos-Zeus (*Seminar IV*, 378). To read his citation requires placing it in a series of references whose interrelations are analogous to the mirrored representations associated with *mise en abîme*: Lacan imports two classical myths about divine first families into his discussion of Hugo's rendition of the Book of Ruth that appears within his reconsideration of the pathology described in Freud's "Analysis of a Phobia in a Five-Year-Old Boy." In short, just as Hugo inventively retells the biblical story, so Lacan rereads Hugo and Freud.

In the gamut of familial disorders I have surveyed thus far, one mother produced a filial perversion, the homosexual inclinations of her son, and another mother an obsessional neurotic for whom indecision was only one symptom in an entire gamut of disabilities. In the twelve-chapter section ("The Structure of Myths in the Observation of Little Hans's Phobia") of *Seminar IV* devoted to an analysis of Freud's case history, Lacan implicates the mother in the formation of a phobic symptomology: "The entire sequence of the game unfolds in the lure, finally unbearable, anxiety-provoking, intolerable, of little Hans's relation to his mother" (*Seminar IV*, 212). The father is unable to assume his symbolic position in this familial structure. According to Lacan, the boy finds himself compelled to introduce a dread of horses that bite as a substitute for his real father, whom his real mother does not want.

In elucidating the substitutive function of little Hans's phobia in his seminar of 19 June 1957, Lacan introduced the concept of the paternal metaphor. The term itself, *la métaphore paternelle*, occurs shortly after Lacan's brief reference to the classical succession myth, a reference embedded in his explication of Hugo's image of the golden sickle (379). "Booz endormi" enters into Lacan's discussion of the case of little Hans via another image. He calls upon the "sheaf" in the third stanza of the poem ("His sheaf was neither miserly nor spiteful" [Sa gerbe n'était point avare ni haineuse]) in order to exemplify the workings of the phallus at the metaphoric level. As Lacan clarifies in "The Agency of the Letter," which was written the month before his June 1957 seminar, the metaphor "sheaf" that replaces the proper name

"Boaz" in the signifying chain emblematizes the structure of paternity: "[I]t is the figure of the burgeoning of fecundity, and it is this that announces the surprise that the poem celebrates, namely, the promise that the old man will receive in the sacred context of his accession to paternity" (*Écrits*, 508 / 157–58).

Moreover, even though Lacan concedes in the two sessions on metaphor and metonymy held the previous year (May 1956) that the image of the sheaf could be understood in its metonymic connection—"never named directly, there is Booz's royal penis"—what endows this sheaf with metaphoricity, he proceeds to argue, is its usurpation of the paternal signifier: "[T]he metaphor is placed in the position of subject, in Booz's place" (*Seminar III*, 257 / 225). The same metaphor, Lacan might have also noted, prepares for the appearance of the oak tree in Hugo's poem. While Ruth lies at Boaz's feet and patiently waits, he sleeps and dreams of a great oak growing out of his stomach toward the sky: "un chêne / Qui, sorti de son ventre, allait jusqu'au ciel bleu; / Une race y montait comme une longue chaîne; / Un roi chantait en bas, en haut mourait un Dieu" (ll. 37–40). The poet interpolates here a dream image that extends the promise, "A race . . . like a long chain," previously intimated in the munificent sheaf. Boaz's dream of the oak paradoxically presages what has already taken place, namely, the founding of a royal lineage: "Below sang a king, above died a God." In medieval iconography, as Jacques Truchet points out in his editorial notes, Boaz's vision is usually attributed to Jesse, grandson of Boaz and father of David.[16] The tree of Jesse (Boaz) represents the genealogy of Jesus Christ *en haut*, at the summit, from David *en bas*, the king at the base. Hugo extracts a historical as well as a prophetic image from the biblical text, but it is not *in* the text.

When Hugo's figure of the patriarch whose position as transcendent signifier is not in doubt reappears in *Seminar IV*, it is by way of contrast to the vacancy left by little Hans's undesired father. This vacancy has invited invasion by the signifier "horse." (Again the symbolic, and not the actual, paternity of the child is called into question by the mother's non-desire.) Lacan thus takes up the sheaf that he has examined twice before and then, for the first time, turns his attention to the sickle:

> Neither in my last year's teaching, nor in what I have recently written ["The Agency of the Letter"] on this sheaf in the poem of Boaz and Ruth, have I

pushed the investigation until the ultimate point to which the poet develops the metaphor. I have left the sickle aside because, out of the context of what we are doing here, it might have appeared somewhat forced to the reader. . . .

It is a question, in effect, of the fine and clear crescent of the moon. But it cannot escape you that, if the thing is pertinent, if it is something other than a very pretty painterly stroke, a touch of yellow on the blue sky, it is insofar as the sickle in the sky is the eternal sickle of maternity, that which has already played her small role between Cronos and Uranos, between Zeus and Cronos. (*Seminar IV*, 378–79)

The "small role" is Lacan's own ironic touch. Immediately after invoking the classical trinity of fathers, he speaks of *la puissance*: "the power . . . represented in the mystic waiting of woman." In conjunction with the "eternal sickle of maternity," this waiting—"l'attente mystique de la femme"—may be correlated neither only with Ruth's patient vigil as Boaz lies sleeping nor only with the generic passivized woman who waits to be given that which she essentially lacks. Lacan's reading of Hugo's reading of the Book of Ruth culminates in an image of active and self-seeking power. He extracts this historic and proleptic image from the poem, but it is not *in* the poem: "With this sickle that trails in the grasp of her hand, the gleaner will effectively slice through the sheaf that's at stake here" ("Avec cette faucille qui traîne à la portée de sa main, la glaneuse tranchera effectivement la gerbe dont il s'agit" [379]). In a chain that stretches behind Ruth, who gleans and gathers in the fields of Boaz, stands Rhea, and behind Rhea, Gaea.

In ancient Greek cosmogony, what Rhea did for Cronos pales before what Gaea (Earth) did for Ouranos (Heaven). In Hesiod's account, "Earth bore first of all one equal to herself, starry Heaven, so that he should cover her all about" (6). The firstborn son who was the first husband was also the starlit sky. When Heaven and Earth mated, they produced the primeval race—the twelve Titans, and then the one-eyed giants—the three Cyclopes, and then the hundred-handed monsters—the three Centimanes. Ouranos (Uranus) was apparently horrified by his own children, "loathed them from the beginning," for he shut them all up in the body of Gaea (Ge, Gaia), in the depths of Earth: "[H]e took pleasure in the wicked work, did Heaven, while the huge Earth was tight-pressed inside, and groaned" (7). Finally, Gaea could no longer wait and bear the strain. She conceived a stratagem against her lusty husband. She took the law, so to speak, into her own hands.

"Without delay," Hesiod writes, "she created the element of grey adamant, and made a great reaping hook, and showed it to her dear children." Félix Guirand, scholar and mythographer, writes that Gaea sought "terrible vengeance," whereas H. J. Rose applies the same epithet to Ouranos, "terrible father" (88; 22).

Be that as it may, Gaea's plan for vengeance (or defense) proceeded to unfold. While her other children hesitated or feared to support her, "the great crooked-schemer" Cronos, her youngest and lastborn son, was ready to undertake the task. After Ouranos had approached his wife, as he did nightly, and fallen into a profound sleep, Cronos arose from his hiding place armed with the gleaming hook: "[Heaven's] son reached out from the ambush with his left hand; with his right he took the huge sickle with its long row of sharp teeth and quickly cut off his father's genitals, and flung them behind him to fly where they might" (7–8). Thus the spiteful sheaf fell before the adamant sickle. She who bore starry Heaven also took back the night. She who gave him life now took that life away. "Cette faucille d'or dans le champ des étoiles": Boaz beware, even as you sow, so may you be reaped.

The sickle in Lacan's re-citations of "Booz endormi" is rife with associative ambiguities. The crescent moon as open and inviting container, as the body-vessel for the phallic hammer (" . . . Boaz begat Obed, / And Obed begat Jesse, and Jesse begat David" [Ruth 4:21–22]), shows its dark and vicious side. The death-dealing scythe severs life at its very root. Just as the sheaf stands in a substitutive relation to "Boaz," so the sickle may serve as a metaphor for "Ruth," for the womb/tomb of the great mother Gaea and, not least, for the seemingly smiling but toothsome mouth of the crocodile. Lacan's fabulated image in *Seminar XVII*, is linked to the sickle of maternity in *Seminar IV* through the sound of delicate bones being munched and crunched between savage maternal jaws.

Yet if the sickle of gold is put back into its poetic context, the image turns out not to be patently a function of the ratio: as "sheaf" is to paternity, so "sickle" is to maternity. In effect, the entire movement of "Booz endormi" leads to a quite different attribution. From the sheaf that was neither miserly nor spiteful to the oak stretching skywards from the aged dreamer's fecund loins, the poem progresses to another metaphor of paternal transcendence: "The cedar feels [smells, senses] not a rose at its base / And he felt not a woman at his feet" ("Le cèdre ne sent pas une rose à sa base, / Et lui ne sentait pas une femme à ses pieds" [ll. 59–60]). His crown is so much closer to heaven than her lovely yet always lowly head. The Moabite rose is surely blessed in her position at his base; in other words, the father's name is in its proper place. Upon seeing the "fine and clear crescent" in the night sky above Bethlehem, Ruth asks herself at the poem's close:

> What god, what harvester of eternal summer,
> Had, in departing, negligently thrown
> This sickle of gold in the field of stars.
>
> *Quel dieu, quel moissonneur de l'éternel été,*
> *Avait, en s'en allant, négligemment jeté*
> *Cette faucille d'or dans le champs des étoiles.* (ll. 86–88)

The sickle is the last in a chain of royal images of paternity anticipating the establishment of the House of David and the birth of Christ.[17] Typological resonances provide a further extension for the father. Hugo also patterns Boaz's dream of paternity, I suggest, after the fulfillment vouchsafed to Abraham in the Book of Genesis. Just as the constellation of sheaf-oak-cedar signals the posterity of Boaz and his seed, so the sickle may be traced back to Abraham and, via Abraham, shifted forward again to Boaz:

> After these things the word of the Lord came unto Abram in a vision, saying, Fear not, Abram: I *am* . . . thy exceeding great reward. / And Abram said, Lord GOD, what wilt thou give me, seeing I go childless . . . ?
> . . . . And he brought him forth abroad, and said, Look now toward heaven, and tell the stars, if thou be able to number them: and he said unto him, So shall thy seed be. (Gen. 15:1–2, 5)

and after the near-sacrifice of Isaac, the Angel of the Lord calls out:

> That in blessing I will bless thee, and in multiplying I will multiply thy seed as the stars of the heaven. . . . (Gen. 22:17)[18]

By means of metaphoric allusion and articulated reference, Hugo assembles a convocation of patriarchs that ensures the accession of the phallic sickle, the posterity of the founding father's astral seed. The sickle is made of that self-metal that crowns the head of kings.

When Lacan briefly returns, in *The Four Fundamental Concepts of Psychoanalysis*, to the sickle and the sheaf, he offers a complex and partial acknowledgment of their continuity as figural representations of a divine or transcendent father. "The dimension of meaning opened up by this metaphor," he writes, citing once again the "neither miserly nor spiteful" sheaf, "is nothing less than what appears to us in the final image, that of the golden sickle carelessly thrown into the field of stars" (*Seminar XI*, 224 / 247–48). However, to arrive at the "hidden" dimension of this image, "it is not enough to refer to the sickle which Jupiter used to flood the world with the blood of Chronos [*sic*]." In the biblical context of (male) genealogies, "present with all the echoes of history," and notwithstanding the "dimension of castration that is involved" in the mythic blood-stained sickle, what Lacan now finds in Hugo's final image is another successful operation, albeit hidden or repressed, of the paternal metaphor. As he puts it, "the Lord with the unpronounceable name is precisely he who sends children to barren women and old men. The fundamentally transbiological character of paternity, introduced . . . by the tradition of the destiny of the chosen people, has something that is originally repressed there, and which always re-emerges . . . with the meaning that remains hidden" (224 / 248). The sickle simultaneously reveals what it conceals: an affirmation of the Name-of-the-Father.

In placing the crescent in *Ruth's* grasp in *Seminar IV*, Lacan neglects not only (what he would later acknowledge as) the poem's steady progression toward the final invocation of the Lord's promise to childless old men. His reading also ignores the biblical characterization of Ruth as one who steadfastly follows in the wake of others. She famously responds, "[W]hither thou goest, I will go; and where thou lodgest, I will lodge" (Ruth 1:16), and later in the land of Naomi's kinsman, she says, "Let me now go to the field, and glean ears of corn after *him* in whose sight I shall find grace. . . . And she went, and came, and gleaned in the field after the reapers" (Ruth 2:2–3).[19] Ruth wields no sickle. She is not among the reapers. She is constrained to pick up Boaz's leavings with nothing more than her hands and a hopeful heart: "Let her glean even among the sheaves, and reproach her not: / And let fall also *some* of the handfuls of purpose for her, and leave *them*, that she may glean" (Ruth 2:15–16).

If the sickle is returned, moreover, to its mythographic context and if memory did not selectively choose its sites of self-authentication, Lacan's reference to Cronos-Saturn could also serve to evoke another adaptation of this tool. I shall give three brief examples of such mythological usage. First, the one festival known to be associated with the ancient God in Greece, the

Kronia, was a harvest festival: "The rare representations of [Kronos] in art show him as a majestic but sorrowful old man, holding a curved object traditionally interpreted as the knife wherewith he wounded Uranos, but which is quite as likely, considering the time of his festival, to be a reaping-hook" (Rose, 43). Second, as a Latin and Roman agricultural divinity, Saturn was of the rank of Janus and Jupiter. In a painting found at Pompeii, the god is depicted standing, "a sickle in his hand. On coins he carries a sickle or ears of corn" (Guirand and Pierre, 205, 207). Third, in a half-alchemical and half-mythological representation, an etching entitled "The *Prima Materia* as Saturn Devouring his Children," he appears in three different aspects with a small child in or near his mouth (Jung, 317, fig. 161).[20] In the last pose, he also holds a curved sword aloft, thereby recalling that his name was linked to the Latin *satur* (stuffed, gorged) as well as to *sator* (a sower) (Guirand and Pierre, 205). The mythic sickle, then, does not solely denote the goddess Gaea, mother and wife of Heaven. What may also be designated, after Lacan, "the eternal sickle of paternity" has left bloody and benevolent traces of its multiple functions.

By now the monster-images have becomes so numerous and implicated in one another that the reader might well worry: who really needs to be rescued? Indeed, should the watchful hunter have spoiled the wolf's slumbers and spared the child? Should Cronos have supported his father and seen his mother swell and suffer? And should Gaea have endured the phallic law of Ouranos and waited mystically, patiently, until she burst under the unbearable weight? Or should the fathers have overcome their dread, jealousy, and *knowledge* that one day their children would survive and supersede them? To the extent that a reply is forthcoming, it lies beyond the realm of ambiguity, beyond the interplay (and sometime consolation) of mutually exclusive categories. The Oedipal stage is congested with monsters. All members may be variously impaled on the mythic nuclear family. The phallic *dentata* no more obviously belong to the mothers than they do to the fathers or the children. So Lacan articulates his symbolic algorithms in an attempt to instill order among these terrible families. The schemas that he proposes try to defer their derangements. The formula of the Name-of-the-Father "over" the Desire of the Mother is neither descriptive nor prescriptive but, in this view, primarily defensive. Thus in the schematic terms of his fable:

The phallus is the privileged latch, the safety catch, the master key that keeps the maternal jaws from clamping down. Only the paternal sheaf stops the crescent womb from engorging herself with her own offspring. The symbolic father boldly enters into the amatory dyad and plays the role of Saint (or *Sein*) George to mother-dragon. Please, tell me another story.

Borders of Language

Kristeva's Critique of Lacan

In "Within the Microcosm of 'The Talking Cure,'" an essay collected in the volume *Interpreting Lacan*, Julia Kristeva presents "her own reading of Jacques Lacan's texts and practice." In spite of—or perhaps in keeping with—her opening promise to examine "Lacan's contributions" (33), Kristeva proceeds to mount a radical critique of the Lacanian project (the linguistic interpretation of the unconscious) and to display the contingencies that limit his voyage of discovery (the return to Freud).

Lacan's (in)version of the Saussurian sign is summarily stated in his well-known "algorithm"

$$\frac{S}{s}$$

"the signifier over the signified, 'over' corresponding to the bar separating the two stages" (*Écrits*, 497 / 149). Throughout her theoretical writings, Kristeva calls into question the relevance of this formula to certain signifying practices, even when she is not overtly concerned with Lacanian psychoanalysis. In particular, she argues that the algorithm inadequately accounts for nondiscursive pathological and creative phenomena, for an experiential dimension (whether lived or, say, literary) that eludes the language function. As she suggests in "Within the Microcosm," the task of the analyst—and of the critic-reader—is to be attentive to "noises," to try to hear "not only through the different *figures* or *spaces* made by those signs which resemble linguistic signs, but also through *other elements* . . . which, although always already caught in the web of meaning and signification, are not caught in same way as the two-sided units of the Saussurean sign and even less so in the manner of linguistico-logical categories" (37).

In this text and others, Kristeva proposes the concept of the "semiotic" in order to designate those other elements and to facilitate study of them. She would shift psychoanalysis away from its fascination with language and toward operations that are "*pre-meaning* and *pre-sign* (or *trans-meaning, trans-sign*)," that "[cut] through language, in the direction of the unspeakable" ("System," 29; *Tales*, 247).

Within this larger, ongoing project, the essay on the "talking cure" presents a concentrated effort to redress what Kristeva views as Lacan's overemphasis, in his teaching and practice, on the symbolic order. She focuses on a specific clinical instance: the analytic encounter with borderline patients. To demonstrate the limitations of a theory by means of a limited example might itself seem a questionable critical procedure. In what follows I try to show that Kristeva's critique of the Lacanian formula, in relation to the borderline patient's discourse, has wide-ranging implications for other forms of communication as well. Furthermore, because Lacan offers his algorithm as the elementary structure of all language and of all unconscious processes, Kristeva's essay, in effect, challenges the ability of his theory to sustain the Freudian insight.

I

"Borderline," in the clinical sense of the term, usually designates a "special category of cases . . . on the fringes of madness" (Clément, 55) and, similarly, "patients whose problems are situated on the frontier between neurosis and psychosis" (Moi, 239). Kristeva's characterization of the borderline reflects her twofold theoretical orientation as a linguist and a psychoanalyst.

First, a distinctive symptom of the borderline condition is the appearance of "bits of discursive chaos" (Kristeva, "Within the Microcosm," 45); the language function disintegrates: "[T]he patient's 'borderline' discourse gives the analyst the impression of something alogical, unstitched, and chaotic—despite its occasionally obsessive appearances—which is almost impossible to memorize" (42). These "bits" appear at the limits of the symbolic order, "outside the transcendental enclosure within which we are otherwise constrained by phenomenology and its relative, linguistics" (40–41). Eluding the inside of the language system, borderline discourse refuses ordered and regulating articulations. It does not cause the patient to transgress the law of language and logic or to foreclose the Name-of-the-Father; rather, symptomatically, it allows such transgression and foreclosure to go into effect. Topographically, the borderline is where the sovereignty of the sign is threatened and something wild, something irreducible to language, emerges. Nevertheless, it should be noted that this is a border, and not a beyond, of language. The dissolution of the sign is, Kristeva stresses, only *"relative,"* and a "semblance of socialization" is sometimes maintained (42–43).

Second, borderline discourse is an effect or outbreak of what Kristeva calls "abjection." Described briefly and oversimply, abjection entails an absence (the normative condition of the pre-mirror-stage *infans*) or a collapse (the condition of the borderline patient) of the boundaries that structure the subject. In the opening pages of *Powers of Horror*, Kristeva repeatedly posits a connection between abjection and the border. She defines abjection as "what disturbs identity, system, order. What does not respect borders, positions, rules" and explains that "abjection is above all ambiguity" (4, 9). This ambiguity develops under the impact of "ruptures" or in the collapse of self-limits. The abject is neither subject nor object, neither inside nor outside, neither here nor there. In other words, the borderline patient is one who *"strays* instead of getting his bearings, desiring, belonging, or refusing." Instead of *"Who* am I?" this patient asks: *"Where* am I?" (8). The "borderlander" is always an exile; "'I' is expelled," or ceases to be, for, "How can I be without a border?" This absence of identity—a psychic wandering or loss of place—is congruent with a discourse produced on the borders of language: "[W]hat is *abject* . . . draws me toward the place where meaning collapses" (2).

For Kristeva, then, the borderline has a complex resonance. It designates a condition that eludes both the mirror stage essential for subject formation and the castration anxiety that (by placing the maternal object under prohibition) generates desire, leaving a "strayed subject . . . huddled outside the paths of desire." The borderline also denotes a corollary effect: "a language that gives up" (11).

II

Now if, as already noted, Kristeva's critique applies only to an exception, only to an interesting but restricted deviation, it would not seriously endanger the Lacanian rule. However, as the word "microcosm" in the title of her essay immediately suggests, this "special" case is an epitome of the speaking subject at large; instead of regarding the borderline as a pathological entity, Kristeva sees in it a pervasive aspect of the human condition. Border effects are to be found in the discourse of everyday life: "The problem of the heterogeneous in meaning, of the unsymbolizable, the unsignifiable, which we confront in the analysand's discourse . . . characterizes the very condition of the speaking being, who is not only split but split into an irreconcilable heterogeneity" ("Within the Microcosm," 35–36).

Nor is that all. The term "heterogeneity" describes more than an effect of the split between the conscious and the unconscious within the subject. The borders of the symbolic system are where art, or certain types of art, emerge as well. In "Within the Microcosm," these relations are briefly indicated: "The analyst's attentiveness to language makes him open to works of art, since it is so-called aesthetic production that *knows how to deal with* [*sait faire avec*] the (de)negation inherent in language, without actually knowing it" (39). This statement alludes to a convergence that Kristeva elaborates elsewhere. She defines poetic language, like borderline discourse, as "a practice *for which any particular language is the margin*" ("Ethics," 25) and, consequently, as eluding a strictly linguistic interpretation: "[T]he very concept of sign, which presupposes a vertical (hierarchical) division between signifier and signified, cannot be applied to poetic language—by definition an infinity of pairings and combinations" ("Word," 69). At times, she makes the connection even more explicit—"poetic language . . . by its very economy borders on psychosis" ("From One Identity," 125)—and, at other times, more general: "[A]ll literature is probably a version of the apocalypse that seems to me rooted . . . on the fragile border (borderline cases) where identities . . . do not exist or only barely so—double, fuzzy, heterogeneous, animal, metamorphosed, altered, abject" (*Powers*, 207).

To insist on the primacy of language is, therefore, to fail to account for preverbal and nonverbal elements that escape the safety net of language, that cannot be subsumed under the Saussurian sign. It is to fail to account for areas of aesthetic and, in particular, literary creation situated beyond signification and meaning (beyond the symbolic). As Kristeva observes in an earlier revisionist essay, "[A] text cannot be grasped through linguistics alone" ("Word," 69). The rhythms and musicality of a literary work, like the colors of a painting, may inscribe "instinctual 'residues' that the understanding subject has not symbolized" ("Giotto's Joy," 221). In brief, Kristeva argues that Lacan's linguistic conceptualization of unconscious processes ("The unconscious is structured like a language") restricts access to essential and hidden elements of experience.

This argument may seem vulnerable at two points. First, Lacan's concept of *lalangue*, introduced rather late in his work (in the seminars of 1972–73), seems to clear a space within the symbolic order for heterogeneity. *Lalangue* is, Kristeva concedes, a "fundamental refinement" of his earlier interpretation of the relations between the unconscious and language. "As something completely different from communication or dialogue," from the symbolic order of experience, *lalangue* is called upon "to represent the real from which linguistics takes its object" ("Within the Microcosm," 34). Kristeva quotes Lacan: "Language is what we try to know about the functioning of *lalangue*" (*Seminar XX: Encore*, 126; quoted in "Within the Microcosm," 34). However, even though *lalangue* seems to be "animated by affects that involve the presence of nonknowledge," and therefore seems "irreducible-to-significance," it remains a fundamentally "thetic" concept: "[I]t exists and can be conceived only through the *position*, the thesis, of language." On what grounds other than her vested interest does Kristeva make this claim? "No matter how impossible the *real* might be, once it is made homogeneous with *lalangue*, it finally becomes part of a topology with the *imaginary* and the *symbolic*, a part of that trinary hold from which nothing escapes" ("Within the Microcosm," 35–36). By assimilating *lalangue* to the realm of the real,

Lacan makes the concept fully coherent with the interrelated orders (symbolic-imaginary-real) central to his thought. *Lalangue*, too, becomes a part of that triadic structure.

Kristeva's argument could be undercut (but also reinforced) from a second point of view. Her complaint is not the first, nor is it likely to be the last, directed at Lacan. As she readily acknowledges: "Critiques of Lacanian theory have included a number of attempts to give status to affect and to the heterogeneity it introduces into the discursive order" ("Within the Microcosm," 34). What, then, does Kristeva's critique add to our understanding of this theory and its limitations? I would suggest that the force and innovation of her reading derive from its specific direction or recourse: the path it takes back to the writings of Freud.

III

A dense footnote, half a page long, gives the first indication of the direction Kristeva's reading will take. It presents new and significant (not marginal) material in support of her critical interpretation. The note's position is therefore somewhat at odds with its content. What appears to be a detour from the main path unpredictably turns into a crucial step in a series of steps:

> We should keep in mind the incredible complexity of Freud's notion of a "sign," which is exorbitant compared with the closure imposed on the sign by Saussure's stoicism. The Freudian "sign" is outlined in *On Aphasia*: *visual*, *tactile*, and *acoustic* images linked to object associations which refer, principally through an auditory connection, to the *word* itself, composed of an *acoustic* and *kinesthetic* image, of *reading* and *writing*. The fact that the *acoustic* image is privileged in this case does not diminish the heterogeneity of this "psychological blueprint of word-presentations," which today we still have difficulty assimilating, even with the rigor of linguistics and analytical attentiveness. And yet, the nature of this "imagery" will remain incomprehensible unless we perceive it as always already *indebted* (in a more or less "primary" or "secondary" way, as he would later say) to that representability specific to language, and therefore to the linguistic *sign* (signifier/signified). While this sign serves as the internal limit upon which Freud structures his notions of *presentation* and *cleavage* (what Lacan makes explicit in his "linghysteria"), it is by no means the most far-reaching of Freud's discover-

ies. Freud's conception of the unconscious derives from a notion of language as both heterogeneous and spatial, outlined first in *On Aphasia* when he sketches out as a "topology" both the physiological underpinnings of speech ("the territory of language," "a continuous cortical area," "centers" seen as *thresholds*, etc.) as well as language acquisition and communication (the after-word, the relation to the Other). ("Within the Microcosm," 37 n. 8)

The note constitutes an essay-within-the-essay, or a kind of subplot in Kristeva's text. In sections III–V of my discussion, I closely study this reference to "Freud's notion of a 'sign'" and examine its immediate intertextual relations, and in section VI, I assess the wider implications of the note for her challenge to Lacan's theory and practice. By "intertextual relations," I mean both the inner play of elements that organizes Kristeva's argument, "the web of relationships which produce the structure of the text (or the subject)," and the outer play, "the web of relationships linking the text (subject) with other discourses" (Zepp, 92–93; see also Kristeva, *Revolution*, 59–60).

The terms "complexity" and "closure" in Kristeva's opening exhortation function in a manner analogous to "heterogeneity" and "homogeneity." These sets of terms also suggest yet another distinction central to her work. *Le sémiotique*, in the sense given it by Kristeva, differs from *la sémiotique*, which is semiotics as a general, traditional science of signs. Her semiotic is a drive-affected dimension of human experience that disrupts (even as it interfuses with) the symbolic: "a disposition that is definitely heterogeneous to meaning but always in sight of it" ("From One Identity," 133). This conception of *le sémiotique* may be postulated as a mediation between the real that is the beyond or other of language and the symbolic, between what is ineffable and what is articulated through language. According to Kristeva's formulations, it is a process rather than a system: "meaning not as a sign-system but as a *signifying process*" ("System," 28); it involves dynamic, prelinguistic operations rather than thetic or static modes of articulation, which are the domain of what she calls "'classical' semiotics" (32). *Le sémiotique* is also characterized by states of archaic mentation, closely linked to infantile symbiosis. Thus, for Kristeva the semiotic encompasses two distinct but related areas of interest: (1) the "semanalysis" or semiology of signifying practices—that is, the study of linguistic phenomena—and of "pre- and translogical breakouts" ("Ethics," 27); and (2), in contrast to thetic consciousness, a condition of instinctual motility that corresponds to the position of the *in-*

fans before the mirror stage permits the elaboration of an ego and, no less crucially, before the fear of castration produces a superego submissive to the interdiction imposed by the father.

Strategically, then, Kristeva enlists the "complexity" of Freud's model of the sign in order to counter the "closure" and hegemony of the Saussurian model privileged by Lacan. She appeals to authority in order to repeal authority. The invocation of Freud's sign will enable her to arrive at the limits (that is to say, the limitations as well as the borders) of the system, and thus to identify operations irreducible to the S/*s* relation. But why is this sign itself deported to a border?

Any attempt to examine the implications of this gesture requires tracing the footnote's progress. For it is a question not only of displacement but also of repetition. Where exactly does the footnote first appear? And where does it go from there? Note 8 is introduced, in the first part of "Within the Microcosm," at the end of a sentence that posits "places of *jouissance* (when it undermines the signifier/signified distinction and predicative synthesis) and of defense (when [*jouissance*] becomes blocked)" (37). By a kind of associative transposition, the reader is then directed to "the other scene"—literally, to a block of small type at the bottom of the page. The material presented in this block reappears a few pages later, within the capital or principal text; that is, in the second part of her essay, Kristeva raises the footnote out of the bottom margin and integrates it into the main line of her argument. (This movement might recall the "upward mobility" of Hamlet after his original appearance in a note in the first edition of *The Interpretation of Dreams*.) Kristeva's footwork now becomes increasingly intricate. Her note on the Freudian sign not only moves from the borders to the body of the essay on Lacan. It also turns up for a third time, in "Something To Be Scared Of," the second chapter of *Powers of Horror*.

This repetition undoubtedly indicates the theoretical importance of Freud's sign for the critical evaluation of Lacan's contributions. Perhaps it is also a trace of the essay's origins in two pieces that were stitched together for the first time in the volume *Interpreting Lacan* ("Within the Microcosm," 33). But, as Freud's founding gesture of autoanalysis demonstrates, it is difficult, if not impossible, to have a theory without the libidinal positioning of the theorist. The odd marginal moment, the emergence of the footnote within her texts, enacts what Kristeva describes: the disruptive relation of borderline phenomena to the symbolic system. This moment could also be said to resemble the interplay between the unconscious and the conscious. I examine the footnote, therefore, in the theoretical context of her critique and subsequently in relation to an anxiety that enables and accompanies its textual reproduction. Such a reading itself cannot avoid repetition, if only because it brings, conceptually and typographically, a border (a footnote) to the center of discussion. My interpretation is constrained to duplicate as well as analyze Kristeva's text. In other words, I cannot step outside (again it is a question of footwork) the circuit of readings I am trying to read.

IV

Freud's interest in a psychical, as well as a physiological, explanation for articulatory disturbances is already evident in his monograph *On Aphasia* (1891). In describing the "speech apparatus," Freud posits a relation between "word-presentation" and "object-presentation." Later, in the 1915 paper "The Unconscious," the same terms enter into different combinations: "word-presentation" is retained, but what was called "object-presentation" becomes "thing-presentation." In "The Unconscious," as the editor of the *Standard Edition* points out, "object-presentation" denotes "a complex made up of the combined 'thing-presentation' and 'word-presentation'—a complex which has no name given to it" in *On Aphasia* (*SE*, 14, Appendix C: 209). This complex, however, is named in Kristeva's footnote and its reiterations. She calls it Freud's "sign," usually indicating her application by means of italics or quotation marks.

Yet to use the term "sign" for what Freud calls "the functional unit of speech" and "a complex concept" in *On Aphasia* seems to underscore the similarity between Freud's and Saussure's linguistic formulations (73; and for an alternative translation, see also *SE*, 14: 210). Such a designation not only suggests that Freud's "functional unit of speech" adumbrated Saussure's but, more crucial for Lacan's linguistic emphasis, that Freud's conception does not fundamentally differ from the signified-signifier distinction set forth in the *Course in General Linguistics* (1915). If so, the monograph provides strong grounds for a defense (rather than a critique) of Lacan's assimilation of the Saussurian schema into his theory.

Kristeva expressly notes these grounds in the second chapter of *Powers of Horror*: "Obviously privileged here [in *On Aphasia*], the *sound* image of word presentation and the *visual* image of object presentation become linked, calling to mind very precisely the matrix of the sign belonging to philosophical tradition and to which Saussurian semiology gave new currency." This recalling, however, emphasizes certain elements in Freud's definitional statements while repressing or neglecting others: "it is easy to forget the other elements belonging to the sets thus tied together" (51). What are these "other elements"? Or what, according to Kristeva, is the difference between the two signs—Freud's and Saussure's?

For a reply it necessary to return, as Kristeva indicates, to the monograph on aphasia, in which Freud defines his "complex concept" (Kristeva's "sign") as "constituted of auditory, visual and kinaesthetic elements" (73; see also *SE*, 14: 210). Freud expands this concept—the word "corresponds to an intricate process of associations entered into by elements of visual, acoustic and kinaesthetic origins"—and then repeats it: "The idea, or concept, of the object is itself another complex of associations composed of the most varied visual, auditory, tactile, kinaesthetic and other impressions" (77–78; and see also *SE*, 14: 213). This is indeed a complex object-presentation. In addition to linking visual and acoustic components, it allows nonverbal elements of expression to be integrated into the "psychological schema of the word concept" (77). For this reason, Kristeva asserts in her footnote that Freud's notions of presentation are among "the most far-reaching" of his discoveries. Certainly Freud, like Saussure (as Derrida shows in *Of Grammatology*), privileges the sound image in his later writings, just as he does in the 1891 monograph. Nevertheless, Kristeva contends, "[t]he fact that the *acoustic* image is privileged in this case does not diminish the heterogeneity of this 'psychological blueprint of word-presentations,' which today we still have difficulty assimilating"—and which Lacan apparently never did.

It should be stressed, however, that Kristeva neither slights nor denies the importance of the Saussurian-Lacanian distinction for linguistics and for psychoanalysis. In the footnote and its permutations, she repeatedly gives credit where it is due. The Freudian sign, she says, is "always already *indebted* . . . to that representability specific to language and therefore to the linguistic *sign* (signifier/signified)" ("Within the Microcosm," 37); "one can say nothing of such (effective or semiotic) heterogeneity without making it homologous with the linguistic signifier" (*Powers*, 51); and, "one should not forget the advantages that centering the heterogeneous Freudian sign in the Saussurian one afforded" (52). Yet she also closely and frequently remarks the disadvantages. The assimilation of Freud's sign to Saussure's leaves out, she observes, "what constitutes all the originality of the Freudian 'semiology' and guarantee[s] its hold on the heterogeneous economy (body and discourse) of the speaking being" (51–52). Lacanian theory, in emphatically insisting on the "unitary bent" of the sign, neglects Freud's notions of "a complicated concept built up from various impressions" (*On Aphasia*, 77): "[W]hen Lacan posits the Name of the Father as the keystone to all sign, meaning, and discourse, he points to the *necessary condition* of one and only one process of the signifying unit, albeit a constitutive one" (*Powers*, 53).

Before discussing other implications of Kristeva's critical position, I would like to recapitulate the argument already presented. In his famous "return to Freud," Lacan does not go far enough, either theoretically or chronologically. Despite the considerable explanatory power of his theory, Lacan does not take in or allow for the full complexity of Freud's insights. Hence Kristeva emphasizes the need to "rehabilitate this Freudian sign; the study of language—in linguistics or in psychoanalysis—can no longer do without it" ("Within the Microcosm," 42). Hence she cautions those who would apply Lacanian formulations indiscriminately that "a reductiveness of this sort amounts to a true castration of the Freudian discovery" (*Powers*, 52). In Kristeva's view, a funny thing happened to Lacan on his way back to Freud. He murdered his father, perhaps without knowing it.

V

A further understanding of the drama that unfolds here requires transposing a different kind of castration onto the one just mentioned. This transposition will lead to the "maternal" mode of reading recommended and practiced by Kristeva as a supplement—in the Derridean sense of addition *and* substitution—to the "paternal" mode that marks Lacan's access to the unconscious.

In the treatment of borderline patients, Kristeva remarks, the analyst often encounters "a language that gives up." This implies that something is surrendered or, more precisely, sundered at the borders of language. The signifier is often cut off from the signified; the material specificity of the sign remains, without any signification and affect. Thus the border is a cutting edge, a place of scission: "It is, in short, a reduction of discourse to the state of 'pure' signifier, which insures the disconnection between verbal signs" (*Powers*, 49). The privileged signifier, the Name-of-the-Father is repudiated, and fragmented, nonverbal elements, or "pure" signifiers, prevail. Language (the patient's or the text's) "keeps breaking up to the point of desemantization, to the point of reverberating only as notes, music, 'pure signifier'"; similarly, "there is a collapse of the nexus constituted by the verbal signifier effecting the simultaneous *Aufhebung* of both *signified* and *affect*" (49–50).

To put it in more strictly psychoanalytic terms, there is a foreclosure (*Verwerfung*) of the paternal function and a regression to a premirror stage in which the individual forms a fusional dyad with what is no longer perceived as an alterity or (m)other. In such regressive states, the unstable ego tends to produce echolalia—that is, an echoing infantile discourse. This semiotic disposition may be heard, according to Kristeva, "in all of these divergences from codified discourse, but also in gestures, laughter and tears, moments of acting out" ("Within the Microcosm," 38). Yet the semiotic does not only appear within and through infantile or divergent modes of expression: "Beneath the seemingly well-constructed grammatical aspects of these patients' discourse we find a futility, an emptying of all affect from meaning—indeed, even an empty signifier" (41).

But if borderline discourse and, by extension, certain types of poetic language are full of the symptom called a "pure" or "empty" signifier, how can the analyst (who is inevitably caught up in the symbolic) respond to such a discourse? How can the "talking cure" or any interpretation take place when the bottom has dropped out of the sign? What kind of analytic technique is called for?

In "Within the Microcosm," Kristeva offers a primarily theoretical account of her work in this area. (She includes more extensive clinical examples in *Tales of Love*, originally published in 1983, the same year that *Interpreting Lacan* appeared.) The title of the second part of the essay—"Two Types of Interpretation in the Cure of a Borderline Patient: Construction and Condensation"—points to her analytic approach. Although Kristeva does not explicitly make the connection, the two types may be considered as correlative to the signs previously contrasted in her essay. The constructive type assumes the Saussurian-Lacanian distinction; the condensed type draws upon the interplay of "other elements." These methods of interpretation do not exclude each other, however. Condensation serves in one of two supplementary capacities: as an optional accessory or a required substitute. That is, just as Kristeva delineates the limitations of the Lacanian "algorithm" but acknowledges its necessity, so she suggests, in this part of her essay, the need for going beyond construction without abandoning it. In the exposition that follows, I do not attempt to evaluate the clinical aspects of construction and condensation. Rather, as a reader trained in literary criticism, I explore some interesting analogies between these techniques and the analysis of literary texts.

Construction resembles a more or less conventional but essential "thematic" criticism. As Kristeva describes it, constructive interpretation entails a "repetition or reordering . . . that builds connections"; "it reestablishes plus and minus signs and, subsequently, logical sequences" (46). Because borderline states often involve a breakdown of the linguistic sign, the emphasis in treating them is on the process of construction. The analyst is a kind of contractor who builds meanings out of disparate, "empty" elements. The task of this contractor is to repair the paternal function, "to *construct relations*, to take up the bits of discursive chaos in order to indicate their relations (temporal, causal, etc.), or even simply to repeat these bits of discourse, thereby already ordering these chaotic themes." By introducing a sequential, relational logic into a discourse that is marked by discontinuity and fragmentation, this type of interpretation attempts to reconstitute "the very capacities of speech to enunciate exterior referential realities." Reactivating the defunct S/s connection, "constructive interpretation reestablishes signification and allows meaning to rediscover affect" (45–46).

In certain respects, condensation seems analogous to deconstruction. It calls for a free "play of signifiers" (46), for puns and other verbal manipulations in the analyst's own interpretive discourse. So why not call it "deconstructive" or "deconstructed" interpretation, especially since such terms bring out the contrast with "constructive" type? As already indicated, construction and condensation do not constitute a diametrical opposition for Kristeva, nor does she in any way enjoin us to view them as such. To assign the label *deconstruction* to the supplement of construction would perpetuate a polarization that Kristeva deliberately and consistently attempts to fore-stall. It is a question not of choosing one and excluding the other (a logic of either/or) but, rather, of deploying the two types (a logic of both/and). Per-haps, more complexly still, the borderline patient is better served when the analyst maintains an interpretive stance that moves freely between the op-tions presented by these forms of logic.

Such a stance is itself close to, and yet not identical with, that of decon-struction. It is like deconstruction in its moments of play and in its move-ments between the either/or and both/and logics of interpretation. It is un-like deconstruction in the ethical position that the analyst takes vis-à-vis the "text," in the analyst's obligation to alleviate suffering, to enable a cure by re-turning meaning and signification to the patient's symbolic universe. The lit-erary critic is, of course, under no such obligation. On the contrary, the ethics of philosophical and, by extension, literary instruction, Derrida writes in "Violence and Metaphysics," is to be found in or founded upon "the dis-cipline of the question." According to Derrida, "[T]he question must be maintained. As a question. . . . A founded dwelling, a realized tradition of the question remaining a question. If this commandment has an ethical mean-ing, it is not in that it belongs to the *domain* of the ethical, but that it ulti-mately authorizes every ethical law in general" (80).

Psychoanalysis maintains the discipline (and the freedom) of the question by calling it into question. There are times, as Kristeva shows in *Tales of Love*, when the question must be superseded, when constructive interpretation or "a knowledge effect," however provisional—"this means such-and-such, for the *moment*" (276)—is required: "To the extent that the analyst not only causes truths to emerge but also tries to alleviate the pains of John or Juliet, he is duty bound to help them in building their own proper space." Note that she speaks of "truths," however, not a single "truth," and of a process, "building." Kristeva adds: "It is not a matter of filling John's 'crisis'—his emptiness—with meaning, or of assigning a sure place to Juliet's erotic wan-derings. But to trigger a discourse where his own 'emptiness' and her own 'out-of-placeness' become essential elements, indispensable 'characters' if you will, of a *work in progress*" (380).

Yet, even if Kristeva's refusal of the term "deconstruction" is understand-able, the question remains: why "condensation"? Kristeva borrows Freud's term for one of the essential mechanisms governing dreamwork and joke work. She quotes from Freud's *Jokes and Their Relation to the Unconscious*, "Condensation . . . [is] a process stretching over the whole course of events till the perceptual region is reached" (*SE*, 8: 164), and immediately continues, "Thus, a condensed interpretation has a more erotic and more binding effect" ("Within the Microcosm," 46). The connection between these two statements is not immediately apparent. Nevertheless, they indicate another important distinction between construction and condensation. Whereas the constructive interpretation would provide a signified (a meaning) for the "empty" signifier, the condensed interpretation evokes wide-ranging, translinguistic associations. In keeping with this distinction in psychical range and with the different roles assumed by the analyst in each interpretive mode, I would suggest that construction may also be characterized as "unitary" intervention and condensation as "complex" participation. Condensation supplements "logico-constructive protection" by colluding with the borderline patient's "manic or narcissistic manipulation of the signifier" (46). The analyst responds to non-sense with non-sense; that is, in the analyst's play of metaphors, puns, and manipulations of words, as in the borderline patient's discourse, "sense does not emerge out of non-sense, metaphorical or witty though [the non-sense] might be" (*Powers*, 50). The analyst imitates or borrows from the patient's rhetoric, rhythms, and intonations, thereby invoking heterogeneous dispositions (the semiotic), in addition to trying to reassemble linguistic signs (the symbolic). In effect, the analyst echoes the echolalia of the patient.

Kristeva briefly suggests why this type of interpretation is effective. By reinforcing archaic modes of articulation, it activates a "maternal" transference in which the patient directs toward the analyst an "entire gamut of . . . desires and needs." Condensation prompts the reemergence of a presymbolic, infantile organization and, therefore, has "a more erotic and more binding effect" ("Within the Microcosm," 46–47). In contrast to the unitary intervention, which attempts to reestablish the paternal function, condensation may be said to comply with the patient's pressure for symbiosis. This participation enables the patient to experience a fusion or "death-in-the-mother" and, then, a second birth.

Thus condensation extends the critique of Lacanian theory and practice. It points to the limitations of an analytic perspective that privileges the paternal function, that stresses the advent of the subject into the discursive

world of desire. Lacan writes in "The Agency of the Letter in the Unconscious" that "man's desire is a metonymy" (*Écrits*, 528 / 175). Kristeva comments in the first part of *Tales of Love*, entitled "Freud and Love: Treatment
and Its Discontents":

> Lacan located idealization solely within the field of the signifier and of de-
> sire; he clearly if not drastically separated it . . . from drive heterogeneity
> and its archaic hold on the maternal vessel. To the contrary, by emphasizing
> the *metaphoricity* of the identifying idealization movement, we can attempt
> to restore to the analytic bond located there (transference and countertrans-
> ference) its complex dynamics. . . . (38)

Kristeva's argument necessitates taking into account the Lacanian alignment of the mechanisms of displacement (*Verschiebung*) and condensation
(*Verdichtung*) with what Lacan calls "their homologous function[s] in discourse": metonymy and metaphor (*Écrits*, 511 / 160). This alignment follows
Freud's definitions of displacement as "the replacing of some one particular
idea by another in some way closely associated with it" and of condensation
as the compression of two or more elements into "a single common element" (*SE*, 5: 339). In a state of love (such as transference), Freud's common
element corresponds to the subject's movement toward identification with or
idealization of the other; in metaphor, this element is the area of overlap in
which two semantic components fuse. Likewise, Kristeva's use of the term
"condensation" suggests both a mode of unconscious mental functioning
and its linguistic correlative, metaphoricity. In contrast to Lacan, who emphasizes the metonymic dimension of desire, the displacements imposed by
a third party, the mythic father of *Totem and Taboo*, Kristeva investigates—
through her condensed interpretations—the metaphoric dimension of love:
the bond with (as well as separation from) the mother.

VI

Kristeva's essay in *Interpreting Lacan* constitutes only one moment, albeit a
significant one, in her effort to challenge the privileged position of the symbolic paternal order as articulated by Lacanian theory. Perhaps inevitably, in
presenting her account of Lacan's "castration of the Freudian discovery,"

Kristeva reduplicates her subject matter. Her essay opens with a brief acknowledgment:

> It would be strange for a psychoanalyst, asked to present her own reading of Jacques Lacan's texts and practice, to consider herself either a propagator or a critic of his work. For the propagation of psychoanalysis . . . has shown us, ever since Freud, that interpretation necessarily represents appropriation, and thus, an act of desire and murder. (33)

Jane Gallop comments on the broader significance of this opening statement: "Outside the immediate context, it reminds us that, psychoanalytically, interpretation is always motivated by desire and aggression, by desire to have and to kill" (*Reading Lacan*, 27). But what does the text have that the reader must kill—or interpret—to possess? The reader wants what the text is supposed to know; or, as Lacan might put it, the reader desires the signifier of desire, the "phallus": "signifier of power, of potency" ("Desire," 51).

In the first sentence of the next paragraph, however, Kristeva may be said to begin "Within the Microcosm" once again, with a modest disclaimer immediately followed by the promise of "contributions": "In the following pages, I will first try to present one possible reading—my own—of Lacan's contributions to the interrelations between language and the unconscious" (33). Yet Kristeva has already noted that every text is an incorporation and transformation of another text. If, as she also reminds us, "every hero is a patricide" (*Powers*, 181), every critic might be one too. The role of the writer as patricide is, of course, what Harold Bloom documents in his poetics of influence. But whereas Bloom, following Freud's *Totem and Taboo*, envisages interpretive appropriation as a father-son conflict, as the struggle between strong male poets or critics and their paternal precursors, Kristeva clears a space for the daughter in this engagement. Kristeva enters into a conflictual relationship with a powerful paternal authority. This daughter is not seduced by the father; instead, she masters and murders him. Her example invites other female descendants who formerly were spectators or objects in the male drama of desire to join in the ritual feast.

Significantly, Kristeva is not only contending with a symbolic, with an already "dead" father. Father Lacan, although legendary, was still alive when the two parts of "Within the Microcosm" were initially presented. The first part appeared in the autumn of 1979 as "Il n'y a pas de maître à langage"

("There Is No Master of Language"), in a special issue of *Nouvelle Revue de Psychanalyse*. The title could be read as a refutation of Lacan's "truth": "Il n'est parole que de langage" ("There is no other speech but language") (*Écrits*, 412 / 124). According to Kristeva, in borderline cases (which, as I have suggested, cover a lot of territory) the speaker is not spoken by or is subjected to language. Moreover, she argues that attempts to assimilate psychoanalysis to linguistic models ignore the radical difference between the two fields: "l'imperméabilité de la ratio linguistique à la découverte freudienne" ("Il n'y a pas de maître," 127). Thus her title could also be understood to announce: Lacan is not the master of (psychoanalytic) language. The second part of her essay was delivered as a seminar at the Centre Hospitalier Sainte Anne in the spring of 1981. Lacan died on 9 September 1981.

However, as theorists and practicing psychoanalysts, both Kristeva and Lacan are—and always remain—the children of Freud. From this standpoint, Lacan is not the father; rather, he is the self-appointed son and hero. Kristeva thus enters into a rivalry with Freud's "French son" (Kerrigan, ix). She finds that the son who guards the paternal power, as it were, avails himself of it. His interpretation is an act of self-empowerment that strips away the full originality of the Freudian insight. Kristeva challenges this appropriation. A defender of the father and his faith, she attempts to resurrect his word (the privileged signifier) after the murderous son's incorporation of it. "It is necessary," as she says, "to go back to the Freudian theory of language."

"Go back" is a marked phrase in this context. At stake, for all sides, is more than how, or more than who knows how, to read Freud well. Recasting King Lear's question, we might also ask, which of them shall we say does return the most? Interpretation is an act of love and devotion, as much as of hate and slaughter, by a son or a daughter. Wherever Kristeva cites Freud's sign, she gives two elements prominence: the suggestion of a return to origins (namely, to a very early Freudian text) and, often in conjunction with this return, the concept of heterogeneity. For example, note 8 of "Within the Microcosm" concludes: "Freud's conception of the unconscious derives from a notion of language as both heterogeneous and spatial, outlined first in *On Aphasia* when he sketches out as a 'topology' both the physiological underpinning of speech . . . as well as language acquisition and communication. . . . " This statement sums up Kristeva's critique of Lacan: it is the "extraterritorial" or semiotic dimension of experience, together with the sphere of symbolic influence, that constitutes the Freudian unconscious. As Lacan himself declares, the Freudian concept of the unconscious is indeed "something different" from his own (*Seminar XI*, 24 / 21).

Kristeva reiterates later in her essay that her return to Freud outdistances Lacan's: "In rereading Freud's initial, preanalytic text on aphasia . . . we find Freud's own model of the *sign* and not the Saussurian signifier/signified distinction" (42). Again, in *Powers of Horror*, she links her return with heterogeneity: "And, returning to the moment when [the Freudian theory of language] starts off from neurophysiology, one notes the heterogeneity of the Freudian *sign*" (51); the documentation reads: "See Freud's first book, *Aphasia (Zur Auffassung der Aphasien*, 1891)" (213 n. 12). In the two-paragraph section of *Powers of Horror* entitled "The 'Sign' According to Freud," the words "heterogeneity" and "heterogeneous" appear five times (51–52). These terms, as already noted, are also among the defining characteristics of *le sémiotique*, Kristeva's major theoretical corrective to the preeminence granted the symbolic order.

Thus Kristeva aligns the complexity of her notion of a semiotic approach with Freud against Lacan and the closure of the Saussurian sign. This observation does not invalidate Kristeva's reading of Lacan or consign it to the category of an intrafamilial disorder. Nonetheless, in the course of her critical assessment, Kristeva enters into a doubly binding relationship with her adversary. Not daughter, but sister; both sister and daughter.

Having gone thus far, it is difficult for me to ignore the double bind that my presentation of Kristeva's critique is itself caught up in. I shall briefly try to step outside—as if I could—and describe this complication.

In choosing to engage Kristeva's work and, particularly, her essay on the "talking cure," I repeat and applaud her criticisms of Lacanian theory as too narrowly enclosed in its linguistic formulations. My reading of Kristeva's reading of Lacan's reading of Freud would establish a communion, a sisterhood. I not only follow the movements of her footnote but also repeat her return to the monograph on aphasia, thereby exhibiting an analogous ambivalence: a defense of the "good" father (Freud) and a challenge to the "bad" (Lacan). But, in situating Kristeva's texts in relation to Lacan's, I am also committed to an act of appropriation. My close reading of Kristeva's subtextual lines of defense is not entirely innocent. It implicates what were formerly omissions at Freud's totemic festival. It raises the specter of a conflictual engagement between mothers and daughters. I have taken pains to defend myself and avoided any footnotes. For the fathers hover dimly, recede into the background, as I find myself in the coils of a transference with a powerful maternal authority. Not sister, but daughter; both daughter and sister.

Nevertheless, no longer silent onlookers at the brothers' banquet, we come up to the table. And we are hungry.

Reference Matter

Notes

INTRODUCTION

1. Where two page numbers are given separated by a slash mark, the first refers to the French edition of Lacan's works and the second to the English. Where only one page reference appears, the work has not been translated into English and, unless otherwise indicated, the excerpt is given in my translation.

2. Elizabeth Grosz concludes her study of Lacan with a brief but important recommendation for feminist readers to develop a critical ambivalence toward his teaching. "A cultivated ambivalence," Grosz writes, "may help to sustain the arduous and pleasurable task of reading Lacan." Such an ambivalence would not result from indecision, from an inability to cease oscillating between acceptance and rejection of Lacanian theory. On the contrary, it might well function as a strategic standpoint: namely, "as a tactical position enabling feminists to use his work where it serves their interests without being committed to its more troublesome presumptions" (191–92). The question this recommendation raises for me is: is it possible "to use his work" without some degree of commitment, however troubled and uneasy, to its "presumptions"?

3. Special thanks are due to Nancy K. Miller for her timely and generous suggestion that led to this investigation of Courbet's *The Origin of the World*.

CHAPTER ONE

1. A reproduction of *The Origin of the World* may be found on-line at http://www.lacan.com/courbet.htm. This truncated mode of representation is analogous to Yves Klein's 1960 performance works that enacted his concept of the *femme pinceau* (female paintbrush) by using naked models covered with paint to produce body-print images. "Very quickly I saw that it was the 'block' of the body itself, that is to say the trunk and also a portion of the thighs, that fascinated me. The hands, the arms, the

head, the legs were unimportant. Only the body lives, all-powerful, and does not think," Klein explains. "In the substitution of the woman's body (and specifically the torso) for the phallic brush, the represented figure is turned into a fetish, so that it becomes a reassuring image rather than one that evokes unpleasure through the threat of sexual difference and castration," Lynda Nead comments (73).

2. Gérard Zwang, a physician and sexologist, published the first of these books, *Le sexe de la femme* (1967); Giuseppe Maria Lo Duca, an expert in eroticism and pornography, the second, *Histoire de l'érotisme* (1969). For further details, see Teyssèdre, 227–29.

3. Whenever excerpts from works in French appear with no translator named in the bibliography, the quotation is given in my translation.

4. See, e.g., Nochlin, "Origin Without an Original," 76, 78–79, and Herz, "Medusa's Head," 171.

5. See http://sunsite.unc.edu/cgfa/courbet/p-courbet7.htm for a depiction of Courbet's *The Painter's Studio*.

6. In a chapter on "Courbet's 'Femininity,'" Michael Fried proposes that the representation of sexual difference in Courbet's *The Painter's Studio* (as in his other gender-coded paintings) "both is and is not culturally stereotypical." While arguing that the painting's central group "confirms a conventional privileging of masculinity as active and productive over against femininity as passive and supportive," Fried also contends that several factors contribute to the destabilization of gender identities represented in this group. For instance, "by depicting the model as the bearer rather than merely the object of the look (standing behind the seated painter she is unavailable to his gaze even while she is exposed to ours), the central group characterizes femininity as implicitly active after all"; and furthermore, "the merging of painter, model, and painting in a single pictorial-ontological entity coextensive with the central group . . . work[s] against the privileging of any one of those elements above the others" (191–92). Contra Fried's extensive attempts to align Courbet's art with the feminine, the subtitle to his chapter greets the reader with the following conflation: "Chiefly Paintings of Women Along with Certain Landscapes and Related Subjects."

7. Francis Haskell provides a biographical sketch of Khalil Bey, with a special emphasis on the important collection of European paintings he amassed during the 1860s in Second Empire Paris and was constrained to sell at auction. After the successful sale of this collection, Khalil Bey recapitulated his "strange" life-adventures as follows: "Women have deceived me, gambling has let me down, and my pictures have brought me money" (quoted in Haskell, 183). As a point of parallel observation, one of the most popular and frequently published (twice in the 1860s) pornographic novels in Victorian England was *The Lustful Turk: a History Founded on Facts, containing an interesting narrative of the cruel fate of two young English ladies named Sylvia Carey and Emily Barlow*. Sylvia and Emily are ravished in the course of their misadventures and installed in the Turk's harem, but a "cruel fate" visits their captor as well: a new member of his harem revolts and castrates him (see Webb, 97–98).

8. Shortly after the installation of *The Origin* at the Musée d'Orsay, J.-B. Pontalis

(coauthor of the monumental *Language of Psycho-Analysis* and a psychoanalyst who did his training analysis under Lacan) told a reporter for *Le Nouvel Observateur* about the one occasion when Lacan showed him the painting: "I believe it was not for the sake of my beautiful eyes but because I was accompanied by Marguerite Duras" (quoted in Teyssèdre, 256). In 1965, Lacan published his "Hommage fait à Marguerite Duras," an unusually laudatory essay on Duras's enigmatic novel *Le ravissement de Lol V. Stein.*

9. According to Bernard Teyssèdre, the title is not out of keeping with Courbet's "pagan vitality, nor with his irreligious cheek": "To make of *man* the origin of the world is a whim no less mystifying than to imagine a creation spun out of God" (145, 140; emphasis added). Unless other information is found, the first documented mention of the title occurs in Charles Leger's inaugural lecture delivered at an exposition of the works of Courbet at the Kunsthaus in Zurich on 14 December 1935 (see Teyssèdre, 428–29).

10. In a 1973 biography of Courbet, Jack Lindsay makes an early analogy between a female nude (*Woman with White Stockings*) and landscape in the artist's oeuvre: "[K]eeping the essential lay-out but transforming the human sections into rocks, tree-clumps and the like, we arrive at a typical landscape of the kind that deeply stirred Courbet—the vagina forming the cave-entry, the water-grotto, which recurs in his scenes . . . a certain symbolism was present in many of the landscapes: for instance, the one in the easel-painting of the *Studio*" (217–18). Herz draws a detailed comparison between *The Source of the Loue* (now in the Albright-Knox Gallery, Buffalo) and *The Origin*: "Courbet's characteristic care in representing the surfaces of his model's body—the care at once painterly and mimetic . . . can be observed in his rendering of the rocks surrounding the cave of the Loue" ("In Reply," 213). Fried offers a concise analysis of several comparable observations along with his counterview (see esp. 209–16).

11. See Ortner, "Is Female to Male as Nature Is to Culture?" for an anthropological analysis of "the woman problem."

12. For an application of the Lacanian concepts of the imaginary and symbolic to the operations of pornographic images in male heterosexual experience, see Mark Bracher's chapter on "Pornography," esp. 90–101.

13. See, e.g., Lacan's chapter "Le maître châtré" (The Castrated Master) in his *Seminar XVII: L'envers de la psychanalyse,* 1969–1970.

CHAPTER TWO

1. Whenever two page citations appear in tandem after quotations from *Les complexes familiaux*, separated by a slash mark, the first refers to the French text and the second to Carolyn Asp's abridged translation, "The Family Complexes." Where only one page citation is given, it refers to material omitted in the English version. Translations of these passages are mine.

2. Lacan's formulation is: "À travers les images, objets de l'intérêt, comment se constitue cette *réalité*, où s'accorde universellement la connaissance de l'homme? à travers les identifications typiques du sujet, comment se constitue le *je*, où il se reconnaît?" (*Écrits*, 92).

3. See, e.g., Lacan's dismissal of attempts to find his later ideas "already there" in his previous work as illusory: "Il arrive que nos élèves se leurrent dans nos écrits de trouver 'déjà là' ce à quoi notre enseignement nous a porté depuis" (*Écrits*, 67). However, as discussed in Chapter 3, Lacan's attitude is more complex than his statement here suggests.

4. Laplanche and Pontalis provide a useful distinction between the terms "imago" and "complex": "[T]hey both deal with the same area—namely, the relations between the child and its social and family environment. The notion of the complex refers, however, to the effect upon the subject of the interpersonal situation as a whole, whereas that of the imago evokes an imaginary residue of one or other of the participants in that situation" (211).

5. Rank's dedication to Freud was also a pledge of continued allegiance: "Presented to the Explorer of the Unconscious" and "Creator of Psychoanalysis" (Lieberman, 202). See also James Strachey's introduction to *Inhibitions, Symptoms and Anxiety* in *SE*, 20: 85–86.

6. In 1926, three weeks before Freud's seventieth birthday, Rank left Vienna with his family and, as he notified the members of the Psychoanalytic Society, "permanently settled" in Paris. Rank remained in Paris from 1926 until 1935 when he moved to the United States (Roazen, 407, 409). I have found no indication that Lacan and Rank ever met in Paris, but it does not seem implausible to assume that some contact took place between them.

7. E. James Lieberman suggests that "Jones and Abraham stand as the jealous and devious siblings" Goneril and Regan to Freud's King Lear. Lieberman also cites a "private" letter (in contradistinction to the *Rundebriefe* circulated among the Committee members) in which Jones writes to Abraham about Freud's hopeless lack of "objectivity where Rank is concerned": "One must recognize with regret that even Freud has his human frailties and that age is bringing with it one-sidedness of vision and diminution of critical power" (letter dated 1 January 1923, quoted in Lieberman, 212). Filling in this analogy, I would recall Goneril's tête-à-tête with Regan at the end of the first scene of *King Lear*: "The best and soundest of his time hath been but rash; then must we look from his age to receive not alone the imperfections of long-engrafted condition, but therewithal the unruly waywardness that infirm and choleric years bring with them" (1.1.297–302).

8. Ernest Jones discusses the birth-trauma controversy from the biased but informative perspective of one of the parties involved (3: 59 ff.). For more balanced favorable discussions of Rank's views and his relation to Freud, see Bókay; Gay, 470–89; Kramer; Lieberman, esp. 193–225; Roazen, 392–418; Rudnytsky; and Taft, esp. 78–120. An interesting account of the clinical relevance of "normal birth expe-

rience" and "grades of traumatic birth" to the analytic situation appears in D. W. Winnicott's "Birth Memories, Birth Trauma, and Anxiety" (1949). Indirectly engaging the still much-debated issue of the after-effects of birth and deferring frequently to the Freudian position, Winnicott describes the dream of a schizophrenic patient in response to reading *The Trauma of Birth*: "The dream itself is a reaction to an impingement (the reading of Rank's book) and the analysis suffered a temporary setback" (186). Elsewhere in this essay, however, Winnicott acknowledges "a relation clinically between anxiety manifestations and the details of birth trauma" that may determine patterns of persecution in paranoid cases, as well as "a link between birth trauma and the psychosomatic disorders" (190–91).

9. See Strachey's chronology: "The title-page of Rank's book bears the date '1924'; but on its title page appear the words 'written in April, 1923,' and the dedication declares that the book was 'presented' to Freud on May 6, 1923 (Freud's birthday). . . . [Freud] had nevertheless been aware of the general line of Rank's ideas as early as in September, 1922" (*SE*, 20: 85–86).

10. Freud's attribution of "Character is Destiny" to Napoleon appears twice: in "Debasement in the Sphere of Love" (1912), *SE*, 11: 189, and in "The Dissolution of the Oedipus Complex" (1924), *SE*, 19: 178. On the authority of George Eliot, however, the saying should be credited to Novalis: "'Character,' says Novalis in one of his questionable aphorisms—'character is destiny'" (*Mill on the Floss*, 420). The epigram is more commonly attributed to Heracleitus (see Bartlett, 77; also Stevenson, 317).

11. For an interesting development of this idea from a feminist perspective, see Marcia Ian, esp. 20–22 and 38–39.

12. In *Les complexes familiaux*, Lacan describes the *Fort/Da* game played by Freud's grandson as an exemplary extension of the acceptance/rejection of weaning. Following Freud, Lacan notes the pleasurable sense of mastery accompanying the child's play; however, he also stresses the structural resemblance of this activity to the bipolar attitude activated by weaning: "the dialectical moment when the subject assumes this discomfort [i.e., human weaning ('le malaise du sevrage humain')] by his first playful acts and, through that, sublimates and overcomes it" (40–41 / 17; trans. modified). Toward the end of the essay, Lacan reiterates that the child's casting the reel to and fro is a gestural symbol signifying a reenactment of the weaning process. It represents an "assumption of the original tearing apart under the guise of a game that consists in rejecting the object" (93 / 25; trans. modified). The terms "assumes" and "assumption" in both passages may be correlated with the pole of acceptance: the *Fort/Da* game repeats the painful process of assuming or accepting *sevrage*, thereby enabling a positive resolution to the weaning crisis. The game allows the child to recreate the rupture—"the original tearing apart"—together with a renewed consent to the primal loss of rapture.

13. Freud addresses the dynamic point of view as follows: "[W]e explain it [i.e., the splitting of the conscious-preconscious system from the unconscious] dynami-

cally, from the conflict of opposing mental forces, and recognize it as the outcome of an active struggling on the part of the two psychical groupings against each other" (*SE*, 11: 26).

14. In a comparable vein, Rank writes: "We believe we have shown, in a bird's-eye view of the essential achievements and developments of civilization, that not only all socially valuable, even over-valued, creations of man but even the fact of becoming man, arise from a specific reaction to the birth trauma" (183).

15. See, e.g., *The Ego and the Id* (1923): "I have lately developed a view of the instincts which I shall here hold to and take as the basis of my further discussion" (*SE*, 19: 40); see also *Civilization and Its Discontents* (1930): "[I]n the course of time [the death instincts] have gained such a hold upon me that I can no longer think in any other way" (21: 119).

16. For accounts of the mixed reception among Freud's contemporaries of his theory of conservative or death instincts, see Jones, 3: 276–78, and Gay, *Freud: A Life*, 402–3.

CHAPTER THREE

1. On the difficulty of translating the German word *nachträglich* and the inadequacy of the terminology used in English, see Bowie, *Lacan*, 180–81.

2. My discussion of Lacan's theory of time and the subject is particularly indebted to conversations with William J. Richardson and the closing paragraphs of his essay "Lacan and the Subject of Psychoanalysis."

3. Ken Frieden notes a resemblance between Freud and the figure of Janus: as a dream interpreter, Freud himself was "two-faced, divided between orientations toward the past and toward the future." While continually looking back "for causes of mental events," he also inspired in his patients the "creation of new meanings" (9).

4. In *Tribute to Freud*, the American poet H.D. (Hilda Doolittle) recalls Freud's showing her the Pallas Athena in his art collection: "'*This* is my favorite' he said. . . . It was a little bronze statue, helmeted, clothed to the foot in carved robe with the upper incised chiton or peplum. One hand was extended as if holding a staff or rod. 'She is perfect,' he said, '*only she has lost her spear*.'" Perhaps the word "only" may also signify here "because": "*because* she has lost her spear"? The collector's item images the notion of genital deficiency, the lack or "always already" castrated condition of female sexuality. The statue is consonant with Freudian (and Lacanian) theory in yet another sense. H.D. adds that when Freud said, "*she is perfect*," his words suggested to her that "the little bronze image was a perfect symbol, made in man's image . . . born without human or even without divine mother, sprung full-armed from the head of her father, our-father, Zeus" (68–70).

5. John Macquarrie and Edward Robinson explain their translation of *Zu-kunft* as follows: "Without the hyphen, 'Zukunft' is the ordinary word for 'the future'; with

the hyphen, Heidegger evidently wishes to call attention to its kinship with the expression 'zukommen auf . . . ' ('to come towards . . .' or 'to come up to . . .') and its derivation from 'zu' ('to' or 'towards') and 'kommen' ('come'). Hence our hendiadys" (Heidegger, 372–73 n. 3).

6. The term "story" here designates the narrated events in their chronological or sequential order; "plot," the actual disposition of this narrative content in the work. In the plot the events are not necessarily presented in sequence but, rather, from a perspective that rearranges them. The formalist critic Boris Tomashevsky similarly distinguishes between the story as "the action itself" and the plot as "how the reader learns of the action" (67). I am suggesting here an analogy between two views of psychical temporality (developmental stages vs. deferred action) and two basic aspects of narrative fiction (story vs. plot).

7. In the section of *Of Grammatology* entitled " . . . That Dangerous Supplement . . .," Derrida discusses the two significations of the concept of the supplement: on the one hand, a dispensable or optional addition ("it is a surplus") and, on the other, a necessary replacement or completion that fills a gap ("its place is assigned in the structure by the mark of an emptiness"). Following Derrida's "logic of supplementarity," I propose that the second of these two significations replaces the first in Ferenczi's text as what is apparently optional "intervenes or insinuates itself *in-the-place-of*" (see *Of Grammatology*, 144–45).

8. See, e.g., Roudinesco, *Jacques Lacan & Co.*, 268, 278, 414, and Borch-Jacobsen, 46–47, 248.

9. For an analysis of three main periods in Ferenczi's conception of therapeutic technique from a Lacanian perspective, see Soler.

10. For a discussion of Ferenczi's differences with Freud that is heavily weighted against Ferenczi, see Jones, 3: 46–81. For alternative accounts of the issues and politics involved, see Balint, 124–26, 149–53; Gay, *Freud: A Life*, 578–86; Lieberman, 193–95; Roazen 363–71.

11. From a contemporary perspective, Ferenczi's insights into the responses of young children to sexual abuse and violence are not only illuminating but all too verifiable. However, in 1932 Freud argued that the essay (which overturned his seduction theory by contending that sexual traumas often resulted from factual rather than fantasized experience) would harm Ferenczi's professional reputation and attempted to dissuade him from presenting it at the International Congress in Wiesbaden. Ferenczi nevertheless read the paper, published it, and bore the consequences. For a varied range of descriptions, see Gay, *Freud: A Life*, 583–84; Jones ("it would be scandalous to read such a paper before a psychoanalytic congress" [3: 173]); Roazen, 368; and This ("Traum n'est pas *Traum*: le rêve . . . Ferenczi s'isole pour protéger sa liberté de pensée" [73]).

12. Melanie Klein is the likely target of Lacan's comment. Neither her clinical intuition nor her investigations into the mother's role in childhood development prevented strife within her own family. In a series of debates held at the British Psychoanalytic Society during the early 1940s, "Melitta Schmideberg, a child analyst,

engaged in unseemly public controversy with the pioneering child analyst, Melanie Klein, who was her mother" (Gay, *Freud: A Life*, 466). These attacks may have engendered Klein's later idea of the infant's "primitive envy" of the feeding breast and all that the mother supposedly withholds: "Some infants obviously have great difficulty in overcoming such grievances" (Klein, "Study of Envy," 213–14). The public rancor displayed by mother and daughter apparently also led to Lacan's sideswipe in the context of his reference to the confusion of tongues.

CHAPTER FOUR

1. My discussion is mainly indebted to Jane Gallop's "Where to Begin?" (*Reading Lacan*, 74–92) for its overall approach and to Roudinesco's biographical work on Lacan for its extensive archival information.

2. On the atmosphere at the Marienbad congress, the conflicts between Anna Freudians and Kleinians, and Lacan's general reception, see Roudinesco, *Esquisse*, 151–61.

3. Gallop gives an acute analysis of this blind entry in *Reading Lacan* (74–76).

4. Hélène Cixous writes of *Through the Looking-Glass*: "[O]ne is immediately tempted . . . to take the whole adventure for a figurative representation of the imaginary construction of self, the ego, through reflexive identification" (238).

5. The single, disparaging reference to Lacan in Girard's *Violence and the Sacred* (1972) is thus quite off the mark: "Lacan, too, failed to discover [the mimetic nature of desire], forced as he was by his linguistic fetishism to reinforce the more rigid . . . aspects of Freudian theory" (185). Nevertheless, Girard's idea of the *mimetic* rival differs from Lacan's *mirror-stage* rival in two basic respects. First, Girard defines mimetic rivalry as a kind of antidialectic, an interminable oscillation that does not lead to any synthesis or progress: "the situation affords no stability of any sort, no synthetic resolution" (154). Second, he subsumes the Oedipus complex under the category of mimetism, stressing the structurally identical positions occupied by the father-brother in relation to the subject (see, e.g., 145). In Girard's view, viable distinctions cannot be made between "primary" and "secondary" identifications and, correlatively, between the two types (fraternal and paternal) of rivalry.

6. Excerpts from Wallon's text are given in my translation.

7. For further discussion of the significance of Matthews's and Chauvin's research for Lacanian theory, see Ver Eecke, 115–16.

8. Roudinesco also notes that "a transition was . . . effected from the description of a concrete experiment to the elaboration of a doctrine" (*Jacques Lacan & Co.*, 143). However, her analysis of this transition does not take into account the differences between Wallon's literal and Lacan's primarily metaphoric concepts of the mirror.

9. In another connection, Gerald Fogel makes the similar point that Winnicott's work "creates not a theory, but an antitheory": "Theories ordinarily explain, but

Winnicott is more interested in grasping or describing the nature of personal experience, not its causes or its components. Almost everything he deals with refers to a relational or existential *process*" (207).

10. On Winnicott's subtle deployment of this analogy in four additional papers published between 1941 and 1971, see First, "Mothering, Hate, and Winnicott."

11. Lacan refers to psychoanalysis as a "conjectural science" on several occasions; see, e.g., *Écrits*, 472, 863.

12. See "From Love to the Libido" in *Seminar XI*: "Whenever the membranes of the egg in which the foetus emerges on its way to becoming a new-born are broken, imagine for a moment . . . that one can do it with an egg as easily as with a man, namely the *hommelette*" (qu'on peut faire avec un oeuf aussi bien qu'un homme, à savoir l'hommelette) (179 / 197). The passage echoes James Joyce's play on words in *Finnegan's Wake* (1939): "*Mon foie*, you wish to ave some homelette, yes, lady! Good mein leber! Your hegg he must break himself" (59). In addition to Joyce's pun, Lacan could also be alluding to one of Freud's favorite French truisms for the need to discuss openly "the facts of normal or abnormal sexual life." As he writes in the case of Dora (1905): "No one can undertake the treatment of a case of hysteria until he is convinced of the impossibility of avoiding the mention of sexual subjects. . . . The right attitude is: 'pour faire une omelette il faut casser des oeufs'"(*SE*, 7: 49; see also Freud's letter to Fliess [6 August 1899] in *Complete Letters*, 365). For Lacan, the connection between the *hommelette* and the facts of origin—that is, the procreative agency of the parents—seems to be again the telling and difficult one.

CHAPTER FIVE

1. This chapter benefited greatly from stimulating discussions with Zephyra Porat and Daniel Boyarin.

2. In the "Index" to Ferenczi's *Further Contributions to the Theory and Technique of Psycho-Analysis*, two separate listings appear for analytic technique: "Technique (*active*)" and "Technique (*classical*)." As this division implies, Ferenczi defines the "classical" approach in terms of its passivity. For example, "Psycho-analysis, as we employ it to-day, is a procedure whose most prominent characteristic is *passivity*. We ask the patient to allow himself to be guided uncritically by his 'ideas.' . . . The doctor should not fix his attention rigidly on any particular intention . . . but should also yield himself passively to the play of his phantasy with the patient's ideas" ("Further Development of an Active Therapy," 199). Ferenczi possibly intended the term "classical" to be complimentary or, at least, inoffensive; but it was, in effect, counterposed to the term "innovation," as well as to "activity"—and so Freud understood it. Ferenczi's correlation of classical technique with the analyst's rule-bound, silent, unresponsive behavior during treatment elicited this equivocal, even irritated response from Freud: "The work [Ferenczi and Rank's *The Development of Psychoanalysis*] has, in my

judgment, the fault that it is incomplete, i.e., it does not work out the changes in technique . . . but only sketches them. There are certainly dangers involved in this deviation from our 'classical technique' as Ferenczi dubbed it in Vienna, but this is not to say that they cannot be avoided" (Freud to Committee, letter dated January 1924; Rank Collection, Rare Books and Manuscript Library, Columbia University).

3. References to Chauvin's and Matthews's experiments also appear in "Remarks on Psychical Causality," 189–91, and "Some Reflections on the Ego," 14. For further discussion, see Chapter 4, 78.

4. I want to thank my student Navah Moshkowitz for sharing her responses to her daughter's first independent flip-flop. For an analysis of the onset and persistence of maternal separation anxiety in a folkloric context, see my "Reading 'Snow White': The Mother's Story."

5. See Derrida, "Le Facteur de la vérité" "The Postman or Factor of Truth", in *The Post Card*; see also "The Purveyor of Truth," in Muller and Richardson, *Purloined Poe*, for an abbreviated version of this essay. For an insightful discussion of the Lacanian reading of "The Purloined Letter" as "no less than an *allegory of psychoanalysis*," see Felman, "On Reading Poetry" (esp. 147–48).

6. On the differences between compositional allegory and interpretive allegory, see Whitman, 3–8 and 263–68 (Appendix II).

7. Contra the "vertical" conception of allegorical narratives as providing a kind of baseline for interpretation, Maureen Quilligan argues for a "horizontal" or progressive view: "It would be more precise to say . . . that allegory works horizontally, rather than vertically, so that meaning accretes serially, interconnecting and crisscrossing the verbal surface long before one can accurately speak of moving to another level 'beyond' the literal" (28). However, it seems to me that whether one conceives the meaning of allegorical compositions as residing in vertically or horizontally organized space, the description remains a figurative convenience, a manner of speaking about the complex interplay between spoken and unspoken, articulated and unarticulated components of the work. The two metaphors of movement (up/down and back/forth) both serve as supplementary rather than strictly opposite views of the interpretive process.

8. Bowie notes that Lacan "savours the ambiguity of prepositions . . . and plays relentlessly upon the alternative meanings of *à* and *de*"; and Dennis Porter similarly remarks, in his "Translator's Note" to *Seminar VII*, that "one of the most difficult words to translate turned out to be '*de*'" (Bowie, "Jacques Lacan," 144; Porter, viii).

9. My reading coincides with Muller and Richardson's explication of the word "passion" in these paragraphs as designating "the submission of man, as signifiable, to the laws of language that structure the unconscious expression of desire" (*Ouvrir*, 164).

10. Cf. Macklin Smith: "It seems to me that no 'synthesis' occurs precisely because the poet cannot conceive his culture apart from his God, that his cultural orientation is exclusively Christian" (5; see also 105, 108).

11. Whitman offers an alternative view: "[W]hile the divided will may be one of the necessary conditions for the personification of the soul, it is clear that something beyond this division is necessary. . . . The forces of the personality need not only to be divided, but to be fully abstracted, removed to their own level of discourse, and capable of diverging from their strict definitions" (31).

12. This notion of existence may be aligned with the opening statement of Bruce Fink's *Lacanian Subject*: "Unlike most poststructuralists, who seek to deconstruct and dispel the very notion of the human subject, Lacan the psychoanalyst finds the concept of subjectivity indispensable and explores what it means to be a subject" (xi). For existence in the opposite sense as "the impossible-real kernel resisting symbolization," see Žižek, 136–37.

13. To cite an exception, see Cynthia Chase's subtle discussion of the ways in which "Lacan's writing inscribes . . . the necessity of a specular moment in the process of signification, and the necessity of its recurrence" (990).

14. Prior to Freud's adoption of the term "narcissism," its first clinical usage appeared in the work of Havelock Ellis in 1898, and its introduction into psychoanalytic circles apparently took place in a paper presented by Isidor Sadger at the Vienna Psychoanalytic Society in 1908. For further discussion of the evolution and applications of narcissism in psychoanalysis, see Pulver, 321–24.

CHAPTER SIX

1. "The maternal theme in Lacan's works is as sparse as the paternal theme is abundant. It might be because, for him, the mother as origin is inconceivable," Marcelle Marini remarks (78). My analysis attempts to show that the absence or curtailment of the mother's role is a development that reverses Lacan's own earlier formulations. The mother as origin is not inconceivable from the outset in his writings.

2. See, e.g., Rank's *Trauma of Birth* and Klein's "Early Stages of the Oedipus Conflict," discussed in Chapter 2.

3. Laplanche and Pontalis were in analysis with Lacan when, in 1958, they undertook to prepare an inventory of Freudian terminology. Their *Vocabulaire* was completed eight years later. However, by the 1970s, members of Lacan's coterie belonging to the EFP (École freudienne de Paris) judged it to be "eclectic" and incompatible with a "Lacanian reading" of Freud's corpus (Roudinesco, *Jacques Lacan & Co.*, 221, 466).

4. Laplanche and Pontalis's definition of "paranoia" is: "Chronic psychosis characterised by more or less systematised delusion, with a predominance of ideas of reference but with no weakening of the intellect and, generally speaking, no tendency towards deterioration" (296). For a helpful commentary on Lacan's expansion of this type of psychosis to a "permanent disposition of the human mind," see Bowie, *Lacan*, 38 ff.

5. The notion of spectral presence derives from Madelon Sprengnether.

6. This term appears, for instance, in Freud's *Group Psychology*: "dann ist die Va-teridentifizierung zum Vorläufer der Objektbindung an den Vater geworden" ("in that event the identification with the father has become the precursor of an object-tie with the father"), and in *The Ego and the Id*: "Die Vateridentifizierung nimmt nun eine feindselige Tönung an" ("His identification with his father then takes on a hos-tile colouring"). See *GW*, 13: 116, 260, and *SE*, 18: 106, 19: 32.

7. Like the rendering of the German *Besetzung* into the neologism "cathexis" (from the Greek *catechein*, to occupy), the terms "anaclisis" and "anaclitic" are an-other example of what Bruno Bettelheim calls, in his *Freud and Man's Soul*, the "mis-translation of Freud's carefully chosen language into gobbledygook English": "Freud shunned arcane technical terms whenever he could, not just because using them was bad style but also because the essence of psychoanalysis is . . . to make hidden ideas accessible to common understanding" (89). On the specific problems involved in Strachey's translation of the everyday noun *Anlehnung* and the verbal form *sich an an-lehnen* into "a 'learned' word, artificially coined" from the Greek, see Laplanche and Pontalis, 29–30.

8. For an analysis of the mother figure in Freud's *Totem and Taboo*, see Sprengnether, 87–105.

9. "Mourning and Melancholia" was written very shortly after the paper on nar-cissism; but, while Freud completed the final draft in 1915, the essay was not pub-lished until two years later ("Editor's Note," *SE*, 14: 239).

10. Cf. Tennyson's "In Memoriam": " 'Tis better to have loved and lost / Than never to have loved at all" (pt. 27, stanza 4; also pt. 85, stanza 1).

11. Bracketed passages are omitted in Asp's version and given in my translation.

12. Cf. Andrea Kahn's translation: "It is also the mother, the first object of the [play of] tendencies, as food to be absorbed and even as breast in which to be reab-sorbed, which is first offered up to the Oedipal desires" (193). Kahn has translated the third section, "Le complexe d'Oedipe," of *Les complexes familiaux*. Her rendition is less idiomatically fluent but often closer in literal meaning to the French text than Asp's.

13. For an analysis of the connection between the weaning complex and castra-tion anxiety in Lacan's 1938 essay, see Chapter 2, esp. 30–32.

14. Lacan's most sustained discussion of the Cartesian "subject of certainty" ap-pears in *Four Fundamental Concepts of Psycho-Analysis*. On the philosophical basis for his critique of the *cogito*, see esp. Lee, 22–24; Ragland-Sullivan, 9–14; and Richard-son, "Lacan and the Subject of Psychoanalysis," 58–59.

15. See also "affective relationships"; "the specular image presents a good symbol of [the subject's] reality, i.e., of its affective value"; and "the subject's affective isola-tion" (*CF*, 17 / 39, 17 / 42, 18 / 45).

16. In "Reading Lacan, or Harlaquanage," I present the contributions of

Borch-Jacobsen's *Lacan* in relation to Bowie's and Grosz's contemporaneous studies of Lacan.

17. In addition to the essay "Femininity" (*SE*, 22: 112–35), Irigaray frequently mentions "The Infantile Genital Organization" (19: 141–45), "The Dissolution of the Oedipus Complex" (19: 172–79), "Some Psychical Consequences of the Anatomical Distinction between the Sexes" (19: 241–58), and "Female Sexuality" (21: 221–43).

18. On the differences between "economic" and "dynamic" points of view in psychoanalysis, see Laplanche and Pontalis, 126–30.

19. Dolto's two case histories on the flower-doll, first published in the *Revue française de psychanalyse* (1949 and 1950), were revised for her collection of essays *Au jeu du désir* (1981). All references in my text are to this revised edition. Cited excerpts from *Au jeu du désir* and Lacan's exchange with Dolto are given in my translation.

20. "Lacan participated actively in the presentations of the S.P.P. His comments were often brief and sometimes funny because whatever subject was discussed, he would generally come back to paranoia, narcissism, and the mirror stage, his main preoccupations," Marini writes (104).

21. Kristeva gives an account of her objections in "Within the Microcosm of 'The Talking Cure.'" For an analysis of Kristeva's sustained debate with Lacan, see Epilogue.

22. After noting that the doll has no mouth, Lacan also remarks that the doll is a sexual symbol: "Il trouve important que la poupée-fleur n'ait pas de bouche et . . . fait remarquer qu'elle est une symbole sexuele" (Miller, 21). He presumably finds a phallic form in the limbless doll. Analogously, while commenting on the little girl's playing with dolls in "Femininity," Freud presents a serial equivalence: doll = baby = penis (*SE*, 22: 128–29). Irigaray proceeds to deconstruct Freud's reading of doll-playing in *Speculum*. Her critical analysis may also be brought to bear on Lacan's view of the symbolism of the flower-doll. Irigaray subverts the masters' lesson that she "repeats" or parodically ventriloquizes as follows: "The girl, let us repeat, has no right to play in any manner whatever with any representation of her beginning, no specific mimicry of origin is available to her: she must inscribe herself in the masculine, phallic way of relating to origin" (78).

23. Leonard Harrison Matthews, "Visual Stimulation and Ovulation in Pigeons," *Proceedings of the Royal Society*, ser. B (Biological Sciences), 126, no. 845 (3 Feb. 1939); cited as "Harrisson" in *Écrits*, 189.

24. See Horney, "Flight from Womanhood": "When one begins, as I did, to analyze men only after a fairly long experience of analyzing women, one receives a most surprising impression of the intensity of this envy of pregnancy, childbirth, and motherhood, as well as of the breasts and of the act of suckling" (60–61). For commentary on this counteranalysis of penis envy, see Quinn, 222 ff.

25. The structuralist physicalism of Gestalt theory is one of the sources of con-

temporary structuralism. Gestalt psychologists reject the assumption that "there are first isolated elements or sensations and then relations between them in the form of associations" (Piaget, 24). A Gestalt formation begins with a perception grasped as a totality rather than separate parts, so that perceptual organization of the whole determines the relations among the parts. This approach to perceptual patterning should therefore be counted among the influences on Lacan's shift to structural analysis. For a sketch of Gestalt theory, see Arnheim.

26. See Chapter 4, n. 12, for the possible sources of this wordplay.

27. My summary draws on Lacan's Seminar IX, "*L'identification, 1961–1962*," available in manuscript. For a helpful discussion of this seminar, see Taillandier.

28. Borch-Jacobsen spins out this intricate chain of animal examples: "Say the word 'lion,' [Hegel] writes, and you create the lion ex nihilo, by abolishing it as a tangible thing. Say the word 'dog,' Kojève comments, and you kill the real dog that barks and wags its tail. Pronounce the word 'cat,' Blanchot continues, and 'death speaks.' Say the word 'elephants,' Lacan concludes, and here comes a herd of elephants, present in its absence and filling up the room" (193; also 169–70).

29. See Ernest Becker on Freud's "*causa-sui* project": "In the normal Oedipal project the person internalizes the parents and the superego they embody, that is, the culture at large. But the genius cannot do this because his project is unique; it cannot be filled up by the parents or the culture. It is created specifically by a renunciation of the parents, a renunciation of what they represent and even of their own concrete persons—at least in fantasy" (110). Becker analyzes how the psychoanalytic movement served as a *causa-sui* vehicle for Freud (115–23).

CHAPTER SEVEN

1. Quotations from the *Confessions* are given in R. S. Pine-Coffin's translation and cited first by book and chapter numbers to facilitate reference, followed by the page number in the 1961 Penguin edition. For the Latin text, see the Loeb Classical Library edition of *St. Augustine's Confessions* in William Watts's translation.

2. As introduced by Freud in 1899, screen memories or images usually belong to the actual lived experience of the individual (see *SE*, 3: 303–22).

3. Derrida, however, also fully acknowledges the value of this exegetical moment: "Doubling commentary should no doubt have its place in a critical reading. To recognize and respect all its classical exigencies is not easy and requires all the instruments of traditional criticism. Without this recognition and this respect, critical production would risk developing in any direction at all and authorize itself to say almost anything" (*Of Grammatology*, 158).

4. In a beautifully nuanced reading of this scene of instruction, Stanley Cavell brings out the factor of isolation, rather than the communal integration, inherent in it: "[W]hat strikes me about Augustine's description is how isolated the child appears,

training its own mouth to form signs (something you might expect of a figure in a Beckett play), the unobserved observer of culture. The scene portrays language as an inheritance but also as one that has, as it were, to be stolen, anyway in which the capacity and the motivation to take it is altogether greater than the capacity and perhaps the motivation to give it. Haunting the entire [Wittgensteinian] *Investigations*, the opening scene and its figure of the child signals that the question 'Where did you learn—what is the home of—a concept?' may at any time arise (and not only in the couple of dozen sections in which the child explicitly appears), that the inheritance of a culture—the process of cultivation . . . comes not to a natural end, or rather to its own end, but to one ended, by poor resources, or by power. . . . At any time I may find myself isolated" (99–100).

5. "The writing of the *Confessions* was an act of therapy" (Brown, 165).

6. Foucault delineates "technologies of the self" as skills and attitudes that "permit individuals to effect by their own means or with the help of others a certain number of operations on their own bodies and souls, thoughts, conduct, and way of being, so as to transform themselves in order to attain a certain state of happiness, purity, wisdom, perfection, or immortality" (18). Foucault also points out that the idea of the self as "something to write about, a theme or object (subject) of writing activity" is not a modern development, "born of the Reformation or of romanticism," but rather is a venerable Western tradition that was "well established and deeply rooted when Augustine started his *Confessions*" (27).

7. In Joan Copjec's reading, Lacan's "televisual" image is intended as a self-parody: "Through his appearance in *Television*, Lacan parodies the image of himself—of his teaching—that we have, to a large extent, received and accepted. Standing alone behind his desk, hands now supporting him as he leans assertively forward, now thrown upward in some emphatic gesture, Lacan stares directly out at us, as he speaks . . . of '*quelque chose, n'est-ce pas?*' . . . [T]his proffered image is parodic" (15). For the reasons given in my analysis, it seems to me that conviction commingles with parody in Lacan's self-presentation.

8. De Certeau pays brief but close attention to Lacan's relationship to Christianity in the section entitled "A Christian Archaeology" of his *Heterologies*: "But what is, after all, this Other whose irreducible brilliance streaks through the entire work? . . . [T]he house is haunted by monotheism" (58). For a concise account of the publication history of Lacan's thesis on paranoid psychosis and his attitudes toward it, see Macey, 211–12.

9. Several scholars have compared Aeneas's abandonment of Dido and Augustine's of Monica at Carthage. For an overview of previous work and further analysis of these parallelisms, see Ziolkowski.

10. Robert O'Connell offers a counterinsight into the possible delaying effects of Monica's perseverance: "Her prayers and tears had much to do with [Augustine's] conversion, but one may be pardoned for wondering how long her possessive importunities did more to keep him away from the faith" (107).

11. On Monica's "extremely seductive" attitude and "incestuous impulses" toward her son, see Kligerman, 474–75.

12. Jesus rejects his earthly family members in order to replace them with a wider spiritual kinship: "'Who is my mother, or my brethren?' And he looked round about on them which sat about him, and said, 'Behold my mother and my brethren! For whosoever shall do the will of God, the same is my brother, and my sister, and mother'" (Mark 3:33–35). Analogously, Jesus says to his mother at Cana of Galilee: "Woman, what have I to do with thee?" (John 2:4).

13. Although Ziolkowski lists several qualifying statements (23 n. 69), he does not take into consideration the ways in which they complicate his argument about the timeliness of Monica's death in sparing her son a conflict between familial and spiritual obligations.

14. Cf. Maggie Kilgour on the *preoedipal* pattern in the *Confessions*: "In the case of Augustine, separation from the mother, the dominant figure in the pre-oedipal oral phase, appears particularly essential" (59). On the sublimation of Monica into the Catholic Church and the figures of Jerusalem and Continence, see Kilgour, 61, and Harpham, 109–11.

15. I am very grateful to my research assistant Hannah Ovnat for her insightful comments on the family-romance aspects of the *Confessions*.

16. Odes of Solomon probably dates from at least as early as the second century (Harris and Mingana, 2: 12). Phyllis Trible's *God and the Rhetoric of Sexuality*, focusing on the Hebrew scriptures, provides a fascinating study of "the image of God male and female" and the psychophysical connections between the biblical deity and the maternal dimension (see esp. 60–71).

17. Warner attributes the latter passage to the Virgin Mary (195); however, the text of the ode itself does not corroborate this attribution.

18. Comparable clusters of God-as-mother images appear in the medieval religious writings of Anselm of Canterbury and Bernard of Clairvaux (Warner, 196–97); see also Eric Auerbach on Bernard's "Epistle 322" (163–64).

CHAPTER EIGHT

1. According to David Macey, the quotation from Augustine's *Confessions* "is consistently used . . . to illustrate the structures of jealousy that are bound up with the transivitism and the mirror stage" (83). Macey includes the anecdote among the "primarily pedagogic devices and illustrations" in Lacan's work that imply no specific philosophical position. My analysis would qualify the "consistency" of Lacan's usage and also show that philosophical concerns arise from his very first quotation of Augustine.

2. In the opening pages of *Civilization and Its Discontents* (1930), Freud contends that "[a]n infant at the breast does not as yet distinguish his ego from the external

world as the source of the sensations flowing in upon him" (*SE*, 21: 66–67). This statement posits a maternal presence that is integral to the "oceanic feeling" described in Romain Rolland's letter to Freud (21: 65 n. 1). However, Freud "forgets" his contention several pages later and reattributes the religious needs that derive from the oceanic feeling to infantile helplessness and to "the longing for the father aroused by it": "I cannot think of any need in childhood as strong as the need for a father's protection" (21: 72). Freud's shift from the image of an infant "at the breast" to a universal "longing for the *father*" anticipates in a single chapter the gradual movement away from an emphasis on the maternal imago to the preeminence of the paternal function in Lacan's writings.

3. Prior to book publication, Wallon gave a two-year course on his research at the Sorbonne (1929–31) and reworked his lectures in a series of articles (1930–32) that appeared in French scholarly journals. See Wallon's introduction ("Avant-Propos") to *Les origines*.

4. "Abjection preserves what existed in the archaism of pre-objectal relationships," Kristeva writes in *Powers of Horror* (10). See Epilogue for further analysis of the "abject" in Kristeva's work.

5. See Chapter 4, 80–81, 83 and Chapter 5, 96–99 for more detailed discussions of this statement.

6. Roudinesco also reports on the basis of a personal conversation that when Kojève died in 1968, "Lacan rushed to his apartment in order to take possession of a copy of the *Phenomenology of Mind* annotated in Kojève's own hand" (*Jacques Lacan & Co.*, 142, 726 n. 75).

7. For accounts of Lacan's activities during the German occupation of France, see Marini, 109–11, and Roudinesco, *Jacques Lacan & Co.*, 147. "The Years of Silence" is Marini's section heading for this period (1939–44) of his professional life.

8. For an exposition of the complex resonances of the *objet* in Lacan's thought, see Juan-David Nasio: "This symbol 'a' does not represent the first letter of the alphabet, but the first letter of the word 'other' [*autre*]. In Lacanian theory, the other is written with a lower-case 'a' and an upper-case 'A.' The upper-case A is one of the anthropomorphic figures capable of overdetermining the signifying chain, while the small other . . . designates our double [*semblable*], our alter ego. Now, the invention of the object *a* responds to several problems, but above all to this question: 'Who is the other? Who is my double?' . . . [T]o be better understood we can make the question of the other more complex and ask: 'Who is the one facing me? Who is it? Is it a body? Is it an image? Is it a symbolic representation?' . . . Since we have not found the solution that we hoped for and required, we mark it with a written notation—a simple letter—the opaque whole of our ignorance; we put a letter in the place of a response that is not given. Object *a* designates thus an impossibility, a point of resistance to theoretical development" (Nasio, *Five Lessons on the Psychoanalytic Theory of Jacques Lacan*, 76–77). However, the *objet* also exceeds the problem of the other in its status as a residue or "surplus" that escapes the laws and logic of the signifying net-

work: "This means that the [symbolic] system produces something which is an excess, and which is heterogeneous or foreign to it" (Nasio, 79).

9. See Stephen Greenblatt's finely detailed discussion of Holbein's painting in *Renaissance Self-Fashioning*. Of the painting's perspectival duality, he remarks: "To see the large death's-head requires . . . radical abandonment of what we take to be 'normal' vision; we must throw the entire painting out of perspective in order to bring into perspective what our usual mode of perception cannot comprehend" (19).

10. Copjec elaborates on this split term in relation to both the discontinuous subject it describes and its difference from the stable subject of contemporary film theory (see *Read My Desire*, 31–38).

11. As Felman observes in another context: "[W]hile it can be said that Lacan wishes to articulate the *continuity* of a logic and a mathematics of the unconscious, it is clear that he goes about it along paths remarkable for their *discontinuity*" (*Writing and Madness*, 135).

12. On possible reasons for the contingent relations between liquids and drying, see Dundes: "From the concept of the 'water of life' to semen, milk, blood, bile, saliva, and the like, the consistent principle is that liquid means life while loss of liquid means death. 'Wet and Dry' as an oppositional pair means life and death" (266).

13. Dundes alternatively proposes that as an "act of insult," spitting functions like a belittling remark and devalues the admired person or object: "If one spits on the baby . . . one is mitigating the praise or admiration expressed. It is as if to say this is not a beautiful, admirable object (and that it should not be subject to an evil eye attack)" (276); see also Gifford: "All of these gestures . . . not only defy the evil eye but also express contempt" (90).

14. Moss and Cappannari further report that in England, at the coronation of Richard the Lion-Hearted (1189), Jews were forbidden to attend for fear that their evil glances might harm the crown. In Germany, the harmful effects of the Jew were so feared that a term for evil eye remains *Judenblick*, "Jew's glance" (8).

CHAPTER NINE

1. Among the critical analyses of the only partially convincing attempts to undo the synonymy between "penis" and "phallus" in psychoanalytic usage, Gallop's commentary remains one of the more trenchant and memorable: "Of course, the signifier *phallus* functions in distinction from the signifier *penis*. It sounds and looks different, produces different associations. *But* it *also* always refers to penis. . . . [A]s long as the attribute of power is a phallus which can only have meaning by referring to and being confused with a penis, this confusion will support a structure in which it seems reasonable that men have power and women do not"; and therefore, it is not surprising "feminists find that central, transcendental phallus particularly hard to swallow" ("Phallus/Penis: Same Difference," 246–47, 244; see also *Daughter's Seduc-*

tion, esp. 96–100). For a concise overview of the term "phallus" in Lacanian theory and some further criticisms, see Evans, 140–44.

2. Jack Zipes deploys the Lacanian idea of the gaze as a function of the male predator and his desire for the reconfirmation of his identity in a mirroring object: "The gaze of the wolf is a phallic mode of interpreting the world and is an attempt to gain what is lacking through imposition and force" ("Epilogue," 379). My emphasis is on Little Red Riding Hood's position in the symbolic field where the gaze functions as a kind of web- or grid-work in which the subject herself is transfixed.

3. For a brief history and description of the tale's variants, see Paul Delarue, "Sources and Commentary," 380–83. Delarue's discussion presents a partial summary of his study, "Les contes merveilleux de Perrault et la tradition populaire: I. Le Petit Chaperon Rouge," *Bulletin folklorique d'Ile-de-France* (1951): 221–28, 251–60, 283–91; (1953): 511–17.

4. An English translation of "The Story of Grandmother" also appears in Delarue's *Borzoi Book of French Fairy Tales*. Several minor but telling differences serve to render a ribald tale more *civile*: e.g., the comment on granny's "big nostrils" is omitted; the girl asks to go outside "to relieve [her]self"; and instead of "Are you making a load?" the werewolf calls out: "Are you making cables?" (232).

5. In Angela Carter's "The Company of Wolves," a late twentieth-century retelling of the old French tale, the success of the girl is repeated—with some difference. She is old enough to have begun "her woman's bleeding, the clock inside her that will strike, henceforward, once a month"; and yet she still "moves within the invisible pentacle of her own virginity" (113–14). The girl, unlike Little Red Cap, immediately "look[s] round the room" when she enters grandmother's house and takes in the full measure of her danger. "No trace at all of the old woman except for a tuft of white hair that had caught in the bark of an unburned log." The stranger who presses his back against the door to block her escape tells her, "There's nobody here but we two, my darling." Fear first assaults her. She takes off her shawl—"the colour of poppies, the colour of sacrifices, the colour of her menses," and then ceases to be afraid since it will not help her. "What shall I do with my shawl? Throw it on the fire, dear one. You won't need it again" (116–17). Her scarlet shawl is as red as the blood she knows must be spilled. But whose blood and which blood will it be?

As her clothes flare up in the fireplace, she stands on tiptoe and begins to unbutton his shirt ("What big arms you have. All the better to hug you with.") and, in keeping with an earlier promise extracted when he ("a fully clothed one, a very handsome young one") sprang into her path in the forest, she freely bestows the kiss she owes him. To her "What big teeth you have!" he responds like a wolf should: "All the better to eat you with." But she discards the symbolic prescription together with the remnants of their clothing: "The girl burst out laughing; she knew she was nobody's meat. She laughed at him full in the face, she ripped off his shirt for him and flung it into the fire, in the fiery wake of her own discarded clothing." Outside the warm room a blizzard rages, or perhaps all the wolves in the world howl a prothalamion, and under the bed where the intruder stowed the grandmother's remains, her old bones "set up a terrible clattering." But the girl pays them no heed. Her story ends with stillness, snowlight, "a confusion of paw prints," and a reciprocally transformed company. Carter conspires, too, to let a young girl retrieve herself from the jaws of a savage wolf. "See! sweet and sound she sleeps in granny's bed, between the paws of the tender wolf" (118).

6. On the French origins of the Grimms' tale, see Delarue, "Sources and Commentary," 381–82.

7. Quoted in Tartar, 37. For an analysis of the ideology of *civilité* in the evolution of European children's literature, see Zipes: "We must remember that the fairy tale for children originated in a period of absolutism when French culture was setting standards of *civilité* for the rest of Europe. Exquisite care was thus taken to cultivate a discourse on the civilization process through the fairy tale for the benefit of well-raised children" (*Fairy Tales*, 9).

8. I am grateful to my student Yoram Laviv for his insightful comments on Nabokov's allusions to the Grimms' tales throughout *Lolita*.

9. The phrase "negative elementary character" serves as the title of Erich Neumann's chapter on psychical reactions to the "Terrible Mother" archetype: "This Terrible Mother is the hungry earth, which devours its own children and fattens on their corpses: it is the tiger and the vulture, the vulture and the coffin" (149). Representations of the Goddess Tà-urt who was also called "The Great" in ancient Egypt show "hippopotamus and crocodile, lioness and woman, in one." Tà-urt the Great bears the head of a crocodile, with a full and toothsome mouth. The dread inspired by this "inhuman, extrahuman, and suprahuman" aspect of the mother is so overwhelming, according to Neumann, that "man can visualize it only through phantoms" (11, 153; see also fig. 34 and pl. 74).

10. Cf. Freud's formulation in his essay on negation (*Verneinung*): "'You ask who this person in the dream can be. It's not my mother.' We emend this to: 'So it *is* his mother'" (*SE*, 19: 235). See Chapter 3, 60–62, for some implications of this statement.

11. "[T]he *Jäger* was hired by the feudal lord to protect his property from poachers and intruders," Zipes writes ("Trials and Tribulations," 35). The lord who sets his hunter to watch over the poacher seems even more game than the lady who asks her cat to protect the cream.

12. Cascardi's vivid proof-text is Goya's *St. Francis Borja at the Deathbed of an Impenitent* (1788): "His body lies across the bed, and the Saint seems to recoil from him. . . . [St. Francis's] right hand remains scarcely able to control the miraculous sign of salvation, the crucifix. Moreover, the crucifix spurts crimson blood. . . . Instead of the saving power of angels, Goya has placed monsters over the dying man, as if to shock the viewer into remembering the drama of transgression and evil that had become normalized in the Enlightenment world" (203).

13. Bettina Knapp provides a detailed Jungian analysis of the complex archetypal

attributes of the Saturn-Kronos figure that inspired "Goya to paint one of his most spectacular canvases and . . . Malraux to write one of his most deeply moving essays" (373).

14. See Freud's "A Child is Being Beaten" (1919) for an analysis of the psychical mechanism that transforms the activity of sadistic fantasies into the passivity of masochistic fantasies whose repressed aim is the assuagement of a sense of guilt originating from the initial sadism (esp. *SE*, 17: 193–94).

15. Cf. Cixous's critique of the Freudian and Lacanian interpretation of the Medusa's head—"They riveted us between two horrifying myths: between the Medusa and the abyss"—as part of the ongoing attempt to induce women to deposit their lives in "banks of lack." Modulating from criticism of male hegemonic discourse to celebration of female sexuality, Cixous demythologizes the motives for the psychoanalysts' "dogma of castration" in this well-known passage: "Too bad for them if they fall apart upon discovering that women aren't men, or that the mother doesn't have one. But isn't this fear convenient for them? Wouldn't the worst be, isn't the worst, in truth, that women aren't castrated, that they have only to stop listening to the Sirens (for the Sirens were men) for history to change its meaning? You only have to look at the Medusa straight on to see her. And she's not deadly. She's beautiful and she's laughing" ("Laugh of the Medusa," 255).

16. The theme of Jesse's tree derives from the vision of the prophet Isaiah: "And there shall come forth a rod out of the stem of Jesse, and a Branch shall grow out of his roots" (Isa. 11: 1). In *Lethal Love*, Mieke Bal proposes that "Hugo's figuration of Boaz's dream" possibly results from a compound assimilation of biblical images: "In the Christian exegetic tradition, a confusion often exists between Boaz's and Jesse's tree. . . . A second confusion, for which Hugo may not have had any source, is the one between this tree and another 'erection,' the ladder also seen in a dream, by Jacob. This condensation is revealing, based as it is on dreams of election, ascension, and posterity as one and the same issue" (71).

17. For tabulated lists of the poem's numerous Judeo-Christian intertexts, see Michel Grimaud, esp. 106–18. Grimaud discusses the parallel pairings between Boaz-Ruth, Judah-Tamar, and Joseph-Marie and, in particular, reinforces the suggestion of previous critics that the poem be read as an Annunciation scene (116–18). "Booz endormi" also abounds in other complex intra- and intertextual repetitions. See, e.g., Georges Combet for a detailed structural analysis of linguistic, syntactic, and rhythmic parallelisms within the poem.

18. Grimaud offers an apocalyptic gloss for the poem's final stanza: "Thrust in thy sickle, and reap: for the time is come for thee to reap; for the harvest of the earth is ripe. And he that sat on the cloud thrust in his sickle on the earth and the earth was reaped" ("Jette ta faucille, & moissonne, car l'heure de moissonner t'est venue: parce ce que la moisson sur la terre est mûre. Alors celui qui était assis sur la nuée, jetta sa faucille sur la terre & la terre fut moissonnée") (Rev. 14:15–16; quoted in Grimaud, 109).

19. In the Hebraic biblical source, the preposition "after" (*achar* and *acharei*) appears so frequently in connection with Ruth's movements (see, e.g., 2:7, 9) along with references to her alien status as "the Moabitess" and the "Moabitish damsel" that these conjunctions may be intended to evoke the phonological proximity of the Hebrew "after" to "other" (*acher*). Mosaic law mandates that a share of the harvest be left for the poor who gather up what remains after reaping. Ruth's "afterness," or poverty, is closely linked to her otherness (both widow and stranger) in Bethlehem.

20. The etching in Jung's *Psychology and Alchemy* is reproduced from the manuscript *Mutus liber* (1702), which is among the rare book holdings of the Mellon Collection of the Alchemical and Occult at the Yale University Library.

Works Cited

Abraham, Karl. "A Short Study of the Development of the Libido, Viewed in the Light of Mental Disorders." In *Selected Papers of Karl Abraham*, trans. Douglas Bryan and Alix Strachey, 418–501. London: Hogarth Press, 1942.

Appignanesi, Lisa, and John Forrester. *Freud's Women*. New York: Basic Books, 1992.

Arnheim, R. "Gestalt Psychology." In *Encyclopedia of Psychology*, ed. Raymond J. Corsini, 2: 58–60. New York: John Wiley, 1984.

Auerbach, Erich. *Mimesis: The Representation of Reality in Western Literature*. 1946. Translated by Willard R. Trask. Princeton, N.J.: Princeton University Press, 1953.

Augustine, Saint. *Confessions*. Translated by R. S. Pine-Coffin. Harmondsworth, Eng.: Penguin Books, 1961.

———. *On Christian Doctrine*. Translated by D. W. Robertson, Jr. New York: Macmillan, 1958.

———. *St. Augustine's Confessions*. Loeb Classical Library. 2 vols. Translated by William Watts. London: William Heinemann; New York: Macmillan, 1912.

Bal, Mieke. *Lethal Love: Feminist Literary Readings of Biblical Love Stories*. Bloomington: Indiana University Press, 1987.

Balint, Michael. *The Basic Fault: Therapeutic Aspects of Regression*. London: Tavistock, 1968.

Bartlett, John. *Familiar Quotations*. 14th ed. Edited by Emily Morison Beck. Boston: Little, Brown, 1968.

Barzilai, Shuli. "Reading Lacan, or Harlaquanage: An Essay Review." *America Imago: Journal of the Association for Applied Psychoanalysis* 52 (1995): 81–106.

———. "Reading 'Snow White': The Mother's Story." *Signs: Journal of Women in Culture and Society* 13 (Spring 1990): 1–20. Reprinted in *Ties That Bind: Essays on Mother and Patriarchy*, ed. Jean O'Barr, Deborah Pope, and Mary Wyer. (Chicago: University of Chicago Press, 1990), 253–72.

Becker, Ernest. *The Denial of Death*. New York: Free Press, 1973.

Bettelheim, Bruno. *The Uses of Enchantment: The Meaning and Importance of Fairy Tales*. New York: Random House, Vintage Books, 1977.
———. *Freud and Man's Soul*. New York: Random House, Vintage Books, 1982.
Bloom, Harold. *The Anxiety of Influence: A Theory of Poetry*. New York: Oxford University Press, 1973.
Blum, Richard, and Eva Blum. *Health and Healing in Rural Greece: A Study of Three Communities*. Stanford: Stanford University Press, 1965.
Bókay, Antal. "Turn of Fortune in Psychoanalysis: The 1924 Rank Debates and the Origins of Hermeneutic Psychoanalysis." Unpublished English translation by Antal Bókay, with Peter Rudnytsky. Originally published as "Sorsfordulo'k a pszicholanali'zisben," *Thalassa* 2 (1991): 25–43.
Borch-Jacobsen, Mikkel. *Lacan: The Absolute Master*. Translated by Douglas Brick. Stanford: Stanford University Press, 1991. Originally published as *Lacan: Le maître absolu* (Paris: Flammarion, 1990).
Borges, Jorge Luis. "Pierre Menard, Author of the *Quixote*." Translated by James E. Irby. In *Labyrinths: Selected Stories and Other Writings*, ed. Donald A. Yates and James E. Irby. New York: New Directions, 1964.
Bottigheimer, Ruth B. "Tale Spinners: Submerged Voices in Grimms' Fairy Tales." *New German Critique* 27 (1982): 141–50.
Bowie, Malcolm. "Jacques Lacan." In *Structuralism and Since: From Lévi-Strauss to Derrida*, ed. John Sturrock, 116–53. Oxford: Oxford University Press, 1979.
———. *Lacan*. London: Fontana, 1991.
Bracher, Mark. *Lacan, Discourse, and Social Change: A Psychoanalytic Cultural Criticism*. Ithaca, N.Y.: Cornell University Press, 1993.
Broumas, Olga. "Little Red Riding Hood." In *Beginning with O*, 67–68. New Haven, Conn.: Yale University Press, 1977.
Brown, Peter. *Augustine of Hippo: A Biography*. London: Faber & Faber; Berkeley and Los Angeles: University of California Press, 1967. Reprint. New York: Dorset Press, 1986.
Brownmiller, Susan. *Against Our Will: Men, Women and Rape*. New York: Bantam Books, 1976.
Burke, Kenneth. "Freud—and the Analysis of Poetry." In *The Philosophy of Literary Form: Studies in Symbolic Action*, 258–92. Berkeley and Los Angeles: University of California Press, 1973.
———. *The Rhetoric of Religion: Studies in Logology*. Berkeley and Los Angeles: University of California Press, 1970.
Burkert, Walter. *Ancient Mystery Cults*. Cambridge, Mass.: Harvard University Press, 1987.
Carroll, Lewis. *The Annotated Alice: Alice's Adventures in Wonderland & Through the Looking Glass*. With an introduction and notes by Martin Gardner. New York: C. N. Potter, 1960. Reprint. New York: New American Library, 1963.

Carter, Angela. "The Company of Wolves." In *The Bloody Chamber and Other Stories*, 110–18. Harmondsworth, Eng.: Penguin Books, 1981.

Cascardi, Anthony J. "The Ethics of Enlightenment: Goya and Kant." *Philosophy and Literature* 15 (1991): 189–211.

Casey, Edward S., and J. Melvin Woody. "Hegel, Heidegger, Lacan: The Dialectic of Desire." In *Interpreting Lacan: Psychiatry and the Humanities*, ed. Joseph H. Smith and William Kerrigan, 6: 75–112. New Haven, Conn.: Yale University Press, 1983.

Cavell, Stanley. "The Argument of the Ordinary: Scenes of Instruction in Wittgenstein and in Kripke." In *Conditions Handsome and Unhandsome: The Constitution of Emersonian Perfectionism. The Carus Lectures, 1988*, 64–100. Chicago: University of Chicago Press, 1990.

Certeau, Michel de. *Heterologies: Discourse on the Other*. Translated by Brian Massumi. Minneapolis: University of Minnesota Press, 1986.

Chase, Cynthia. "The Witty Butcher's Wife: Freud, Lacan, and the Conversion of Resistance to Theory." *MLN* 102 (1987): 989–1013.

Cixous, Hélène. "Introduction to Lewis Carroll's *Through the Looking-Glass* and *The Hunting of the Snark*." Translated by Marie Maclean. *New Literary History* 13 (1982): 231–51.

———. "The Laugh of the Medusa." Translated by Keith Cohen and Paula Cohen. In *New French Feminisms: An Anthology*, ed. Elaine Marks and Isabelle de Courtivron, 245–64. Sussex, Eng.: Harvester Press, 1981.

Clark, Michael. *Jacques Lacan: An Annotated Bibliography*. New York: Garland, 1988.

Clément, Catherine. *The Lives and Legends of Jacques Lacan*. Translated by Arthur Goldhammer. New York: Columbia University Press, 1983. Originally published as *Vie et légendes de Jacques Lacan* (Paris: Grasset, 1981).

Combet, Georges. "Les parallélismes de 'Booz endormi.'" *Revue des lettres modernes*, nos. 693–97 (1984): 81–99.

Copjec, Joan. *Read My Desire: Lacan Against the Historicists*. Cambridge, Mass.: MIT Press, 1995.

Delarue, Paul, ed. "Sources and Commentary." In *The Borzoi Book of French Fairy Tales*, trans. Austin E. Fife, 359–403. New York: Knopf, 1956.

———. "The Story of Grandmother." In *The Borzoi Book of French Fairy Tales*, trans. Austin E. Fife, 230–32. New York: Knopf, 1956.

Derrida, Jacques. "Le facteur de la vérité." In *La carte postale: De Socrate à Freud et au-delà*. Paris: Flammarion, 1980. Translated by Alan Bass in *The Post Card: From Socrates to Freud and Beyond* (Chicago: Chicago University Press, 1987), 411–96. Abbreviated and reprinted as "The Purveyor of Truth" in *The Purloined Poe: Lacan, Derrida, and Psychoanalytic Reading*, ed. John P. Muller and William J. Richardson (Baltimore: Johns Hopkins University Press, 1988), 173–212.

———. *Of Grammatology*. Translated by Gayatri Chakravorty Spivak. Baltimore:

Johns Hopkins University Press, 1976. Originally published as *De la gramma-tologie* (Paris: Éditions de Minuit, 1967).

————. "Violence and Metaphysics: An Essay on the Thought of Emmanuel Lev-inas." In *Writing and Difference*, trans. Alan Bates, 79–153. Chicago: University of Chicago Press, 1978. Originally published as *L'écriture et la différence* (Paris: Éditions du Seuil, 1967).

Des Cars, Laurence. "Gustave Courbet: *L'Origine du monde*." In *De l'Impression-nisme à l'Art nouveau: Acquisitions du Musée d'Orsay 1990–1996*, 26–35. Gen. dir. Henri Loyrette. Paris: Éditions de la Réunion des musées nationaux, 1996.

Dolto, Françoise. "Cure psychanalytique à l'aide de la poupée-fleur." In *Au jeu du désir: Essais cliniques*, 133–93. Paris: Éditions du Seuil, 1981.

Doolittle, Hilda [H.D.]. *Tribute to Freud*. New York: New Directions, 1956, 1974.

Dor, Joël. *Le père et sa fonction en psychanalyse*. Paris: Point Hors Ligne, 1989.

Dumas, Ann. "The Source of the Loue 1864 [Catalogue nos. 47–48]." In *Courbet Reconsidered*, ed. Sarah Faunce and Linda Nochlin, 153–56. New York: Brooklyn Museum, 1988.

Dundes, Alan. "Wet and Dry, the Evil Eye: An Essay in Indo-European and Se-mitic Worldview." In *The Evil Eye: A Folklore Casebook*, ed. Alan Dundes, 257–312. New York and London: Garland, 1981.

Eifermann, Rivka R. "'Germany' and the 'Germans': Acting Out Fantasies and Their Discovery in Self-Analysis." *International Review of Psycho-Analysis* 14 (1986): 245–62.

————. "Interactions Between Textual Analysis and Related Self-Analysis." In *Dis-course in Psychoanalysis and Literature*, ed. Shlomith Rimmon-Kenan, 38–56. Lon-don: Methuen, 1987.

————. "Varieties of Denial: The Case of a Fairy Tale." In *Denial: A Clarification of Concepts and Research*, ed. E. L. Edelstein, Donald L. Nathanson, and Andrew M. Stone, 155–70. New York: Plenum, 1987.

Eigen, Michael. "The Area of Faith in Winnicott, Lacan and Bion." *International Journal of Psycho-Analysis* 62 (1981): 413–33.

Eliot, George. *The Mill on the Floss*. 1860. Reprint. New York: New American Li-brary, 1965.

Evans, Dylan. *An Introductory Dictionary of Lacanian Psychoanalysis*. London: Rout-ledge, 1996.

Faunce, Sarah and Linda Nochlin, eds. *Courbet Reconsidered*. New York: Brooklyn Museum, 1988.

Felman, Shoshana. "On Reading Poetry: Reflections on the Limits and Possibilities of Psychoanalytic Approaches." In *The Purloined Poe: Lacan, Derrida, and Psycho-analytic Reading*, ed. John P. Muller and William J. Richardson, 133–56. Balti-more: Johns Hopkins University Press, 1988.

————. "The Originality of Jacques Lacan." *Poetics Today* 2 (1980–81): 45–57.

————. *Writing and Madness: Literature/Philosophy/Psychoanalysis*. Translated by

Martha Noel Evans and Shoshana Felman. Ithaca, N.Y.: Cornell University Press, 1985.

Ferenczi, Sándor. "Confusion of Tongues Between Adults and the Child." Translated by Eric Mosbacher. In *Final Contributions to the Problems and Methods of Psycho-Analysis*, ed. Michael Balint, 156–67. London: Hogarth Press and the Institute of Psycho-Analysis, 1955.

———. "The Elasticity of Psycho-Analytic Technique." Translated by Eric Mosbacher. In *Final Contributions to the Problems and Methods of Psycho-Analysis*, ed. Michael Balint, 87–101. London: Hogarth Press and the Institute of Psycho-Analysis, 1955.

———. "The Further Development of an Active Therapy in Psycho-Analysis." Translated by Jane Isabel Suttie. In *Further Contributions to the Theory and Technique of Psycho-Analysis*, ed. John Rickman, 198–217. London: Leonard and Virginia Woolf at the Hogarth Press and the Institute of Psycho-Analysis, 1926.

———. "Introjection and Transference." In *First Contributions to Psycho-Analysis*, trans. Ernest Jones, 35–93. London: Hogarth Press and the Institute of Psycho-Analysis, 1952.

———. "The Problem of Acceptance of Unpleasant Ideas—Advances in Knowledge of the Sense of Reality." Translated by Cecil M. Baines. In *Further Contributions to the Theory and Technique of Psycho-Analysis*, 366–79. London: Leonard and Virginia Woolf at the Hogarth Press and the Institute of Psycho-Analysis, 1926.

———. "Psycho-Analysis of Sexual Habits." Translated by Edward Glover. *Further Contributions to the Theory and Technique of Psycho-Analysis*, 259–97. London: Leonard and Virginia Woolf at the Hogarth Press and the Institute of Psycho-Analysis, 1926.

———. "Stages in the Development of the Sense of Reality." In *First Contributions to Psycho-Analysis*, trans. Ernest Jones, 213–39. London: Hogarth Press and the Institute of Psycho-Analysis, 1952.

Fink, Bruce. *The Lacanian Subject: Between Language and Jouissance*. Princeton, N.J.: Princeton University Press, 1995.

First, Elsa. "Mothering, Hate, and Winnicott." In *Representations of Motherhood*, ed. Donna Bassin, Margaret Honey, and Meryle Mahrer Kaplan, 147–61. New Haven, Conn.: Yale University Press, 1994.

Fletcher, Angus. *Allegory: The Theory of a Symbolic Mode*. Ithaca, N.Y.: Cornell University Press, 1964.

Fogel, Gerald I. "Winnicott's Authority and Winnicott's Art: His Significance for Adult Analysis." *Psychoanalytic Study of the Child* 47 (1992): 205–22.

Forrester, John. *The Seductions of Psychoanalysis: Freud, Lacan and Derrida*. Cambridge, Eng.: Cambridge University Press, 1990.

Foucault, Michel. *Technologies of the Self: A Seminar with Michel Foucault*, ed. Luther H. Martin, Huck Gutman, and Patrick H. Hutton. Amherst: University of

Massachusetts Press, 1988.

Freccero, John. "Autobiography and Narrative." *Reconstructing Individualism: Autonomy, Individuality, and the Self in Western Thought*, ed. Thomas C. Heller, Morton Sonsa, and David E. Wellbery. Stanford: Stanford University Press, 1986.

Freud, Sigmund. "Analysis of a Phobia in a Five-Year-Old Boy." In *SE*, 10: 5–147. London: Hogarth Press, 1955.

————. *Beyond the Pleasure Principle*. In *SE*, 18: 7–64. London: Hogarth Press, 1955.

————. "'A Child is Being Beaten': A Contribution to the Study of the Origin of Sexual Perversions." In *SE*, 17: 177–204. London: Hogarth Press, 1955.

————. *Civilization and Its Discontents*. In *SE*, 21: 57–146. London: Hogarth Press, 1961.

————. *The Complete Letters of Sigmund Freud to Wilhelm Fliess, 1887–1904*. Translated and edited by Jeffrey Moussaieff Masson. Cambridge, Mass.: Harvard University Press, 1985.

————. "The Dissolution of the Oedipus Complex." In *SE*, 19: 173–79. London: Hogarth Press, 1961.

————. *The Ego and the Id*. In *SE*, 19: 3–66. London: Hogarth Press, 1961.

————. "Family Romances." In *SE*, 9: 236–41. London: Hogarth Press, 1959.

————. "Femininity." In *New Introductory Lectures on Psycho-Analysis*. *SE*, 22: 112–35. London: Hogarth Press, 1964.

————. "Five Lectures on Psycho-Analysis." In *SE*, 11: 9–55. London: Hogarth Press, 1957.

————. *Fragment of the Analysis of a Case of Hysteria [Dora]*. In *SE*, 7: 7–122. London: Hogarth Press, 1953.

————. *Gesammelte Werke*. Edited by Anna Freud et al. 17 vols. in 16. London: Imago Pub. Co., 1940–52. Cited as *GW*.

————. *Group Psychology and the Analysis of the Ego*. In *SE*, 19: 69–143. London: Hogarth Press, 1955.

————. *Das Ich und das Es*. In *Gesammelte Werke*, 13: 235–89. London: Imago, 1940.

————. "The Infantile Genital Organization." In *SE*, 19: 139–45. London: Hogarth Press, 1961.

————. *Inhibitions, Symptoms and Anxiety*. In *SE*, 20: 87–172. London: Hogarth Press, 1959.

————. *The Interpretation of Dreams*. *SE*, vols. 4–5. London: Hogarth Press, 1953.

————. *Jokes and Their Relation to the Unconscious*. *SE*, vol. 8. London: Hogarth Press, 1960.

————. *Massenpsychologie und Ich-Analyse*. In *Gesammelte Werke*, 13: 71–161. London: Imago, 1940.

————. "Medusa's Head." In *SE*, 18: 273–74. London: Hogarth Press, 1955.

————. "Mourning and Melancholia." In *SE*, 14: 239–58. London: Hogarth Press, 1957.

———. "Negation." In *SE*, 19: 235–39. London: Hogarth Press, 1961.

———. *On Aphasia: A Critical Study*. Translated by E. Stengel. New York: International Universities Press, 1953. Originally published as *Zur Auffassung der Aphasien: Eine kritische Studie* (Leipzig: F. Deuticke, 1891).

———. "On the History of the Psychoanalytic Movement." In *SE*, 14: 7–66. London: Hogarth Press, 1957.

———. "On Narcissism: An Introduction." In *SE*, 19: 73–102. London: Hogarth Press, 1957.

———. *The Origins of Psycho-Analysis: Letters to Wilhelm Fliess, Drafts and Notes, 1877–1902*, ed. Marie Bonaparte, Anna Freud, and Ernest Kris. Translated by Eric Mosbacher and James Strachey. New York: Basic Books, 1954.

———. *Project for a Scientific Psychology*. In *SE*, 1: 295–387. London: Hogarth Press, 1966.

———. "Screen Memories." In *SE*, 3: 303–22. London: Hogarth Press, 1962.

———. *The Standard Edition of the Complete Psychological Works of Sigmund Freud*. Edited and translated by James Strachey. 24 vols. London: Hogarth Press, 1953–74. Cited as *SE*.

———. *Three Essays on the Theory of Sexuality*. In *SE*, 7: 3–245. London: Hogarth Press, 1953.

———. *Totem and Taboo: Some Points of Agreement Between the Mental Lives of Savages and Neurotics*. In *SE*, 13: 1–161. London: Hogarth Press, 1955.

———. "The 'Uncanny,'" In *SE*, 17: 217–56. London: Hogarth Press, 1955.

———. "The Unconscious: Appendix C." In *SE*, 14: 209–15. London: Hogarth Press, 1957.

———. "The Universal Tendency to Debasement in the Sphere of Love." In *SE*, 11: 179–190. London: Hogarth Press, 1957.

Fried, Michael. *Courbet's Realism*. Chicago: University of Chicago Press, 1990.

Frieden, Ken. *Freud's Dream of Interpretation*. Albany, N.Y.: State University of New York Press, 1990.

Froula, Christine. *Modernism's Body: Sex, Culture, and Joyce*. New York: Columbia University Press, 1996.

Frye, Northrop. *Anatomy of Criticism: Four Essays*. Princeton, N.J.: Princeton University Press, 1957.

Fuss, Diana. *Identification Papers*. New York: Routledge, 1995.

Gallop, Jane. "Phallus/Penis: Same Difference." In *Men by Women*, ed. Janet Todd, 243–51. New York and London: Holmes & Meier, 1981.

———. *Reading Lacan*. Ithaca, N.Y.: Cornell University Press, 1985.

———. *The Daughter's Seduction: Feminism and Psychoanalysis*. Ithaca, N.Y.: Cornell University Press, 1982.

Gay, Peter. *Freud, Jews and Other Germans: Masters and Victims in Modernist Culture*. Oxford: Oxford University Press, 1978.

———. *Freud: A Life for Our Time*. New York: Norton, 1988.

Gifford, Edward, S. *The Evil Eye: Studies in the Folklore of Vision*. New York: Macmillan, 1958.

Girard, René. *Violence and the Sacred*. Translated by Patrick Gregory. Baltimore: Johns Hopkins University Press, 1977. Originally published as *La violence et le sacré* (Paris: Grasset, 1972).

Goux, Jean-Joseph. *Symbolic Economies after Marx and Freud*. Translated by Jennifer Curtiss Cage. Ithaca, N.Y.: Cornell University Press, 1990. This volume contains selections from Jean-Joseph Goux, *Freud, Marx: Économie et symbolique* and *Les iconoclastes* (Paris: Éditions du Seuil, 1973, 1983).

Greenblatt, Stephen. *Renaissance Self-Fashioning: From More to Shakespeare*. Chicago: University of Chicago Press, 1980.

Grimaud, Michel. *Poétique et érudition: Microlecture du "Booz endormi" de Victor Hugo*. Paris: Lettres modernes, 1991.

Grimm, Jacob, and Wilhelm Grimm. *Grimms' Tales for Young and Old*. 1819. Translated by Ralph Manheim. New York: Doubleday, 1977.

———. *Kinder- und Hausmärchen*. Munich: Winkler, 1984.

Grosz, Elizabeth. *Jacques Lacan: A Feminist Introduction*. London: Routledge, 1990.

Guirand, Félix, and A.-V. Pierre. "Roman Mythology." In *New Larousse Encyclopedia of Mythology*, ed. Félix Guirand et al., 199–221. Translated by Richard Aldington and Delano Ames. London and New York: Hamlyn, 1959.

Harpham, Geoffrey Galt. *The Ascetic Imperative in Culture and Criticism*. Chicago: University of Chicago Press, 1987.

Harris, Rendel, and Alphonse Mingana, eds. *The Odes and Psalms of Solomon*. 2 vols. Manchester: Longmans, Green & Co., and Bernard Quaritch, 1920.

Haskell, Francis. "A Turk and his Pictures in Nineteenth-Century Paris." In *Past and Present in Art and Taste: Selected Essays*, 175–85. New Haven, Conn.: Yale University Press, 1987.

Hegel, G. W. F. *Phenomenology of Spirit*. Translated by A. V. Miller. Oxford: Oxford University Press, 1977. Originally published in 1807 as *Phänomenologie des Geistes*; reprint, from 5th ed., ed. J. Hoffmeister, Philosophische Bibliothek, 114 (Hamburg: Felix Meiner, 1952).

Heidegger, Martin. *Being and Time*. Translated by John Macquarrie and Edward Robinson. New York: Harper & Row, 1962. Originally published as *Sein und Zeit* (1927; reprint, Tübingen: Neomarius, 1977).

Herz, Neil. "In Reply." In *The End of the Line: Essays on Psychoanalysis and the Sublime*, 206–15. New York: Columbia University Press, 1985.

———. "Medusa's Head: Male Hysteria under Political Pressure." In *The End of the Line: Essays on Psychoanalysis and the Sublime*, 161–92. New York: Columbia University Press, 1985.

Hesiod. *Theogony*. In *Theogony and Works and Days*, trans. M. L. West, 3–33. Oxford: Oxford University Press, 1988.

Horney, Karen. "The Flight from Womanhood: The Masculinity-Complex in

Women as Viewed by Men and by Women." In *Feminine Psychology*, ed. Harold Kelman, 54–70. New York: Norton, 1967.

Hugo, Victor. "Booz endormi." In *La légende des siècles*, ed. Jacques Truchet, 33–36. Paris: Gallimard, 1950.

Ian, Marcia. *Remembering the Phallic Mother: Psychoanalysis, Modernism, and the Fetish*. Ithaca, N.Y.: Cornell University Press, 1993.

Irigaray, Luce. *Speculum of the Other Woman*. Translated by Gillian C. Gill. Ithaca, N.Y.: Cornell University Press, 1985. Originally published as *Speculum de l'autre femme* (Paris: Éditions de Minuit, 1974).

Johnson, Barbara. "The Frame of Reference: Poe, Lacan, Derrida." In *The Purloined Poe: Lacan, Derrida, and Psychoanalytic Reading*, ed. John P. Muller and William J. Richardson, 213–51. Baltimore: Johns Hopkins University Press, 1988.

Jones, Ernest. *The Last Phase: 1919–1939*. Vol. 3 of *The Life and Work of Sigmund Freud*. New York: Basic Books, 1957.

Joyce, James. *Finnegans Wake*. 1939. Reprint. London: Penguin Books, 1992.

Jung, Carl Gustave. *Psychology and Alchemy*. Translated by R. F. C. Hull. 2d ed. London: Routledge & Kegan Paul, 1968.

Kerrigan, William. "Introduction." In *Interpreting Lacan: Psychiatry and the Humanities*, ed. Joseph H. Smith and William Kerrigan, 6: ix–xxvii. New Haven, Conn.: Yale University Press, 1983.

Kilgour, Maggie. *From Communion to Cannibalism: An Anatomy of Metaphors of Incorporation*. Princeton, N.J.: Princeton University Press, 1990.

King, Pearl, and Ricardo Steiner, eds. *The Freud-Klein Controversies, 1941–45*. London and New York: Tavistock/Routledge, 1991.

Klein, Melanie. "Early Stages of the Oedipus Conflict." In *The Selected Melanie Klein*, ed. Juliet Mitchell, 69–83. New York: Macmillan, 1987.

———. "A Study of Envy and Gratitude." In *The Selected Melanie Klein*, ed. Juliet Mitchell, 211–29. New York: Macmillan, 1987.

Kligerman, Charles. "A Psychoanalytic Study of the *Confessions* of St. Augustine." *Journal of the American Psychoanalytic Association* 5 (1957): 469–84.

Knapp, Bettina L. "Archetypal Saturn/Kronos and the Goya/Malraux Dynamis." *Kentucky Romance Quarterly* 30 (1983): 373–87.

Kojève, Alexandre. *Introduction to the Reading of Hegel: Lectures on* The Phenomenology of Spirit. Assembled by Raymond Queneau. Edited by Allan Bloom. Translated by James H. Nichols, Jr. New York: Basic Books, 1969. Originally published as *Introduction à la lecture de Hegel: Leçons sur La phénoménologie de l'esprit, professées de 1933 à 1939 à l'École des Hautes-Études* (Paris: Gallimard, 1947).

Kramer, Robert. "The Birth of Client-Centered Therapy: Carl Rogers, Otto Rank, and 'The Beyond.'" *Journal of Humanistic Psychology* 35 (1995): 54–110.

Kristeva, Julia. "The Ethics of Linguistics." In *Desire in Language: A Semiotic Ap-*

proach to Literature and Art, trans. Thomas Gora, Alice Jardine, and Leon S. Roudiez, ed. Leon S. Roudiez, 23–35. New York: Columbia University Press, 1980.

———. "Freud and Love: Treatment and Its Discontents." In *Tales of Love*, trans. Leon S. Roudiez, 21–56. New York: Columbia University Press, 1987. "Freud and Love" was first published in English in *The Kristeva Reader*, ed. Toril Moi, 238–71 (New York: Columbia University Press, 1986).

———. "From One Identity to an Other." In *Desire in Language: A Semiotic Approach to Literature and Art*, trans. Thomas Gora, Alice Jardine, and Leon S. Roudiez, ed. Leon S. Roudiez, 124–47. New York: Columbia University Press, 1980.

———. "Giotto's Joy." In *Desire in Language: A Semiotic Approach to Literature and Art*, trans. Thomas Gora, Alice Jardine, and Leon S. Roudiez, ed. Leon S. Roudiez, 210–36. New York: Columbia University Press, 1980.

———. "Il n'y a pas de maître à langage." *Regards sur la psychanalyse en France. Nouvelle Revue de Psychanalyse* 20 (1979): 119–40.

———. *Powers of Horror: An Essay on Abjection*. Translated by Leon S. Roudiez. New York: Columbia University Press, 1982. Originally published as *Pouvoirs de l'horreur* (Paris: Éditions du Seuil, 1980).

———. *Revolution in Poetic Language*. Translated by Margaret Waller. New York: Columbia University Press, 1984. Originally published as *La révolution du langage poétique* (Paris: Éditions du Seuil, 1974).

———. "The System and the Speaking Subject." In *The Kristeva Reader: Julia Kristeva*, ed. Toril Moi, 24–33. New York: Columbia University Press, 1986.

———. *Tales of Love*. Translated by Leon S. Roudiez. New York: Columbia University Press, 1987. Originally published as *Histoires d'amour* (Paris: Denoël, 1983).

———. "Within the Microcosm of 'The Talking Cure.'" Translated by Thomas Gora and Margaret Waller. In *Interpreting Lacan: Psychiatry and the Humanities*, ed. Joseph H. Smith and William Kerrigan, 6: 33–48. New Haven, Conn.: Yale University Press, 1983.

———. "Word, Dialogue, and Novel." In *Desire in Language: A Semiotic Approach to Literature and Art*, trans. Thomas Gora, Alice Jardine, and Leon S. Roudiez, ed. Leon S. Roudiez, 64–91. New York: Columbia University Press, 1980.

Lacan, Jacques. *Les complexes familiaux dans la formation de l'individu*. 1938. Paris: Navarin, 1984. Translated by Carolyn Asp in abridged form under the title "The Family Complexes," *Critical Texts* 5 (1988): 12–29. Cited as *CF*.

———. "Desire and the Interpretation of Desire in *Hamlet*." Translated by James Hulbert. In *Literature and Psychoanalysis: The Question of Reading, Otherwise*, ed. Shoshana Felman, 11–52. Baltimore: Johns Hopkins University Press, 1982. First published in English in 1977 in Yale French Studies nos. 55–56.

———. *Écrits*. Paris: Éditions du Seuil, 1966. Translated by Alan Sheridan under the title *Écrits: A Selection* (New York: Norton, 1977).

————. "The Family Complexes." Translated by Carolyn Asp. *Critical Texts* 5 (1988): 12–29. An abridged translation of *Les complexes familiaux dans la formation de l'individu* (Paris: Navarin, 1984).

————. "Guiding Remarks for a Congress on Feminine Sexuality." Translated by Jacqueline Rose. In *Feminine Sexuality: Jacques Lacan and the École Freudienne*, ed. Juliet Mitchell and Jacqueline Rose, 87–98. London: Macmillan, 1982.

————. "Hommage fait à Marguerite Duras, du *Ravissement de Lol V. Stein*." *Cahiers Renaud-Barrault* 52 (1965): 7–15. Reprinted in *Ornicar? Revue du Champ freudien* 34 (1985): 7–13.

————. "De l'impulsion au complexe." *RFP* 11 (1939): 137–41. Reprinted in *Ornicar? Revue du Champ freudien* 31 (1984): 14–19.

————. "The Oedipus Complex." Translated by Andrea Kahn. *Semiotext(e)* 4 (1980): 190–200. Section 3 of *Les complexes familiaux dans la formation de l'individu* (Paris: Navarin, 1984).

————. *Le séminaire de Jacques Lacan, Livre I: Les écrits techniques de Freud, 1953–1954.* Edited by Jacques-Alain Miller. Paris: Éditions du Seuil, 1975. Translated with notes by John Forrester under the title *Freud's Papers on Technique, 1953–1954* (New York : Norton, 1988).

————. *Le séminaire de Jacques Lacan, Livre II: Le moi dans la théorie de Freud et dans la technique de la psychanalyse, 1954–1955.* Edited by Jacques-Alain Miller. Paris: Éditions du Seuil, 1978. Translated by Sylvana Tomaselli under the title *The Ego in Freud's Theory and in the Technique of Psychoanalysis, 1954–1955*, with notes by John Forrester (New York: Norton, 1988).

————. *Le séminaire de Jacques Lacan, Livre III: Les psychoses, 1955–1956.* Edited by Jacques-Alain Miller. Paris: Éditions du Seuil, 1981. Translated by Russell Grigg under the title *The Psychoses, 1955–1956* (New York: Norton, 1993).

————. *Le séminaire de Jacques Lacan, Livre IV: La relation d'objet, 1956–1957.* Edited by Jacques-Alain Miller. Paris: Éditions du Seuil, 1994.

————. *Le séminaire de Jacques Lacan, Livre VII: L'éthique de la psychanalyse, 1959–1960.* Edited by Jacques-Alain Miller. Paris: Éditions du Seuil, 1986. Translated by Dennis Porter under the title *The Ethics of Psychoanalysis, 1959–1960* (New York: Norton, 1992).

————. "Le séminaire de Jacques Lacan, Livre IX: L'identification, *1961–1962*." Unpublished.

————. *Le séminaire de Jacques Lacan, Livre XI: Les quatre concepts fondamentaux de la psychanalyse, 1964.* Edited by Jacques-Alain Miller. Paris: Éditions du Seuil, 1973. Translated by Alan Sheridan under the title *The Four Fundamental Concepts of Psycho-Analysis* (London: Hogarth Press and the Institute of Psycho-Analysis, 1977; New York: Norton, 1978, 1981).

————. *Le séminaire de Jacques Lacan, Livre XVII: L'envers de la psychanalyse, 1969–1970.* Edited by Jacques-Alain Miller. Paris: Éditions du Seuil, 1991.

————. *Le séminaire de Jacques Lacan, Livre XX: Encore, 1972–1973.* Edited by Jacques-Alain Miller. Paris: Éditions du Seuil, 1975. Translated with notes by Bruce Fink under the title *Feminine Sexuality: The Limits of Love and Knowledge, 1972–1973* (New York: Norton, 1998).

————. "Seminar on 'The Purloined Letter.'" Translated by Jeffrey Mehlman. In *The Purloined Poe: Lacan, Derrida, and Psychoanalytic Reading*, ed. John P. Muller and William J. Richardson, 28–54. Baltimore: Johns Hopkins University Press, 1988.

————. "Some Reflections on the Ego." Translated by Nancy Elisabeth Beaufils. *International Journal of Psycho-Analysis* 34 (1953): 11–17.

————. "Le stade du miroir comme formateur de la fonction du *Je* telle qu'elle nous est révélée dans l'expérience psychanalytique." 1949. In *Écrits* (Paris: Éditions du Seuil, 1966), 93–100; translated by Alan Sheridan in *Écrits: A Selection* (New York: Norton, 1977), 1–7.

Langdon, Stephen. "An Incantation in the 'House of Light' Against the Evil Eye." In *The Evil Eye: A Folklore Casebook*, ed. Alan Dundes, 39–40. New York: Garland, 1981.

Laplanche, Jean, and J.-B. Pontalis. *The Language of Psycho-Analysis.* Translated by Donald Nicholson-Smith. London: Hogarth Press and the Institute of Psycho-Analysis, 1983. Originally published as *Vocabulaire de la psychanalyse* (Paris: Presses Universitaires de France, 1967).

Leclaire, Serge. "Philo, or the Obsessional and His Desire." In *Returning to Freud: Clinical Psychoanalysis in the School of Lacan*, ed. and trans. Stuart Schneiderman. New Haven, Conn.: Yale University Press, 1980, 114–29. Reprinted from *Evolution Psychiatrique* 3 (1959): 383–411.

Lee, Jonathan Scott. *Jacques Lacan.* Amherst: University of Massachusetts Press, 1990.

Lewis, C. S. *The Allegory of Love: A Study in Medieval Tradition.* London: Oxford University Press, 1936.

Lieberman, E. James. *Acts of Will: The Life and Work of Otto Rank.* New York: Macmillan, 1985.

Lindsay, Jack. *Gustave Courbet: His Life and Art.* New York: Harper & Row, 1973.

Macey, David. *Lacan in Contexts.* London: Verso, 1988.

Maloney, Clarence. "Don't Say 'Pretty Baby' Lest You Zap It with Your Eye—The Evil Eye in South Asia." In *The Evil Eye*, ed. Clarence Maloney, 102–48. New York: Columbia University Press, 1976.

Malraux, André. *Saturn: An Essay on Goya.* Translated by C. W. Chilton. London and New York: Phaidon Press, 1957. Originally published as *Saturne: Essai sur Goya* (Paris: Gallimard, 1950).

Marini, Marcelle. *Jacques Lacan: The French Context.* Translated by Anne Tomiche. New Brunswick, N.J.: Rutgers University Press, 1992. Originally published as *Jacques Lacan* (Paris: Éditions Pierre Belford, 1986).

Merleau-Ponty, Maurice. "The Child's Relations with Others." Translated by

William Cobb. In *The Primacy of Perception and Other Essays on Phenomenological Psychology, the Philosophy of Art, History and Politics*, ed. J. M. Edie, 96–155. Evanston, Ill.: Northwestern University Press, 1964. Originally published as *Les relations avec autrui chez l'enfant* (Paris: Centre de documentation universitaire, 1958).

Miller, Jacques-Alain. "Interventions de Lacan à la Société Psychanalytique de Paris." *Ornicar? Revue du Champ freudien* 31 (1984): 7–27.

Moi, Toril, ed. *The Kristeva Reader: Julia Kristeva*. New York: Columbia University Press, 1986.

Moss, Leonard W., and Stephen C. Cappannari. "*Mal'occhio, Ayin ha ra, Oculus Fascinus, Judenblick*: The Evil Eye Hovers Above." In *The Evil Eye*, ed. Clarence Maloney, 1–15. New York: Columbia University Press, 1976.

Muller, John P., and William J. Richardson, eds. *The Purloined Poe: Lacan, Derrida, and Psychoanalytic Reading*. Baltimore: Johns Hopkins University Press, 1988.

———. *Ouvrir les Écrits de Jacques Lacan*. Adapted by Philippe Julien. Toulouse: Érès, 1987.

Murgoci, A. "The Evil Eye in Roumania, and Its Antidotes." In *The Evil Eye: A Folklore Casebook*, ed. Alan Dundes, 124–29. New York: Garland, 1981.

Nabokov, Vladimir. *Lolita*. New York: Putnam, 1955.

Nasio, Juan-David. *Five Lessons on the Psychoanalytic Theory of Jacques Lacan*. Translated by David Pettigrew and François Raffoul. Albany, N.Y.: State University of New York Press, 1998. Originally published as *Cinq leçons sur la théorie de Jacques Lacan* (Paris: Editions Rivages, 1992).

Nead, Lynda. *The Female Nude: Art, Obscenity and Sexuality*. London: Routledge, 1992.

Neumann, Erich. *The Great Mother: An Analysis of the Archetype*. Translated by Ralph Manheim. Princeton, N.J.: Princeton University Press, 1963.

Nochlin, Linda. "Courbet's *L'origine du monde*: The Origin Without an Original." *October* 37 (1986): 76–86. Cited as "Origin Without an Original."

———. "Courbet's Real Allegory: Rereading 'The Painter's Studio.'" In *Courbet Reconsidered*, ed. Sarah Faunce and Linda Nochlin, 17–41. New York: Brooklyn Museum, 1988.

———. "The Origin of the World 1866 [Catalogue no. 66]." In *Courbet Reconsidered*, ed. Sarah Faunce and Linda Nochlin, 177–79. New York: Brooklyn Museum, 1988.

O'Connell, Robert J. *St. Augustine's Confessions: The Odyssey of Soul*. Cambridge, Mass.: Harvard University Press, 1969.

Ogilvie, Bertrand. *Lacan: La formation du concept de Sujet (1932–1949)*. Paris: Presses Universitaires de France, 1987.

Ortner, Sherry. "Is Female to Male as Nature is to Culture?" In *Woman, Culture, and Society*, ed. Michelle Zimbalist Rosaldo and Louise Lamphere, 67–87. Stanford: Stanford University Press, 1974.

Perrault, Charles. "The Little Red Riding-Hood." Translated by Robert Samber. In *The Classic Fairy Tales*, ed. Iona and Peter Opie, 95–97. Oxford: Oxford University Press, 1974.

Piaget, Jean. *Main Trends in Psychology*. London: George Allen & Unwin, 1973. Originally published as chapter 3 in *Main Trends in the Social and Human Sciences* (Mouton/UNESCO, 1970).

Pitrè, Giuseppe. "The Jettatura and the Evil Eye." In *The Evil Eye: A Folklore Casebook*, ed. Alan Dundes, 130–42. New York: Garland, 1981.

Pliny. *Natural History*. Translated by W. H. S. Jones. Vol. 8. London: Heineman; Cambridge, Mass.: Harvard University Press, 1963.

Poe, Edgar Allan. "The Purloined Letter." In *The Purloined Poe: Lacan, Derrida, and Psychoanalytic Reading*, ed. John P. Muller and William J. Richardson, 6–23. Baltimore: Johns Hopkins University Press, 1988.

———. "William Wilson." In *Great Tales and Poems of Edgar Allan Poe*, 351–73. New York: Washington Square Press, 1940.

Porter, Dennis. "Translator's Note." In *The Seminar of Jacques Lacan, Book VII: The Ethics of Psychoanalysis*, 1959–1960, vii–viii. New York: Norton, 1992.

Prudentius, Aurelius Clemens. "Psychomachia The Fight for Mansoul." Ca. C.E. 405. In *Prudentius*, trans. H. J. Thomson, 1: 274–343. London: William Heinemann; Cambridge, Mass.: Harvard University Press, 1962.

Pulver, Sydney E. "Narcissism: The Term and the Concept." *Journal of the American Psychoanalytic Association* 18 (1970): 319–41.

Quilligan, Maureen. *The Language of Allegory: Defining the Genre*. Ithaca, N.Y.: Cornell University Press, 1979.

Quinn, Susan. *A Mind of Her Own: The Life of Karen Horney*. Reading, Mass.: Addison-Wesley, 1988.

Ragland-Sullivan, Ellie. *Jacques Lacan and the Philosophy of Psychoanalysis*. Urbana: University of Illinois Press, 1987.

Rank, Otto. *The Trauma of Birth*. Translator unknown. London: Kegan Paul, Trench, Trubner, 1929. Originally published as *Das Trauma der Geburt* (Leipzig: Internationaler Psychoanalytischer Verlag, 1924).

Rendon, Mario. "Narcissus Revisited: A Venture Outside the Intrapsychic." *American Journal of Psychoanalysis* 41 (1981): 347–54.

Richardson, William J. "Lacan and the Subject of Psychoanalysis." In *Interpreting Lacan*, ed. Joseph H. Smith and William Kerrigan, 51–74. New Haven, Conn.: Yale University Press, 1983.

Rimbaud, Arthur. *Rimbaud: Complete Works, Selected Letters*. Translated by Wallace Fowlie. Chicago: University of Chicago Press, 1966.

Roazen, Paul. *Freud and His Followers*. New York: Knopf, 1975.

Roberts, John M. "Belief in the Evil Eye in World Perspective." In *The Evil Eye*, ed. Clarence Maloney, 223–78. New York: Columbia University Press, 1976.

Róheim, Géza. "The Evil Eye." *American Imago* 9 (1952): 351–63. Reprinted in *The*

Evil Eye: A Folklore Casebook, ed. Alan Dundes (New York: Garland, 1981), 211–22.

Rollinson, Philip. *Classical Theories of Allegory and Christian Culture*. Pittsburgh, Pa.: Duquesne University Press, 1981.

Rose, H. J. *A Handbook of Greek Mythology Including Its Extension to Rome*. New York: Dutton, 1959.

Roudinesco, Elisabeth. *La bataille de cent ans: Histoire de la psychanalyse en France*. Vol. 2. Paris: Éditions du Seuil, 1986. Translated by Jeffrey Mehlman under the title *Jacques Lacan & Co.: A History of Psychoanalysis in France, 1925–1985* (Chicago: University of Chicago Press, 1990).

———. *Jacques Lacan: Esquisse d'une vie, histoire d'un système de pensée*. Paris: Fayard, 1993. Translated by Barbara Bray under the title *Jacques Lacan* (Cambridge, Eng.: Polity Press; New York: Columbia University Press, 1997).

Roustang, François. *The Lacanian Delusion*. Translated by Greg Sims. New York: Oxford University Press, 1990. Originally published as *Lacan, de l'équivoque à l'impasse* (Paris: Éditions de Minuit, 1986).

Rowe, Karen E. "To Spin a Yarn: The Female Voice in Folklore and Fairy Tale." In *Fairy Tales and Society: Illusion, Allusion, and Paradigm*, ed. Ruth B. Bottigheimer, 53–74. Philadelphia: University of Pennsylvania Press, 1986.

Rudnytsky, Peter L. "Rank: Beyond Freud?" *American Imago* 41 (1984): 325–41.

Saussure, Ferdinand de. *Course in General Linguistics*. 1915–16. Translated by Wade Baskin. Edited by Charles Bally and Albert Sechehaye. New York: Fontana/Collins, 1974.

Sexton, Ann. *Transformations*. Boston: Houghton Mifflin, 1971.

Smith, Macklin. *Prudentius' Psychomachia: A Reexamination*. Princeton, N.J.: Princeton University Press, 1976.

Soler, Colette. "L'acte manqué de Ferenczi." *Ornicar? Revue du Champ freudien* 35 (1985): 81–90.

Sprengnether, Madelon. *The Spectral Mother: Freud, Feminism, and Psychoanalysis*. Ithaca, N.Y.: Cornell University Press, 1990.

Stein, Howard F. "Envy and the Evil Eye: An Essay in the Psychological Ontogeny of Belief and Ritual." In *The Evil Eye*, ed. Clarence Maloney, 193–222. New York: Columbia University Press, 1976. Reprinted in *The Evil Eye: A Folklore Casebook*, ed. Alan Dundes (New York: Garland, 1981), 223–56.

Stevenson, Burton. *The Macmillan Book of Proverbs, Maxims & Famous Phrases*. New York: Macmillan, 1966.

Sturrock, John. *The Language of Autobiography: Studies in the First Person Singular*. Cambridge, Eng.: Cambridge University Press, 1993.

Taft, Jessie. *Otto Rank: A Biographical Study Based on Notebooks, Letters, Collected Writings, Therapeutic Achievements and Personal Associations*. New York: Julian Press, 1958.

Taillandier, Gérôme. "Présentation brève du séminaire de J. Lacan sur l'identification." In *Les identifications: Confrontation de la clinique et de la théorie de Freud à Lacan. L'espace analytique*, ed. Patrick Guyomard and Maud Mannoni, 11–22. Paris: Denoël, 1987.

Tatar, Maria. *Off With Their Heads! Fairy Tales and the Culture of Childhood*. Princeton, N.J.: Princeton University Press, 1992.

Teyssèdre, Bernard. *Le roman de l'Origine*. Paris: Gallimard, 1996.

This, Bernard. "Touchant Ferenczi." *Ornicar? Revue du Champ freudien* 35 (1985): 72–80.

Tomashevsky, Boris. "Thematics." 1925. In *Russian Formalist Criticism: Four Essays*, ed. and trans. Lee T. Lemon and Marion J. Reis, 61–95. Lincoln: University of Nebraska Press, 1965.

Trible, Phyllis. *God and the Rhetoric of Sexuality*. Philadelphia: Fortress Press, 1978.

Ver Eecke, Wilfried. "Hegel as Lacan's Source for Necessity in Psychoanalytic Theory." In *Interpreting Lacan*, ed. Joseph H. Smith and William Kerrigan, 113–38. New Haven, Conn.: Yale University Press, 1983.

Wallon, Henri. *Les origines du caractère chez l'enfant*. 1933. Reprint. Paris: Presses Universitaires de France, 1949.

Warner, Marina. *Alone of All Her Sex: The Myth and the Cult of the Virgin Mary*. New York: Random House, Vintage Books, 1983.

Webb, Peter. "Victorian Erotica." In *The Sexual Dimension in Literature*, ed. Alan Bold, 90–121. London: Vision;Totowa, N.J.: Barnes & Noble, 1983.

Weber, Samuel. *Return to Freud: Jacques Lacan's Dislocation of Psychoanalysis*. Translated by Michael Levine. Cambridge, Eng.: Cambridge University Press, 1991. Originally published as *Rückkehr zu Freud: Jacques Lacans Entstellung du Psychoanalyse* (Vienna: Passagen Verlag, 1990).

Whitman, Jon. *Allegory: The Dynamics of an Ancient and Medieval Technique*. Cambridge, Mass.: Harvard University Press, 1987.

Winnicott, D. W. "Mirror-Role of Mother and Family in Child Development." In *Playing and Reality*, 130–38. Harmondsworth, Eng.: Penguin Books, 1971.

———. "Birth Memories, Birth Trauma, and Anxiety." In *Through Paediatrics to Psycho-Analysis*, 174–93. London: Hogarth Press and the Institute of Psycho-Analysis, 1975.

Wittgenstein, Ludwig. *Philosophical Investigations*. 1953. Translated by G. E. M. Anscombe. Oxford: Basil Blackwell, 1967.

Zepp, Evelyn H. "The Criticism of Julia Kristeva: A New Mode of Critical Thought." *Romanic Review* 73 (1982): 80–97.

Ziolkowski, Eric J. "St. Augustine: Aeneas' Antitype, Monica's Boy." *Literature and Theology* 9 (1995): 1–23.

Zipes, Jack. "Epilogue: Reviewing and Re-Framing Little Red Riding Hood." In *The Trials and Tribulations of Little Red Riding Hood*, ed. Jack Zipes, 343–83. 2d ed. New York: Routledge, 1993.

———. *Fairy Tales and the Art of Subversion: The Classical Genre for Children and the Process of Civilization*. New York: Methuen, 1988.

———. "The Trials and Tribulations of Little Red Riding Hood." In *The Trials and Tribulations of Little Red Riding Hood*, ed. Jack Zipes, 17–88. 2d ed. New York: Routledge, 1993.

Žižek, Slavoj. *Looking Awry: An Introduction to Jacques Lacan Through Popular Culture*. Cambridge, Mass.: MIT Press, 1991.

Index

In this index an "f" after a number indicates a separate reference on the next page, and an "ff" indicates separate references on the next two pages. A continuous discussion over two or more pages is indicated by a span of page numbers, e.g., "57–59."

Augustine, Saint, 6, 101, 154, 160,
164–65, 166f, 187, 191f; *Confessions*, 3,
5, 144ff, 147–50, 153ff, 157–59, 188,
198, 264n1; and Monica (mother),
154–57, 159f, 198, 263n10,
264nn13,14; and Patricius (father),
155ff; on sibling jealousy, 160, 168ff,
170–71, 176, 177–79, 182–83, 185,
190, 262–63n4; and evil eye, 193, 192,
196, 198
Autobiography, 5, 181; Freud and, 73–74;
Lacan, 73, 151–55

Balint, Michael, 64
Bataille, Georges, 80
Bataille, Sylvia, *see* Lacan, Sylvia
Bataille de cent ans, La (Roudinesco), 9
Being and Time, see Sein und Zeit
(Heidegger)
Bettelheim, Bruno, 260n7; *The Uses of
Enchantment*, 212–13
Bey, Khalil (Khalil Sherif Pacha), 9, 13,
250n7
Beyond the Pleasure Principle (Freud), 3,
38, 44f
"Beyond the 'Reality Principle'" (Lacan),
20, 178
Biology, 33, 45, 78, 93, 133; anti-biolo-
gism, 78f
Birth trauma, 23, 28ff, 35f, 252–53n8,
254n14
Bisexuality, 186
Bleuler, Eugen, 181
Bloom, Harold, 66f, 243
Boaz, 200, 224. *See also* "Booz endormi"
Body-image, 93, 111, 143; fragmented,
11, 37–38, 79, 87, 130, 132, 134, 167;
total, 46–47, 79, 86–87, 160, 167, 183;
and mirror stage, 83–86, 93–94. *See
also* Fragmentation; Gestalt
"Booz endormi" (Hugo), 7, 219–20, 221,
222–23, 269nn16, 17
Borch-Jacobsen, Mikkel, 88, 126
Borderline discourse, 228–29, 234–35,
237–38, 241, 244; and art, 230–31, 238
Borges, Jorge Luis: "Pierre Menard, Au-
thor of the *Quixote*," 166–67
Bottigheimer, Ruth, 211, 213
Bowie, Malcolm, 54, 139, 153
Breast, 33, 61f, 119, 136–37, 154, 158f,

177, 195, 198f, 264–65n2; imago of, 1,
4, 23, 45, 49, 56, 91, 121, 123, 129,
171, 174, 196; withdrawal of, 22,
26–27, 37f, 43, 184
Breton, André, 80
Broumas, Olga: "Little Red Riding
Hood," 215
Brown, Peter, 154, 159, 192
Brownmiller, Susan: *Against Our Will*,
209
Bühler, Charlotte, 75, 178
Burke, Kenneth, 116–17; "Verbal Action
in St Augustine's *Confessions*," 158–59
Burkert, Walter, 94

Caillois, Roger, 191
Cain, and Abel, 76, 145
Camp, Maxime du, 9–10
Cannibalism, 117–18, 194; identification
and, 119–20, 123, 141
Carroll, Lewis, 75, 76–77, 85, 154
Cars, Laurence des, 10f
Carter, Angela: "The Company of
Wolves," 267–68n5
Cascardi, Anthony, 216, 268n13
Castration, 6, 21, 37, 188, 203, 224, 237;
anxiety, 11, 15, 33, 38, 46, 66–67, 218,
230; fantasies of, 32, 35, 123. *See also*
Phallus
Castration complex, 24–25, 26, 37, 23,
188, 218, 237; redefinition of, 6, 28;
genitalia and, 11, 26–28, 31–32, 40, 66,
128; Rank on, 30–31, 36
Cavell, Stanley, 262–63n4
Certeau, Michel de, 153, 263n8
*CF, see Complexes familiaux dans la forma-
tion de l'individu, Les* (Lacan)
Château of Blonay, The (Courbet), 13
Chauvin, Remy, 78, 93, 258n3
Children, childhood, 58, 255n11; sexual
abuse of, 6, 53, 208; developmental
stages of, 21–22, 40, 56, 78, 90–91, 183;
and primal scene, 50, 52; and mirror
image, 78, 83–84, 96, 106–7; communication and aggression between, 168–69,
175f; jealousy in, 171–72, 177–78. *See
also* Mother-child relationship
"Child's Relations with Others, The"
(Merleau-Ponty), 84–85
Chose, la, see Ding, das

31f, 41, 47, 67, 88, 148, 180f, 185ff,
200f, 203, 214, 256n5, 260n12; castration and, 6, 24; redefinition of, 6, 201;
Klein on, 33f, 35–36; and superego, 40,
138; paternal imago and, 90, 109,
262n29; identification and, 120–21,
138; Little Red Riding Hood and,
212–13
Oedipus Rex (Sophocles), 108, 110
Ogilvie, Bertrand, 75, 88
Oral erotism, 119–20
Origines du caractère chez l'enfant, Les
(Wallon), 75, 77–78, 79, 82, 84–85, 95,
171, 172–73, 183
Origin of the World, The (Courbet), 3, 7,
9–11, 249–50n1, 250–51n8; Lacan and,
13–15, 16–18; in Museé d'Orsay,
14–15; title of, 15–16, 251n9
Originality, 75, 173–74
Origins: issues of, 34–36, 63, 74, 171,
257n12; of religion and society, 41,
164, 18, 264–65n26; of superego and
repression, 35, 41–44, 118; as production and reproduction, 132–35,
179–80; as *causa-sui* project, 143,
262n29
Othello (Shakespeare), 172–73
Other, 80, 98, 114, 139, 184, 190f, 196,
265–66n8; desire of, 77, 97; subject
and, 81, 122, 147, 184, 242; big Other,
86, 208. *See also* Counterpart,
semblable
"Our Antecedents, Of" (Lacan), 69, 73
Ouranos (Uranos), 221–22, 225

Painter's Studio: A Real Allegory, The
(Courbet), 11–12, 13, 250n6
Paradise: as intrauterine state, 35, 91
Paranoia, paranoid knowledge, 105,
114–15, 138–39, 178, 225, 259n4
Paternal metaphor, 6, 20, 40f, 90,
159, 199, 201, 203; and "Little Red
Cap," 212–14; and "little Hans," 219,
220–21; images of, 222–25
Patriarchy, patriarchal authority, 12,
36–37, 138, 220, 223
Patricide, 111, 116, 118, 222, 237, 243
Penis, 22, 31–32, 36f, 128, 204, 220,
266n1
Penis envy, 31–32, 34

Perrault, Charles: "Le Petit Chaperon
Rouge," 211–13
Persephone, 94
"Petit Chaperon Rouge, Le" (Perrault),
211–13
Phallic signifier, 2, 7, 17, 243. *See also* Pa-
ternal metaphor
Phallus, 18, 36, 128, 200, 205, 209,
266–67n1; and mother's desire, 2, 201,
204, 225; and lack, 6, 190; representa-
tional status of, 189, 215, 217, 219–20,
225–26, 249–50n1, 267n2; imaginary
vs. symbolic, 201–4
Phenomenology of Spirit, The (Hegel), 80,
97, 174, 265n6
Philo, philosopher, 109
Philo, case of, 200
"Philo, or the Obsessional and His De-
sire" (Leclaire), 203–5
Philosophical Investigations (Wittgenstein),
149, 262–63n4
Pitrè, Giuseppe, 193
Plato, 13, 101
Pliny: *Natural History*, 193
Plutarch, 101
Poe, Edgar Allan: "The Purloined Let-
ter," 13, 95, 105–6; "William Wilson,"
184
Pontalis, J.-B., 50, 53, 250–51n8, 252n4,
259nn3, 4; *The Language of Psycho-
Analysis*, 112–13
Pornography, 10f, 18, 250n7, 251n12
Powers of Horror (Kristeva), 229, 234, 236,
245
Prägnanz, laws of, 134f
Pregnancy, 5, 111, 132, 134
Preyer, W. T., 75
Priority, 49–50, 63. *See also* Origins
Primal horde, 41, 44, 111, 116, 118, 185
Primordial ambivalence, *see* Ambivalence
Primordial weaning, *see* Sevrage
"Problem of Acceptance of Unpleasant
Ideas-Advances in Knowledge of the
Sense of Reality, The" (Ferenczi), 60,
62f
Project for a Scientific Psychology (Freud),
53
Projection, 194–95, 215
Prudentius: *Psychomachia*, 3, 5, 101–2,
103–4, 105

244, 252n7; *Hamlet*, 108, 110, 145, 234; *Othello*, 172–73
Sheridan, Alan, 71
Sign, 227–28, 229ff, 241; Freud and, 232–34, 236–37, 244–45
"Signification of the Phallus, The" (Lacan), 49, 100
Signification, signifier, 99 105, 140–41, 162, 227–28; passion of, 99–100, 147; and signified, 227, 230, 234ff, 238, 245; and semiotic, 233–34
Signifying chain, 7, 100, 105, 141, 161, 207, 217, 220
Single stroke (*trait unaire*), 140–41
Société Psychanalytique de Paris (SPP), 71, 74, 130f, 261n20
"Some Reflections on the Ego" (Lacan), 70, 75, 177f, 182f
Sophocles: *Oedipus Rex*, 108, 110
Soul, 99, 101, 104f; fight for, 5. *See also Psychomachia* (Prudentius)
Source of the Loue, The (Courbet), 16, 251n10
Spatial relations, 78, 83–84
Specular image, 4f, 20, 83, 86–87, 106, 109, 122f, 126, 128, 182; confrontation with, 48, 99; assumption of, 70, 80, 93, 103; identity of, 83–86, 88. *See also* Conflict; Counterpart (or semblable)
Speculum of the Other Woman (Irigaray), 128
Speech, 56, 100, 124, 131, 137, 148, 150
Sphincter control, 41–42, 43; and bodily functions, 54
SPP, *see* Société Psychanalytique de Paris
"Stade du miroir, Le," *see* "Mirror Stage, The" (Lacan)
"Stages in the Development of the Sense of Reality" (Ferenczi), 3–4, 57, 60
Stärcke, A., 27
"Story of Grandmother, The," 209–10, 211, 267–68nn4, 5
Structural (or deferred-action) viewpoint, 3, 59, 70, 103
Struggle (or fight) for "pure prestige," 5, 76, 81, 92, 108, 175, 180
"Study of Envy and Gratitude, A" (Klein), 197
Study of the Development of the Libido (Abraham), 57, 60

Subject, *ubique*: advent of ("coming-into-being"), 2, 20, 66, 92f, 99, 160, 241; sight and, 20, 124, 129; inner world of, 49, 96; discourse of, 55–56; split, 170, 175, 182, 184, 191, 214, 230; barred, 175, 214. *See also* Other
Subjectivity, 68, 124, 146, 173, 259n12; constitution of, 38, 47, 83, 88, 124, 150, 191; mind-time and, 55–56, 58–59; and deferred action, 48, 59–60
Sublimation, 22–23, 40; Lacan on, 43, 163
"Subversion of the Subject, The" (Lacan), 58
Superego, 40, 46; formation of, 34, 41–44, 118, 234
Symbolic, 43, 45, 54, 56, 131, 207, 228, 229–30, 242; as constitutive of subject, 47, 105, 124, 139, 150

Taft, Jesse, 26
Tales of Love (Kristeva), 238, 240, 242
Tatar, Maria, 206, 209f
Temporality, 58–59, 189; and causality, 3, 48; Freud and Lacan on, 54–55; of Lacan's teaching, 73; of mirror stage, 80, 97–98
Teyssèdre, Bernard, 15
Three Essays on the Theory of Sexuality (Freud), 117f
Totem and Taboo (Freud), 40–41, 110, 115, 117, 119, 129, 164, 185–86, 242f
Totemism, 115–17, 118
Transitivism, 176, 178
Trauma of Birth, The (Rank), 3, 24–25, 28f, 35, 64, 252–53n8
Truchet, Jacques, 220
Truth, 49, 56, 94, 195, 240

Umbilical connection, 36f, 74, 179
Umwelt (outer world), 96, 98, 103, 191
"'Uncanny,' The" (Freud), 190, 194
Unconscious, 7, 85, 177, 230, 233, 245; structured as a language, 227f, 231
"Unconscious, The" (Freud), 235
Uses of Enchantment, The (Bettelheim), 212–13

"Verbal Action in St. Augustine's *Confessions*" (Burke), 158

Library of Congress Cataloging-in-Publication Data

Barzilai, Shuli.
     Lacan and the matter of origins / Shuli Barzilai.
        p.   cm.
     Includes bibliographical references and index.
        ISBN 0-8047-3381-3 (alk. paper). — ISBN 0-8047-3382-1 (pbk. :
     alk. paper)
        1. Psychoanalysis. 2. Lacan, Jacques, 1901– . I. Title.
     BF17.B2145 1999
     150.19'5—dc21   99-39702

♾ This book is printed on acid-free, archival quality paper.

Original printing 1999
Last figure below indicates year of this printing:
08   07   06   05   04   03   02   01   00   99

Typeset by Robert C. Ehle in 10/14 Janson, with Franklin Gothic display.